T0321838

Multi-Disciplinary Applications of Fog Computing:

Responsiveness in Real-Time

Debi Prasanna Acharjya
Vellore Institute of Technology, India

Kauser Ahmed P.
Vellore Institute of Technology, India

A volume in the Advances in Computational
Intelligence and Robotics (ACIR) Book Series

Published in the United States of America by
IGI Global
Engineering Science Reference (an imprint of IGI Global)
701 E. Chocolate Avenue
Hershey PA, USA 17033
Tel: 717-533-8845
Fax: 717-533-8661
E-mail: cust@igi-global.com
Web site: http://www.igi-global.com

Library of Congress Cataloging-in-Publication Data

Names: Acharjya, D. P., 1969- editor. | Kauser, P. Ahmed, 1983- editor.
Title: Multi-disciplinary applications of fog computing : responsiveness in
    real-time / Debi Prasanna Acharjya, and P. Ahmed Kauser, editors.
Description: Hershey, PA : Engineering Science Reference, an imprint of IGI
    Global. [2023] | Includes bibliographical references and index. |
    Summary: "The objective of this edited book is to provide the
    researchers with the recent advances in the fields of data analysis
    processing through fog computing, which are required to achieve in-depth
    knowledge in the field of concern to solve problems in real-time
    applications"-- Provided by publisher.
Identifiers: LCCN 2022032327 (print) | LCCN 2022032328 (ebook) | ISBN
    9781668444665 (h/c) | ISBN 9781668444672 (s/c) | ISBN 9781668444689
    (ebook)
Subjects: LCSH: Cloud computing.
Classification: LCC QA76.585 .M85 2023 (print) | LCC QA76.585 (ebook) |
    DDC 004.67/82--dc23/eng/20220815
LC record available at https://lccn.loc.gov/2022032327
LC ebook record available at https://lccn.loc.gov/2022032328

This book is published in the IGI Global book series Advances in Computational Intelligence and Robotics (ACIR) (ISSN: 2327-0411; eISSN: 2327-042X)

British Cataloguing in Publication Data
A Cataloguing in Publication record for this book is available from the British Library.

For electronic access to this publication, please contact: eresources@igi-global.com.

Advances in Computational Intelligence and Robotics (ACIR) Book Series

Ivan Giannoccaro
University of Salento, Italy

ISSN:2327-0411
EISSN:2327-042X

MISSION

While intelligence is traditionally a term applied to humans and human cognition, technology has progressed in such a way to allow for the development of intelligent systems able to simulate many human traits. With this new era of simulated and artificial intelligence, much research is needed in order to continue to advance the field and also to evaluate the ethical and societal concerns of the existence of artificial life and machine learning.

The **Advances in Computational Intelligence and Robotics (ACIR) Book Series** encourages scholarly discourse on all topics pertaining to evolutionary computing, artificial life, computational intelligence, machine learning, and robotics. ACIR presents the latest research being conducted on diverse topics in intelligence technologies with the goal of advancing knowledge and applications in this rapidly evolving field.

COVERAGE

- Evolutionary Computing
- Computational Intelligence
- Automated Reasoning
- Artificial Life
- Brain Simulation
- Neural Networks
- Adaptive and Complex Systems
- Pattern Recognition
- Computational Logic
- Heuristics

IGI Global is currently accepting manuscripts for publication within this series. To submit a proposal for a volume in this series, please contact our Acquisition Editors at Acquisitions@igi-global.com or visit: http://www.igi-global.com/publish/.

Titles in this Series

For a list of additional titles in this series, please visit: www.igi-global.com/book-series

Stochastic Processes and Their Applications in Artificial Intelligence
Christo Ananth (Samarkand State University, Uzbekistan) N. Anbazhagan (Alagappa University, India) and Mark Goh (National University of Singapore, Singapore)
Engineering Science Reference • copyright 2023 • 220pp • H/C (ISBN: 9781668476796) • US $270.00 (our price)

Handbook of Research on Deep Learning Techniques for Cloud-Based Industrial IoT
P. Swarnalatha (Department of Information Security, School of Computer Science and Engineering, Vellore Institute of Technology, India) and S. Prabu (Department Banking Technology, Pondicherry University, India)
Engineering Science Reference • copyright 2023 • 432pp • H/C (ISBN: 9781668480984) • US $335.00 (our price)

Handbook of Research on AI-Based Technologies and Applications in the Era of the Metaverse
Alex Khang (Global Research Institute of Technology and Engineering, USA) Vrushank Shah (Institute of Technology and Engineering, Indus University, India) and Sita Rani (Department of Computer Science and Engineering, Guru Nanak Dev Engineering College, India)
Engineering Science Reference • copyright 2023 • 517pp • H/C (ISBN: 9781668488515) • US $345.00 (our price)

Handbook of Research on Thrust Technologies' Effect on Image Processing
Binay Kumar Pandey (Department of Information Technology, College of Technology, Govind Ballabh Pant University of Agriculture and Technology, India) Digvijay Pandey (Department of Technical Education, Government of Uttar Pradesh, India) Rohit Anand (G.B. Pant DSEU Okhla-1 Campus, India & Government of NCT of Delhi, New Delhi, India) Deepak S. Mane (Performance Engineering Lab, Tata Research, Development, and Design Center, Australia) and Vinay Kumar Nassa (Rajarambapu Institute of Technology, India)
Engineering Science Reference • copyright 2023 • 320pp • H/C (ISBN: 9781668486184) • US $350.00 (our price)

Advanced Interdisciplinary Applications of Machine Learning Python Libraries for Data Science
Soly Mathew Biju (University of Wollongong, UAE) Ashutosh Mishra (Yonsei University, South Korea) and Manoj Kumar (University of Wollongong, UAE)
Engineering Science Reference • copyright 2023 • 300pp • H/C (ISBN: 9781668486962) • US $275.00 (our price)

Predicting Pregnancy Complications Through Artificial Intelligence and Machine Learning
D. Satish Kumar (Nehru Institute of Engineering and Technology , India) and P. Manilarasan (Nehru Institute of Engineering and Technology, India)
Medical Information Science Reference • copyright 2023 • 350pp • H/C (ISBN: 9781668489741) • US $350.00 (our price)

701 East Chocolate Avenue, Hershey, PA 17033, USA
Tel: 717-533-8845 x100 • Fax: 717-533-8661
E-Mail: cust@igi-global.com • www.igi-global.com

Dedicated to

My Beloved Family Members, Asima, Aditi, Aditya

D. P. Acharjya

My Beloved Father Late P. Nisar Ahmed

Kauser Ahmed P

Editorial Advisory Board

Table of Contents

Section 1
Fog Computing Foundations and Applications

Section 2
Fog Computing for Data Analytics

Section 3
Multi-Disciplinary Applications of Fog Computing

Detailed Table of Contents

Section 1
Fog Computing Foundations and Applications

Chapter 1

    Muhammad Ehsan Rana, Asia Pacific University of Technology and Innovation, Malaysia
    Nirase Fathima Abubacker, Asia Pacific University of Technology and Innovation, Malaysia

Fog computing is a paradigm that extends cloud computing capabilities to the network edge. Its foundations lie in understanding the theoretical principles and key concepts driving its development. This includes exploring architectural aspects which facilitate efficient and distributed data processing at the network edge. It involves examining the device and hardware support required for seamless fog computing operations, including edge devices, fog nodes, and network infrastructure. Different deployment approaches such as centralized, distributed, and hierarchical deployments bring their own advantages, limitations, and considerations. Evaluating these strategies and associated metrics aids in informed decision-making for fog infrastructure deployment. Understanding these foundations is crucial for building efficient, scalable, and resource-rich fog computing systems that address challenges in modern computing. This chapter investigates these concepts and highlights the significance of fog computing in enabling low-latency and resource-rich processing in smart infrastructure setups.

Cloud computing has already demonstrated its effectiveness in managing internet of things (IoT) applications and computationally intensive tasks and resources. Due to the substantial delay imparted by the network, cloud computing is not recommended for latency-critical applications. Excessive data flow and connections to data centers may clog up the system. Fog computing was developed to meet this difficulty. It is designed to expand the cloud computing capabilities to increase the quality of service (QoS) of such computing applications with a high latency requirement. In comparison to cloud datacenters, fog devices are dynamic and varied. In this chapter, the authors provide a solution to resource allocation issue in fog computing. The performance metrics such as scalability, reliability, and availability are optimized compared to the existing approaches.

The adoption of IoT has increased rapidly due to the abundance in the availability, affordability, and capability of different components like sensors, processors, and communication technologies. This growth has subsequently resulted in the development of the industrial internet of things (IIoT). When it comes to IoT there are four primary paradigms each with its own perks and drawbacks — cloud, edge, fog, and mist computing. This chapter focuses on fog computing, exploring its applications, services, and the current state of fog computing with emerging technologies. Fog computing extends its capabilities by distributing processing, storage, and networking tasks across cloud, fog, and edge nodes. It enables localized data analysis, real-time decision-making, and improved bandwidth utilization. This chapter focuses on the architectural principles, key components, and use cases of fog computing. It also highlights integrating emerging technologies with fog computing, such as artificial intelligence, machine learning, and blockchain that supports diverse IoT applications.

The thyroid is a part of the endocrine system that is placed toward the front of the neck and produces thyroxine, which is essential for our overall health. Recent advancements in computational approaches have facilitated the storage and collection of medical data for disease diagnosis. Various machine learning technology has a major role in making processes easy and efficient. Fog computing could be used to monitor and help to detect disease at an early stage, reduce the diagnosis time, and prevent complicated diseases. To strengthen thyroid patient prediction, machine learning can be integrated with fog computing for practical solutions. In this chapter, a fog-assisted internet of things-based quality of service framework is presented to prevent and protect against the thyroid. It provides real-time processing of users' health data to predict the thyroid disease by observing their symptoms and immediately generates an emergency alert, medical reports, and significant precautions for the user, their guardian, as well as doctors.

Section 2
Fog Computing for Data Analytics

Chapter 5

Madhusmita Mishra, Dr. Sudhir Chandra Sur Institute of Technology and Sports Complex, JIS Group, Kolkata, India
Amrut Ranjan Jena, Guru Nanak Institute of Technology, JIS Group, Kolkata, India
Himadri Biswas, Budge Budge Institute of Technology, Kolkata, India

The present days passes through Industry 4.0. It emphasizes on intelligent computing, smart computing, cloud computing, internet of things (IoT), artificial intelligence (AI), and machine learning (ML). In addition, the function of smart devices in these computing techniques make the work user friendly. Nowadays, health issues are a big challenge in society. In this industry revolution period, smart devices play significant role to provide health assistance in a finger touch. It is possible due to the increase in the number of smart devices and use of IoT, cloud, AI, and ML. Fog computing is the mechanism of providing quality services through optimization of the resources. This paper presents the hybridization of cloud computing with fog computing in the field of healthcare applications.

Chapter 6

Riyam Patel, SRM Institute of Science and Technology, India
Aditi Acharjya, SRM Institute of Science and Technology, India
Punyaban Patel, CMR Technical Campus (Autonomous), Hyderabad, India
Borra Sivaiah, CMR College of Engineering and Technology, India
Bibhudatta Sahoo, National Institute of Technology, Rourkela, India

Health care organisations must now understand the problems of assessing health care quality and establishing programmes to improve it. The literature covers quality and performance measures in primary, quaternary, public health, and voluntary healthcare. Due to healthcare expansion, reaction time, security, and data volume, latency has become an issue. This systematic study examines fog-based healthcare system approaches. IoT, cloud, and fog computing have created many medical care platforms. Thus, an internet of things and fog computing-based diabetes monitoring system was created to aid diagnosis and prediction. The fog computing-based diabetes monitoring and prediction system includes logistic regression and a decision tree. ML methods can identify if the patient has diabetes. Diabetic patients apply the Donabedian method to improve healthcare quality. This chapter explores, classifies, discusses, and proposes a way to improve Donabedian model, analyses and critique current healthcare metrics, indicators, quality and safety measures, and challenges in measuring health care systems.

Chapter 7

Yönal Kirsal, Electrical and Electronics Engineering Department, Faculty of Engineering, European University of Lefke, Lefke, Cyprus

This book chapter focuses on the analysis of quality of service (QoS) and performance modelling in the context of fog computing. The chapter proposes analytical frameworks for QoS analysis and performance modelling of fog computing systems. The chapter starts with an introduction to fog computing and the importance of QoS analysis in such systems. The next section presents a literature review of related work and different approaches to QoS analysis in fog computing. The proposed analytical frameworks are then described in detail, including their different components and assumptions. Case studies are also presented to demonstrate the application of the analytical frameworks. The case studies include a scenario of a fog computing system with a specific architecture and different performance metrics and models used for the analysis. The results and analysis of the case studies are then presented. Finally, the chapter concludes with a discussion of the key findings and contributions of the analytical frameworks.

Chapter 8

Munir Ahmad, Survey of Pakistan, Pakistan
Asmat Ali, Survey of Pakistan, Pakistan
Malik Sikander Hayat Khiyal, Preston University Kohat, Islamabad, Pakistan

Fog computing is a promising approach to address the challenges faced by traditional spatial data infrastructure when processing large-scale and real-time data. This chapter examined the opportunities and challenges of using fog computing in SDI through the service dominant logic framework. The study showed that fog computing can improve SDI by providing real-time data processing, improved data security and privacy, and increased accessibility of geospatial data. However, challenges such as data quality and interoperability, collaboration, technical infrastructure, and governance policies need to be addressed. The chapter suggested ways to improve the value co-creation process between fog computing and SDI users, including collaboration and partnership, investment in technical infrastructure, and capacity building initiatives. Future research can investigate the practical implementation and evaluation of fog computing in SDI applications.

Section 3
Multi-Disciplinary Applications of Fog Computing

Chapter 9

Sreekumar, Rourkela Institute of Management Studies, India
Swati Das, Rourkela Institute of Management Studies, India
Rema Gopalan, CMR Institute of Technology, India
Bikash Ranjan Debata, Kirloskar Institute of Management, India

Retail industry plays an important role in global economic scenario and contributes around 27 percent of world economy. The use of information technology enhances customer self-awareness, and it is a proven fact that consumers who enjoy their shopping experience end up buying more and more things. Retail is one of the sectors that has seen significant change since the introduction of Industry 4.0 technologies like cloud computing, IoT, fog computing, artificial intelligence, etc. This change can be seen in supermarkets like Amazon Go store, Alibaba Hema store, IKEA, and many more. The study focuses on various technological advancement including application of fog computing for giving the Indian retail industry a competitive advantage. The study also observes that store organizations that emphasize store design and adoption of technological innovations to simplify the purchasing process have been very successful in creating loyal customers for their stores.

One of the many applications of machine learning in healthcare is the analysis of large amounts of data to reveal new therapeutic insights. Once doctors have this data, they can better serve their patients. Therefore, satisfaction can be raised by using deep learning to enhance the quality of care provided. This work aims to integrate machine learning and AI in healthcare into a single system. Predictive algorithms based on machine learning could revolutionize healthcare by allowing doctors to avoid unnecessary treatments. Various libraries, including those for machine learning algorithms, were used to develop this work. Because of its extensive library and user-friendliness, Python has emerged as the preferred language. syntax. The authors used various classification techniques to train machine learning models and then select the one that provided the best balance between accuracy and precision while avoiding prediction error and autocorrelation problems, the two main causes of bias and variance.

The objective of the current study is to choose the best model with the highest accuracy rate using three robust hybrid artificial intelligence-based models: the ANN-GA, ANN-PSO and ANN-RSA. To do so, a sample of COVID-19 confirmed cases in India between August 1, 2021, and July 26, 2022, is first compiled. A random allocation of 70% (30%) of the total observation has been chosen as training (testing) data. After that, the LM method is used to train an ANN model. Accordingly, the appropriate number of hidden neurons is determined to be 9 using the R^2 and RMSE criterion. To achieve the highest accuracy rate, ANN-GA, ANN-PSO, and ANN-RSA models are developed using the presented ANN model. The optimized model's R-values during the training and test phases, according to ANN-GA and ANN-PSO, are 0.99 and 0.95, respectively. The R-values for ANN-RSA varied from 0.99 to 0.96. hence, the ANN-RSA demonstrated superior performance in forecasting COVID-19 cases in India.

Preface

Fog computing is defined as a distributed computing paradigm that extends the services provided by the cloud to the edge of the network. It uses network switches and routers, gateways, and mobile base stations to provide cloud service with the minimum possible network latency and response time. Simultaneously, it provides data, computing, storage, and application services to end-users that can be hosted at the network edge. Besides, it is capable of filtering and processing a considerable amount of incoming data on edge devices, making the data processing architecture distributed and thereby scalable. Recently, several fog computing applications are developed like IoT-based healthcare, 5G, block chains, autonomous driving, and mobile wireless applications. It also addresses the challenges such as data management, scalability, regulations, interoperability, device network human interfaces, security, and privacy. From the above observation, researchers can provide a better understanding of fog computing and its challenges. This edited book focuses on fog computing problems and solutions for various applications. It will cover the new approaches, architecture, and theoretical foundations in the fog paradigm of storage, communication, and computing. The book explores recent trends and challenges leading to a potential course for the ideas, practices, norms, and strategies related to fog computing. Keeping this in mind, the objective of this edited book is set to provide researchers of various fields like computer science, electrical, electronics, and information technology with the recent advances and approaches of fog computing and its applications. To achieve these objectives, theoretical background, advances, and applications to real-time problems are emphasized. We believe that our effort can make this collection interesting and highly attractive to the research community.

In recent years data are accumulated at a dramatic pace. The data can be qualitative, quantitative, graphic images, or in terms of videos. But, the real challenge lies in converting huge data into knowledge. Therefore, it is essential to develop new computational theories and tools to assist humans in extracting knowledge from high-dimensional data. The study of these new theories in data analytics is quite interesting and challenging. Therefore, there is a growing demand for data analytics in diverse application areas, such as secured data communication, data privacy, and security. For the last few decades fog computing for data analytics has been considered as an important research area to find solutions in many real-life applications. The importance of data analysis is exhibited in almost all existing engineering and scientific fields. It will help those researchers who have an interest in this field to keep an insight into different concepts and their importance for applications in real life. This has been done to make the edited book more flexible and to stimulate further interest in topics.

While these are a few examples of issues, our intention in editing this book is to offer concepts of fog computing: architecture, applications, and research challenges in a precise and clear manner to the research community. In editing the book, we attempt to provide frontier advances and applications of fog computing. The conceptual basis required to achieve in-depth knowledge in the field of computer science and information technology relating to fog computing is stressed.

The editors of the present volume are inspired to compile what the research community is thinking about fog computing and its application in various contexts. The book would come to benefit several categories of students and researchers. At the student level, this book can serve as a reference book for the special papers at the masters level aimed at inspiring possibly future researchers. At the researcher level, those interested in interdisciplinary research would also be benefited by the book. After all, the enriched interdisciplinary contents of the book would be a subject of interest to the faculties, existing research communities, and new research aspirants from diverse disciplines of the concerned departments of premier institutes across the globe. Above all, the availability of the book should be ensured to as many universities and research institutes as possible through whatever graceful means it may be. The edited book is divided into three sections such as fog computing foundations and applications, fog computing for data analytics, and multi-disciplinary applications of fog computing. We trust and hope that the edited book will offer a unified view of fog computing. Therefore, it is suitable as a reference for engineers, researchers, and graduate students.

In Chapter 1, the fundamentals of fog computing are defined. A brief introduction to theoretical foundations, architecture, devices, infrastructure, deployment, and programming models and a brief review of fog computing development is discussed. This is an effective foundation for researchers particularly engaged newly in the relevant field.

Chapter 2 of the book provides a solution to the resource allocation issue in Fog computing. The performance metrics such as scalability, reliability, and availability are compared to the existing approaches. Three significant difficulties that need to be addressed in the resource allocation issue in fog computing are discussed. These issues include decentralized solutions that better match the dynamicity and heterogeneity of fog nodes; resource allocation between fog nodes and from fog to the cloud for horizontal scalability; and functional constraints in addition to time metrics for optimal resource allocation.

Chapter 3 deals with an important present-day application of fog computing. An impressive review in this respect, particularly the novel application of fog computing, its recent trends, and emerging technologies with fog computing has been reported. This chapter also provides case studies of fog computing applications in smart agriculture, autonomous driving, and healthcare.

In Chapter 4, a sincere effort has been made to integrate fog computing with machine learning techniques for the diagnosis of thyroid disease. It presents a fog-assisted IoT-based quality of service framework to prevent and protect from thyroid in real-time. In fog computing, the use of machine learning algorithms is discussed as a tool for QoS-aware resource management in real-time disease prediction. It generates a real-time message to the government health agencies for controlling the outbreak of chronic illness and for taking quick and timely actions.

The present days passes through industry 4.0. It emphasizes on intelligent computing, smart computing, cloud computing, internet of things (IoT), and artificial intelligence, and machine learning. In addition, the function of smart devices in these computing techniques make the work user friendly. Now-a-days health issue is a biggest challenge in the society. In this industry revolution period, the smart devices play significant role to provide health assistance in a finger touch. It is possible due to increase in the number of smart devices and use of IoT, cloud, AI, and ML. Fog computing is the mechanism of providing quality services through optimization of the resources. Chapter 5 presents a model health preventive measure as a service (HPMaaS) for detection of diseases. It uses an intelligent fog-cloud-based approach for the detection of diseases through smartphone sensors. HPMaaS provides a low-cost, detection of diseases via smartphone with minimum cross-infection.

Chapter 6 offers an informative platform where a systematic review of fog-based healthcare systems, their analysis, applications, and challenges are presented. In addition, classification and discussion of different applications are provided. It also attempted to address the effectiveness of fog computing in healthcare. This chapter is devoted to exploring how fog computing can be implemented in healthcare. Challenges, and issues in fog-based healthcare are also discussed.

The main contribution of Chapter 7 is to provide a comprehensive overview of analytical approaches for QoS analysis and performance modeling in fog computing. An analytical model such as the Markov reward model is developed to study the exact spectral expansion solution and successive over-relaxation approaches for QoS evaluation and estimation in fog computing architectures. Moreover, it also discusses the QoS metrics and models specific to fog computing environments. Real-world case studies and examples are illustrated related to QoS analysis in fog computing.

The opportunities and challenges of using fog computing in spatial data infrastructures (SDI) are discussed in Chapter 8. It also establishes a theoretical framework for understanding the relationship between fog computing and spatial data infrastructures using the service-dominant logic framework. An extensive review of fog computing and spatial data infrastructures is carried out. Further, it is applied to the service-dominant logic framework to analyze the potential benefits and limitations of fog computing for spatial data infrastructures.

The retailers of today focus on building robust business processes and delightful customer service. They should understand their customer completely. Identifying the customer's preferences and creating a unique personalized shopping experience for them is a challenging task. The challenge before the brick-and-mortar store is technology adoption to take on online shopping. Customers don't want to spend too much time in shops, they want smart, fast, and efficient services be it online or in-store. Retailers can increase computer use at the edge by providing a better experience for customers. With fog computing all the retailers can have the flexibility of network and scalability which is necessary for its growth. Therefore, fog and edge computing with IoT is one of the best ways to grow business and bring customers back from the mall. Chapter 9 presents an application of fog computing in the Indian retail industry. It addresses the effectiveness of fog computing in the retail industry.

Chapter 10 illustrates the challenges and methodologies of developing a remote healthcare system with advanced machine-learning techniques. The development of healthcare applications, benefits, and challenges of implementing machine learning in disease prediction is discussed in this chapter.

In Chapter 11, a predictive mode to predict COVID-19 new instances using a combination of three reliable metaheuristic methods genetic algorithm, particle swarm optimization, reptile search algorithm, and ANN is presented to achieve the highest forecasting precision. A sincere effort has been made to identify various challenges associated with this kind of computation and justified the robustness and performance of the ANN-RSA as best.

Last, but not the least, the book is intended to bring a broad spectrum of application domains under the purview of fog computing so that it can trigger further inspiration among various research communities to contribute in their respective fields of applications. The recent advance in fog computing has been exploited to a greater extent to solve real-life problems. In nature, it is cumbersome to perform analysis of digital data by its heterogeneity in terms of modality. To solve many real-life problems, the analysis of digital data is mandatory through the fog computing methodology. The key to realizing the benefits of fog computing is the real-life applications and it leads to modern computing environments that help different organizations. Obtaining recent advances is an important goal but cannot always be achieved. The publication presents existing methodologies of fog computing to identify, extract and describe best practices to foster further research.

Many researchers in different organizations across the globe have been doing research in fog computing, its architecture, and applications. To keep abreast with this development, it is an effort to bring the recent advances in fog computing and its emerging applications in a cohesive manner. The main objective is to bring most of the major developments in the above-mentioned area in a precise manner so that it can serve as a handbook for many researchers. Also, many of the universities have introduced this topic as a course at the postgraduate level. We trust and hope that this book will help the researchers, who have an interest in fog computing: architecture and its applications, to keep insight into recent advances and their importance in real-life applications. Further, a larger number of research communities may be brought under one umbrella to share their ideas in a more structured manner. In that case, the present endeavor may be seen as the beginning of such an effort in bringing various research applications close to one another.

D. P. Acharjya
Vellore Institute of Technology, India

Kauser Ahmed P.
Vellore Institute of Technology, India

Acknowledgment

We would like to thank all the authors and publishers whose books and periodicals the contributors consulted while writing. Additionally, we appreciate VIT University in India for giving the resources needed to finish this project. For their assistance during the review process, the editorial board and reviewers have our sincere gratitude. Last but not least, we would like to express our gratitude to the IGI Global production team for supporting us and offering their assistance in order to complete this edited book on schedule.

D. P. Acharjya
Vellore Institute of Technology, India

Kauser Ahmed P
Vellore Institute of Technology, India

Section 1
Fog Computing Foundations and Applications

Chapter 1
Fog Computing Foundations

Muhammad Ehsan Rana

Asia Pacific University of Technology and Innovation, Malaysia

Nirase Fathima Abubacker

Asia Pacific University of Technology and Innovation, Malaysia

ABSTRACT

Fog computing is a paradigm that extends cloud computing capabilities to the network edge. Its foundations lie in understanding the theoretical principles and key concepts driving its development. This includes exploring architectural aspects which facilitate efficient and distributed data processing at the network edge. It involves examining the device and hardware support required for seamless fog computing operations, including edge devices, fog nodes, and network infrastructure. Different deployment approaches such as centralized, distributed, and hierarchical deployments bring their own advantages, limitations, and considerations. Evaluating these strategies and associated metrics aids in informed decision-making for fog infrastructure deployment. Understanding these foundations is crucial for building efficient, scalable, and resource-rich fog computing systems that address challenges in modern computing. This chapter investigates these concepts and highlights the significance of fog computing in enabling low-latency and resource-rich processing in smart infrastructure setups.

1. INTRODUCTION

In today's rapidly evolving technological landscape, where the Internet of Things (IoT) is revolutionizing the way we interact with the digital world, traditional cloud computing paradigms are facing significant challenges. The exponential growth of IoT devices, the increasing demand for real-time and low-latency applications, and the massive amounts of data generated at the network edge have prompted the need for a new computing paradigm that can address these unique requirements. The proliferation of the Internet of Things (IoT) has led to the deployment of a large number of sensors, enabling the creation of numerous smart infrastructure setups. The concept of cloud computing has played a crucial role in managing vast amounts of big and fast streaming data.

Fog computing has emerged as a promising solution to bridge the gap between IoT devices and the cloud, enabling efficient and decentralized processing and storage capabilities at the network edge. Fog

DOI: 10.4018/978-1-6684-4466-5.ch001

computing extends cloud computing capabilities to the edge of the network, closer to the data source and end-users. It brings computation, storage, and networking resources closer to the data generation points, reducing the latency and bandwidth constraints associated with cloud-centric architectures. By leveraging the distributed computing power of edge devices, fog computing enables real-time data analysis, faster response times, and enhanced user experiences for a wide range of applications, including smart cities, industrial automation, healthcare, transportation, and more (Varshney & Simmhan, 2017).

Fog computing is defined as a distributed computing architecture that profoundly extends the services provided by cloud computing to the edge of the network (Dastjerdi et al., 2016). To support fundamental network operations and applications, users can rent out a vast collection of heterogeneous and decentralized devices that communicate with each other to store data and process tasks. Figure 1 shows the Cisco invented Fog computing concept, which extends and moves the Cloud platform closer to the end-user's device (Khan et al., 2017).

At its core, fog computing aims to address the limitations of traditional cloud computing models by pushing intelligence, processing, and storage closer to the edge. This paradigm shift brings numerous benefits, such as reduced network congestion, improved data privacy and security, enhanced scalability, and the ability to operate in disconnected or intermittently connected environments. By utilizing edge devices such as routers, gateways, edge servers, and IoT devices, fog computing enables efficient data processing, analytics, and decision-making, leading to improved operational efficiency and better utilization of network resources. Moreover, fog computing introduces a collaborative and distributed approach to data processing. Instead of relying solely on centralized cloud infrastructures, fog computing encourages peer-to-peer communication and collaboration among edge devices. This enables efficient sharing

Figure 1. Fog computing by Cisco
(Khan et al., 2017)

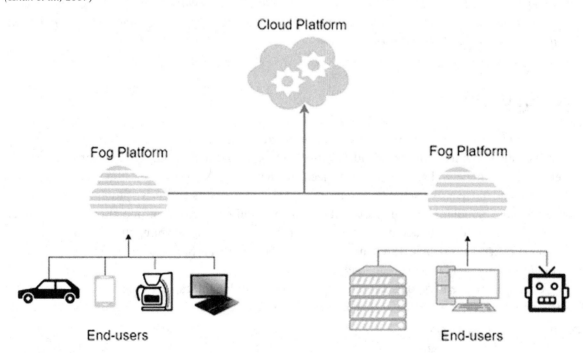

of data, task offloading, and cooperative processing, allowing edge devices to leverage their collective capabilities and enhance the overall system performance.

Despite its immense potential, fog computing also presents unique challenges. These challenges include resource constraints of edge devices, ensuring data security and privacy in decentralized environments, managing the heterogeneity and scale of edge deployments, and seamlessly integrating fog computing with existing cloud infrastructures (Alzoubi et al., 2022). Overcoming these challenges requires innovative research, development of robust algorithms, and the establishment of industry standards.

The objective of this book chapter is to provide a comprehensive understanding of fog computing by exploring its theoretical foundations, architecture, device and hardware support, deployment strategies, programming models, abstraction techniques, and future research directions. The chapter begins with an introduction to fog computing and its significance in enabling low-latency and resource-rich processing in smart infrastructure setups. Theoretical foundations of fog computing systems are then explored, followed by an in-depth examination of fog computing architecture, including hierarchical and layered architectures. The chapter also discusses device and hardware support for fog computing, focusing on edge devices, fog nodes, and network infrastructure. Deployment strategies for fog infrastructures, such as centralized, distributed, and hierarchical deployments, are examined, along with their characteristics, advantages, limitations, and case studies. Evaluation metrics for deployment strategies are presented, including performance, cost, scalability, and reliability metrics. Programming models for fog computing, such as event-driven, message passing, stream processing, and edge analytics models, are discussed, highlighting their architectures, advantages, and challenges. Abstraction techniques in fog computing are explored, followed by a review of fog computing development and future research directions. The chapter concludes with a summary of key findings and insights into the foundations of fog computing.

2. THEORETICAL FOUNDATIONS FOR FOG COMPUTING SYSTEMS

The theoretical foundations of fog computing draw from various disciplines such as distributed systems, cloud computing, queuing theory, formal methods, and cyber-physical systems. These disciplines provide a solid framework for understanding the fundamental principles and concepts underlying fog computing and enable the application of formal techniques to ensure correctness, reliability, and security. By leveraging these foundations, fog computing systems can be designed, optimized, and verified to meet performance, scalability, and safety requirements. Overall, these theoretical foundations provide researchers and designers with the necessary tools and concepts to address the challenges and complexities of fog computing systems, ensuring their efficiency, reliability, and security.

Distributed systems form the basis for understanding and designing fog computing systems, involving concepts like concurrency, consistency and replication, fault tolerance, distributed algorithms, scalability, and communication protocols. Firstly, concurrency management is vital to handle multiple tasks simultaneously and ensure consistency in fog computing systems. Consistency and replication techniques guarantee fault tolerance and reliability by maintaining data consistency across multiple replicas. Fault tolerance mechanisms safeguard the system against failures, ensuring availability and reliability. Distributed algorithms address coordination and synchronization challenges in tasks like load balancing and data processing. Scalability techniques enable fog computing systems to handle large-scale deployments efficiently. Communication protocols facilitate seamless data exchange and coordination between nodes, promoting efficient collaboration in fog computing systems.

Cloud computing provides a theoretical foundation with its concepts of virtualization, scalability, service models, service level agreements (SLAs), resource management, and data management (Hajibaba & Gorgin, 2014). Virtualization enables efficient resource management and allocation in fog computing systems. Scalability techniques ensure that fog nodes can handle increasing workloads and dynamically scale their resources. Cloud service models can be extended to the edge, allowing fog nodes to offer services and act as platforms for fog applications. Service level agreements define quality standards and expectations in fog computing. Resource management techniques optimize resource utilization in dynamic and heterogeneous environments. Data management principles from cloud computing apply to efficient and scalable data storage, retrieval, and processing in fog computing systems.

Computer networks play a crucial role in the design and optimization of fog computing systems, covering network topologies, routing algorithms, network performance analysis, network protocols, and network optimization (Al-Doghman et al., 2016). Network topologies determine the arrangement of nodes and links, allowing efficient resource distribution and communication. Routing algorithms ensure timely data delivery and can be optimized for fog computing environments. Performance analysis helps identify bottlenecks and optimize resource allocation. Network protocols enable seamless communication and coordination among fog nodes, edge devices, and cloud resources. Network optimization techniques enhance resource allocation and system performance in fog computing.

Queuing theory is a mathematical discipline that analyzes and models waiting lines or queues, which is essential for understanding and optimizing fog computing systems. It encompasses concepts like arrival and service processes, queueing models, queueing networks, performance measures, and optimization and control (Mas et al., 2022). In fog computing systems, queueing theory helps model and optimize various aspects, including resource allocation, task scheduling, and system performance. It allows researchers to analyze the arrival process of tasks, understand the service process, and apply queueing models to characterize system behaviour. Queueing networks help model interactions between fog nodes, while performance measures evaluate system efficiency. Optimization techniques based on queueing theory enable researchers to find optimal configurations and control policies, maximizing throughput and minimizing waiting times in fog computing systems.

Cyber-physical systems (CPS) are vital for modelling, analyzing, and optimizing the interactions between the physical world and computational components in fog computing systems. CPS contributes to the understanding of physical processes, sensor integration, control and actuation, cyber-physical co-ordination, security and privacy, and resilience and fault tolerance (Bouachir et al., 2020). Cyber-Physical Systems (CPS) are essential for understanding and designing fog computing systems. By leveraging CPS theory, researchers can create fog computing systems that effectively monitor, control, and respond to the physical world, ensuring accurate data acquisition, real-time decision-making, and reliable operation in dynamic environments.

Formal methods are mathematical techniques used to rigorously analyze, model, and verify the correctness of software and hardware systems. In the context of fog computing systems, formal methods ensure reliability, safety, and security. They enable precise system specification, verification of system properties, design refinement, safety and security analysis, runtime monitoring, and analysis of safety-critical and autonomous systems. By applying formal methods, designers can eliminate errors, ensure system correctness, and enhance the dependability of fog computing systems in various domains.

3. FOG COMPUTING ARCHITECTURE

Fog computing architecture extends cloud computing to edge devices and users, addressing limitations like high latency and privacy concerns. It leverages resources at the network edge, including edge devices, fog nodes, and cloud servers, for efficient and real-time data processing. Edge devices serve as the interface between the physical world and the fog computing infrastructure, performing lightweight computations and data preprocessing. Fog nodes, located at the network edge, are responsible for processing and analyzing data, hosting fog applications, and providing low-latency interactions. Cloud servers in data centers handle heavy-duty computations, data storage, and act as the backend infrastructure (Hu et al., 2017).

Fog computing relies on a middleware layer for communication and coordination between edge devices, fog nodes, and cloud servers. It facilitates data routing, device discovery, security, and resource management, ensuring integration and fault tolerance. Robust networking infrastructure with high-speed and low-latency connectivity is crucial for real-time interactions. Security measures like authentication, encryption, and secure communication protocols are implemented to protect data, and privacy concerns are addressed through privacy-enhancing technologies and policies. Fog computing architecture supports various applications like smart cities, industrial IoT, healthcare monitoring and utilizes programming models for efficient and scalable data processing at the edge (Lai et al., 2021).

3.1 Hierarchical Architecture

In hierarchical fog computing architecture, the fog nodes are grouped into different tiers based on their proximity to the edge devices and their computing capabilities. Typically, the architecture consists of three tiers: the edge tier, the intermediate tier, and the cloud tier as shown in Figure 2 (Wani et al., 2019).

3.1.1 Edge Tier

The edge tier consists of fog nodes that are closest to the edge devices. These nodes are responsible for performing low-latency and real-time processing tasks directly at the network edge. They are capable of handling lightweight computations, data preprocessing, and immediate response to local events. Edge nodes are deployed in close proximity to the edge devices, enabling faster data processing and reducing network latency.

3.1.2 Intermediate Tier

The intermediate tier is positioned between the edge tier and the cloud tier. It comprises fog nodes with higher computational capabilities and storage capacities compared to the edge tier. These nodes are responsible for aggregating and processing data from multiple edge nodes before forwarding it to the cloud tier. The intermediate tier performs more complex computations, data analytics, and decision-making tasks. It acts as a bridge between the edge tier and the cloud tier, providing a balance between low-latency processing at the edge and resource-intensive tasks in the cloud.

3.1.3 Cloud Tier

The cloud tier represents the highest level in the hierarchical fog computing architecture. It consists of cloud servers located in data centers that provide scalable computing and storage resources. Cloud servers handle resource-intensive tasks, such as big data analytics, machine learning, and complex simulations. They store historical data, provide long-term storage, and serve as a centralized backend for the fog computing infrastructure. The cloud tier is responsible for processing data that requires significant computational power and storage capacity, which may not be feasible at the edge or intermediate tiers.

3.2 Layered Architecture

According to (Naha et al., 2018), the best way to depict fog architecture is through layered representation. He depicted fog computing architecture using eight layers as shown in Figure 3:

The Description of these layers are as follows:

Figure 2. Hierarchical fog computing architecture
(Wani et al., 2019)

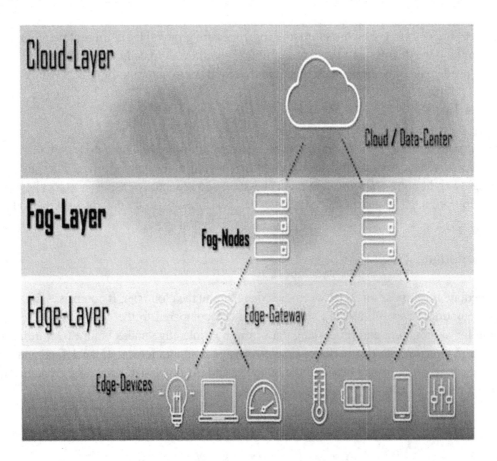

Fog Computing Foundations

Figure 3. Components of layered fog computing architecture
(Naha et al., 2018)

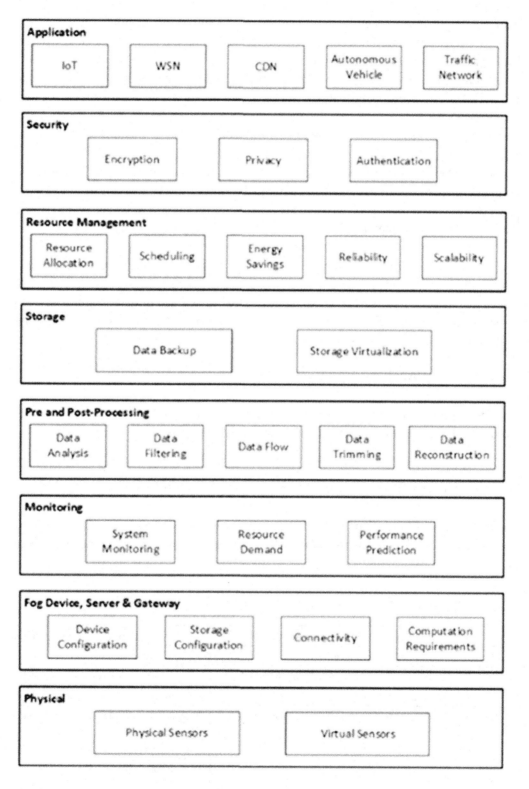

7

a.   Application Layer: This layer has IoT, Wireless Sensor Network, Content Delivery Network, Autonomous vehicle, Traffic network, to name a few.

b.   Security Layer: It performs encryption, privacy checks and user authentication.

c.   Resource Management Layer: It helps in resource allocation, task scheduling, energy savings. This also improves reliability and scalability.

d.   Storage Layer: It consists of storage hardware for backup and can function as virtual storage.

e.   Pre- and Post-Processing: Data analysis, filtering, data flow and other transformations of data takes place in this layer.

f.   Monitoring: The metrics such as system performance, resource demand and predication will be made here.

g.   Fog Device, Server, and Gateway: The hardware and software configurations, connectivity and computation requirements are determined in this layer.

h.   Physical: This layer consists of physical and virtual sensor points which act as the entry and exit points of data to fog computing device.

The Layered Fog Computing Architecture proposed by Naha et al. offers several advantages such as modularity, resource management, security, data processing, and monitoring. However, the architecture's limitations, including the lack of detailed implementation guidelines, limited evaluation, complexity, potential performance bottlenecks, and adaptability challenges, need to be considered when implementing and assessing its suitability for fog computing systems.

3.3 Comparison of Architectures

Table 1 provides a concise comparison of the two architectures in terms of their design, communication patterns, scalability, flexibility, resource management, and deployment/configuration.

4. DEVICE AND HARDWARE SUPPORT FOR FOG COMPUTING

Fog computing brings computation, storage, and networking resources closer to the edge devices, enabling real-time data processing, improved response time, enhanced security, and efficient bandwidth

Table 1. Comparison of layered and hierarchical fog computing architectures

	Layered Fog Computing Architecture	**Hierarchical Fog Computing Architecture**
Architecture Design	Based on a layered approach	Based on a hierarchical structure
Communication	Vertical communication and data flow between layers	Horizontal and vertical communication and data flow
Scalability	Modular and scalable structure	Scalability through distributed hierarchical structure
Flexibility	Independent customization and adaptability of each layer	Flexibility through distribution across hierarchical tiers
Resource Management	Managed independently at each layer	Hierarchical resource management at different levels
Deployment and Configuration	Layers can be deployed and configured independently	Placement and configuration based on hierarchical levels

utilization. In order to effectively implement fog computing, robust device and hardware support is essential (Lawal et al., 2020). This section explores the key aspects of device and hardware support for fog computing and their significance in enabling this paradigm.

4.1 Edge Devices

Edge devices are the foundational components of fog computing. They include sensors, actuators, smartphones, gateways, routers, and other embedded systems. Edge devices play a crucial role in collecting data from the physical world and preprocessing it before transmitting it to fog nodes or the cloud. They need to be capable of handling real-time data processing, communication, and storage (Aazam et al., 2018).

The characteristics of edge devices include:

a. Computational Power: Edge devices should possess sufficient computational power to perform data processing tasks locally. This involves executing complex algorithms, running machine learning models, and performing analytics.
b. Memory and Storage: Adequate memory and storage capacity are required to store and manage the data locally. Edge devices should have enough RAM and non-volatile storage options to handle the workload efficiently.
c. Connectivity Options: Edge devices should support various connectivity options such as Wi-Fi, Bluetooth, cellular networks, and Ethernet. This enables seamless communication with other devices and fog nodes.
d. Energy Efficiency: Many edge devices operate on limited power sources such as batteries or renewable energy. Hence, energy-efficient designs are essential to ensure long battery life and sustainable operation.

4.2 Fog Nodes

Fog nodes serve as intermediaries between edge devices and the cloud infrastructure. They receive data from edge devices, perform processing and analysis, and provide localized services. Fog nodes are typically located at various network points, such as access points, base stations, or network switches (Atlam et al., 2018).

The characteristics of fog nodes include:

a. Processing Power: Fog nodes require sufficient processing power to handle the computational demands of fog computing applications. This involves executing complex algorithms, running virtualized environments, and supporting real-time analytics.
b. Memory and Storage: Fog nodes should have ample memory and storage capacity to store and manage data. This includes both RAM and storage devices like solid-state drives (SSDs) for efficient data access.
c. Networking Capabilities: High-speed networking interfaces are crucial for efficient data transmission between edge devices, fog nodes, and the cloud. Fog nodes should support various communication protocols and have the ability to handle high volumes of data traffic.

d.   Scalability: Fog nodes should be scalable to accommodate the growing number of edge devices and changing workload requirements. This ensures that the fog computing infrastructure can handle increasing data processing demands effectively.

4.3 Network Infrastructure

A robust network infrastructure is vital to support fog computing. The network should provide low-latency and high-bandwidth connectivity between edge devices, fog nodes, and the cloud (Bonomi et al., 2012). The characteristics of the network infrastructure include:

a.   Low Latency: Fog computing requires low-latency communication to enable real-time data processing and response. Network infrastructure should minimize delays in data transmission and ensure timely delivery of data packets.

b.   High Bandwidth: Fog computing generates and processes a significant amount of data. The network infrastructure should provide high bandwidth to handle the data traffic efficiently and avoid congestion.

c.   Communication Protocols: The network should support various communication protocols such as Wi-Fi, cellular networks, Ethernet, and wireless sensor networks. This accommodates different types of edge devices with diverse connectivity requirements.

d.   Resilience: The network infrastructure should be resilient to failures and disruptions. Redundancy, fault tolerance mechanisms, and effective routing protocols are necessary to ensure continuous operation of fog computing services.

5. DEPLOYMENT STRATEGIES OF FOG INFRASTRUCTURES

The deployment strategies of fog infrastructures involve strategically placing fog nodes, edge devices, and network components to optimize performance, reliability, and scalability. There are three main deployment strategies: centralized fog deployment, distributed fog deployment, and hierarchical fog deployment.

5.1 Centralized Fog Deployment

Centralized fog deployment involves placing a central fog node or cluster of fog nodes in a central location, such as a data center or cloud infrastructure, to serve multiple edge devices. This strategy leverages the computational power of the central fog node, enables data aggregation, and simplifies resource management. It offers improved performance, efficient resource utilization, simplified management, and enhanced security (Manju & Sumathy, 2019). However, it has limitations such as single point of failure, network congestion, and scalability challenges (Pierre & Ahmed, 2020).

5.2 Distributed Fog Deployment

Distributed fog deployment distributes fog computing resources across the network, closer to the edge devices. Each fog node independently performs data processing, storage, and computing tasks. It offers lower latency, scalability, improved reliability, and data localization and privacy benefits (Wobker et al.,

2018). However, it presents challenges in resource management complexity, increased network overhead, and integration and interoperability (Lin & Yang, 2018).

5.3 Hierarchical Fog Deployment

Hierarchical fog deployment organizes fog nodes in a hierarchical structure, with multiple levels based on proximity and computing capabilities. It enables efficient resource management, data aggregation, and decision making across different levels of the fog network. It provides efficient resource management, scalability, reduced network traffic, and improved decision making. However, managing the hierarchy can be complex, there can be increased overhead in data aggregation, and a single point of failure at the central level (Shaik & Baskiyar, 2018).

5.4 Recommendations for Selecting Fog Deployment Strategy

There are several best practices and recommendations that organizations can follow to ensure successful implementation. By adhering to these best practices and recommendations, organizations can maximize the benefits of fog computing and achieve improved performance, scalability, and reliability in their deployments.

a.   Before selecting a fog deployment strategy, it is essential to thoroughly assess the specific requirements of the applications to be deployed. Consider factors such as latency sensitivity, data volume, security needs, and computational requirements to determine the most suitable fog deployment approach.
b.   Analyze the network topology to identify the locations and distribution of edge devices and fog nodes. This analysis helps determine the optimal placement of fog nodes for efficient data processing, reduced latency, and improved overall system performance.
c.   Evaluate the availability and capacity of computing resources at different levels of the fog infrastructure. Consider factors such as processing power, memory, storage, and network bandwidth to ensure sufficient resources are allocated for each fog node and application.
d.   Utilize optimization techniques and tools to enhance the efficiency and effectiveness of fog deployment strategies. These techniques include load balancing, task scheduling algorithms, and resource allocation algorithms. Such optimizations can improve performance, scalability, and resource utilization in fog environments.

6. PROGRAMMING MODELS FOR FOG COMPUTING

Fog computing requires specialized programming models to effectively handle the distributed and real-time nature of edge devices. This section explores several programming models commonly used in fog computing and their applications.

6.1 Event-driven Programming Model

The event-driven programming model involves event sources and event handlers for asynchronous and event-driven processing. It enables efficient handling of asynchronous events, offers flexibility and scalability, and allows for loose coupling between components. It also facilitates the integration of diverse devices and technologies. However, challenges arise in ensuring the reliability and availability of event handling mechanisms and maintaining consistency and coherence across distributed components. Event-driven programming enables the application to respond in real-time to changes or inputs, making it well-suited for time-sensitive tasks and applications that require immediate action (Bermbach et al., 2018).

6.2 Message Passing Model

The message passing model involves the exchange of messages between fog nodes, edge devices, and cloud servers. It operates based on standardized rules and protocols for message creation, transmission, and handling. The model offers advantages such as flexibility and scalability, dynamic interactions between components, fault tolerance and resilience, and support for distributed algorithms and parallel processing. However, challenges include ensuring message integrity and security, managing overhead in message handling, and employing efficient message processing techniques (Srirama et al., 2021). Common message passing protocols used in fog computing include Message Queueing Telemetry Transport (MQTT), Advanced Message Queuing Protocol (AMQP), and Data Distribution Service (DDS) (Dizdarević et al., 2019). Message passing models are suitable for applications that require reliable communication, event synchronization, and data sharing among distributed components.

6.3 Stream Processing Model

The stream processing model treats data as a continuous stream of events or records and processes it incrementally in real-time. It involves processing stages that operate on incoming data streams, allowing for immediate insights and actions. The advantages of this model include real-time handling of high-velocity data streams, data parallelism, distributed processing, and flexibility. However, challenges include handling out-of-order events, managing data skew, and ensuring fault tolerance in distributed stream processing. In fog computing, the stream processing model is well-suited for scenarios where data is generated and collected from distributed sensors, devices, or edge nodes. The model enables data to be processed and analyzed at the edge of the network, closer to the data source, reducing the latency and bandwidth requirements for transmitting data to the cloud (Cardellini et al., 2019).

6.4 Edge Analytics Programming Model

The edge analytics programming model involves deploying analytical algorithms and models directly on edge devices, allowing for real-time data processing and analytics at the edge (Yi et al., 2015). It reduces reliance on cloud resources, improves privacy and security, and enables context-aware and adaptive actions. However, there are challenges related to the limited computational and storage capabilities of edge devices, optimizing resource utilization, developing efficient algorithms, ensuring data security and privacy, and managing the heterogeneity of edge devices. One of the key characteristics of the edge analytics programming model is its ability to process data in near real-time. Instead of transmitting the data to a centralized server or the cloud for analysis, the data is processed locally at the edge, enabling immediate insights and actions. This is particularly beneficial in applications that require timely decision-making or in scenarios where network connectivity may be limited or unreliable (Ma et al., 2019).

6.5 Comparative Analysis and Selection of Programming Models

The selection of a programming model for fog computing depends on the specific requirements and characteristics of the application. Each programming model has its strengths and weaknesses, and a comparative analysis can help in choosing the most appropriate model. Factors to consider include the nature of data processing (event-based, stream-based, or analytics-driven), real-time requirements, resource constraints, scalability, fault tolerance, and programming language support. Table 2 provides a concise overview of the different programming models in fog computing, allowing for a systematic evaluation of their characteristics and suitability for various applications.

7. ABSTRACTION IN FOG COMPUTING

Abstractions in fog computing play a vital role in simplifying complex underlying technologies and resources. They provide higher-level representations that enable developers and users to interact with the fog computing environment without dealing with intricate details. This summary will cover the key abstractions in fog computing: resource abstractions, data abstractions, service abstractions, security abstractions, and mobility abstractions.

Resource abstractions in fog computing focus on providing higher-level representations of computing, storage, and networking resources in the fog environment. They enable efficient resource management and allocation, facilitating the deployment and scaling of fog applications. Resource abstractions include mechanisms for resource discovery, modeling, allocation and scheduling, optimization, monitoring and control, as well as promoting interoperability and portability (Choi et al., 2017).

Data abstractions in fog computing are essential for handling and processing data efficiently within the distributed fog environment. They provide higher-level representations of data sources, data formats, and data processing mechanisms. Data abstractions cover aspects such as data source representations, data format handling, data processing interfaces, data storage management, data security and privacy considerations, and data lifecycle management (Moysiadis et al., 2018).

Table 2. Comparison of programming models for fog computing

	Event-driven	Message Passing	Stream Processing	Edge Analytics
Concurrency	Supports parallel processing and enhances responsiveness.	Allows for parallel execution of tasks through message passing.	Enables parallel processing and real-time analysis of data streams.	Utilizes edge devices for local processing, reducing latency.
Integration	Facilitates loose coupling between components in a fog computing system.	Enables communication and coordination between distributed components.	Works well with distributed and parallel processing environments.	Leverages computational capabilities of edge devices for local analysis.
Real-time Processing	Well-suited for time-sensitive tasks and immediate actions.	Supports real-time communication and coordination.	Designed for continuous and real-time processing of data streams.	Enables real-time analysis and decision-making at the edge.
Application Examples	IoT data processing, real-time analytics, smart grid monitoring.	Distributed systems, collaborative environments.	Real-time data processing, IoT applications, financial analysis.	Predictive maintenance, anomaly detection, personalized recommendations.

Service abstractions in fog computing enable the composition, orchestration, and management of services within the fog environment. They abstract the complexities of service interactions and resource management. Service abstractions include service representation, composition and orchestration mechanisms, service discovery and management interfaces, quality of service (QoS) considerations, service interoperability, as well as service security and privacy mechanisms (Qu et al., 2020).

Security abstractions in fog computing ensure secure communication, protect data privacy, and enforce access control in the fog environment. They provide higher-level representations of security mechanisms and policies, simplifying their implementation and management. Security abstractions cover aspects such as secure communication, access control, data privacy, threat detection and prevention, security policy management, as well as secure data storage and processing (Lee et al., 2015).

Mobility abstractions in fog computing address the challenges posed by the mobility of edge devices within the fog infrastructure. They ensure seamless handoff management, dynamic resource allocation, location awareness, and network resilience. Mobility abstractions enable fog applications to adapt to changing resource availability, maintain uninterrupted service delivery during device movement, leverage location information for context-aware services, and handle intermittent network connectivity or disruptions (Yi et al., 2015).

Table 3 provides an overview of different levels of abstraction in fog computing, ranging from the physical devices and network infrastructure to higher-level concepts such as application services and security considerations. Each level of abstraction plays a crucial role in understanding, designing, and optimizing fog computing systems.

Table 3. Comparison of abstractions for fog computing

Level of Abstraction	Description	Example
Physical Devices	Represents the physical devices in the fog computing system, including fog nodes, edge devices, and sensors.	Raspberry Pi, Smartphones, Industrial IoT Devices
Network Topology	Abstract representation of the network connectivity between fog nodes, edge devices, and cloud resources.	Star Topology, Mesh Topology, Tree Topology
Communication Protocols	Defines the rules and procedures for data exchange and communication between fog nodes, edge devices, and cloud resources.	MQTT, CoAP, HTTP
Data Processing	Represents the processing and analytics capabilities of fog nodes and edge devices.	Data filtering, Data aggregation, Machine learning algorithms
Resource Management	Deals with the allocation and utilization of computational resources, such as CPU, memory, and storage, in fog computing systems.	Load balancing, Task scheduling, Resource provisioning
Application Services	Represents the higher-level services and applications running on fog computing systems.	Video surveillance, Smart city applications, Industrial automation
Security and Privacy	Deals with the protection of data, communication, and system resources in fog computing systems.	Authentication, Encryption, Access control
QoS and Service Level Agreements	Defines the performance metrics and guarantees for fog computing services, such as latency, reliability, and availability.	Response time, Throughput, Service uptime

8. REVIEW OF FOG COMPUTING DEVELOPMENT

Fog computing has emerged as a promising paradigm to address the challenges posed by the growing demand for real-time data processing, low latency, and efficient resource utilization in the era of the Internet of Things (IoT) and edge computing. One significant aspect of fog computing development is the advancement in hardware and infrastructure. The availability of powerful and energy-efficient edge devices has enabled the deployment of fog nodes closer to the data sources, allowing for faster data processing and reduced network latency. Moreover, the development of edge computing platforms and gateways has facilitated the seamless integration of edge devices into the fog infrastructure. These advancements in hardware and infrastructure have paved the way for the widespread adoption of fog computing in various domains and industries (Laghari et al., 2021).

Another important area of development in fog computing is the evolution of programming models and abstractions. The development of programming models tailored for fog computing, such as event-driven programming, message passing, and stream processing models, has provided developers with the necessary tools and frameworks to design and deploy fog-based applications. These programming models abstract the complexities of distributed computing, allowing developers to focus on the application logic rather than the underlying infrastructure. Additionally, the development of abstractions for resource management, data processing, service composition, and security has further facilitated the development of fog applications, enabling efficient resource utilization, seamless data processing, and secure communication (Dastjerdi et al., 2016).

The advancement in fog computing has also been supported by the development of various communication protocols and networking technologies. Fog computing relies on efficient and reliable communication between fog nodes, edge devices, and cloud servers. Therefore, the development of protocols such as MQTT (Message Queuing Telemetry Transport) and CoAP (Constrained Application Protocol) that are lightweight, low-latency, and suitable for constrained environments has been crucial for enabling efficient data transmission and communication in fog computing environments (Tuli et al., 2019). Additionally, advancements in wireless networking technologies, such as 5G, have further enhanced the communication capabilities of fog computing systems, enabling faster data transfer rates, lower latency, and improved network reliability (Meng et al., 2020).

Furthermore, the development of analytics and machine learning techniques tailored for fog computing has played a significant role in extracting valuable insights from the vast amount of data generated by edge devices. Fog-based analytics and machine learning algorithms enable real-time data processing, predictive analytics, and decision-making at the edge, reducing the need for data transmission to centralized cloud servers. These developments have been instrumental in enabling fog computing to support various applications, including smart cities, industrial automation, healthcare monitoring, and autonomous vehicles (Guevara et al., 2020).

Despite the progress made in fog computing development, several challenges and open research areas remain. These include addressing issues related to scalability, resource allocation, interoperability, security, and privacy (Wang et al., 2019). Scalability challenges arise when dealing with a large number of edge devices and fog nodes, requiring efficient resource management and load balancing techniques. Interoperability challenges involve integrating heterogeneous edge devices and fog nodes into a cohesive fog infrastructure, ensuring seamless communication and cooperation. Security and privacy concerns need to be addressed to protect sensitive data, ensure secure communication, and mitigate potential attacks in fog computing environments (Wani et al., 2019).

In conclusion, the development of fog computing has witnessed significant progress in terms of hardware infrastructure, programming models, communication protocols, and analytics techniques. These advancements have laid the foundation for the adoption of fog computing in various domains and have paved the way for realizing the vision of edge intelligence and real-time data processing. However, further research and development are required to overcome the remaining challenges and make fog computing more scalable, secure, and interoperable, thus unlocking its full potential in the era of IoT and edge computing.

9. FUTURE RESEARCH DIRECTIONS

In the rapidly evolving field of fog computing, the future research directions include incorporating advanced machine learning and artificial intelligence techniques to enhance edge intelligence, exploring collaboration and communication among edge devices, optimizing resource allocation and energy efficiency and improving fog-cloud integration and interoperability. Moreover, exploring fog computing in specific application domains such as healthcare, transportation, smart cities, industrial automation, and agriculture needs a thorough research focus. These research directions aim to advance fog computing systems and enable their effective utilization in various domains, addressing domain-specific challenges and improving operational efficiency. Following is a brief description of these areas:

- Edge Intelligence and AI: Integrating advanced machine learning and artificial intelligence techniques at the edge is a key research direction. This includes developing intelligent algorithms and models that can efficiently process and analyze data at the edge, enabling real-time decision-making, predictive analytics, and autonomous behaviour in fog computing systems.
- Edge Device Collaboration and Communication: Investigating efficient collaboration and communication mechanisms among edge devices is essential for distributed processing and resource sharing. Research can focus on developing protocols, algorithms, and architectures that facilitate seamless communication, data sharing, and task offloading between edge devices, enabling cooperative and coordinated behaviour.
- Resource Allocation and Energy Efficiency: Optimizing resource allocation in fog computing systems is crucial to ensure efficient utilization of computational resources, minimize latency, and enhance system performance. Future research can explore dynamic resource allocation algorithms, workload balancing strategies, and energy-efficient techniques to optimize resource usage, reduce energy consumption, and prolong the lifespan of edge devices.
- Fog-Cloud Integration and Interoperability: Enhancing the integration and interoperability between fog and cloud resources is a significant research direction. This involves developing standardized interfaces, protocols, and architectures that enable seamless communication, data exchange, and resource management between fog nodes and cloud platforms. Ensuring compatibility and interoperability will facilitate the efficient utilization of both fog and cloud resources in a unified manner.
- Security and Privacy in Fog Computing: Addressing security and privacy challenges in fog computing systems remains a critical research area. This includes developing robust security mechanisms, privacy-preserving techniques, and authentication protocols to protect data, ensure system

integrity, and mitigate security threats. Research can also focus on developing intrusion detection and prevention systems tailored for fog computing environments.

- Domain-Specific Applications: Exploring fog computing in specific application domains such as healthcare, transportation, smart cities, industrial automation, and agriculture requires dedicated research efforts. Understanding the unique requirements, challenges, and constraints of each domain will enable the development of tailored fog computing solutions that address domain-specific needs and enhance operational efficiency.

10. CONCLUSION

In conclusion, the rapid growth of Internet of Things (IoT) devices and the need for real-time applications have exposed limitations in traditional cloud computing. As a solution, fog computing extends cloud capabilities to the network edge, enabling real-time data analysis and faster responses. Its distributed approach promotes collaboration among edge devices, reducing network congestion and enhancing data privacy. Fog computing's potential applications span various fields, such as smart cities, healthcare, and industrial automation. However, it faces challenges like resource constraints and data security. The chapter provided a comprehensive understanding of fog computing, exploring its foundations, architecture, deployment, programming models, and future directions. Fog computing presents a compelling alternative, unlocking the full potential of IoT and revolutionizing how data and computing are handled in an interconnected world.

REFERENCES

Aazam, M., Zeadally, S., & Harras, K. A. (2018). Offloading in fog computing for IoT: Review, enabling technologies, and research opportunities. *Future Generation Computer Systems*, 87, 278–289. doi:10.1016/j.future.2018.04.057

Al-Doghman, F., Chaczko, Z., Ajayan, A. R., & Klempous, R. (2016). A review on Fog Computing technology. *2016 IEEE International Conference on Systems, Man, and Cybernetics (SMC)*. IEEE. 10.1109/SMC.2016.7844455

Alzoubi, Y. I., Al-Ahmad, A., & Kahtan, H. (2022). Blockchain technology as a Fog computing security and privacy solution: An overview. *Computer Communications*, 182, 129–152. doi:10.1016/j.comcom.2021.11.005

Atlam, H., Walters, R., & Wills, G. (2018). Fog computing and the Internet of Things: A review. *Big Data and Cognitive Computing*, 2(2), 10. doi:10.3390/bdcc2020010

Bermbach, D., Pallas, F., Pérez, D. G., Plebani, P., Anderson, M., Kat, R., & Tai, S. (2018). A research perspective on fog computing. In *Service-Oriented Computing – ICSOC 2017 Workshops* (pp. 198–210). Springer International Publishing. doi:10.1007/978-3-319-91764-1_16

Bonomi, F., Milito, R., Zhu, J., & Addepalli, S. (2012). Fog computing and its role in the internet of things. *Proceedings of the First Edition of the MCC Workshop on Mobile Cloud Computing*. ACM. 10.1145/2342509.2342513

Bouachir, O., Aloqaily, M., Tseng, L., & Boukerche, A. (2020). Blockchain and fog computing for cyber-physical systems: The case of smart industry. *Computer, 53*(9), 36–45. doi:10.1109/MC.2020.2996212

Cardellini, V., Mencagli, G., Talia, D., & Torquati, M. (2019). New landscapes of the data stream processing in the era of fog computing. *Future Generation Computer Systems, 99*, 646–650. doi:10.1016/j.future.2019.03.027

Choi, N., Kim, D., Lee, S.-J., & Yi, Y. (2017). A fog operating system for user-oriented IoT services: Challenges and research directions. *IEEE Communications Magazine, 55*(8), 44–51. doi:10.1109/MCOM.2017.1600908

Dastjerdi, A. V., Gupta, H., Calheiros, R. N., Ghosh, S. K., & Buyya, R. (2016). Fog Computing: principles, architectures, and applications. In Internet of Things (pp. 61–75). Elsevier. doi:10.1016/B978-0-12-805395-9.00004-6

Dizdarević, J., Carpio, F., Jukan, A., & Masip-Bruin, X. (2019). A survey of communication protocols for Internet of Things and related challenges of fog and cloud computing integration. *ACM Computing Surveys, 51*(6), 1–29. doi:10.1145/3292674

Guevara, J. C., Torres, R. da S., & da Fonseca, N. L. S. (2020). On the classification of fog computing applications: A machine learning perspective. *Journal of Network and Computer Applications, 159*(102596), 102596. doi:10.1016/j.jnca.2020.102596

Hajibaba, M., & Gorgin, S. (2014). A review on modern distributed computing paradigms: Cloud computing, jungle computing and fog computing. *CIT. Journal of Computing and Information Technology, 22*(2), 69. doi:10.2498/cit.1002381

Hu, P., Dhelim, S., Ning, H., & Qiu, T. (2017). Survey on fog computing: Architecture, key technologies, applications and open issues. *Journal of Network and Computer Applications, 98*, 27–42. doi:10.1016/j.jnca.2017.09.002

Khan, S., Parkinson, S., & Qin, Y. (2017). Fog computing security: A review of current applications and security solutions. *Journal of Cloud Computing (Heidelberg, Germany), 6*(1), 19. doi:10.118613677-017-0090-3

Laghari, A. A., Jumani, A. K., & Laghari, R. A. (2021). Review and state of art of fog computing. *Archives of Computational Methods in Engineering. Archives of Computational Methods in Engineering, 28*(5), 3631–3643. doi:10.100711831-020-09517-y

Lai, K. L., Chen, J. I. Z., & Zong, J. I. (2021). Development of smart cities with fog computing and internet of things. [UCCT]. *Journal of Ubiquitous Computing and Communication Technologies, 3*(01), 52–60. doi:10.36548/jucct.2021.1.006

Lawal, M. A., Shaikh, R. A., & Hassan, S. R. (2020). An anomaly mitigation framework for IoT using fog computing. *Electronics (Basel), 9*(10), 1565. doi:10.3390/electronics9101565

Lee, K., Kim, D., Ha, D., Rajput, U., & Oh, H. (2015). On security and privacy issues of fog computing supported Internet of Things environment. *2015 6th International Conference on the Network of the Future (NOF)*. ACM.

Lin, C.-C., & Yang, J.-W. (2018). Cost-efficient deployment of fog computing systems at logistics centers in industry 4.0. *IEEE Transactions on Industrial Informatics*, *14*(10), 4603–4611. doi:10.1109/TII.2018.2827920

Ma, K., Bagula, A., Nyirenda, C., & Ajayi, O. (2019). An IoT-based fog computing model. *Sensors (Basel)*, *19*(12), 2783. doi:10.339019122783 PMID:31234280

Manju, A. B., & Sumathy, S. (2019). Efficient load balancing algorithm for task preprocessing in fog computing environment. In *Smart Intelligent Computing and Applications* (pp. 291–298). Springer Singapore. doi:10.1007/978-981-13-1927-3_31

Mas, L., Vilaplana, J., Mateo, J., & Solsona, F. (2022). A queuing theory model for fog computing. *The Journal of Supercomputing*, *78*(8), 11138–11155. doi:10.100711227-022-04328-3

Meng, Y., Naeem, M. A., Almagrabi, A. O., Ali, R., & Kim, H. S. (2020). Advancing the state of the fog computing to enable 5G network technologies. *Sensors (Basel)*, *20*(6), 1754. doi:10.339020061754 PMID:32245261

Moysiadis, V., Sarigiannidis, P., & Moscholios, I. (2018). Towards distributed data management in fog computing. *Wireless Communications and Mobile Computing*, *2018*, 1–14. doi:10.1155/2018/7597686

Naha, R. K., Garg, S., Georgakopoulos, D., Jayaraman, P. P., Gao, L., Xiang, Y., & Ranjan, R. (2018). Fog computing: Survey of trends, architectures, requirements, and research directions. *IEEE Access : Practical Innovations, Open Solutions*, *6*, 47980–48009. doi:10.1109/ACCESS.2018.2866491

Pierre, G., & Ahmed, A. (2020). Docker-pi: Docker container deployment in fog computing infrastructures. *International Journal of Cloud Computing*, *9*(1), 6. doi:10.1504/IJCC.2020.105885

Qu, Y., Gao, L., Luan, T. H., Xiang, Y., Yu, S., Li, B., & Zheng, G. (2020). Decentralized privacy using blockchain-enabled federated learning in fog computing. *IEEE Internet of Things Journal*, *7*(6), 5171–5183. doi:10.1109/JIOT.2020.2977383

Shaik, S., & Baskiyar, S. (2018). Hierarchical and autonomous fog architecture. *Proceedings of the 47th International Conference on Parallel Processing Companion*. ACM. 10.1145/3229710.3229740

Srirama, S. N., Dick, F. M. S., & Adhikari, M. (2021). Akka framework based on the Actor model for executing distributed Fog Computing applications. *Future Generation Computer Systems*, *117*, 439–452. doi:10.1016/j.future.2020.12.011

Tuli, S., Mahmud, R., Tuli, S., & Buyya, R. (2019). FogBus: A blockchain-based lightweight framework for edge and fog computing. *Journal of Systems and Software*, *154*, 22–36. doi:10.1016/j.jss.2019.04.050

Varshney, P., & Simmhan, Y. (2017). Demystifying fog computing: Characterizing architectures, applications and abstractions. *2017 IEEE 1st International Conference on Fog and Edge Computing (ICFEC)*. IEEE.

Wang, H., Wang, L., Zhou, Z., Tao, X., Pau, G., & Arena, F. (2019). Blockchain-based resource allocation model in fog computing. *Applied Sciences (Basel, Switzerland)*, *9*(24), 5538. doi:10.3390/app9245538 PMID:32944385

Wani, U. I., Batth, R. S., & Rashid, M. (2019). Fog computing challenges and future directions: A mirror review. *2019 International Conference on Computational Intelligence and Knowledge Economy (ICCIKE)*. IEEE. 10.1109/ICCIKE47802.2019.9004428

Wobker, C., Seitz, A., Mueller, H., & Bruegge, B. (2018). Fogernetes: Deployment and management of fog computing applications. *NOMS 2018 - 2018 IEEE/IFIP Network Operations and Management Symposium*.

Yi, S., Hao, Z., Qin, Z., & Li, Q. (2015). Fog computing: Platform and applications. *2015 Third IEEE Workshop on Hot Topics in Web Systems and Technologies (HotWeb)*. IEEE. 10.1109/HotWeb.2015.22

Chapter 2
Resource Allocation in Fog Computing

Gopal K. Shyam
Presidency University, India

Priyanka Bharti
Reva University, India

ABSTRACT

Cloud computing has already demonstrated its effectiveness in managing internet of things (IoT) applications and computationally intensive tasks and resources. Due to the substantial delay imparted by the network, cloud computing is not recommended for latency-critical applications. Excessive data flow and connections to data centers may clog up the system. Fog computing was developed to meet this difficulty. It is designed to expand the cloud computing capabilities to increase the quality of service (QoS) of such computing applications with a high latency requirement. In comparison to cloud datacenters, fog devices are dynamic and varied. In this chapter, the authors provide a solution to resource allocation issue in fog computing. The performance metrics such as scalability, reliability, and availability are optimized compared to the existing approaches.

1. INTRODUCTION

We are getting closer to a highly linked modern society where everything and everyone will be online. By 2025, Statista projects that there shall be more than 75 billion linked devices worldwide. According to Cisco VNI global mobile data forecast, by 2022, the monthly volume of just mobile Internet traffic may be 77 Exabyte's (Mouradian et al., 2018). If we do not concentrate on data processing close to the users, the sudden development of IoT devices and Internet traffic would experience unexpected chaos. The idea behind fog computing is created for this purpose. Applications are executed close to users or the edge by using either edge devices or the distributed computing paradigm. Such devices are obviously heterogeneous, not specialized equipment, and connected utilizing a variety of network connections.

DOI: 10.4018/978-1-6684-4466-5.ch002

Additionally, user behavior in the fog environment has the potential to change over time. Users may alter their criteria even after making an application request depending on their present circumstances. Real-time traffic applications and augmented reality applications, for instance, are two examples of such applications where users' behavior may change constantly, depending on their changing requirements as well as the present situation. Resource allocation is challenging due to the issues with changing user behavior and the unstable characteristics of the available resources in the devices (Naha et al., 2018; Zhenyu et al., 2017).

For the application to run effectively and consistently, resource allocation in the fog should discover and choose resources as well as take these factors into account. Failure to complete the duties by the deadline can result in financial loss and may even endanger human life if the application is for an emergency system. For example, the emergency fire response service, driverless cars, emergency vehicle management, and many more.

The majority of research on fog computing ignored the interaction of user and resource challenges as it relates to dynamic user behavior. This study intends to close this gap by creating a resource allocation method that is an improvement over static resource allocation models. In summary, this research has the following contributions: a. to suggest an answer to the issue of application placement when user behavior is changing dynamically; b. to suggest a novel resource allocation for fog applications that will take various fog characteristics into account. The remainder of the article is structured as follows. The literature on resource scheduling and allocation for fog is presented in section 2. The problem and solution techniques are then described in section 3. Section 4 discusses the results obtained. Finally, section 5 offers a conclusion.

2. LITERATURE ON RESOURCE SCHEDULING AND ALLOCATION

By taking into account the hierarchical composition of the fog and cloud environments, Bittencourt et al. presented mobility-aware application scheduling. They did not, however, take into account other unique features of the Fog computing environment, such as CPU availability fluctuations and the arrival of applications in the future. Fog-cloud resource allocation is proposed (Silva et al., 2018) which would take into account available system resources.

Gaussian Process Regression for Fog-Cloud Allocation (GPRFCA) is the name of their suggested mechanism. For resource allocation, GPRFCA examines prior submission requests and latency. It also reduces the amount of energy used by fog nodes. Du et al., (2018) proposed resource allocation for the fog-cloud environment that ensured min-max fairness in another research work. That work's major purpose is to ensure that transmitted power, radio bandwidth, and computation resources are optimized. Table 1 shows the performance parameters and their optimization considered in various research works.

Due to virtualization's ability to represent diverse systems, fog computing typically depends on it. A whole Operating System (OS) and all of its applications can be executed on a virtual computer thanks to the notion of virtualization. As a result, anytime a new Virtual Machine (VM) needs to be constructed, resource consumption in Fog nodes may be delayed unnecessarily. VMs require some startup time to run on hardware platforms (Ahmed et al., 2021). A lightweight virtualization platform called containers is used which has several advantages over standard virtualization (Jianbo et al., 2018).

Since containers start up significantly faster than VMs, they have a quicker response time such as milliseconds vs. seconds in terms of CPU, memory, and storage performance, containers outperform VMs

Table 1. Performance metrics and reference

Performance parameters	References
Resource consumption	Lina et al., (2018)
Number of tasks	Carlos et al., (2019)
Network delay	Redowan, et al., (2020)
Resource availability	Redowan, et al., (2020)
Bandwidth	Antonio et al., (2017)
Execution Time	Souza et al., (2018)
Latency	Yigitoglu et al., (2018)
Energy consumption	Pooranian et al., (2018)

(Yin et al., 2018). Game theory is a powerful mathematical framework widely used to solve resource allocation problems. Zhang et al., (2017) considered a fog computing architecture, where a set of Data Service Operators (DSO) controls the Fog Nodes (FN), providing data service requested by a set of Data Service Subscribers (DSS). The authors proposed a joint optimization framework for all FN, DSO, and DSS to achieve an optimal resource allocation scheme in a distributed fashion.

The proposed approach consists of the pricing problem analysis for all DSOs and the resource allocation for DSSs. The use case has been selected to focus on unique events in the smart transportation system and applications linked to augmented reality. We need to identify suitable resources to fulfill the tasks that the program needs to complete in order to address the resource allocation challenge for time-sensitive applications with deadline constraints and dynamic user behavior in the fog environment.

An approach for resource allocation method is what we present as a solution. To determine the delay and expense for the experiments and simulations, a mathematical framework is used. Three performance measures are finally discussed in order to assess the effectiveness of the system.

3. PROPOSED WORK

How can deadlines be met based on user demands for time-sensitive applications, taking into account users' unpredictable behavior in the fog computing environment is addressed in this chapter. To schedule time-sensitive applications in the fog environment, there is a need of some intelligence; otherwise, it would not be able to meet the requirements of the applications' time sensitivity. The user may alter the due date for finishing the submitted job while the application is being used. Application processing would be done in several instances with more processing capacity to handle the deadline constraint request. Because those greater capacity nodes require more processing power, the customer must pay more. However, control resource supply can be controlled such that the user would not have to pay extra.

Assuming a user submits a task at *TASK_ initial*, the user demands that the task be finished within *TASK_deadline* time at both the beginning and any subsequent points in the processing of the work. Let *TASK_completed* represent the percentage of tasks that have been completed. As a result, the fog resource would finish the task *TASK_TO_COMPLETE* in *TASK* deadline time, where *TASK_TO_COMPLETE = TASK_initial– TASK_*completed, and it would also satisfy the requirement that *TIME NEEDED TASK_TO_COMPLETE ≤TASK* deadline, where *TIME_NEEDED_TASK_ TO_COMPLETE* represents the amount of time required to finish the tasks *TASK_TO_COMPLETE*. The notation along with its meaning is presented in Table 2.

3.1 Network Model

The bandwidth of a link, *BW_LINK*, in Eqn. (1) is defined as the minimum bandwidth of the ports of nodes *CONNECTION_A* and *CONNECTION_B*. The following definitions describe the bandwidth of paths connected by several connections and nodes.

$$BW\_LINK_{port} = \min_{i=CONNECTION\_A, CONNECTION\_B} \left(BW_i \right) \tag{1}$$

Where, *BW_LINK* port represents the bandwidth of a path which is the minimum bandwidth of the ports of nodes *CONNECTION_A, CONNECTION_B, CONNECTION_N*, bandwidth will be further allocated using the Max-Min fairness policy. This Policy allows using minimum bandwidth between all links while competing with other users for the bandwidth of the same link. Thus the available bandwidth of a link or the path for a user is given in Eqn. 2.

Table 2. Notation and its meaning

Notation	Meaning
UCP	Unit Connectivity Price
CTTC	Connection Time To Cloud
CTFS	Connection Time to Fog Server
FSC	Fog Server Cost
FDC	Fog Device Cost
UPM	Unit Price Messaging
MCR	Messaging Cloud Request
DSU	Data Size Unit
MRFD	Messaging Request Fog Device,
MRFS	Messaging Request Fog Server
FSC	Fog Server Cost
FDC	Fog Device Cost
PRTC	Processing Request to Cloud
PRTF	Processing Request to Fog
UPM	Unit Price Messaging
FDC	Fog Device Cost
FSC	Fog Server Cost
DSU	Data Size Unit
TPC	Total Processing Cost

$$BW\_LINK_{port} = \min_{i=CONNECTION_{-A},CONNECTION_{-B},CONNECTION_{-N}} \left(BW_i\right) \tag{2}$$

Propagation time, transmission time, queue time, and processing delay are the four fundamental factors that affect network latency. Depending on the type of medium, propagation latency varies (wired or wireless). Eqn. 3 is the overall delay for a link of a single communication unit:

$$NETWORK_{delay} = 2\left(QUEING_{\_delay} + TRANSMISSION_{\_delay} + PROPAGATION_{\_delay} + PROCESSING_{\_delay}\right) \tag{3}$$

All intermediary links and nodes must be taken into account when calculating the network delay of a path. In that case, a path's network delay will be as in Eqn. 4.

$$NETWORK_{path_{delay}} = (QUEING_{path_{delay}} + TRANSMISSION_{path_{delay}} + PROPAGATION_{path_{delay}} +$$
$$PROCESSING_{path_{delay}}) \tag{4}$$

3.2 Pricing Model

Due of its varied mak+eup, the Fog resource's pricing is crucial. The computing and data transfer tasks are carried out by various node types and networking hardware. We assume that the Fog device costs one-third of the half price when computation occurs on the fog server. The possible problem is that users of time- sensitive applications pay less than users of the cloud. On the other hand, the cloud's infrastructure and upkeep are expensive. Hence, we give time-sensitive apps in the Fog environment priority in order to address this issue. We can develop prices for connectivity, messages, registries, and rules or actions based on our presumption. The cost of connectivity (connectivity cost) can be calculated using Eqn. 5.

$$CHARGE_{total} = UCP\left(\sum CTTC + \frac{1}{FSC_x}\sum CTFS + \frac{1}{FDC_x}\sum CTTF\right)*10^{-6} \tag{5}$$

In our example, the cost variable for the Fog server is 2 and the cost variable for the fog device is 3. The cost of messaging (Messaging cost) is calculated using Eqn. 6.

$$MESSAGING\_COST_{total} = UPM\left(\sum_{i=1}^{n}\left\lceil\frac{MCR_i}{DSU}\right\rceil\right) + \frac{1}{FSC}\sum_{i=1}^{n}\left\lceil\frac{MRFS}{i}DSU\right\rceil + 1\frac{1}{FDC\sum_{i=1}^{n}\left\lceil\frac{MRFD}{i}DSU\right\rceil*10^{-6}} \tag{6}$$

The cost of processing (Processing Cost) is calculated using Eqn. 7. Similarly, in simulation, the connectivity, processing and messaging are only considered. Hence, the total cost per application is calculated using Eqn. 8.

$$TPC = UPM\left(\sum_{i=1}^{n}\left\lceil\frac{PRTC_i}{DSU}\right\rceil + \frac{1}{PRTF_x}\sum_{i=1}^{n}\left\lceil\frac{FSC}{i}U\right\rceil + \frac{1}{FDC_x}\sum_{i=1}^{n}\left\lceil\frac{P_{FD_i}}{U}\right\rceil\right)*10^{-6} \tag{7}$$

$$AT_{cost} = CHARGE_{total} + MESSAGING_{total} + PROCESSING_{total} \qquad (8)$$

Due to the changing nature of the resources in the Fog environment, we use priority-based algorithms to choose the best resources by taking into account their specific properties.

Fog devices are not only used for processing fog applications. The majority of these devices are primarily in charge of processing native applications. The participating Fog devices may use any current computational resources they have for processing fog data. Depending on how busy the native apps are, CPU usage may change even while processing a fog application. This is referred to as the CPU's availability varying. The term "CPU availability fluctuation rate" refers to the rate at which CPU availability varies when a fog application is running. Such a situation might occur in a fog environment when the users' requirements alter dynamically over time. Tasks should be able to be scheduled by the application broker so that the application may fulfil user requests. So, it is advisable to set aside some resources for potential future application demands.

We anticipate that the Fog application services would not be in charge of bulk processing, also known as long-term processing. As a result, based on user queries to the application, the reservation will occasionally be modified. The proposed work will be able to deal with fundamental Fog computing characteristics including restricted resource capacity, dynamic resource availability, and mobility throughout the resource allocation and scheduling process.

4. RESULTS AND DISCUSSIONS

We require 500 MIPS of pushing power for a specific amount of time to finish an application, but the Fog environment does not provide such resources. We also assume that there would not be any circumstances in which the cloud resources are required to fulfil a user request since the Fog resources are entirely exhausted. That is, using fog infrastructure, all time-sensitive processing will be carried out within the Fog environment. Naturally, the system depends on the cloud for bulk processing and long-term archiving because these tasks are not time-sensitive. Each fog device will run a sensor application to keep an eye on the resources being used by the fog platform. The resources and data will all be on the fog server. Table 3 lists the specifications of local machine. Table 4 lists the specifications of Amazon instances. The following algorithm is used for resource allocation and scheduling.

Algorithm (Resource Allocation and Scheduling)

1. Obtain a list of the resources that are accessible.

Table 3. Specifications of local machine

Resource	Specifications
Processor Intel Core	i5-2430M
RAM	2GB DDR3
Operating System	Window 8, 32bit

Table 4. Specifications of Amazon instance

Resource	Specifications
Processor	Intel Xeon
Processor Speed	2.5 GHz to 3.3 GHz
CPU Credit/Hour	6
RAM	1 GB
Operating System	Linux
Storage	ESB

2. Locate the best resources while taking into account response speed, usage, and availability, proximity, and CPU availability.
3. Find all combination that can accommodate the specified resource allocation in the given time (T).
4. To determine a potential optimal allocation, determine the Shapley value based on resource availability.
5. Utilize resource allocation that is objective-based.
6. Reserve resources based on the application request while taking various goals into account.
7. Observe how the local resources are being used and reassign the task if needed.

The performance metrics considered are resource utility, resource availability, and resource scalability. Resource utility refers to the percentage of resource utilization. Likewise, resource availability is the percentage of resource available at any time for allocation. Similarly, resource scalability is the percentage of resource that can be scaled up during peak times of resource requirements.

The existing research focuses on a specific performance parameter and a static values, while the proposed system considers dynamic tasks. The algorithm shows a 11-13% improvement in resource utility, 7% improvement in resource availability, and 6% improvement in resource scalability over static resource allocation. Compared to the multi-agent systems work in the field, the algorithm shows 3-5% improvement with regard to these performance parameters. Table 5 depicts the comparative study on different resource factors.

5. CONCLUSION

Because of the changing nature of users and computation devices, placing applications in the fog environment is difficult. We cannot be confident that the application that has been submitted to a device will be

Table 5. Comparative study on different resource factors

Ref.	Utility	Availability	Scalability
Lina et al., (2018)	69.00%	NA	NA
Carlos et al., (2019)	71.00%	NA	NA
Redowan, et al., (2020)	NA	77.00%	79.80%
Proposed system	82.00%	84.00%	85.00%

finished by that device in the fog. User requirements, on the other hand, may change in the interim. As a result, before deploying an application in the fog environment, we must examine several fog computing features. We have identified three significant difficulties that need to be addressed in this field. These issues include the need for: (i) decentralized solutions that better match the dynamicity and heterogeneity of Fog nodes; (ii) resource allocation between Fog nodes as well as from the Fog to the cloud for horizontal or vertical scalability; and (iii) functional constraints in addition to time or capacity metrics for optimal resource allocation. Finally, these many challenges should be considered to achieve better resource allocation in fog computing.

REFERENCES

Ahmed, K. D., & Zeebaree, S. R. M. (2021). Resource allocation in fog computing: A review. *International Journal of Science and Business*, *5*(2), 54–63.

Brogi, A., & Forti, S. (2017). QoS aware deployment of IoT applications through the fog. *IEEE Internet of Things Journal*, *4*(5), 1185–1192. doi:10.1109/JIOT.2017.2701408

Du, J., Zhao, L., Feng, J., & Chu, X. (2018). Computation offloading and resource allocation in mixed fog/cloud computing systems with min-max fairness guarantee. *IEEE Transactions on Communications*, *4*(4), 1594–1608. doi:10.1109/TCOMM.2017.2787700

Guerrero, C., Lera, I., & Juiz, C. (2019). Lightweight decentralized service placement policy for performance optimization in fog computing. *Journal of Ambient Intelligence and Humanized Computing*, *10*(6), 2435–2452. doi:10.100712652-018-0914-0

Bittencourt, L., Diaz-Montes, J., Buyya, R., Rana, O., & Parashar, M. (2018). Mobility aware application scheduling in fog computing. *IEEE Cloud Computing, 4*(2), 26-35.

Mahmud, R., Srirama, S. N., Ramamohanarao, K., & Buyya, R. (2020). Profit aware application placement for integrated fog- cloud computing environments. *Journal of Parallel and Distributed Computing*, *135*, 177–190. doi:10.1016/j.jpdc.2019.10.001

Mouradian, C., Naboulsi, D., Yangui, S., Glitho, R. H., Morrow, M. J., & Polakos, P. A. (2018). A comprehensive survey on fog computing: State-of-the-art and research challenges. *IEEE Communications Surveys and Tutorials*, *20*(1), 416–464. doi:10.1109/COMST.2017.2771153

Naha, R. K., Garg, S. K., Georgakopoulos, D., Jayaraman, P. P., Gao, L., Xiang, Y., & Ranjan, R. (2018). Fog computing: Survey of trends, architectures, requirements, and research directions. *IEEE Access : Practical Innovations, Open Solutions*, *6*, 47980–48009. doi:10.1109/ACCESS.2018.2866491

Ni, L., Zhang, J., Jiang, C., Yan, C., & Yu, K. (2017). Resource allocation strategy in fog computing based on priced timed Petri Nets. *IEEE Internet of Things Journal*, *4*(5), 1216–1228. doi:10.1109/JIOT.2017.2709814

Pooranian, Z., Shojafar, M., Paola, G. V. N., Chiaraviglio, L., & Conti, M. (2016). A novel distributed fog-based networked architecture to preserve energy in fog data centres. In: *Proceedings of 14th IEEE International Conference on Mobile Ad Hoc and Sensor Systems*. IEEE.

Rodrigo AC da Silva & Nelson LS da Fonseca. (2018). Resource allocation mechanism for a fog-cloud infrastructure. In: *Proceedings of the IEEE International Conference on Communications*, (pp. 1-6). IEEE.

Souza, V. B., Masip-Bruin, X., Marín-Tordera, E., Sànchez-López, S., Garcia, J., Ren, G. J., Jukan, A., & Juan Ferrer, A. (2018). Towards a proper service placement in combined fog-to-cloud architectures. *Future Generation Computer Systems*, *87*, 1–15. doi:10.1016/j.future.2018.04.042

Wen, Z., Yang, R., Garraghan, P., Lin, T., Xu, J., & Rovatsos, M. (2017). Fog orchestration for Internet of Things services. *IEEE Internet Computing*, *21*(2), 16–24. doi:10.1109/MIC.2017.36

Yigitoglu, E., Mohamed, M., Liu, L., & Ludwig, H. (2017). Foggy: A framework for continuous automated IoT application deployment in fog computing. In: *Proceedings of IEEE International Conference on AI Mobile Services*, (pp. 38-45). IEEE. 10.1109/AIMS.2017.14

Yin, L., Luo, J., & Luo, H. (2018). Tasks scheduling and resource allocation in fog computing based on containers for smart manufacturing. *IEEE Transactions on Industrial Informatics*, *14*(10), 4712–4721. doi:10.1109/TII.2018.2851241

Zhang, H., Xiao, Y., Bu, S., Niyato, D., Yu, F. R., & Han, Z. (2017). Computing resource allocation in three-tier IoT fog networks: A joint optimization approach combining stackelberg game and matching. *IEEE Internet of Things Journal*, *4*(5), 1204–1215. doi:10.1109/JIOT.2017.2688925

Chapter 3
Fog Computing Applications

Nirase Fathima Abubacker
Asia Pacific University of Technology and Innovation, Malaysia

Muhammad Ehsan Rana
Asia Pacific University of Technology and Innovation, Malaysia

Mafas Raheem
Asia Pacific University of Technology and Innovation, Malaysia

ABSTRACT

The adoption of IoT has increased rapidly due to the abundance in the availability, affordability, and capability of different components like sensors, processors, and communication technologies. This growth has subsequently resulted in the development of the industrial internet of things (IIoT). When it comes to IoT there are four primary paradigms each with its own perks and drawbacks — cloud, edge, fog, and mist computing. This chapter focuses on fog computing, exploring its applications, services, and the current state of fog computing with emerging technologies. Fog computing extends its capabilities by distributing processing, storage, and networking tasks across cloud, fog, and edge nodes. It enables localized data analysis, real-time decision-making, and improved bandwidth utilization. This chapter focuses on the architectural principles, key components, and use cases of fog computing. It also highlights integrating emerging technologies with fog computing, such as artificial intelligence, machine learning, and blockchain that supports diverse IoT applications.

1. INTRODUCTION

Fog computing is one among many layers of the IoT computing paradigm that sits between the cloud and mist layer. There are several factors and areas where fog computing brings in significant value. The devices involved in the fog computing paradigm are often commonly available devices like personal computers or micro-computers. This keeps the geographical proximity close to the edge devices which helps take load off the cloud by processing data in the fog computing layer as well as reducing latency. The fog computing paradigm is implemented at the edge of the IoT network and is near the edge devices. Instead of sending raw data directly to the cloud for processing, it can be processed in the fog layer which

DOI: 10.4018/978-1-6684-4466-5.ch003

has a significant improvement in the speed of communication and processing subsequently resulting in a lower latency. This is a critical factor for time-sensitive applications where small amounts of time can have a notable impact. (Habibi et al., 2020)

There is an enormous amount of data being generated by edge devices in an IoT architecture. A cloud infrastructure usually handles the data for processing and analysis, followed by which the data is often sent back to the devices carrying some instructions or information for decision making. This large amount of data can sometimes congest the network bandwidth and might have a fatal impact on time-sensitive applications. Fog computing not only reduces the amount of raw data being sent but processes the raw data to send only relevant and processed data to streamline the processing and optimize data transmission.

Fog Computing is an extension that aims to move the processing and execution closer to the source of the data. It helps in improving the service and delivery time while reducing the bandwidth of data and processing sent to the cloud. Fog computing serves as a bridge layer between the edge devices and cloud computing infrastructures by utilizing the computational power from consumer devices like personal computers, or micro-computers — referred to as fog nodes — within the edge network to handle and process small amounts of critical data to reduce the latency and provide more robust and sustainable service. Another significant benefit fog computing provides is reducing the data traffic between the edge nodes and cloud datacentres. In the instance when many IoT devices initiate data-driven interaction with the cloud, there is a high probability of network congestion which can have fatal repercussions on the delivery of processed data or commands which can further lead to possible failures (Mahmud et al., 2021).

The objective of this book chapter is to provide a comprehensive understanding of fog computing by exploring its novel applications and services, advancing the state of fog computing with emerging technologies and fog computing applications: case studies and future research directions. the chapter begins with an introduction to fog computing with its recent trends. novel fog applications are then explored for smart homes, video surveillance and education followed by an in-depth examination of advancing the state of fog computing with emerging technologies that focuses on the application of fog computing on iot-based and blockchain-based applications in smart cities context. in addition, the topic explores mobile computing under fog computing and the significant impact in combining fog computing and 5g technology. The chapter also discusses fog computing applications in depth with some case studies on smart agriculture, autonomous driving, and healthcare.

2. TRENDS IN FOG COMPUTING

Habibi et al. (2020) carried out a survey on fog computing architecture to explore the architectural, technological, and algorithmic aspects of this computing paradigm. They mention that the concept of fog computing was introduced to address the computing and communication limitations present in the edge-to-cloud model. Abdulqadir et al. (2021) brings up the concern that with the exponential growth in the adoption and development of IoT, there are various obstacles and challenges presented to the traditional and centralized cloud computing paradigm. Fog computing addresses a lot of these limitations. They investigate the complexities and advantages of moving from classical cloud computing to integrating fog computing. With the enormous amounts of data generated by IoT and the interconnectivity of nodes in fog computing, resource management is one of the most crucial obstacles that requires making sequential decisions continuously. The integration of machine learning algorithms has been considered by many to overcome this obstacle by making decisions taking into consideration various factors. However, machine learning algorithms also introduce some new challenges like high variance and online training. Iftikhar et al. (2022) conducted a review of these studies to analyze the role and effect of machine learning in addressing the challenge of resource management in fog computing.

Alraddady et al. (2019) observed the issue of bottlenecks in network bandwidth occurring during the Hajj season as there are millions of people gathering in a small geographical location for a short period of time. However, many time-sensitive services like security and healthcare are dependent on the large influx of data generated. To overcome this issue of bottleneck, a fog computing-based framework is proposed for streamlined and efficient data processing and information retrieval. Abdulkareem et al. (2019) state that the number of applications and infrastructures built upon the fog computing architecture is increasing rapidly and they produce a large amount of data. They also mention the fact that the domain of machine learning has experienced significant growth in terms of developments and applications. Several studies have been conducted exploring ways to merge machine learning into fog computing architecture to address some of its drawbacks. However, they observed that the role of machine learning in the fog computing paradigm was not investigated yet.

Rawat et al. (2023) make a very interesting proposal for integrating a distributed deep-learning method with the fog computing architecture to detect cyber-attacks and vulnerability injection (CAVID). They bring up the fact that IoT devices generate large amounts of data which is ideal for training deep-learning algorithms that are more robust compared to shallower machine-learning algorithms. CAVID is an intelligent machine learning-based security architecture used for predicting cybersecurity attacks in fog computing. Based on their evaluation, implementing deep learning over classical machine learning algorithms demonstrated a significant improvement in accuracy, effectiveness, and scalability. There are various applications for IoT and its underlying computing architecture. Rani et al. (2021) shares one such interesting application of using fog computing to provide storage as a service. They affirm that the storage and computing performance of fog computing is like that of cloud computing, and fog computing has more benefits by being in closer proximity to the edge of the network. They conduct a review around using fog computing to provide storage as a service while highlighting the numerous benefits it provides over cloud computing such as speed, efficiency, and security to name a few.

Building smart cities is another application of IoT that has attained a lot of attention from researchers, engineers, and the public alike due to the possibilities of added convenience and ease of everyday life. Traditionally, the technologies for smart cities were based on cloud computing architectures, which brought along the limitations and drawbacks of cloud computing. Javadzadeh and Rahmani (2020) observed the lack of a survey around the implementation of fog computing in smart cities and developed systematic literature while making analytical comparisons and noting the relevant trends as well as directions for future research. Another integration of fog computing for building smart cities is explored by Naranjo et al. (2019) where they present a Fog Computing Architecture Network (FOCAN) where several IoT devices process and communicate using a fog computing architecture for efficiency in terms of latency and energy while providing a smooth service. One of the primary reasons for presenting this architecture was to improve efficiency compared to traditional cloud computing architectures. The proposed architecture demonstrated tremendous improvement in efficiency across multiple devices deployed in the smart city network.

Fog computing is a wing of cloud computing that leads to meeting users' demands to provide actionable insight in real-time. Internet of everything (IoE), Industrial Internet of Things (IIoT), IoT applications are the main pillars of fog computing. The application of fog computing had gradually become prevalent in organisations. In this line, many fog computing applications do exist among which some are prominent such as smart homes, Video surveillance and education.

3. NOVEL FOG APPLICATIONS AND SERVICES

This section focuses on the application and services of fog computing in smart homes, video surveillance and education. The authors have looked critically at the significance, impact, and potential use cases in applying fog computing for these technologies. Moreover, the challenges that need to be addressed in this regard have also been emphasized.

Smart Homes

Smart homes are residences that are equipped with the goal of providing appropriate services through smart technologies. It employs internet-connected gadgets to allow online tracking and control of systems and utilities, such as lighting and heating. It is straightforward to recognize how important smart houses are to making people's lives more comfortable (Rahimi et.al, 2020). Using smart home, people can virtually manage every gadget they have in their home from a distance, such as sprinklers, webcams, and home security systems are programmed using a smart home system, including devices like air conditioners, heaters, and refrigerators. The Figure 1 below shows the smart home system.

Any electronic device linked to your smart house system, connect with other devices, and make some own choices is considered a smart device. Televisions, stoves, security systems, doorbells, garage doors, and stereos are examples of Smart devices. However, the integration of these devices becomes difficult due to their functionalities of distinctive operating systems. Fog computing is used to execute these smart houses. Smart homes are linked to fog nodes that transfers data to the cloud as given in Figure 2, which handle data sent by smart devices. In other terms, smart home devices transmit different metrics and statuses to the fog node. Fog connects all the various devices through a single user interface and provides smart home applications adaptable resources in providing increased security, extremely low latency, and cost- and energy-effectiveness.

Video Surveillance

Video surveillance is a security management system that uses video cameras to monitor the interior and exterior smart home environment to completely protect against burglary, damage, and breach (Qiu et.al, 2018). A smart home video surveillance system is made up of several devices that may capture a lot of surveillance-related data, including photos and videos. This might cause significant network congestion and create a heavy computational burden on various appliances and computers (Ni et.al, 2018). Several recent studies have proved that an effective solution to this problem is possible via an IoT-integrated intelligent video surveillance framework. However, they struggle with the bandwidth and latency demands of video surveillance applications. This demand necessitates IoT nodes close to the visual data source (Sultana et.al, 2019). To deal with these problems, fog computing (Vaquero et.al, 2014) has been developed. The latest enhancement to cloud technology is fog computing. It is an intermediate layer that exists between the cloud and the edge. A networking technique called edge computing enables remote devices to process data and carry out operations in real time. When edge computers transmit massive

Figure 1. Smart home system
Source: http://visioforce.com/smarthome.html

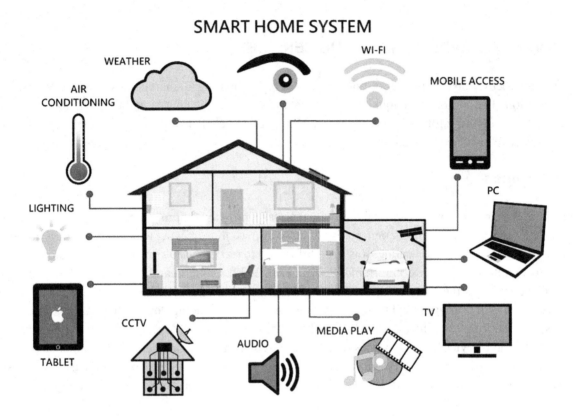

volumes of data to the cloud Fog nodes receive the same data but prioritize only the vital information. Then these vital data is transferred to the cloud by fog node to be stored and either delete or preserve the unnecessary data on their own for additional analysis. This is how fog computing transfers essential data rapidly while saving a lot of space on the cloud. Figure 3: Illustration of IoT-fog assisted security management system.

Any movement of any kind in above Figure 2 will be detected by the edge node's camera sensor, which will also take motion-object pictures and send them to the fog node. The fog node subsequently compiles and delivers criminal data (i.e., the labelled picture, crime event location, and camera position) to the closest crime assistance or police unit. In addition, it sends a real-time alarm message to the protective service. On the other hand, updated crime data models are created by the cloud and made available to the fog node as they become available.

Education

Platform built on fog that offers a comprehensive answer for seamless real-time educational cooperation amongst students, whether they are in the same school building or not. The use of fog computing provides quick and adaptable interactions between professors and students by bringing processing near to their devices. It enables lower latency real-time response. Additionally, it enables educational

Figure 2. The IoT of a smart home based on the fog
(Zhang, et al., 2019)

institutions speedier data storage and access capabilities. The fog nodes have significance in offering real-time analytics as well as in acquiring real-time data. After including fog computing technology in IoT educational settings, system may respond in milliseconds. Any question posed by students will be answered by teachers swiftly, and teachers can also respond to questions instantaneously.

Each classroom is a fog node in the revolutionary teaching platform of the fog model. The adoption of the widely used cloud computing model simply causes many users to visit remote servers at the same time and handles students' requests like inquiries or downloads during the process of online teaching

Figure 3. Illustration of IoT-fog-enabled security management system
(Sultana &Wahid, 2019)

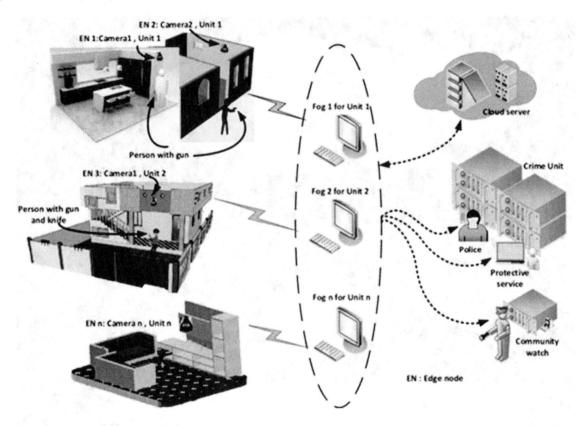

within a short period of time. This not only results in a long communication distance and long delay, but it also easily causes network congestion, which has an impact on the experience of the teaching process. (Cai et.al, 2018)

4. ADVANCING THE STATE OF FOG COMPUTING WITH EMERGING TECHNOLOGIES

Fog Computing Application in Smart Cities

This section spotlights on the fog computing applications on IoT-based and blockchain-based applications in smart cities context. The authors have looked critically at the significance, impact, and potential use cases in applying fog computing for these technologies. Moreover, the challenges that need to be addressed in this regard have also been emphasized. Further, this topic also explores mobile computing under fog computing. Smartphone-based applications offer a significant number of services which are now supported by fog computing. This is also referred to as mobile-edge-computing using a specific approach and will be discussed in this topic.

Figure 4. Architecture of the innovative teaching platform
(Cai, et al, 2018)

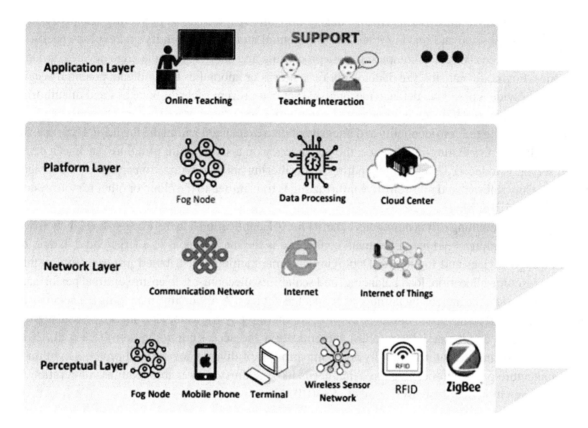

Internet of Things

Fog computing plays a vital role in enabling real-time analysis of IoT data in smart cities. In a smart city environment, numerous IoT devices are deployed throughout the urban infrastructure, generating a massive amount of data. Fog computing brings computational resources closer to these edge devices, which allows data processing and analysis to occur locally or in nearby fog nodes. It reduces the latency associated with transmitting data to remote cloud servers for analysis. By processing data at the edge, fog computing enables real-time analysis, facilitating timely decision-making and responsiveness in various smart city applications (Aazam et al., 2018). For example, in a smart traffic management system, fog nodes deployed at intersections can analyze data from traffic sensors in real-time, detecting traffic congestion or accidents and triggering immediate responses such as adjusting signal timings or rerouting vehicles. This timely analysis and response are critical for optimizing traffic flow and ensuring efficient transportation within the city. Furthermore, fog computing allows for distributed intelligence in smart cities. This distribution of intelligence enables faster and more localized decision-making, as critical data analysis can be performed closer to the source of data. For instance, in an environmental monitoring application, fog nodes equipped with sensors can analyze air quality data locally and trigger actions like adjusting ventilation systems or issuing alerts in real-time (Bonomi et al., 2012).

By leveraging fog computing, IoT applications can benefit from privacy and security enhancements. Fog computing reduces the need to transmit sensitive data to remote cloud servers, minimizing the risk of data interception or unauthorized access during transmission. It helps in protecting sensitive data by limiting its distribution and making it harder for potential attackers to identify and exploit specific individuals or devices. With fog computing, data processing and analysis occur at edge devices or nearby fog nodes. Fog nodes can analyze data locally for patterns or anomalies that indicate potential security threats to provide a proactive defence mechanism that can prevent security breaches and unauthorized access before they reach the cloud. Encrypted communication protocols and secure channels can be established, ensuring the confidentiality and integrity of data exchanged within the fog layer. By processing data locally and distributing intelligence, the dependency on a single point of failure, such as a central cloud server, is reduced. Using fog computing, data filtering and anonymization can also be enabled at the edge. Only relevant and non-sensitive information is transmitted to the cloud or other remote systems (Atlam et al., 2018, Ma et al., 2019).

While fog computing offers numerous benefits for IoT applications, there are also several challenges that need to be addressed. One of the main challenges is the management of a large and dynamic network of edge devices and fog nodes. Deploying and maintaining a distributed infrastructure requires efficient resource allocation, load balancing, and scalability mechanisms to ensure optimal performance and accommodate the increasing number of connected devices. Additionally, managing the security and privacy of data becomes more complex in a fog computing environment, as it involves securing multiple edge points and maintaining a robust authentication and access control system (Lee et al., 2015). Moreover, ensuring the interoperability and compatibility of diverse devices and protocols within the fog architecture poses another challenge that needs to be addressed to enable seamless integration and data exchange in IoT ecosystems (Lawal et al., 2020).

Blockchains

Blockchain is a decentralized and distributed digital ledger technology that records and stores transactions across multiple computers or nodes in a network. Each transaction, or block, is cryptographically linked to the previous block, forming a chain of blocks. This chain is maintained and validated by a network of participants, known as nodes, who reach a consensus on the validity of transactions through consensus algorithms. Blockchain is characterized by its transparency, immutability, and security, as once a block is added to the chain, it is extremely difficult to alter or tamper with the recorded information. By leveraging fog computing, blockchain applications can bring numerous benefits to smart cities. Firstly, fog computing enables efficient and real-time data processing at the edge, reducing latency and enhancing the responsiveness of blockchain-based smart city applications. This allows for timely decision-making and enables faster transaction confirmations, improving the overall efficiency of services such as energy management, traffic control, waste management, and more. Secondly, fog computing enhances data privacy and security by keeping sensitive data localized and reducing the reliance on centralized servers. The distributed nature of fog nodes in smart cities adds an additional layer of security and resilience to the blockchain network (Bouachir et al., 2020). Furthermore, fog computing enables the integration of various IoT devices, sensors, and data sources within the smart city infrastructure, creating a seamless ecosystem for data collection, analysis, and sharing, which can be further enhanced by the immutability and transparency provided by blockchain technology (Tuli et al., 2019).

By applying fog computing for blockchain-based systems, several compelling use cases for smart cities can be observed. One such use case is in energy management, where fog nodes located near power generation sources can facilitate real-time monitoring, optimization, and trading of energy resources through blockchain-based smart contracts, enabling efficient energy distribution and reducing costs. Another use case is in traffic control, where fog nodes deployed near intersections can collect and analyze data from sensors, cameras, and vehicles, enabling real-time traffic management and optimizing transportation systems. Moreover, fog computing and blockchain can be utilized in waste management, where fog nodes integrated with sensors and IoT devices can track waste levels, optimize collection routes, and incentivize recycling through blockchain-based reward systems. To leverage fog computing for these use cases, several steps can be taken. Firstly, identify the requirements of the specific use cases, such as energy management, traffic control, or waste management. Then, strategically deploy fog nodes across the city infrastructure to bring computing capabilities closer to the data sources and end-users, enabling real-time data processing and reducing latency. Establish secure communication channels between the fog nodes and the blockchain network to ensure data integrity and privacy. Utilize blockchain technology to enable decentralized and transparent transactions, data sharing, and smart contracts within the smart city ecosystem. Additionally, integrate various sensors, IoT devices, and data sources with the fog computing infrastructure and blockchain network to enable seamless data collection, aggregation, and analysis (Wang et al., 2019).

The main challenge in using fog computing for blockchain applications is the issue of data integrity and security. Fog computing involves distributing computing resources closer to the edge of the network, which can introduce vulnerabilities and increase the risk of unauthorized access or tampering with data (Alzoubi et al., 2022). Blockchain applications heavily rely on the immutability and trustworthiness of the data stored on the distributed ledger and ensuring the integrity and confidentiality of this data becomes more complex in a fog computing environment. Additional security measures and protocols need to be implemented to protect the data and ensure the validity of transactions, increasing the complexity and potential points of failure in the system (Qu et al., 2020).

Mobile Computing

The adoption of smartphones has experienced tremendous growth in the last decade and access to a smartphone and in turn, connectivity has become wider and faster in this digital world. Furthermore, mobile technology has been advancing at a breakneck speed catching up with computer-level performance and even surpassing it in some cases, while keeping a significantly smaller footprint. This is true not only for smartphones but also for other mobile computing devices. However, smartphones are the primary focus of mobile computing due to the accessibility of the countless different functions that can be performed with just one device along with a strong processing power. Many researchers, companies and industries have been integrating mobile computing into their architecture to make services more accessible to the end user as they don't have to add any additional hardware. Smartphones nowadays are packed with a range of different sensors along with attachable accessories, if not found for better connectivity using both wired and wireless, etc.

The focus of IoT in the domain of healthcare provides stable, reliable, and effective connectivity between the available medical resources by providing smart healthcare services with tracking and alerting facilities in case of emergency, especially for aged people with chronic diseases (Nazir et al., 2019). Mobile computing helps in making these services more accessible to a wide range of people with the use of smartphones and applications based on its mass adoption. Similarly, excessive requirements of patients within an in-home health monitoring system can result in communication overload and insufficiency in the available resources. In this line, a cost-efficient in-home health monitoring system based on mobile-edge computing was developed to over the previously mentioned issues by dividing the architecture into two sub-systems of wireless body area networks (WBANs) — intra-WBANs and beyond-WBANs — using decentralized game theory-based approach (Ning et al., 2021). A cooperative game is formulated for intra-WBANs to assign the resources in the wireless channel. Whereas in beyond-WBANs, a non-cooperative game is asserted to minimize the cost throughout the system. The proposed algorithm is further proven to reach a Nash equilibrium and the evaluation demonstrates positive effects of the proposed algorithm.

The advancement in Location Based Services (LBS) plays an important role in the future of smart cities. And rightly so, including location data can help in adding context to the data and provide more appropriate services to the users making the experience significantly rich. Based on this idea, Spatharakis et al. (2020) suggested to provide computer resources for the remote execution of LBS, to develop a two-level edge computing architecture. and the architecture was evaluated on a smart touristic application scenario. First, an offloading decision is made at the device level considering the estimated position and quality of the connection between each user. Then at the edge layer, a resource profiling mechanism dynamically maps the workload to different computing resources available in edge computing.

The full potential of a mobile-edge computing architecture cannot be utilized if the connectivity link used for offloading computation tasks is compromised. Bai et al. (2020) proposed using intelligent reflecting surfaces (IRS) which can improve the efficiency in terms of spectrum and energy consumption. The IRS uses a controller to adjust many reflective elements where each element can induce a phase shift on the incoming signal, hence cooperatively enhancing the signal in terms of strength and direction. One of the benefits of implementing an IRS is further explored where a single antenna can provide a more accurate and efficient performance compared to conventional systems. Based on the evaluation, an improvement of around 20% was observed in terms of latency with a single cell covering an area with a radius of 300m and 5 active devices.

Wang et al. (2019) propose a three-tier cooperative computing network by leveraging vertical cooperation among devices, edge nodes and the cloud. The offloading decision and computation resources are optimized concurrently to minimize the task duration for the limited battery capacity on mobile devices. The presented problem, however, is a large-scale and non-linear problem usually referred to as an NP-hard problem. A reformulation linearization technology (RLT) is implemented for efficient offloading with lower complexity and a parallel optimization framework is proposed which utilizes the alternating direction method of multipliers (ADMM) and difference of convex functions (DC) programming. The underlying concept behind the proposed framework is to divide a large-complex problem into smaller problems that can be distributed among devices for efficient computation. The proposed framework demonstrated an improvement of over 24% compared to other techniques.

Microservices are an emerging service architecture where a larger web service is decomposed into smaller lightweight services that can act independently and mobile-edge computing can help by distributing these services dynamically to provide a quick and better service to the users. However, Wang et al. (2021) stated that user mobility can lead to frequent switching of edge cloud which can result in increased latency and delays in the service. To overcome this limitation, a novel microservice coordination algorithm was proposed based on the concept of the Markov decision process framework along with a reinforcement learning model to determine an optimal solution from different variations. Based on the evaluation conducted, the proposed framework demonstrated a significant improvement in performance and a cost reduction.

The inception of the concept of fog computing by Cisco in 2012 helped the Internet of Things (IoT) and Industry 4.0 to advance by leaps and bounds by addressing the shortcomings of cloud computing and bridging the gap between the edge of the network and the cloud infrastructure. The most notable benefit, however, was making it feasible to integrate IoT into time-sensitive applications by reducing the latency as well as reducing the processing load on the cloud infrastructure and avoiding network bandwidth congestions. The introduction of a new computing paradigm such as mobile-edge-computing brought in a host of new devices that are relatively efficient and secure. Several studies are being conducted around the latest technologies like artificial intelligence, blockchains, and cybersecurity to understand and explore how the introduction of these technologies can address various services and be implemented into the existing architectures. Similarly, research around efficient processing and communication is being conducted to optimize the energy efficiency of devices involved in the fog computing paradigm. Various technologies were implemented to deploy mobile-edge computing to support fog computing such as in-home health monitoring systems, two-level edge computing architecture for LBS, and mobile computing using IRS. It has become more vibrant

5G

In recent times, fog computing has grown as a promising approach to meet the growing demand for edge computing, furnishing a decentralized design for processing and storing of data at the edge of the network. With the exponential growth in data generation and consumption every day, the current state of fog computing faces several challenges, including scalability, security, and resource operation. A distributed computing approach called fog computing will be closer to user unlike cloud computing and enables data processing near the source of the data, at the network's edge. Compared to the conventional centralized computing approach, where all processing and storage occur in a distant data center, this represents a paradigm change (Naha et al., 2018).

Fog computing has emerged as a crucial technology for processing and analysing the enormous quantity of data created by Internet of Things (IoT) devices in real-time (Varshney & Simmhan, 2017). The amount of data produced by sensors has greatly expanded with the growth of IoT. Big data analytics has gained a lot of interest recently because of the sudden surge in data production and the inadequacy of traditional databases to handle different types of structured and unstructured data. To gain insights and make critical decisions, every organization is now giving priority to data analysis especially due to the migration towards cloud computing. The information technology and hardware infrastructure used in the business to accommodate the growing needs and size of data that is being generated by the IoT must be scalable and secure.

5G in Big Data Streaming

The big data streaming is one of the important and main features of fog computing, especially over internet. The mobile devices are the major contributors of big data streaming over internet either through wi-fi or through mobile network. (Baccarelli et al., 2017). Fog computing and 5G technology is expected to have a significant impact on the way we process and analyze data in the future.

Figure 5. Big data streams
(Baccarelli,2017)

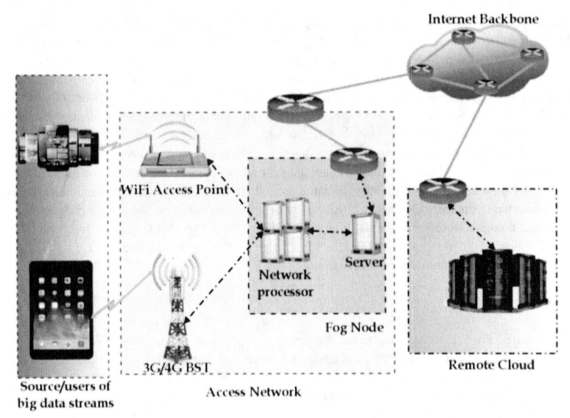

The big data streaming is represented effectively in the figure 5. The dotted line denotes the Transmission Control Protocol / Internet Protocol commonly referred as TCP/IP transmission of data typically through ethernet. The mobile network connectivity through base station (BST) has begun to support 5G along with Voice over LTE (4G) and 3G. By incorporating 5G, the transaction per second (TPS) will improve and will require real-time offloading of data and/or code to nearby data centers via the available wireless networks (Baccarelli et al., 2017). It should also be energy and computing efficient so that we can make it more prevalent among the users. The major challenges of this setup would be energy and resource consumption and latency.

5G is the next generation of wireless technology that promises to revolutionize the way we communicate and interact with the world. 5G is also critical for the advancement of fog computing because it enables faster and more reliable communication between fog nodes and edge devices (Jain et al., 2022). One of the key features of 5G is its ability to support massive machine-type communications which is critical for IoT applications because it enables the connectivity of many devices in a single network. This is particularly important for fog computing because it enables the deployment of many edge devices that can process and analyze data in real-time (Meng et al., 2020).

5G technology is well suited for Fog computing because it enables computation to be performed closer to the edge devices. The advantages low latency makes it significantly faster than previous generations of wireless technology. This is important for Fog computing because it helps reduce latency and improve overall network efficiency (Meng et al., 2020). Both the 5G network and the widespread use of fog computing technology in 5G systems are still in developmental phase and is being envisioned. 5G and fog computing has potential to improve the radio access network data services which can serve a wide range of applications (Meng et al., 2020).

Impacts of 5G in Fog Computing

Along with its capabilities, the fog computing framework also carries over several security weaknesses from the cloud computing paradigm that must be fixed for the benefit of the user.

- **Security Risks:** as the distributed nature of the architecture makes it vulnerable to attacks from multiple entry points. To address this challenge, emerging technologies such as blockchain and secure hardware can provide a secure and tamper-proof environment for data processing and storage (Mukherjee et al., 2017). Fog computing broadens the attack surface for hackers. New security flaws brought on by emerging technologies like 5G, the possibility of more malware and phishing assaults, are also present. These security concerns may risk sensitive information, resulting in monetary loss, harm to one's reputation, and legal consequences.
- **Decreased Privacy:** Controlling the sensitive data is difficult as computer resources are distributed over the network. Additionally, new privacy threats including the possibility of enhanced tracking and spying are brought on by upcoming technologies like 5G. These privacy problems may cause consumers to lose faith in the system and steer clear of fog computing. (Mukherjee et al., 2017).
- **Increased Energy Consumption**: 5G and other emerging technologies in Industry 4.0 need a lot of energy to operate, which might raise the system's carbon footprint. The distribution of computational and storage resources throughout the network may also lead to inefficient resource utilization, which wastes energy (Baccarelli et al., 2017).
- **Regulatory Compliance Requirements:** As the system becomes more complex and involves the distribution of sensitive data, organizations may be subject to increased regulatory compliance requirements, such as data protection laws and cybersecurity regulations. Meeting these compliance requirements can be time-consuming and costly, further adding to the overall cost of the system.

Organizations should carefully evaluate these disadvantages before adopting fog computing to ensure that they can manage the associated risks and costs.

5. FOG COMPUTING APPLICATIONS: CASE STUDIES

Smart Agriculture Application

Agriculture serves as a major source of income, in addition, it also plays a crucial part in the world's food supply chain. It is necessary for maintaining life for humans. Compared to other sectors, the agriculture sector's growth is highly successful up to 4 times in increasing the earnings of the poorest people. It is also an important factor in economic growth, which accounts for 4% of global GDP and up to more than 25% of GDP in the least developed nations. However, several issues, including population expansion, increased industrialization, and fluctuations in the climate, limit the growth of agriculture (Namho et.al, 2017). Farmers, scientists, agronomists, and the agriculture industry use cutting-edge technology like drones, IoT, big data, artificial intelligence, cloud computing, edge computing, and fog computing to solve agriculture-related problems and meet annual global agricultural production needs.

The term "smart agriculture" refers to the management of agriculture that makes use of cutting-edge information and communication technologies to boost product quantity and quality in addressing the rising demand while reducing production losses. Smart Agriculture promises to combine services in rural areas and make intelligent use of their resources through the deployment of IoT technology (Elijo et.al, 2018 & Mekala et.al, 2017). Smart applications can be used in the agriculture sector, to perceive pertinent data, such as weather conditions, soil moisture, or crop development stage, to make an irrigation decision (Garcia, 2020).

Every device that can be controlled via the Internet, is considered an IoT device. The Internet of Things (IoT) in agriculture uses robots, drones, remote sensors, computer imaging, and constantly improving machine learning and analytical tools to monitor crops, survey, and map fields, as well as provide farmers with data they can use to create optimal agriculture management plans that save them time and money. The smart agriculture is processed in four stages such as Data collection: where the farmers install sensors on their farms to collect information on the moisture content of the soil. Then at the next stage in diagnostics, the data is transferred and processed in clouds. The processed data will be analysed for better decision making at the third stage. At the final stage, essential steps will be carried to achieve the objectives of the decisions made in previous stage.

Over the past few years, several IoT apps for agriculture have been released. Based on recent findings, these applications are categorized based on the objectives such as monitoring, tracking and traceability. An example for the Internet of Things-based approach is illustrated for smart agriculture monitoring in Figure 6.

Figure 6. IOT-based smart agriculture monitoring system
(Rehman et.al, 2022)

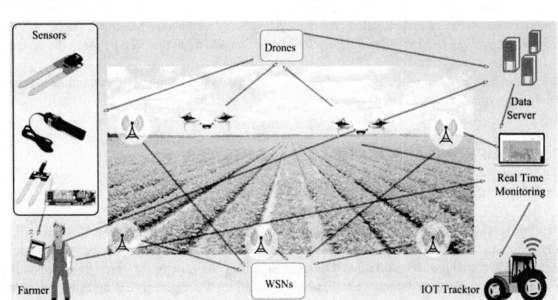

Soil Monitoring

Soil monitoring is one of the most challenging areas of agriculture today, for both producers and farmers. Agriculture production is impacted by a number of environmental issues relating to soil monitoring. Accurately identifying these types of hurdles makes it straightforward to acquire farming customs and practises. Farmers can boost crop output by using the results of a soil monitoring test report. (Rehman et.al, 2022).

Crop Monitoring

Sensors can also be used to keep an eye on crops. Throughout the farms, sensors keep an eye out for variations in temperature, humidity, light, shape, and size. The sensors scan for anomalies and alert the farmer. Remote sensing can therefore track crop growth and help to stop the spread of disease.

Water Monitoring

Crops that receive less water develop more slowly and take up less calcium. Roots are killed by frequent watering and water is wasted. As a result, precise crop irrigation becomes quite challenging (Rajaram et.al, 2020). Cost-effective automatic sensor systems are available to determine if plants need watering based on data collected from monitoring and controlling soil water levels to reduce dryness or overflow (Abba et.al, 2019). Table 1 summarizes few recent smart agricultural applications.

All the smart agriculture applications could boost productivity, raise quality, and reduce expenses. However, the drawback of smart agriculture is that it has certain limitations in using technologies in agriculture as such it is not a perfect system. Few issues and challenges in smart agriculture are discussed in the next section.

Table 1. List of few selected applications based on smart agriculture

Reference	Application Name	Description
(Frida et.al, 2021)	Soil Analysis Fertilizer Management	Based on the climate, topography, and relatively constant soil properties (such as soil texture, depth, and mineralogy), land management holds promise over the long run. With the help of this application, farmers are better able to assess the potential of their land and climate change mitigation strategies. To maximise the usage of fertiliser, Eco Fert offers management assistance. It chooses the best fertiliser combination to cover the required nutrient suspension and takes the needs of various yields into account. Additionally, it considers the price of fertiliser based on current market rates.
(Saba et.al, 2017)	Pest Management Agrippa Farm Manager	(Frida et.al, 2021) Village Tree offers clever pest management methods by gathering data on pest occurrence from farms. Additionally, it uses a crowdsourcing technique, distributing photographs and location information to additional farmers who might be impacted. (Saba et.al, 2017) By using the eFarmer Application, a farmer can create electronic field maps, maintain a history of the crops they have grown there (such as planting, fertilising, harvesting, warehouses, and petrol stations), and locate objects in the field (such as soil samples for agrochemical labs). Before planting begins, the farmers can choose which techniques to use with the use of the Farm Manager App. This programme allows you to examine, organise, and change any field-related data, including yield, planting, and spraying conditions without using your handheld device.

Open Issues and Key Challenges in Smart Agriculture

In this section of the article, the challenges of implementing IoT-based systems for agricultural production are addressed. The expense and durability of the sensors are explained. The Internet of Things device needs a steady supply of energy. It might take a lot of energy, depending on size. However, it can be difficult to find such power in remote and village areas. Alternative energy sources like sun and wind must be used to satisfy the energy demand. Additionally, this will greatly increase the cost. In remote and village areas, a reliable internet link is essential. It is the most important step in setting up an IoT-based system. The connection needs to have enough bandwidth to transfer data as needed by the programme. Farmers need instruction in using rudimentary computers and tablets (HID devices) as well as knowledge of how the Internet of Things works. Additionally, appropriate instruction regarding the innovative IoT deployment in their farm must be given (Rahman, 2020).

Autonomous Driving

Vehicles have become more integral to people's everyday lives, there has been an increase in demand for a more secure and pleasurable driving experience. Autonomous driving has a possibility to render transportation systems safer, more environmentally friendly, and more productive. The emergence of Internet of Things (IoT), along with advancements of computing power and wireless communication facilitates the development of autonomous vehicles also known as self-driving cars. The vehicle must understand its surroundings and operate in real time by using the massive amounts of data collected through cameras, Radar, Lidar, and other IoT sensors. The information collected is transmitted to servers for analysis to determine the next course of action based on these signals, such as moving, controlling speed, avoiding obstacles, and many more. The process of analysing sensor data involves object detection, pedestrian identification, traffic sign recognition, and many more. These tasks which consume high computing power cannot be handled in local due to the capacity restrictions of local machines (Zhou et al., 2020).

Furthermore, autonomous cars necessitate a rapid response to assure that the safety aspect is robust. Cloud computing has been leveraged to support real-time processing of the data collected from a variety of sensors and actuators that are interconnected with one another and to their surroundings that ensures the efficiency of autonomous vehicles. It is a cost-effective method that can provide more robust computational capability while also being easily maintained due to its centralised nature. However, the centralised characteristics make it challenging to achieve reliable communication with minimal latency (Mokhtarian et al., 2021).

The extensive amount of data gathered from sensors and decision-making processes which rely on Artificial Intelligence algorithms generate a huge load on the cloud servers where Fog Computing helps to overcome. Many advanced in-car applications, such as augmented reality, dynamic route planning, and cognitive driving systems, are necessary for implementing autonomous driving. These applications require enormous computational resources along with close to real-time reaction. This case study will provide an examination of the application of fog computing in the autonomous driving domain.

Autonomous Driving

Autonomous vehicles run software and travels between destinations without the assistance of humans by utilising a combination of sensors, actuators, machine learning systems, and sophisticated algorithms

(Singh & Saini, 2021). The fundamental architecture of autonomous vehicles is composed of hardware such as sensors, actuators, Global Positioning System (GPS), cameras, Radar, and Lidar that perceive internal and external environments of an autonomous vehicle and provide raw information about its surroundings. On the other hand, software includes the control unit which can process information and control the autonomous driving system based on input data.

Potential Application in the Context of Autonomous Driving

Case Study: Vehicular Fog Computing Architecture for Cooperative Sensing

Wang et al. (2020a) implemented a Vehicular Fog Computing (VFC) architecture to enable cooperative sensing among numerous neighbouring vehicles travelling in a platoon. Platooning indicates that cooperative automated vehicles (CAVs) drive closely behind each other using on-board sensors and vehicle-to-vehicle communication (Scholte et al., 2022). This can be achieved when multiple cars travelling at similar speeds in the same direction from a line. Each vehicle in a platoon can be linked together and share sensing information with the help of the Internet of Vehicle (IoV) (Du et al., 2020). To maintain safety and traffic efficacy, communication between these vehicles should be conducted with minimum latency.

Fog computing can offer proximity to end users, extensive geographical distribution, and great mobility support, the researcher used this strategy to enhance the sensing coverage and accuracy of self-driving vehicles. To assess the effectiveness of the proposed VFC structure, the researcher focused on the lane change detecting aspect. Greedy algorithms were used for selecting cars in the platoon to facilitate vehicle coordination and increase sensor coverage at the beginning. The Support Vector Machine method was then employed to combine sensing data from many vehicles, producing a precise state of the vehicles. Deep learning algorithms such as Light Gated Recurrent Unit (Li-GRU), GRU, and Long-Short Term Memory (LSTM) were adopted, and the model performances were evaluated using a real-world traffic dataset.

The proposed VFC architecture can reduce computer complexity by offloading sensing, data processing, and training tasks to several autonomous vehicles in a platoon (Wang et al., 2020a). To execute training tasks and evaluate the performance of the proposed VFC architecture, centralised and distributed structures are used. Centralised implies that data processing and training takes place solely in the lead vehicle, whereas distributed indicates that training is delegated to the vehicles in the platoon. By comparing the training duration, the proposed VFC architecture was found with the potential to substantially decrease computing time by allowing distributed learning. This, in turn, demonstrates the capacity of fog computing in supporting seamless data transmission between multiple vehicles where the proposed approach be further enhanced such that communication, processing, sensing, and vehicle operating conditions can all be scheduled synthetically.

Case Study: Connected Autonomous Vehicles (CAVs)

The increasing number of connected automobiles necessitates additional network connectivity, computation, and storage resources. The fog computing can be used to overcome inadequacies in traditional cloud computing to deliver real-time control in CAVs (Wang et al., 2020b). Conventional cloud-based architecture may have a long delay in responding and is inadequate for time-critical applications, thus motivates to develop a distributed network architecture based on fog computing. The aim was to enhance

Figure 7. Proposed fog-based architecture
(Wang et al., 2020b)

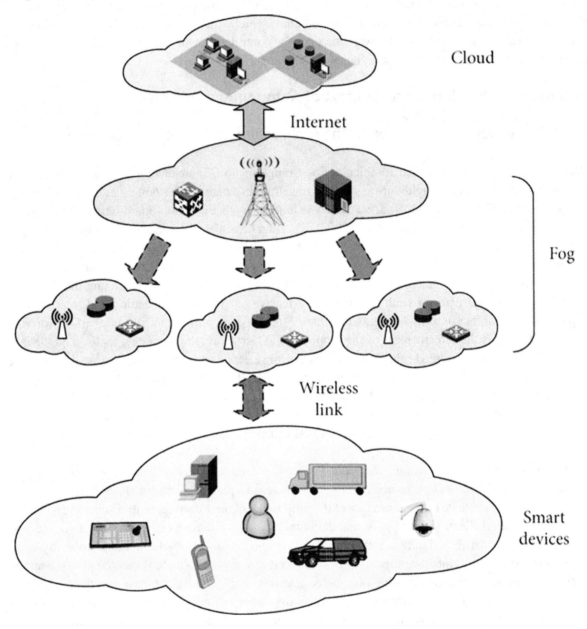

the communication among vehicles by integrating Vehicular Ad Hoc Networks (VANETs) with the fog computing concept. VANET is a type of network in which multiple moving vehicles communicate with one another via a wireless medium and exchange important information (Sandeep, 2020). Cruise control is a feature that maintain the vehicle at a constant speed and an investigation on the connected cruise control (CCC) to show the efficacy of the proposed architecture was crucial. CCC is based on the wireless vehicle-to-vehicle (V2V) communication, thus ensuring a smooth traffic flow and involves gathering real-time status information from automobiles ahead, such as distance, speed, and acceleration (Liu et al., 2021).

As illustrated in figure 7, the novel architecture consists of 3 logical levels, including the cloud, fog nodes, and edge smart devices. The fog nodes can manage the local network by allocating resources, planning transmission paths, and controlling congestion, further, to providing real-time decision making in the CCC system. The scenarios were simulated involving three-vehicle platoon with varying initial state to evaluate the performance of the proposed architecture. The outcomes demonstrated that all vehicles could achieve an ideal state in few seconds with minor delay, thus proving that fog computing can reduce latency successfully. At the same time, some technical obstacles such as the conformity of control algorithms with the variable state of the communication network, the possibility of data security issues, and high energy consumption with increasing number of fog nodes should also be taken into consideration.

Case Study: Supporting Autonomous Driving Assist

An edge twin architecture on a fog-based was designed to facilitate auto-drive assist tasks, particularly emphasis on trajectory prediction of human-piloted vehicles and road space allocation for autonomous vehicles (Maheswaran et al., 2019). The location of autonomous cars collected by the vehicle's sensors, as well as human-piloted cars and other road objects captured by overhead cameras, would be updated to the edge twin. This massive quantity of data in real time and use this information to provide driving assistance was done by employing fog computing for edge twin.

The concept of the edge twin is inspired by the concept of the digital twin and described it as a network of digital twins distributed across the fogs. In general, a digital twin comprises three major components: the physical entity, the virtual component, and the communication between them. It allows for the seamless connectivity of the physical and cyber worlds, along with real-time monitoring, simulation, optimisation, and reliable prediction (Sharma et al., 2022). Besides, the outside-the-car observer offers a bird's-eye perspective of the roadway conditions, such as forecasting how pedestrians would act within a road area.

A machine learning model was first created based on the XGBoost method to predict vehicle trajectory. The box algorithm was used to determine a suitable road space for autonomous vehicles, which can be used to recommend lane changes and accelerations for the vehicles. The performance of proposed framework was evaluated on a dataset that contains vehicle trajectories on highways. The results shown that the vehicles can receive outputs that relate to the moment they are at and apply them to make driving decisions. Hence, it can be concluded that fog computing can reduce the time it takes for data to be transmitted between the auto-drive assist application within the edge twin and the video camera. This enables the edge twin to adequately track real-time traffic circumstances. Meanwhile, fog computing reduced latency in sending decisions from the edge twin to autonomous vehicles.

Open issues in Autonomous Driving

This case study provides an overview of fog computing's potential and how it may be applied to autonomous driving. As the number of vehicles on the road grows exponentially, a large amount of data used to get generated. Additionally, autonomous vehicles require more data to make informed driving decisions to ensure safety. As a result, fog computing emerges as an excellent alternative for processing enormous volumes of data at or close to real-time rates. The fog computing can considerably minimise data transmission latency benefitting time-critical applications such as self-driving automobiles to avoid delays in decision making. As a result, catastrophic consequences may be mitigated. However, while a fog-based framework involves substantial information sharing, it also introduces hurdles such as data privacy concerns. With the swift development of technology, the likelihood of cyberattacks grows. Future study could concentrate on this aspect to improve its implementation in a variety of real-world applications.

Fog Computing in Healthcare

Fog computing is a new computing paradigm in the growing field of computing systems. In this digital era, many domains get benefitted from the Internet of Things (IoT) driven Fog Computing infrastructure among which healthcare is not exceptional. Even though cloud computing has become famous among many industry domains, Fog Computing offers a better latency reduction due to the use of personal computers, mobile devices, and other hand-held personal devices (Elhadad et al., 2022). The development of science and technology brought human development via advanced medical and healthcare applications. Healthcare expects the services to be delivered quickly in both spatial and temporal dimensions using Fog Computing with reduced latency and service response time. Therefore, integrating fog computing into the IoT, especially Internet of Health Things (IoHT) applications would improve system performance and energy efficiency. According to the trend in computing systems, a huge potential for IoHT applications based on fog computing has been witnessed in the contemporary digital era.

Computing and Technology applications are widely used in the healthcare domain to collect & analyse data, monitor & control patient status remotely and make treatment decisions for patients (Kumar et al., 2020) (Qadri et al., 2020). With the advent of 5G, IoT formed a series of smart applications among which smart healthcare has become more vibrant as it serves humanity (Qureshi et al., 2021). It's a novel standard in the healthcare monitoring system where it facilitates data processing with its quantity while preventing network congestion. In a smart healthcare system, IoT sensors are usually mounted on the body of the patient to collect blood pressure, heart rate, mobility, temperature, etc. and pass it to the fog computing platform (Ahad et al., 2019). These perfectly positioned sensors monitor the patient's health status by judging certain signs and assisting them in getting exact solutions.

Case Study: ECG Feature Analysis

A smart healthcare system with the support of a wearable device embedded with the sensors, monitors the patient's body temperature, heart rate, and blood pressure values. A fundamental IoHT technology named Wireless Body Area Networks (WBAN) will be used in the case of obtaining an Electrocardiogram (ECG) and Electromyography (EMG) (Gia et at., 2015). The smart healthcare system is expected to perform real-time analytics using machine learning models and to offer real-time notifications to medical practitioners or paramedical staff if any contradictions are found in the normal threshold value. The patients can also get notifications to alert them about the periodical medications or diet to be maintained.

The smart healthcare system can be set as illustrated in Figure 1 with different types of layers to perform dedicated tasks (Elhadad et al., 2022). A sensor layer will handle all the IoHT sensors connected with the body and collect the relevant data in regular intervals and pass it to the fog layer. The fog layer will perform all the analytical tasks along with data security and notification management to the decision-makers. The results will be then sent to the cloud layer which handles a large amount of data with analytics at a large scale and stores data for future references for the hospitals and the researchers.

It is very vital to define the purpose of the smart healthcare system to offer crucial diagnosis or detection and to offer intelligent patient treatment management. In this line, Electrocardiogram (ECG) feature analysis has been discussed as a case study as it plays an important role in diagnosing many cardiac diseases.

ECG feature analysis helps medical practitioners to diagnose, monitor and prescribe treatment for many cardiovascular-related diseases. Heart rate is one of the most concerned features extracted from ECG thus this data provides much sometimes-in-depth information regarding daily activities. This helps to detect some abnormalities of the heart using heart rate whereby an emergency action can be suggested if needed. The features such as heart rate, P wave and T wave were obtained from the ECG signals via a flexible template based on a lightweight wavelet transform mechanism. Three main parts including ECG preprocessing, wavelet transformation, and ECG feature extraction were carried out based on the used template (Gia et al., 2015).

P wave, T wave and heart rate from original ECG signals will be extracted using a lightweight algorithm for the reason of fast computation and low hardware resources consumption. This would help to keep track of the heart's activities and verify the smart gateway's warning service. The algorithm

Figure 8. Architecture of the fog-based health monitoring using ECG – adopted
(Elhadad et al., 2022)

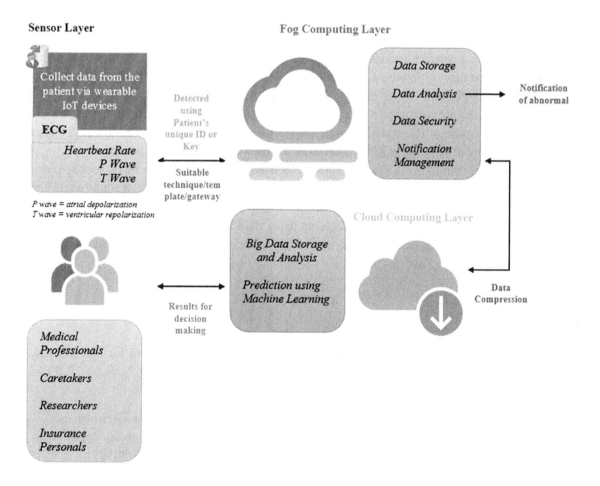

incorporates the appropriate threshold value by scanning the ECG signal and extracting the number of pulses to calculate the heart rate using the following formula (Gog et al., 2005):

$$Heart\ rate = \frac{60}{R - R\ Interval}$$

R-R Interval = time elapsed between two successive R-waves of ECG

Based on the obtained results, fog computing enables low-latency real-time reaction at the network's edge and helps achieve more than 90% bandwidth efficiency.

CONCLUSION

The effective use of fog computing using sensor-based data in medical decision-making has been more vibrant with the advanced IoHT-wearable devices. The outcome of this technological advancement drastically supports humanity's development in detecting or early diagnosing abnormal health conditions and suggesting treatment plans. This has become a solid aid to medical practitioners and caretakers to save lives.Fog Computing is one among many computing paradigms introduced by Cisco in 2012 which addresses many of the shortcomings of cloud computing. Being close to the edge of the network helps in reducing the latency which benefits time-sensitive applications. Furthermore, it shares the processing load with cloud computing and helps in reducing the amount of raw data being sent directly to the cloud infrastructure avoiding network bandwidth congestion. However, along with the numerous benefits of fog computing, some new limitations are introduced regarding the energy efficiency and sustainability of the devices. And with the inclusion of more devices which are usually personal computers and micro-computers, the architecture is exposed to more security vulnerabilities. Many studies are being conducted to leverage the latest state-of-the-art technologies like artificial intelligence, blockchains, cybersecurity and efficient data streaming to help address some of the drawbacks of fog computing.

In conclusion, fog computing is a promising approach to meet the growing demand for edge computing, but it faces several challenges that need to be addressed to enable its widespread adoption. Emerging technologies such as 5G, blockchain, secure hardware, machine learning, and artificial intelligence can help advance the state of fog computing, addressing these challenges and enabling new applications and use cases. As these technologies continue to evolve, fog computing is poised to become an even more powerful tool for processing and storing data at the edge of the network.

REFERENCES

Aazam, M., Zeadally, S., & Harras, K. A. (2018). Offloading in fog computing for IoT: Review, enabling technologies, and research opportunities. *Future Generation Computer Systems*, 87, 278–289. doi:10.1016/j.future.2018.04.057

Abba, S., Wadumi Namkusong, J., Lee, J. A., & Liz Crespo, M. (2019). Design and Performance Evaluation of a Low-Cost Autonomous Sensor Interface for a Smart IoT-Based Irrigation Monitoring and Control System. *Sensors (Basel)*, 19(17), 3643. doi:10.339019173643 PMID:31438597

Abdulkareem, K. H., Mohammed, M. A., Gunasekaran, S. S., Al-Mhiqani, M. N., Mutlag, A. H., Mostafa, S. A., Ali, N. S., & Ibrahim, D. A. (2019). A Review of Fog Computing and Machine Learning: Concepts, Applications, Challenges, and Open Issues. *IEEE Access : Practical Innovations, Open Solutions*, *7*, 153123–153140. doi:10.1109/ACCESS.2019.2947542

Abdulqadir, H. R., Zeebaree, S. R. M., Shukur, H. M., Sadeeq, M. M., Salim, B. W., Salih, A. A., & Kak, S. F. (2021). A Study of Moving from Cloud Computing to Fog Computing. *Qubahan Academic Journal*, *1*(2), 60–70. doi:10.48161/qaj.v1n2a49

Ahad, A., Tahir, M., & Yau, K. L. A. (2019). 5G-based smart healthcare network: Architecture, taxonomy, challenges and future research directions. *IEEE Access : Practical Innovations, Open Solutions*, *7*, 100747–100762. doi:10.1109/ACCESS.2019.2930628

Alraddady, S., Li, A. S., Soh, B., & AlZain, M. A. (2019). Deployment of Fog Computing During Hajj Season: A Proposed Framework. *Procedia Computer Science*, *161*, 1072–1079. doi:10.1016/j.procs.2019.11.218

Alzoubi, Y. I., Al-Ahmad, A., & Kahtan, H. (2022). Blockchain technology as a Fog computing security and privacy solution: An overview. *Computer Communications*, *182*, 129–152. doi:10.1016/j.comcom.2021.11.005

Atlam, H., Walters, R., & Wills, G. (2018). Fog computing and the Internet of Things: A review. *Big Data and Cognitive Computing*, *2*(2), 10. doi:10.3390/bdcc2020010

Baccarelli, E., Naranjo, P. G. V., Scarpiniti, M., Shojafar, M., & Abawajy, J. H. (2017). Fog of Everything: Energy-Efficient Networked Computing Architectures, Research Challenges, and a Case Study. *IEEE Access : Practical Innovations, Open Solutions*, *5*, 9882–9910. doi:10.1109/ACCESS.2017.2702013

Bai, T., Pan, C., Deng, Y., Elkashlan, M., Nallanathan, A., & Hanzo, L. (2020). Latency Minimization for Intelligent Reflecting Surface Aided Mobile Edge Computing. *IEEE Journal on Selected Areas in Communications*, *38*(11), 2666–2682. doi:10.1109/JSAC.2020.3007035

Bonomi, F., Milito, R., Zhu, J., & Addepalli, S. (2012). Fog computing and its role in the internet of things. *Proceedings of the First Edition of the MCC Workshop on Mobile Cloud Computing*. 10.1145/2342509.2342513

Bouachir, O., Aloqaily, M., Tseng, L., & Boukerche, A. (2020). Blockchain and fog computing for cyber-physical systems: The case of smart industry. *Computer*, *53*(9), 36–45. doi:10.1109/MC.2020.2996212

Cai, J., Qin, B., Zheng, F., Li, S., Luo, Y., & Zhang, J. (2018, December). Design and application of innovative teaching platform based on fog computing. In *2018 2nd International Conference on Education Innovation and Social Science (ICEISS 2018)* (pp. 227-231). Atlantis Press. 10.2991/iceiss-18.2018.56

Du, H., Leng, S., Wu, F., Chen, X., & Mao, S. (2020). A New Vehicular Fog Computing Architecture for Cooperative Sensing of Autonomous Driving. *IEEE Access : Practical Innovations, Open Solutions*, *8*, 10997–11006. doi:10.1109/ACCESS.2020.2964029

Elhadad, A., Alanazi, F., Taloba, A. I., & Abozeid, A. (2022, March 15). Fog Computing Service in the Healthcare Monitoring System for Managing the Real-Time Notification. *Journal of Healthcare Engineering, 5337733*, 1–11. Advance online publication. doi:10.1155/2022/5337733 PMID:35340260

Elijah, O., Rahman, T. A., Orikumhi, I., Leow, C. Y., & Hindia, M. N. (2018, October). An Overview of Internet of Things (IoT) and Data Analytics in Agriculture: Benefits and Challenges. *IEEE Internet of Things Journal, 5*(5), 3758–3773. doi:10.1109/JIOT.2018.2844296

Friha, O., Ferrag, M. A., Shu, L., Maglaras, L., & Wang, X. (2021). Internet of things for the future of smart agriculture: A comprehensive survey of emerging technologies. *IEEE/CAA Journal of Automatica Sinica, 8*(4), 718-752.

García, L., Parra, L., Jimenez, J. M., Lloret, J., & Lorenz, P. (2020). IoT-based smart irrigation systems: An overview on the recent trends on sensors and IoT systems for irrigation in precision agriculture. *Sensors (Basel), 20*(4), 1042. doi:10.339020041042 PMID:32075172

Gia, T. N., Jiang, M., Rahmani, A. M., Westerlund, T., Liljeberg, P., & Tenhunen, H. "Fog Computing in Healthcare Internet of Things: A Case Study on ECG Feature Extraction," 2015 IEEE International Conference on Computer and Information Technology; Ubiquitous Computing and Communications; Dependable, Autonomic and Secure Computing; Pervasive Intelligence and Computing, Liverpool, UK, 2015, pp. 356-363 10.1109/CIT/IUCC/DASC/PICOM.2015.51

Goh, K., Lavanya, J., Kim, Y., Tan, E., & Soh, C. (2005). A pda-based ecg beat detector for home cardiac care. *27th Annual International Conference of the Engineering in Medicine and Biology Society*, IEEE. 10.1109/IEMBS.2005.1616423

Habibi, P., Farhoudi, M., Kazemian, S., Khorsandi, S., & Leon-Garcia, A. (2020). Fog Computing: A Comprehensive Architectural Survey. *IEEE Access : Practical Innovations, Open Solutions, 8*, 69105–69133. doi:10.1109/ACCESS.2020.2983253

Iftikhar, S., Gill, S. S., Song, C., Xu, M., Aslanpour, M. S., Toosi, A. N., Du, J., Wu, H., Ghosh, S., Chowdhury, D., Golec, M., Kumar, M., Abdelmoniem, A. M., Cuadrado, F., Varghese, B., Rana, O., Dustdar, S., & Uhlig, S. (2022). AI-based fog and edge computing: A systematic review, taxonomy and future directions. *Internet of Things, 21*, 100674. doi:10.1016/j.iot.2022.100674

Jain, S., Gupta, S., Sreelakshmi, K. K., & Rodrigues, J. J. P. C. (2022). Fog computing in enabling 5G-driven emerging technologies for development of sustainable smart city infrastructures. *Cluster Computing, 25*(2), 1111–1154. doi:10.100710586-021-03496-w

Javadzadeh, G., & Rahmani, A. M. (2020). Fog Computing Applications in Smart Cities: A Systematic Survey. *Wireless Networks, 26*(2), 1433–1457. doi:10.100711276-019-02208-y

Kugali, S. N. (2020). Vehicular ADHOC Network (VANET):-A Brief Knowledge. *International Journal of Engineering Research & Technology (Ahmedabad), 9*(6), 1026–1029. doi:10.17577/IJERTV9IS060784

Kumar, A., Krishnamurthi, R., Nayyar, A., Sharma, K., Grover, V., & Hossain, E. (2020). A novel smart healthcare design, simulation, and implementation using healthcare 4.0 processes. *IEEE Access : Practical Innovations, Open Solutions, 8*, 118433–118471. doi:10.1109/ACCESS.2020.3004790

Lawal, M. A., Shaikh, R. A., & Hassan, S. R. (2020). An anomaly mitigation framework for IoT using fog computing. *Electronics (Basel)*, *9*(10), 1565. doi:10.3390/electronics9101565

Lee, K., Kim, D., Ha, D., Rajput, U., & Oh, H. (2015). On security and privacy issues of fog computing supported Internet of Things environment. *2015 6th International Conference on the Network of the Future (NOF)*. IEEE.

Liu, L., Xue, Y., Chen, H., Wang, Z., Fang, C., Sun, Y., & Sun, Y. (2021). Optimal Connected Cruise Control Design with Time-Varying Leader Velocity and Delays. *Journal of Sensors*, *2021*, 1–14. doi:10.1155/2021/5618538

Ma, K., Bagula, A., Nyirenda, C., & Ajayi, O. (2019). An IoT-based fog computing model. *Sensors (Basel)*, *19*(12), 2783. doi:10.339019122783 PMID:31234280

Maheswaran, M., Yang, T., & Memon, S. (2019). A Fog Computing Framework for Autonomous Driving Assist: Architecture, Experiments, and Challenges. *CASCON '19: Proceedings of the 29th Annual International Conference on Computer Science and Software Engineering*, (pp. 24–33). IEEE.

Mahmud, R., Ramamohanarao, K., & Buyya, R. (2021). Application Management in Fog Computing Environments. *ACM Computing Surveys*, *53*(4), 1–43. doi:10.1145/3403955

Mekala, M. S., & Viswanathan, P. (2007). A Survey: Smart agriculture IoT with cloud computing. 2017 International conference on Microelectronic Devices, Circuits and Systems (ICMDCS). IEEE. 10.1109/ICMDCS.2017.8211551

Meng, Y., Naeem, M. A., Almagrabi, A. O., Ali, R., & Kim, H. S. (2020). *Advancing the state of the fog computing to enable 5g network technologies*. Sensors. doi:10.339020061754

Mokhtarian, A., Kampmann, A., Lueer, M., Kowalewski, S., & Alrifaee, B. (2021). A Cloud Architecture for Networked and Autonomous Vehicles. *IFAC-PapersOnLine*, *54*(2), 233–239. doi:10.1016/j.ifacol.2021.06.028

Mukherjee, M., Matam, R., Shu, L., Maglaras, L., Ferrag, M. A., Choudhury, N., & Kumar, V. (2017). Security and Privacy in Fog Computing: Challenges. *IEEE Access : Practical Innovations, Open Solutions*, *5*, 19293–19304. doi:10.1109/ACCESS.2017.2749422

Naranjo, P. G. V., Pooranian, Z., Shojafar, M., Conti, M., & Buyya, R. (2019). FOCAN: A Fog-supported smart city network architecture for management of applications in the Internet of Everything environments. *Journal of Parallel and Distributed Computing*, *132*, 274–283. doi:10.1016/j.jpdc.2018.07.003

Nazir, S., Kumam, P., Nadeem, S., & García-Magariño, I. (2019). Internet of Things for Healthcare Using Effects of Mobile Computing: A Systematic Literature Review. *Wireless Communications and Mobile Computing*, *2019*, 1–20. doi:10.1155/2019/5931315

Nhamo, N., & Chikoye, D. (2017). Smart Agriculture: Scope, Relevance, and Important Milestones to Date. In *Smart Technologies for Sustainable Smallholder Agriculture* (pp. 1–20). Elsevier. doi:10.1016/B978-0-12-810521-4.00001-3

Ni, J., Zhang, K., Lin, X., & Shen, X. S. (2018). Securing fog computing for Internet of Things applications: Challenges and solutions. IEEE Commun. Surveys Tuts., 20(1), 601–628.

Ning, Z., Dong, P., Wang, X., Hu, X., Guo, L., Hu, B., Wilkinson, A. J., Qiu, T., & Kwok, R. Y. K. (2021). Mobile Edge Computing Enabled 5G Health Monitoring for Internet of Medical Things: A Decentralized Game Theoretic Approach. *IEEE Journal on Selected Areas in Communications*, *39*(2), 463–478. doi:10.1109/JSAC.2020.3020645

Qadri, Y. A., Nauman, A., Zikria, Y. B., Vasilakos, A. V., & Kim, S. W. (2020). The future of healthcare internet of things: A survey of emerging technologies. *IEEE Communications Surveys and Tutorials*, *22*(2), 1121–1167. doi:10.1109/COMST.2020.2973314

Qiu, T., Chen, N., Li, K., Atiquzzaman, M., & Zhao, W. (2018). How can heterogeneous Internet of Things build our future: A survey. IEEE Commun. Surveys Tuts., 20(3). doi:10.1109/COMST.2018.2803740

Qu, Y., Gao, L., Luan, T. H., Xiang, Y., Yu, S., Li, B., & Zheng, G. (2020). Decentralized privacy using blockchain-enabled federated learning in fog computing. *IEEE Internet of Things Journal*, *7*(6), 5171–5183. doi:10.1109/JIOT.2020.2977383

Qureshi, H. N., Manalastas, M., Zaidi, S. M. A., Imran, A., & Al Kalaa, M. O. (2021). Service level agreements for 5G and beyond: Overview, challenges and enablers of 5G-healthcare systems. *IEEE Access : Practical Innovations, Open Solutions*, *9*, 1044–1061. doi:10.1109/ACCESS.2020.3046927 PMID:35211361

Rahaman, S. H., & Biswas, S. (2020). Advantages of Internet of Things (IoT) and It's Applications in Smart Agriculture System. *Int. Res. J. Adv. Sci. Hub*, *2*(10), 4–10. doi:10.47392/irjash.2020.181

Rahimi, M., Songhorabadi, M., & Kashani, M. H. (2020). Fog-based smart homes: A systematic review. *Journal of Network and Computer Applications*, *153*, 102531. doi:10.1016/j.jnca.2020.102531

Rahimi, M., Songhorabadi, M., & Kashani, M. H. (2020). Fog-based smart homes: A systematic review. *Journal of Network and Computer Applications*, *153*, 102531. doi:10.1016/j.jnca.2020.102531

Rajaram, K., & Sundareswaran, R. (2020). IoT Based Crop-Field Monitoring and Precise Irrigation System Using Crop Water Requirement. *In International Conference on Computational Intelligence in Data Science,* Springer: Cham, Switzerland. 10.1007/978-3-030-63467-4_23

Rani, R., Kumar, N., Khurana, M., Kumar, A., & Barnawi, A. (2021). Storage as a service in Fog computing: A systematic review. *Journal of Systems Architecture*, *116*, 102033. doi:10.1016/j.sysarc.2021.102033

Rawat, R., Chakrawarti, R. K., Vyas, P., Gonzáles, J. L. A., Sikarwar, R., & Bhardwaj, R. (2023). Intelligent Fog Computing Surveillance System for Crime and Vulnerability Identification and Tracing. *International Journal of Information Security and Privacy*, *17*(1), 1–25. doi:10.4018/IJISP.317371

Rehman, A., Saba, T., Kashif, M., Fati, S. M., Bahaj, S. A., & Chaudhry, H. (2022). A revisit of internet of things technologies for monitoring and control strategies in smart agriculture. *Agronomy (Basel)*, *12*(1), 127. doi:10.3390/agronomy12010127

Saba, T., Rehman, A., & AlGhamdi, J. S. (2017). Weather forecasting based on hybrid neural model. *Applied Water Science*, *7*(7), 3869–3874. doi:10.100713201-017-0538-0

Scholte, W. J., Zegelaar, P. W. A., & Nijmeijer, H. (2022). A control strategy for merging a single vehicle into a platoon at highway on-ramps. *Transportation Research Part C, Emerging Technologies, 136,* 103511. doi:10.1016/j.trc.2021.103511

Sharma, A., Kosasih, E., Zhang, J., Brintrup, A., & Calinescu, A. (2022). Digital Twins: State of the art theory and practice, challenges, and open research questions. *Journal of Industrial Information Integration, 30,* 100383. Advance online publication. doi:10.1016/j.jii.2022.100383

Singh, S., & Saini, B. S. (2021). Autonomous cars: Recent developments, challenges, and possible solutions. *IOP Conference Series. Materials Science and Engineering, 1022*(1), 012028. doi:10.1088/1757-899X/1022/1/012028

Spatharakis, D., Dimolitsas, I., Dechouniotis, D., Papathanail, G., Fotoglou, I., Papadimitriou, P., & Papavassiliou, S. (2020). A scalable Edge Computing architecture enabling smart offloading for Location Based Services. *Pervasive and Mobile Computing, 67,* 101217. doi:10.1016/j.pmcj.2020.101217

Sultana, T., & Wahid, K. A. (2019). Choice of application layer protocols for next generation video surveillance using Internet of video things. *IEEE Access : Practical Innovations, Open Solutions, 7,* 41607–41624. doi:10.1109/ACCESS.2019.2907525

Tuli, S., Mahmud, R., Tuli, S., & Buyya, R. (2019). FogBus: A blockchain-based lightweight framework for edge and fog computing. *Journal of Systems and Software, 154,* 22–36. doi:10.1016/j.jss.2019.04.050

Vaquero, L. M., & Rodero-Merino, L. (2014, October). Finding your way in the fog: Towards a comprehensive definition of fog computing. *Computer Communication Review, 44*(5), 27–32. doi:10.1145/2677046.2677052

Wang, H., Liu, T., Kim, B., Lin, C.-W., Shiraishi, S., Xie, J., & Han, Z. (2020a). Architectural Design Alternatives based on Cloud/Edge/Fog Computing for Connected Vehicles. *IEEE Communications Surveys and Tutorials, 22*(4), 2349–2377. doi:10.1109/COMST.2020.3020854

Wang, H., Wang, L., Zhou, Z., Tao, X., Pau, G., & Arena, F. (2019). Blockchain-based resource allocation model in fog computing. *Applied Sciences (Basel, Switzerland), 9*(24), 5538. doi:10.3390/app9245538 PMID:32944385

Wang, S., Guo, Y., Zhang, N., Yang, P., Zhou, A., & Shen, X. (2021). Delay-Aware Microservice Coordination in Mobile Edge Computing: A Reinforcement Learning Approach. *IEEE Transactions on Mobile Computing, 20*(3), 939–951. doi:10.1109/TMC.2019.2957804

Wang, Y., Tao, X., Zhang, X., Zhang, P., & Hou, Y. T. (2019). Cooperative Task Offloading in Three-Tier Mobile Computing Networks: An ADMM Framework. *IEEE Transactions on Vehicular Technology, 68*(3), 2763–2776. doi:10.1109/TVT.2019.2892176

Wang, Z., Guo, Y., Gao, Y., Fang, C., Li, M., & Sun, Y. (2020b). Fog-Based Distributed Networked Control for Connected Autonomous Vehicles. *Wireless Communications and Mobile Computing, 2020,* 1–11. doi:10.1155/2020/8855655

Zhang, Y., Qu, Y., Gao, L., Luan, T. H., Zheng, X., Chen, S., & Xiang, Y. (2019). APDP: Attack-Proof Personalized Differential Privacy Model for a Smart Home. *IEEE Access : Practical Innovations, Open Solutions*, 1–13. doi:10.1109/ACCESS.2019.2943243

Zhou, Z., Liao, H., Wang, X., Mumtaz, S., & Rodriguez, J. (2020). When Vehicular Fog Computing Meets Autonomous Driving: Computational Resource Management and Task Offloading. *IEEE Network*, *34*(6), 70–76. doi:10.1109/MNET.001.1900527

Chapter 4

An Integrated Fog Computing With Machine Learning Techniques for Diagnosis of Thyroid Disease

Nancy Kumari

https://orcid.org/0000-0002-4857-8106

VIT Bhopal University, India

ABSTRACT

The thyroid is a part of the endocrine system that is placed toward the front of the neck and produces thyroxine, which is essential for our overall health. Recent advancements in computational approaches have facilitated the storage and collection of medical data for disease diagnosis. Various machine learning technology has a major role in making processes easy and efficient. Fog computing could be used to monitor and help to detect disease at an early stage, reduce the diagnosis time, and prevent complicated diseases. To strengthen thyroid patient prediction, machine learning can be integrated with fog computing for practical solutions. In this chapter, a fog-assisted internet of things-based quality of service framework is presented to prevent and protect against the thyroid. It provides real-time processing of users' health data to predict the thyroid disease by observing their symptoms and immediately generates an emergency alert, medical reports, and significant precautions for the user, their guardian, as well as doctors.

1. INTRODUCTION

Thyroid illness is an endocrinology subgroup that is one among the diseases that are the most misunderstood and undiagnosed (Azar et al., 2021). According to the WHO, after diabetes, Thyroid gland disease is the second most common endocrine ailment in the world. About 2% and 1% of people, respectively, suffer with hyper functioning hyperthyroidism and hypothyroidism. Men's prevalence is around a tenth that of women (Keleş & Keleş, 2008). Hyperthyroidism and hypothyroidism can be caused by thyroid

DOI: 10.4018/978-1-6684-4466-5.ch004

gland malfunction, which can be after pituitary gland malfunction or third to hypothalamus dysfunction. In some locations, goitre or functional thyroid nodules can form as a result of a dietary iodine deficiency, with an occurrence of about 15 percent. Endogenous antibodies (autoantibody) can cause havoc in the thyroid gland, and it can also be the site of a number of malignancies (Sonuç, 2021).

Experts claim that initially illness identification, diagnosis, & treatment, are crucial in reducing the progression of the disease and mortality. For a number of disorders, early diagnosis and possible treatments improves successful therapy. Despite several clinical, trials detection is generally seemed as a challenging job (Kourou et al., 2015). The butterfly- shaped thyroid gland found towards the bottom of the throat. It is made up of levothyroxine (T4), two functional thyroid hormones, and triiodo thyroxine (T3), which regulate blood pressure, heart rate and body temperature. Thyroid disease, moreover, is among the most popular disease in the country, and it's usually triggered by iodine shortage, however this can ever be triggered by some other factors. Whereas thyroid gland seems to be a hormone-producing endocrine organ that transports hormones all around the body. It is positioned in the front center of the human body. Hormones of thyroid gland are mainly responsible for metabolism, and also keeping the moisture of body balanced. Thyroid problems are of two different types: hyperthyroidism & hypothyroidism. Mining of data (Shukla et al., 2009) seems to be a technique of searching that is semi-automated relationships in large databases. ML techniques are one among the most powerful approaches to a wide range of complicated problems (Aswad & Sonuç, 2020). Classification seems to be a method of data gathering (machine learning) that is used for detecting & recognizing various diseases, which include thyroid disease, something that we explored and classified here simply as ML algorithms play a very critical part in characterizing thyroid disease as they are effective and successful and in classifying (Banu, 2016). Despite the fact that artificial intelligence & machine learning have been used in medical since its inception (Chandio et al., 2016), recently, there has been a push to address the need for machines to comprehend solution of healthcare. Due to this, experts anticipate that ML would turn into standard healthcare system in the coming years (Murdoch & Detsky, 2013). Thyroid hyperthyroidism occurs when the thyroid gland generates too many hormones related to thyroid. A rise in thyroid hormone levels causes hyperthyroidism (Vanderpump, 2011). Increased temperature sensitivity, dry skin, weight loss, thinning of hair, elevated heart rate, excessive sweating, high blood pressure (BP), neck expansion, nervousness, shorter menstrual cycles, hands shaking, and abnormal stomach motions are only a few of the symptoms. Hypothyroidisms are disordered in that thyroid gland does not function properly. A decrease in thyroid hormones generation causes hypothyroidism. Whereas Hypo means "insufficient" or "less" not medical jargon. Thyroid gland problem and inflammation are twice major sources of hypothyroidism. Low heart rate, obesity, neck swelling, enlarged temperature sensitivity, hand numbness, hair problems, dry skin, heavy menstrual cycles, and digestive nuisance are all just a couple of small symptoms. If these symptoms aren't handled, they can get worse with time (Prerana & Taneja, 2015).

The main function of the thyroid is to produce hormones that body temperature, control weight, diabetes, blood pressure and heart rate (Cabanillas et al., 2016). Thyroid cases have been increased from 6.8 to 10.7 percent as compared to previous years (Cabanillas et al., 2016) and this disease is getting magnificent worldwide. In today's era, fog computing generates huge amount of data due to which a large number of fog computing services & apps are developing (Samann et al., 2021). The process of using machine learning to improve fog computing applications and provide fog services like effective resource management, traffic modelling, and energy consumption, among others. But there is some problem that integrate fog computing with machine learning has not yet investigate (Samann et al., 2021). This chapter generates thyroid data using the technique of fog computing. Internet apps running on smart devices already create a large amount of data that can be sent to the Cloud for processing (Rouhani & Mansouri, 2009). In addition, machine learning techniques are used to predict thyroid disease whether a patient has thyroid or not. However, a Cloud's communication with end devices is a basic restriction. By dispersing computing, communication, and storage services, Fog Computing overcomes this barrier and satisfied the needs of time-sensitive applications (Rouhani & Mansouri, 2009). The Figure 1 shows that fog computing is an extension of cloud computing, but closer to the end devices such as phones, cars, mobiles, laptops and many other devices. FC supplements cloud computing activities to improve end-user Quality of Service (QoS) and Quality of Experience (QoE) (Samann et al., 2021).

2. LITERATURE SURVEY

Several researches in the literature focus with the detection of thyroid illnesses using hormonal measures and private data from the patient, such as age and sex. Some research, for example, employee machine learning classifications and predictive model, whilst others use deeper CNN architectures.

In this study, Thyroid disorder is diagnosed with several classified models based on factors including TSH, T4U, as well as goitre. In argument is supported by a number of grouping algorithms, including

Figure 1. Integrated fog computing with machine learning techniques

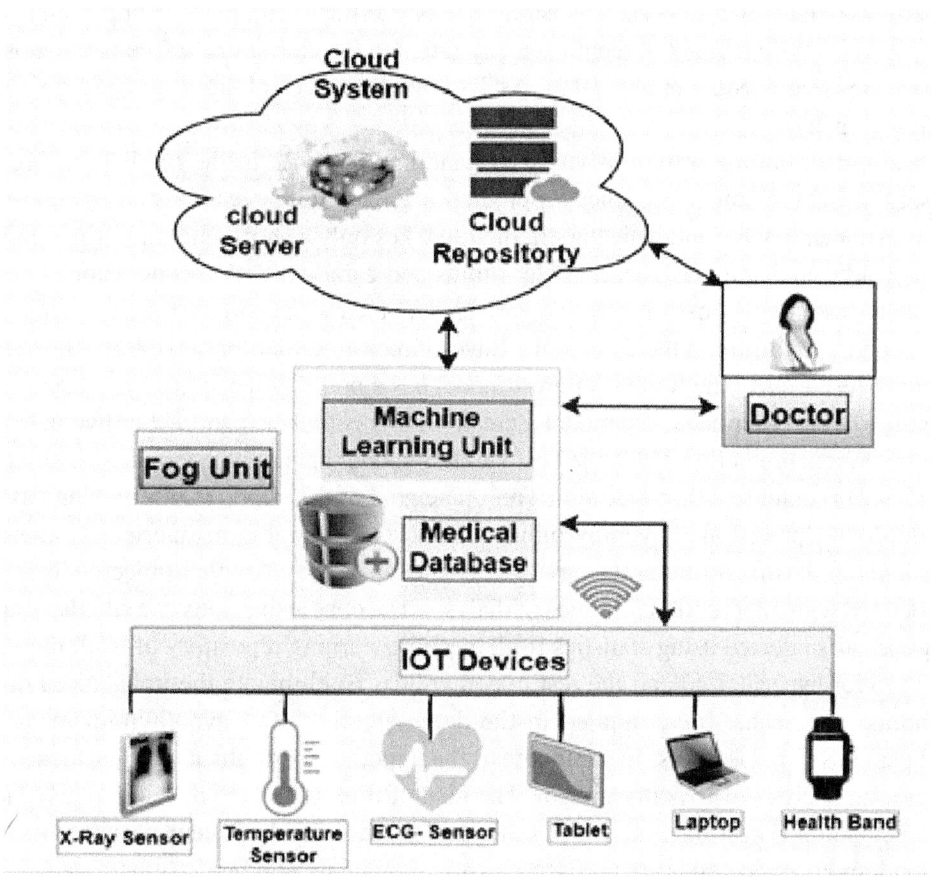

Naive Bayes (Chandel et al., 2016). The algorithm Decision Tree, Random Forest and Support vector machine is used. These studies were conducted with the rapid miner tool, and these results show to Random Forest Algorithm is more successful than Naive Bayes in diagnosing thyroid problems. In this work, Naive Bayes, ANN, SVM, Decision Tree and Random Forest classifiers were utilised. These five classifiers are comparing with the Rapid miner programme. The Random Forest Algorithm with 98.87% accuracy was found to be the most dependable against other four classifiers. The suggested Random Forest approach results in better outcomes by enhancing accuracy of classification. Due to this, Naive Bayes gives linear, elliptical, or parabolic decision boundary. Because the components are interrelated. Thyroid disease are most common affecting human. The thyroid data utilised in this study has been taken from Irvine's data repository (UCI) of University of California. The decision stump tree approach was proven to be less successful than the J48 technique. Diagnosing disease in the field of medicine is a daunting task. A variety of data mining approaches are employed in the decision-making procedure. We reduced dimensionality to decide selection of characteristics from the earlier findings, and we defined thyroid using J48 and different classification approaches for decision stump data mining. The uncertainty matrix is used to evaluate the precision and error rate of a classifier's output. The J48 Algorithm offers higher accuracy percentage (98.87%) and lower rate of error, than that of the decision stump tree (Banu, 2016). Classification is the important data mining approaches under supervised learning and is used to describe preset data sets. The categorization is extensively used in the healthcare industry to help take decision in medical diagnosis as well as supervision. The data for this research came from a renowned laboratory in Kashmir. The ANACONDA3-5.2.0 platform will be used for the whole research study. Different methods of Classification viz. Decision Tree, Naive Bayes etc. may be employed in an experimental investigation. With a 98.87 percent accuracy rate, the Random Forest Tree is the most accurate of the other classes (Umar Sidiq et al., 2019). As Thyroid disease is a long-term condition that affects the population globally.

In healthcare, data mining proves to yield outstanding outcomes in the prediction (prognosis) of multiple diseases. Data mining approaches for prediction have a high level of accuracy and a cheap cost of prediction. Another key advantage is that prediction takes only a short amount of time. In this study, I analyzed thyroid data using classification algorithms and came up with a conclusion. The effectiveness of a model is essentially governed by two variables. Forecast precision is the first, while prediction time is the second. According to the data, Nave Bayes forecasting took only 0.04 sec. It is less precise than Random Forest & J48. The Random Forest model has a prediction accuracy of 98.8 percent when we looked at it. On the other hand, the model's creation time is higher than further two iterations. As a result, for hypothyroid prediction J48 is the best yielding model having 98.87% accuracy and its execution time (0.2 sec) is quite less than Decision Tree . The goal of this job is to offer a plan based on data mining for improving precision of hypothyroidism diagnostic by combining queries of patients and test findings throughout the diagnostic procedure (Peterson et al., 2018). Another objective is lowering the hazards associated with interventional studies of dialysis. The conclusive outcome whether new samples are hypothyroid, was inferred using statistics from machine learning repository of UCI, providing 1212 sample data (155of hyperthyroid and the rest hypothyroid). To eliminate the imbalanced distribution, several sampling approaches were applied in the data gathering, and hypothyroidism models were constructed using, SVM classifiers. In this context, the hypothesis established the influence of sample methodologies on analysis of hypothyroidism. The goal of this study is to develop a machine learning system using Random Forest method to detect thyroid disease inside patient near the beginning and correctly. Random Forest methods are used for classification phase and regression phase of application.

The performance ratio is greater when compared to other methods. The proposed model produces the best prediction results for thyroid disease diagnosis, and the findings show that the system is accurate, effective and, quick in diagnosing the thyroid disease (Chaudhary et al., 2016; Poppe & Glinoer, 2003). Incorporating recent scientific developments into survival prediction models. To build prediction models, we employed a large dataset and three standard data mining methods. We utilized 10-folded cross-validation procedures to test the impartial estimate of all the predictive models in subject for accuracy evaluation. According to the findings, the Bay is safe area to visit. The RBF Networks are the next-best predictors by 93.44% accuracies on the propose sample, followed by the Nave Bayes with 97.36% on the holdout sample. We used two criteria in this study to assess varying thyroid disease survivorship prediction (Yadav & Pal, 2019). The more recent study focuses on the categorization of thyroid-illness in two most common thyroid dysfunctions in the common people. Radial Basis Function networks, Naive Bayes, Multilayer Perceptron's, Decision Tress, were four classification models, researchers looked at and compound. The results show that all of the above-mentioned classification models are very accurate, with the Decision Tree model yielding uppermost categorization of score. Data from UCI machine learning repository and Romanian data website were used to build and evaluate the classifier (Begum & Parkavi, 2019). KNIME Analysis Platform along with Weka is two datasets. The categorization models were developed and tested using data mining techniques as the base. With literature survey, a range of learning in the subject of categorization of thyroid employs different data mining approaches to build strong classifiers. The authors examined how four classification models may be used on thyroid data to assist categorize thyroid dysfunctions including hyperthyroidism along with hypothyroidism. The decision tree model was proper categorization model in all scenarios that were examined.

This paper has studied machine learning algorithm in real world application (Sarker, 2021). In recent times digital world has produce large amount of data from mobile, social media, cyber security, health and so on. This chapter gives an in-depth look at machine learning algorithms, to increase the capabilities of an application in real world application such as healthcare, ecommerce, smart cities. This work as a reference point from research scholars, professionals and Decision Support makers in a real situation.

In Fog Computing, used a machine learning algorithm as a tool for Quality-of-Service aware Resource Management (Guevara et al., 2020). This study examined how the internet offers a wealth of applications that generate large amounts of data that may be forwarded to cloud computing for additional processing. This paper discussed the problem of connectivity with end devices in cloud. Fog computing has addressed this barrier by processing, communicating, and delivering Storage Services, empowering with the C2T (Cloud to Things) Continuum Smart cities, augmented reality (AR), and virtual reality are examples of potential new uses. This study provides an implementation of a common machine learning Classification approach for fog computing application discrimination: Their QoS requirements are a factor.

This chapter has reviewed machine learning and fog computing on behalf of applications, concepts and challenges (Singh et al., 2021). Fog computing generates a large amount of data a large amount of fog computing apps and services are emerged. As fog computing generates large amount of data, leading to large amount of fog computing apps and services. In today's world, an increasing trend in machine learning adoption has been noticed to boost for delivering smog services such as computational applications and efficient resource management, security, latency and energy consumption reduction, and traffic modelling. To achieve deeper analysis and better answers to vital activities, the ML application for fog computing becomes robust end-user and high-level services.

3. IMPLEMENT MACHINE LEARNING ALGORITHM IN THYROID

Machine learning algorithms are being used to distinguish between three types of thyroid illness. Hyperthyroidism is the very first, hypothyroidism is the second, and stable people with no thyroid disorders are the third. Machine Learning (ML) is a field of Artificial Intelligence that has trained a computer by learning from patients' data and making predictions based on past samples. The algorithms of machine learning are divided into methods such as supervised and unsupervised learning. Supervised learning is also called labelled dataset which consists of input labels with target labels in the dataset. On the other hand, unsupervised learning is also called as unlabeled dataset in which dataset needs only input labels. (Choi et al., 2017)

3.1 Naive Bayes Algorithm

This approach is based on Bayes' theorem, which assumes predictor independence. This algorithm predicts the patients have thyroid cancer or not (Keleş & Keleş, 2017). Naive Bayes theorem is inspired by Bayes theorem which states the following equation.

$P(A|B) = P(B/A) * P(A)/P(B)$

Naive Bayes Algorithm is easy and helpful for large data sets. In simple terms, the Naive Bayes classifier implies that the presence of a specific attribute in a class has nothing to do with one's look or other characteristics (Yadav & Pal, 2020).

Using Nave Bayesian, several generalized additive models incorporating subject selection independent variables, variables having the biggest relative impact on classification, and a mixture of different factors from both can be compared. The Figure 2 shows the training and testing set of thyroid disease. It directly compared each one of the best model's prediction accuracies. By fit naive Bayes through varying combination of splines, two-degree polynomials, and sequential predictor's variable, it limited correlations among individual predictors and responses. To construct predictors with nonlinear links to our response variable, we use much more polynomials and splines.

Figure 2. Naïve Bayes representation

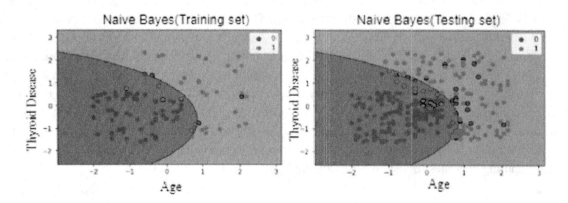

3.2 Random Forest Algorithm

In the problems of regression and classification the random forest (RF) has becomes popular. It is an ensemble learning methods by constructing a multiple of decision trees (Dittman et al., 2011). Random forest was created by multiple classification and regression (CART) trees. The cart tree consists of a binary decision tree, which is constructed by repeatedly dividing the data in the node into child nodes, starting from the root node (Mishra et al., 2021). The root node represents thyroid patients and branch node present whether the patients have cancer or not.

The Figure 3 random forest calculates the average response of each energy consumption predictor. The relative distance between every response was in the mean of every predictor is then added by a random forest for merely a total amount of distance between each response would be from the database's averages from each sample. Those who were regularly distant from the response variable in each sample will have a high maximum distance. A programmed that determined the mode of each answer was used to detect rates that repeatedly categorize the data. The research labelled an answer as possible high in power consumption if the style of response accounted for more than 90% of the overall number of ques-

Figure 3. Flowchart of random forest classification

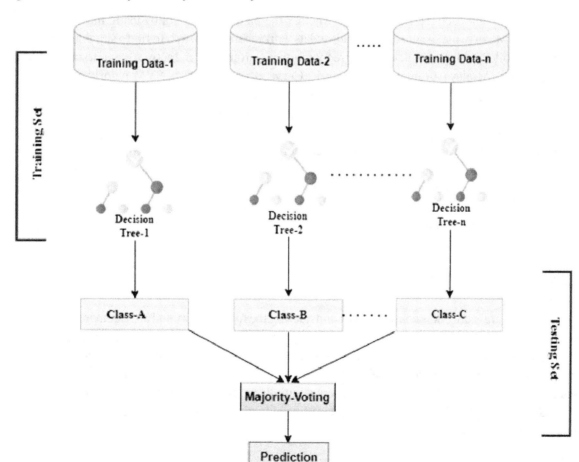

tions. There are a lot of replies that have been noted. A visual analysis of these replies revealed that the subjects had all selected same response.

3.3 Decision Tree Algorithm

It's a set of divide-and-conquer problems that employ a tree-like structure to predict whether or not a patient has thyroid cancer. To predict this outcome various algorithm are used in decision tree such as ID3, C4.5, CHAID. This research paper used CHAID algorithm. This CHAID algorithm is used to find the most dominant features. In CHAID Algorithm, chi square tests are used to find the difference between expected and observed values.

The Figure 4 decision tree-based algorithm is relying on the decision-boosting system that evaluated for forecasting energy usage component, with the purpose of finding the most significant predictors of consumption using a tree-based method. I utilized the decision tree technique to accomplish this. Hundreds of trees should be fitted in order for the product to develop over time, which are grown using knowledge from the past tree. Tuning parameters include shrinkage parameter, the quality of trees, and quantity of breaks in every tree.

3.4 Support Vector Machine

It is a traditional approach a classify disease whether the patient has or not by using machine learning algorithm. SVM is a two-classification model, and its working mechanism is to find a suitable hyperplane to divide the collected data samples. Pattern recognition is a prominent and active research subject among scholars, and SVM plays an important role in it (Cervantes et al., 2020). SVM algorithm is machine learning based algorithm which is associates with supervised learning and data mining approach that may be used to find the best predictors of energy usage. To address our query, the researchers employed prominent categorization approaches such as best boosting trees, subset selection, and generalized additive model. To choose a subset of predictor which more significantly predicted consuming with a linear association, we used backward, forward and optimal subset selection. The Figure 5 SVM proposed a method that used iterative binary splitting to categorize the predictor spaces into sample areas using a tree-based algorithm. The boosting tree approach was chosen since it is regarded to be once among the mostly used tree-based algorithm solutions. SVM is too effective at dealing with data with a lot of dimensions.

3.5 Artificial Neural Network

An artificial neural network is constructed by considering the functionality and arrangement of biological neural networks. In the Figure 6 weights associated with neurons are fixed, and the network categorizes a different data group. In ANN, the blocks are separated into three groups: input that receives information to be processed; output that contain the processing results; and hidden are in the middle to identify input-output relation; the network model is trained initially using a balanced training dataset (Rouhani & Mansouri, 2009). After that, the "test" dataset is utilized to objectively assess the last model appropriate to the training dataset.

Figure 4. Decision tree classification

4. RESEARCH METHODOLOGY

Promising technology of fog computing (FC) could massively solve the issue of networking and computing bottlenecks in IOT application (Samann et al., 2021). In today's era Machine Learning (ML) has focused on enabling FC to settle its issues (Samann et al., 2021). When it comes to autonomous administration and operation, machine learning plays a critical part in establishing a smart/intelligent environment (Samann et al., 2021). Following that, ML techniques were employed to improve the FC paradigm's performance. The goal of ML-based classification approaches is to map a set of input data to a set of discrete or continuous valued output data. Machine learning has used in various fields such as healthcare, agriculture, smart cities and many more (Chandel et al., 2016). In healthcare, machine learning plays a major role in predicting disease, diagnosing the patient, monitoring disease, and prescribing the right treatment for the patient. In healthcare there are various complicated disease such as

Figure 5. Support vector machine classifiers

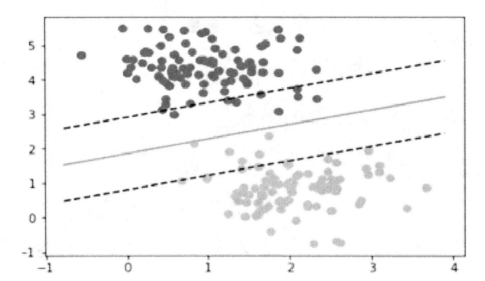

Figure 6. Artificial neural network classifier

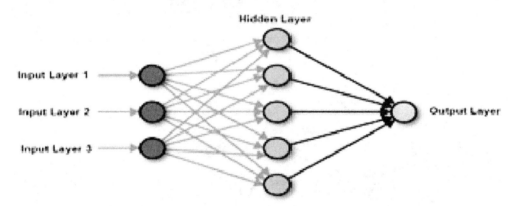

cancer, lung cancer, thyroid, breast cancer, diabetes and so on. Machine learning is a tool used to study and identify patterns in thyroid patients to identify ways to determine whether a patient has a thyroid or not has shown in Figure 7.

The Initial step is to create a thyroid dataset with QoS properties, such as: Delay sensitivity, Data Storage, Bandwidth, Loss sensitivity, Security, Data location, Mobility, Scalability, and Reliability of fog application that can be real or synthetic data. In this data set, 80 percent of the data is used for training, while 20% is used for testing. In pre-processing the irrelevant number of attributes are reduced by using classification algorithm. Disease detection algorithms include logistic regression, nave bayes, random forest, Decision Tree and Support Vector Machine. This method, known as dimensionality reduction, removes, irrelevant, redundant, and noisy data from data, resulting in improved learning and classification performance (Salimi et al., 2018).

Figure 7. Classification of integrated fog computing and machine learning for diagnosis Thyroid disease

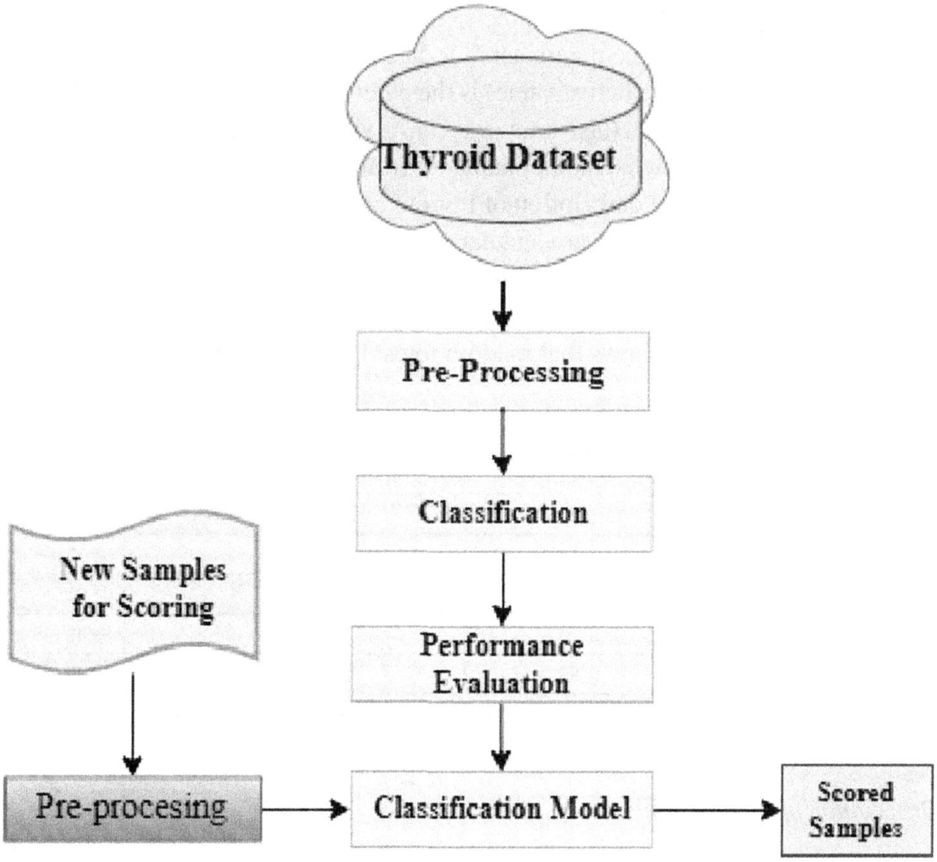

Integrating machine learning with fog computing using python (mainly Scikit-learn and Tensor Flow libraries) takes data, and computing at same level as it will increase the performance of machine learning model. After induction of machine learning with fog computing the performance of overall model and security issues ca be improved. The thyroid dataset is implemented in fog computing environment using machine learning approach. It has been observed that the accuracy of model is improved up to 5%, 3%, 1%, 1% for Support vector machine, Naive Bayes, Random Forest and Decision Tree respectively. This overall accuracy of models is 98.8%, 98.3%, 99.8%, 99% for Support vector machine, Naive Bayes, Random Forest and Decision Tree respectively in fog computing environment.

5. RESULTS AND DISCUSSION

Thyroid disease affects more women than males, with over half of all women and a quarter of all men in India dying from an inflamed thyroid. The thyroid dataset has taken from UCI machine learning repository [https://archive.ics.uci.edu/ml/datasets/thyroid+disease] and Kaggle. To identify the best performing algorithms, the classifier accuracy is the only factor that can be considered. The accuracy of the classifier must be high for the algorithm to be recognized as well performing algorithm. On a jupyter notebook in

Python, this study implements for machine learning algorithms: the Nave Bayes method, the decision tree algorithm, the random forest technique, and the support vector machine algorithm. The classification matrix of machine learning algorithm such as precision, Recall, F1-score, accuracy has shown in table 1. Precision and recall are performance parameters for data retrieved from a fog computing collection. Precision (also known as positive predictive value) is the percentage of relevant examples found among the recovered instances, whereas recall (also known as sensitivity) is the percentage of relevant instances found. The F1-Score or F1- Measure is another name for it. In other words, the F1 score represents the balance of precision and recall. The description of thyroid dataset. Different machine learning models are applied, and the performance metrics are and data set as shown in Figure 8.

The accuracy of classification machine learning algorithms such as Naive Bayes algorithm is 95.21%, random forest algorithm is 98.87%, decision tree algorithm is 98.32%, Support vector machine is 93.82% has shown in Figure 9. This figure shows that random forest has highest accuracy among others.

Table 1.Comparison of performance of different models

Model	Precision	Recall	F1-Score	Accuracy
SVM	94	100	97	93.82
Naïve Bayes	95	96	98	95.21
Decision Tree	86	90	95	98.32
Random Forest	86	86	86	98.87
ANN	90	88	84	92.51

Figure 8. Description of thyroid dataset

```
n [10]:
        df.info()

        <class 'pandas.core.frame.DataFrame'>
        RangeIndex: 1212 entries, 0 to 1211
        Data columns (total 18 columns):
         #   Column             Non-Null Count   Dtype
        ---  ------             --------------   -----
         0   patient_id         1212 non-null    int64
         1   age                1212 non-null    int64
         2   sex                1212 non-null    int64
         3   sick               1212 non-null    int64
         4   pregnant           1212 non-null    int64
         5   query_hypothyroid  1212 non-null    int64
         6   query_hyperthyroid 1212 non-null    int64
         7   lithium            1212 non-null    int64
         8   goitre             1212 non-null    int64
         9   tumor              1212 non-null    int64
         10  hypopituitary      1212 non-null    int64
         11  TSH                1212 non-null    int64
         12  T3                 1212 non-null    float64
         13  TT4                1212 non-null    int64
         14  T4U                1212 non-null    int64
         15  FTI                1212 non-null    int64
         16  TBG                1212 non-null    int64
         17  target             1212 non-null    int64
        dtypes: float64(1), int64(17)
        memory usage: 170.6 KB
```

Figure 9. Accuracy of classification ML algorithm

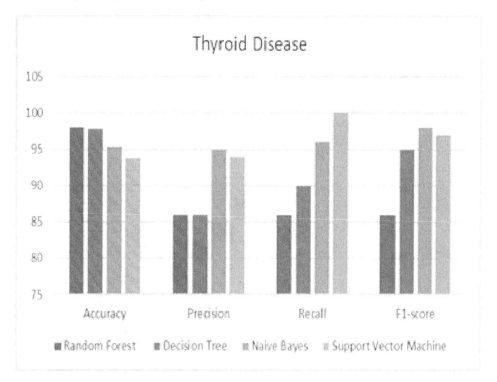

The Correlation matrix of thyroid dataset has shown in Figure 10.

5. CONCLUSION

The disease is most common disorders afflicting the entire nation peoples, and the amount of the cases is rising. Our research focuses on the categorization of the thyroid disease into hypothyroidism and hyperthyroidism in light of medical details that demonstrate major abnormalities in thyroid disorders. In Fog computing, this work introduces the use of ML classification algorithms as a tool for QoS-aware resource management. Algorithms were used to classify this illness. Machine learning produced good results by combining various techniques and constructing two models. The accuracy value of the random-forest method was 98.97 percent that was the greatest accuracy value between all different algorithms tested, in the first model, which had 16 inputs and one output. This machine learning-based categorization methodology enables the use of Qos to control traffic in Fog, which is the first step toward the definition of QoS provisioning mechanisms in the C2T continuum. The definition of the intervals that each QoS requirement applicable for a certain Class is integrated into a Kaggle database of Fog apps.

The research work studies on thyroid patients using machine learning approach to classify and prediction of thyroid disease. In recent years, several accepted analyses for the adequate and professional diagnosis of thyroid disease have led to developed and used. Many researchers around the world have significantly improved the diagnosis of thyroid disease, but it is recommended that the number of criteria patients can use to diagnose thyroid disorders may be limited. The thyroid is defined as the "powerhouse"

Figure 10. Correlation matrix of thyroid disease

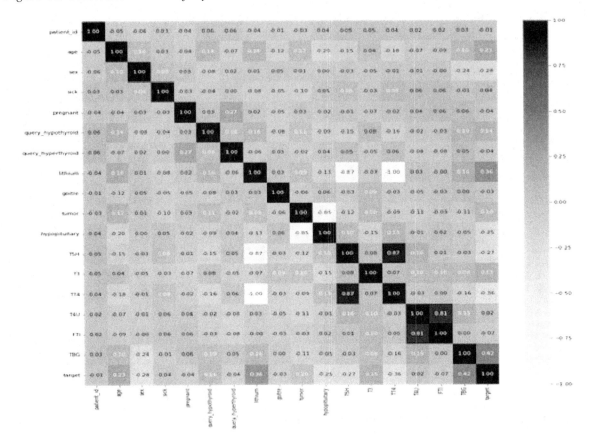

of our body: if the gland in the neck fails, the whole body survives. Therefore, early diagnosis plays a fundamental role in predicting the treatment of a thyroid patient which can be of great help to doctors. Who have patients under treatment? This chapter proposed an approach to predict the thyroid disease treatment. Out task is to classify the prognosis of thyroid patient and predict the accuracy, recall, F1-score, specificity, sensitivity using machine learning techniques that can be used to diagnose thyroid disease. Gender and age have been considered important traits in thyroid disease. It is more common in women and occurs during a certain age range (25-64 years).

REFERENCES

Aswad, S. A., & Sonuç, E. (2020). Classification of VPN network traffic flow using time related features on Apache Spark. In *2020 4th International Symposium on Multidisciplinary Studies and Innovative Technologies (ISMSIT)* (pp. 1-8), IEEE.

Azar, A. T., Hassanien, A. E., & Kim, T. H. (2021). Expert system based on neural-fuzzy rules for thyroid diseases diagnosis. In *Computer Applications for Bio-technology, Multimedia, and Ubiquitous City* (pp. 94–105). Springer.

Banu, G. R. (2016). A Role of decision Tree classification data Mining Technique in Diagnosing Thyroid disease. *International Journal on Computer Science and Engineering, 4*(11), 64–70.

Begum, A., & Parkavi, A. (March,2019). Prediction of thyroid disease using data mining techniques. In *2019 5th International Conference on Advanced Computing & Communication Systems (ICACCS)* (pp. 342-345), IEEE.

Cabanillas, M. E., McFadden, D. G., & Durante, C. (2016). Thyroid cancer. *Lancet, 388*(10061), 2783–2795. doi:10.1016/S0140-6736(16)30172-6 PMID:27240885

Cervantes, J., Garcia-Lamont, F., Rodríguez-Mazahua, L., & Lopez, A. (2020). A comprehensive survey on support vector machine classification: Applications, challenges, and trends. *Neurocomputing, 408*, 189–215. doi:10.1016/j.neucom.2019.10.118

Chandel, K., Kunwar, V., Sabitha, S., Choudhury, T., & Mukherjee, S. (2016). A comparative study on thyroid disease detection using K-nearest neighbor and Naive Bayes classification techniques. *CSI Transactions on ICT, 4*(2), 313–319. doi:10.100740012-016-0100-5

Chandio, J. A., Sahito, A., Soomrani, M. A. R., & Abbasi, S. A. (April,2016). TDV: Intelligent system for thyroid disease visualization. In 2016 International Conference on Computing, *Electronic and Electrical Engineering (ICE Cube)* (pp. 106-112). IEEE.

Chaudhary, A., Kolhe, S., & Kamal, R. (2016). An improved random forest classifier for multi-class classification. *Information Processing in Agriculture, 3*(4), 215–222. doi:10.1016/j.inpa.2016.08.002

Choi, Y. J., Baek, J. H., Park, H. S., Shim, W. H., Kim, T. Y., Shong, Y. K., & Lee, J. H. (2017). A computer-aided diagnosis system using artificial intelligence for the diagnosis and characterization of thyroid nodules on ultrasound: Initial clinical assessment. *Thyroid, 27*(4), 546–552. doi:10.1089/thy.2016.0372 PMID:28071987

Dittman, D., Khoshgoftaar, T. M., Wald, R., & Napolitano, A. (2011). Random forest: A reliable tool for patient response prediction. In *2011 IEEE International Conference on Bioinformatics and Biomedicine Workshops (BIBMW)* (pp. 289-296). IEEE. 10.1109/BIBMW.2011.6112389

Guevara, J. C., Torres, R. D. S., & da Fonseca, N. L. (2020). On the classification of fog computing applications: A machine learning perspective. *Journal of Network and Computer Applications, 159*, 102596. doi:10.1016/j.jnca.2020.102596

Keleş, A., & Keleş, A. (2008). ESTDD: Expert system for thyroid diseases diagnosis. *Expert Systems with Applications, 34*(1), 242–246. doi:10.1016/j.eswa.2006.09.028

Keleş, A., & Keleş, A. (2017). ESTDD: Expert system for thyroid diseases diagnosis. *Expert Systems with Applications, 34*(1), 242-246,2008.

Kourou, K., Exarchos, T. P., Exarchos, K. P., Karamouzis, M. V., & Fotiadis, D. I. (2015). Machine learning applications in cancer prognosis and prediction. *Computational and Structural Biotechnology Journal, 13*, 8–17. doi:10.1016/j.csbj.2014.11.005 PMID:25750696

Mishra, S., Tadesse, Y., Dash, A., Jena, L., & Ranjan, P. (2021). Thyroid disorder analysis using random forest classifier. In *Intelligent and Cloud Computing* (pp. 385–390). Springer. doi:10.1007/978-981-15-5971-6

Murdoch, T. B., & Detsky, A. S. (2013). The inevitable application of big data to health care. *Journal of the American Medical Association*, *309*(13), 1351–1352. doi:10.1001/jama.2013.393 PMID:23549579

Peterson, S. J., Cappola, A. R., Castro, M. R., Dayan, C. M., Farwell, A. P., Hennessey, J. V., Kopp, P. A., Ross, D. S., Samuels, M. H., Sawka, A. M., Taylor, P. N., Jonklaas, J., & Bianco, A. C. (2018). An online survey of hypothyroid patients demonstrates prominent dissatisfaction. *Thyroid*, *28*(6), 707–721. doi:10.1089/thy.2017.0681 PMID:29620972

Poppe, K., & Glinoer, D. (2003). Thyroid autoimmunity and hypothyroidism before and during pregnancy. *Human Reproduction Update*, *9*(2), 149–161. doi:10.1093/humupd/dmg012 PMID:12751777

Prerana, P. S., & Taneja, K. (2015). Predictive data mining for diagnosis of thyroid disease using neural network. *International Journal of Research in Management, Science & Technology*, *3*(2), 75–80.

Rouhani, M., & Mansouri, K. (2009). Comparison of several ANN architectures on the Thyroid diseases grades diagnosis. In *2009 International Association of Computer Science and Information Technology-Spring Conference* (pp. 526-528). IEEE.

Salimi, A., Ziaii, M., Amiri, A., Zadeh, M. H., Karimpouli, S., & Moradkhani, M. (2018). Using a feature subset selection method and support vector machine to address curse of dimensionality and redundancy in hyperion hyperspectral data classification. *The Egyptian Journal of Remote Sensing and Space Sciences*, *21*(1), 27–36. doi:10.1016/j.ejrs.2017.02.003

Samann, F. E., Abdulazeez, A. M., & Askar, S. (2021). Fog Computing Based on Machine Learning: A Review. *International Journal of Interactive Mobile Technologies*, *15*(12), 21. doi:10.3991/ijim.v15i12.21313

Sarker, I. H. (2021). Machine learning: Algorithms, real-world applications and research directions. *SN Computer Science*, *2*(3), 1–21. doi:10.100742979-021-00592-x PMID:33778771

Shukla, A., Tiwari, R., Kaur, P., & Janghel, R. R. (2009). Diagnosis of thyroid disorders using artificial neural networks. In *2009 IEEE International Advance Computing Conference* (pp. 1016-1020). IEEE. 10.1109/IADCC.2009.4809154

Singh, J., Singh, P., & Gill, S. S. (2021). Fog computing: A taxonomy, systematic review, current trends and research challenges. *Journal of Parallel and Distributed Computing*, *157*, 56–85. doi:10.1016/j.jpdc.2021.06.005

Song, X., Liu, Z., Li, L., Gao, Z., Fan, X., Zhai, G., & Zhou, H. (2021). Artificial intelligence CT screening model for thyroid-associated ophthalmopathy and tests under clinical conditions. *International Journal of Computer Assisted Radiology and Surgery*, *16*(2), 323–330. doi:10.100711548-020-02281-1 PMID:33146848

Sonuç, E. (2021). Thyroid Disease Classification Using Machine Learning Algorithms. Journal of Physics: Conference Series, 1963(1), 012140.

Umar Sidiq, D., Aaqib, S. M., & Khan, R. A. (2019). Diagnosis of various thyroid ailments using data mining classification techniques. *Int J Sci Res Coput Sci Inf Technol*, *5*, 131–136.

Vanderpump, M. P. (2011). The epidemiology of thyroid disease. *British Medical Bulletin*, *99*(1), 39–51. doi:10.1093/bmb/ldr030 PMID:21893493

Yadav, D. C., & Pal, S. (2019). To generate an ensemble model for women thyroid prediction using data mining techniques. *Asian Pacific Journal of Cancer Prevention*, *20*(4), 1275. PMID:31031212

Yadav, D. C., & Pal, S. (2020). Prediction of thyroid disease using decision tree ensemble method. *Human-Intelligent Systems Integration*, *2*(1), 89–95. doi:10.100742454-020-00006-y

Section 2
Fog Computing for Data Analytics

Chapter 5

Health Preventive Measure as a Service (HPMaaS):
An Intelligent Fog–Cloud–Based Approach for Detection of Diseases Through Smart Phone Sensors

Madhusmita Mishra
Dr. Sudhir Chandra Sur Institute of Technology and Sports Complex, JIS Group, Kolkata, India

Amrut Ranjan Jena
Guru Nanak Institute of Technology, JIS Group, Kolkata, India

Himadri Biswas
https://orcid.org/0000-0003-1685-971X
Budge Budge Institute of Technology, Kolkata, India

ABSTRACT

The present days passes through Industry 4.0. It emphasizes on intelligent computing, smart computing, cloud computing, internet of things (IoT), artificial intelligence (AI), and machine learning (ML). In addition, the function of smart devices in these computing techniques make the work user friendly. Nowadays, health issues are a big challenge in society. In this industry revolution period, smart devices play significant role to provide health assistance in a finger touch. It is possible due to the increase in the number of smart devices and use of IoT, cloud, AI, and ML. Fog computing is the mechanism of providing quality services through optimization of the resources. This paper presents the hybridization of cloud computing with fog computing in the field of healthcare applications.

INTRODUCTION

The internet practically connects everyone on the planet. The two key technologies employed in human living to make daily tasks easy are cloud computing and the internet of things. Every time a health is-

DOI: 10.4018/978-1-6684-4466-5.ch005

sue occurs in a person's life, it requires greater care. Because a human being now needs treatment, care, and support from other humans. Sometimes a person's busy schedule and workload prevent them from receiving the right direction, attention, and support. Smart gadgets are employed in healthcare to provide affordable patient support as a solution to this issue. The fast diagnostic system, data analytics, cloud computing, Internet of Things, and block chain are the main elements used to develop such a support system. Additionally, applications of fog computing (FC) in healthcare are very popular. Fog computing was initially employed as additional resources to speed up the computation with more storage space (Bhambri et al., 2022). Cloud computing is where FC comes from (Abdulqadir et al., 2021). The basic Mobile-Fog-Cloud computing (MFCC) structural design is revealed in Figure 1.

Figure 1 shows the three layers of the FC architecture, which are the device layer, fog layer, and cloud layer. Data collection, real-time data processing, data storage, and data transmission to the fog layer are all functions of the device layer. Numerous fog nodes are embedded in the fog layer. These are employed in the processing and reduction of data in the fog layer. The higher layer recognizes the cloud layer and saves the information given by the nodes of the fog layer. In this three-layer architecture, the cloud layer responds more quickly than the device and fog layers. The network's fog layer is geographically dispersed and connects to various communicating devices. High latency and data privacy problems plague cloud computing (Laghari et al., 2021). FC was created to overcome this issue (Sharma & Sajid, 2021). Anyone can access direct consulting over FC and IoT in the healthcare sector (Jain et al., 2021). When a user transmits health-related data using an IoT device, the fog nodes that are nearby collect, analyze, and resend the clean data to the cloud for problem solving. For the analysis, classification, and prediction of data, machine learning is crucial. As a result, it aids the fog node in carrying out data analysis to categorize the outcome.

Numerous disastrous outbreaks have taken place over the world (e.g., the Spanish flu, Black Death, SARS, influenza, Asian flu, Zika, and Ebola virus). historically speaking, some of the affects are remarkable, including the most recent COVID-19. Since December 2019 to the present, there have been COVID-19 outbreaks, or corona virus-induced respiratory illnesses. As a result, in this pandemic condition, almost everyone in every country needs to be active in making their test mandatory.

Currently, smart phones have fast processing speeds and are equipped with memory, cameras, microphones, cameras, inertial sensors, proximity sensors, colour sensors, humidity sensors, and wireless chipsets/sensors. In this research, we propose a low-cost, fog-cloud-based, intelligent framework called "Health Preventive Measure as a Service" for disease detection using smartphone sensors. Users can conduct the initial test to prevent cross-infection on their smartphones with minimal effort from anywhere in the world. Therefore, using the necessary sensors, the government may implement the necessary steps for a mandated test of smart phone users. It aids with early disease detection, keeps track of users' whereabouts, and prompts them to take precautionary measures.

The Smart Disease Analyzer (SDA) in the proposed model offers fog-cloud based services to diagnosis various health conditions, including respiratory, ocular, skin, and mental conditions, as well as lung function, body temperature, and cardiovascular activity. Additionally, it can detect diseases including COVID-19, SARS, and EBOLA. The sample collecting phase (by Smartphone sensors) is completed by SDA, and it is then sent to the decision segment for disease diagnosis. Finally, the report is sent to the agency through the Health Monitoring System (HMS) for preventative measures.

Figure 1. Mobile-Fog-Cloud computing architecture

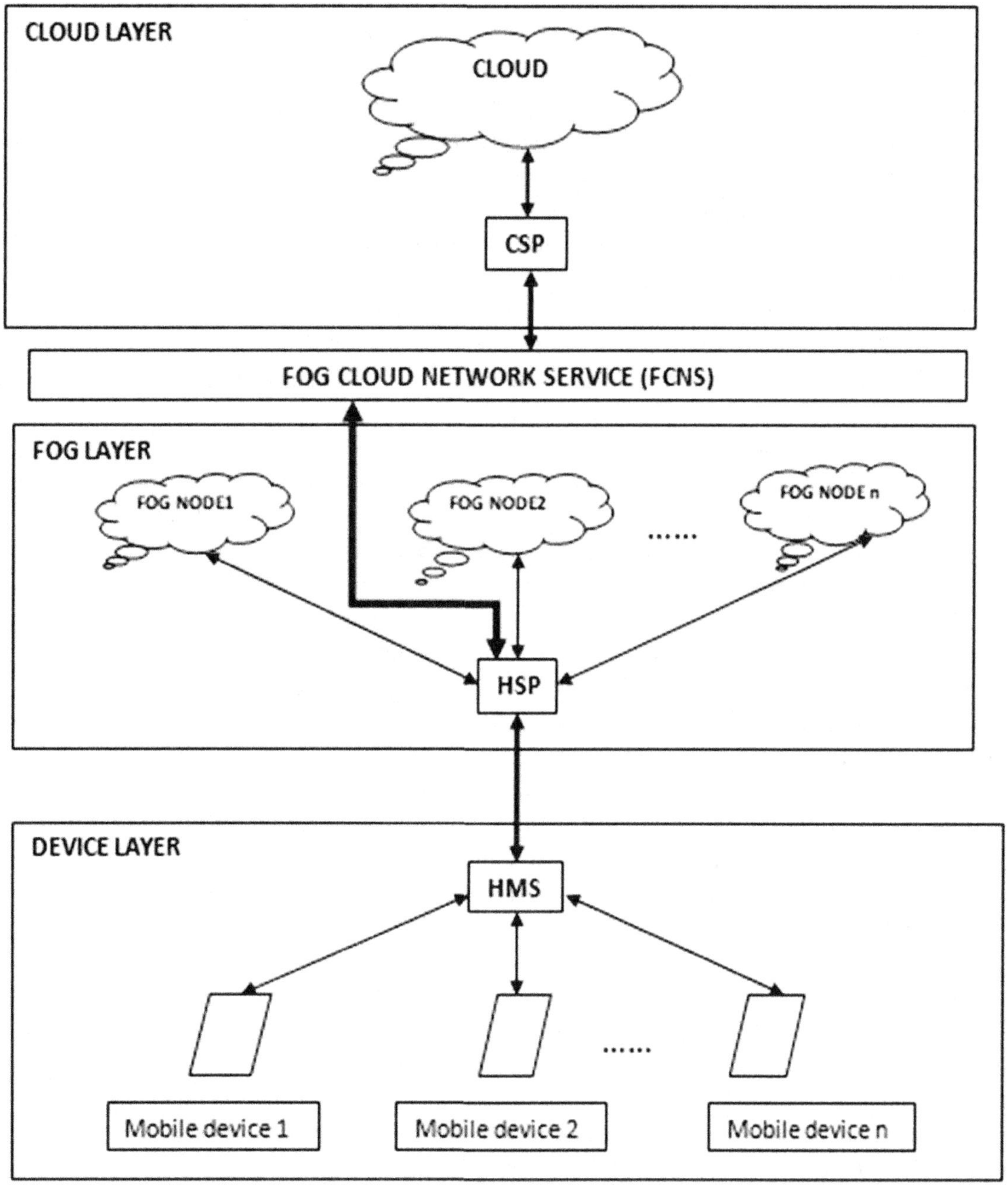

LITERATURE SURVEY

The digital era is now in existence. Technology today has a significant impact on many industries. With the convenience of information and services at the touch of a finger, smart devices improve lifestyle. According to estimates, there will be between 60 and 70 billion linked gadgets by the end of 2022 (Jain et al., 2021). Therefore, regardless of the service industry, an appropriate computer model must be able to handle this load and offer superior service. Because it is impossible for standard computing methods like distributed computing and cloud computing to handle such a heavy load (El-Sayed et al., 2017). Therefore, fog computing is introduced to deal with such a problem. In the modern world, technology has significantly changed several aspects of the healthcare business. As a result, academics are working to develop novel ideas for improving services and applications in the healthcare sector. The challenges and problems that the healthcare sector in society is facing are discussed in this section. Smart devices are also utilised to treat healthcare issues. Today's smart phones are essential to achieving this goal. Researchers state the use of smart phone for monitoring the health issues of the patients (Kumar et al., 2012). Here, fog computing is used to quickly analyse the patient's health according to the data gathered. Three kinds of patients, including those who are hospitalised, injured, and in critical condition, are examined. Finding the patient categories that require additional treatment using IoT and fog computing is the goal of their effort. As a case study, researchers offer various uses of fog computing in healthcare (Mutlag et al., 2019). They discussed several fog models, including platform, infrastructure, and software services. Their primary goal is to advise the platform designer to select a certain application in accordance with the platform design. To offer users consistent services, researchers examined the significance of cloud computing, fog computing, and IoT (Mahmud et al., 2020). The authors discussed a mobile fog computing application for avoiding potential problems in rural areas. Their primary goal is to identify the gap between cloud and fog platforms, and they outline the design approach for quicker access to a problem's solution (Bhardwaj & Krishna, 2021). Researchers use cloud computing, IoT, and cloud computing to analyse healthcare concerns (Dang et al.,2019). They are attempting to analyse the unbroken services for the user according to their requirements. Patients with long-term illnesses who also require many hospital visits for general, recurrent check-ups typically have higher treatment costs. Therefore, using fog computing, cloud computing, and IoT, academics are working on this field to reduce the cost of the treatment. Research is being done in the area of fog computing's scalability (Mahmud et al., 2018; Haghi et al., 2020). Researchers work to address challenges with fog node intercommunication, network dependability, and service quality as they relate to the fog architecture. As seen in Figure 1, fog nodes are capable of receiving both structured and unstructured data from end users. The fog nodes are now analysing this data. Data grouping and categorization are aided by machine learning (ML) (Nguyen et al., 2015). To forecast heart illness, researchers use fuzzy sets and support vector machines (Nilashi et al., 2020).

A wide range of sensors and powerful computers may be found in modern smart phones. Smart phones can be used to record visual data as well as information about daily activities (Purswani et al., 2019). Data from the temperature-fingerprint sensor can be used to forecast the severity of a fever (Maddah & Beigzadeh, 2020). Data from onboard embedded sensors and videos and pictures captured with a smart phone's camera are combined to assess human tiredness (Karvekar, 2019; Roldan et al., 2019). Similar to this, Story et al. (Story et ai., 2019) predicted illness using smartphone movies. Lawanont et al. employ measurements from inertial sensors and camera images to evaluate neck posture and estimate the intensity of human headaches (Lawanont et al., 2018). Audio data from the smartphone is utilised to identify the type of cough (Nemati et al., 2019; Vhaduri et al., 2019; Rao and Vazquez, 2020). It recommends a technique for gathering fundamental travel information regarding individuals and their normal travel-related activities. These data help identify high-risk individuals for isolation early on by enabling machine learning algorithms to learn about and predict each person's risk of infection.

In view of all these circumstances, we suggest employing a smart phone-based technique to allow people to test at home and eliminate the possibility of illness transmission to others. As a result, we want to use the Health Service Provider (HSP) that the Health Monitoring System (HMS) recommends to stop the disease from spreading.

OVERVIEW AND RATIONALE

Smart Phone Sensors

The increasing availability of smart phones equipped with sensors and contemporary technologies makes it possible to monitor people's health-related issues remotely and continuously at a low cost (Chan et al., 2012). The smart phones come with a variety of sensors, including picture sensors, ambient light sensors, and GPS sensors. These sensors can be used to track a variety of medical conditions, as shown in Table 1.

Internet of Things (IoT)

The Internet of Things (IoT) concept is not new; it is just pervasive. The Internet of Things (IoT) is actually made up of many different traditional built-in systems, tiny wireless microsensors, automated control systems, and many other parts that come together to form a massive network. The fusion of wireless networking with internet-connected micro-electromechanical tools has facilitated the invention of new items on the internet. Each entity has a unique identification that may be used to identify it, and it can be accessed online. With the advancement of digital technology, the concept of the Internet, also known as the "Internet of Computers," as a global network of services provided on top of the fundamental structure as a "world wide web," would be established and new innovation in the early 1990s. Over time, the idea of "Computer Internet" has given way to "People's Internet" due to the growth of Web 2.0, in which billions of people are connected via various social networks. The Internet spectrum is constantly growing thanks to the advancement of "Micro Electro Mechanical Devices" (MEMs) and wireless networking technologies, and computers are becoming smaller than the original PCs while having greater processing and storage power. These gadgets serve as computers, mobile phones, and other computing

Table 1. Smart phone sensors applications in various health issues

Typical Smart Phone Sensors	Health Issues
Temperature, thermal camera	Body temperature measurement
Camera with image sensor, microphone	Cardiovascular activity – heart Rate, heart rate variability, respiratory and lung health
Image sensor	Eye health, skin health
Microphone sensor	Sneezing and runny nose, blowing the nose, lung functions, ear health, asthma, cough, shortness of breath, fatigue level
GPS	Track location
Motion sensors, GPS, camera, light sensor	Cognitive function and metal health sssessment
Motion sensors, GPS	Physical activity and movements
Motion sensors	Sleep

equipment. Once these devices, along with actuators, are equipped with sensors, other devices can be given the ability to detect, compute, and communicate across a whole network.

According to Cisco, the "Internet of Things" concept links together people, things, data, and devices to increase the relevance and significance of networked interactions by bringing information closer to reality than before. Over the next ten years, cities might demand $1.9 trillion in value from the IoT. The "International Telecommunications Union" (ITU) asserted in a 2005 report that the "Internet of Things" would connect the world's items in a sensory and intellectual way (Kooistra, 2018). By incorporating numerous technological advancements such as "object recognition," "sensors and wireless sensor networks," "embedded systems," and "nanotechnology," the ITU has identified four dimensions in IoT as, in that order, tagging things, feeling things, thinking things, and shrinking things. Therefore, the idea of IoT is not limited to a certain area, yet it is difficult to define the broad term. It can be defined as the combination of intelligent nodes that communicate with one another, with objects, with environments, and, as a final thought, with large amounts of data. Such information is transformed into practical actions that provide command and control over things that improve quality of life. The various IoT components are shown in Figure 4.

Cloud Service Models

Figure 2 represents the default Cloud Service Models and the proposed Cloud Service Model. In general, the models of cloud computing operation are as follows.

Software as a service (SaaS):

This SaaS model provides a readymade application along with any necessary software, operating system, hardware, and network.

Platform as a service (PaaS):

This PaaS model provides hardware, network, and an operating system facilitates to install or create users develop software and applications.

Infrastructure as a service (IaaS):

The IaaS model provides only the hardware and networks, and the user creates or constructs own operating systems, software and applications.

Health Preventive Measure as a Service (HPMaaS) the Proposed Model

Under Private Cloud, HPMaaS provides low-cost, detection of diseases via smart phone with minimum cross-infection. The key idea is to map the implicit tools (from data collection to decision process) to the real physical resources through the cloud service providers (CSP). Besides, the customers or cloud service provider enrolled in the HPMaaS model have to go through it.

Figure 2. HPMaaS model

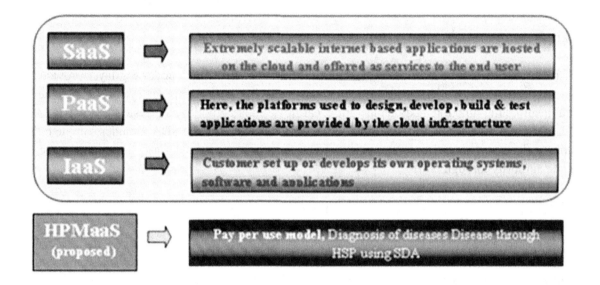

Fog Computing

Targeting services effectively provided by cloud computing (CC) and edge computing (EC), healthcare 4.0. When accessing cloud-based data, there is an unavoidable delay and insufficient real-time response. Because fog computing relies on distributed architectures, it is very reliable (Maddah & Beigzadeh, 2020). It stands in the middle of wearable medical technology and wireless networks. It provides edge devices with a bigger space interface with shorter time delays (Parihar et al., 2017). To provide the greatest e-Health services, it collaborates with other technologies. In addition, FC combines big data, CC, IoT, sensors, and telephony. Through applications and services, healthcare 4.0 has given patients access to a cutting-edge telemedicine experience (Miah et al., 2015). Sensors and actuators in IoT-based medical equipment communicate with cloud, fog, and EC services to exchange health data. When treating patients remotely, this dynamic data is quite helpful.

Health Monitoring System

The state's authorities may create a system known as the health monitoring system (HMS) to track and monitor health-related issues. A planned system called the HMS includes smart gadgets for local health monitoring. According to the authority's protocol, HMS employees keep track of the data and take the appropriate action. The HMS is suggested proposal to the relevant authority.

Health Service Provider

The health service provider (HSP) under HPMaaS has major role at the fog layer for providing health services. It also plays the important role to set up a smooth communication between the users and the

HMS by using the cloud assets from its intended CSP. So before allocating the resources on the cloud server, HSP registered the users, HMS and the CSP to prevent potential conflicts.

Smart Disease Analyzer

After receiving the request from HSP the smart disease analyzer (SDA) under fog layer provides the fog-cloud based services to diagnose different health status like nasal symptom, eye health, skin health, mental health, lung function, body temperature, cardiovascular activities etc. Besides, COVID, SARS, EBOLA like other virus are also diagnosed. The services govern by the SDA includes sample collection phase (by smart phone sensors), decision phase for diagnosing the disease, and report transfer to the state authority through HMS.

PROPOSED WORK

We are aware that the COVID-19 virus is present everywhere. This virus has a terrible impact on human health, education, and the global economy. In order to address this worrying scenario, we need immediately prevent this virus from becoming cross-infected. The proposed fog-cloud computing-based HPMaaS model, which is based on the current situation and past observations on various cloud management services (Bailey et al., 2020), allows for initial testing as well as the early diagnosis of any ailments and accommodates mobile users and their associates. The HPMaaS model as proposed is shown in Figure 3. Users can collect samples and send them to the testing phase using the services offered by the HSP under the fog layer in the model. The report is then given to the HMS so they can take the appropriate action.

The purpose of this work is to provide the public with a reliable service that will enable the state to take the initiative to require all smart phone users to use it in order to profit from early disease detection.

Working Procedure of HPMaaS Model

Figure 3 represents the HPMaaaS working model, where the CSPs are sending periodic signals, recording details and available resources to SDA following successful contract agreements and offering resources. Upon receiving details from the CSP, SDA provides the Fog-Cloud based services to diagnose different Health issues such as Nasal symptom, Eye Health, Skin Health, Mental Health, Lung Function, Body Temperature, Cardiovascular activities etc., and not only that, COVID-19, SARS, EBOLA like other Pandemic diseases are also diagnosed. Besides, getting requests from HSP regarding on-demand services, SDA provides the specific "Disease App" with the necessary guidelines to diagnose their tests.

At first, the users of smart phones make a request to the HMS for diagnosing their disease. After checking the user's authentication, HMS sends information of all smart phone users to the HSP and after getting authorization from the HSP, HMS instructs the users to perform diagnosis with the contact of HSP. In receipt of the information from HMS, HSP either makes a service level agreement (SLA) as a new user or checks as an existing customer upon receipt of the request from the HMS. In this regard, the USER-HSP mapping chart is maintained by the HSP, and the HSP-CSP mapping chart is maintained to get any future reference to known about the service request details.

Figure 3. Proposed architecture of HPMaaS model

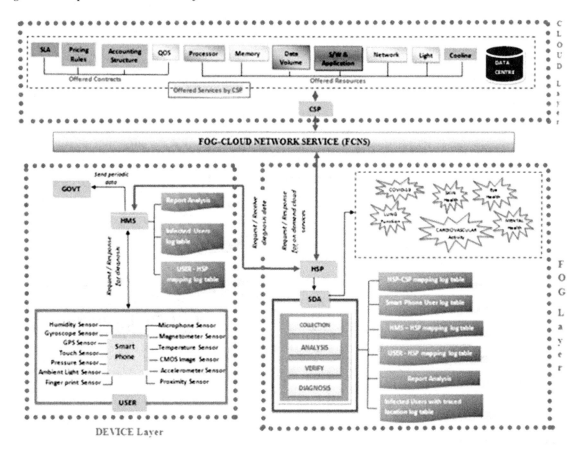

The SDA module under HSP now periodically collects the required symptoms through its "COLLECTION MODULE" via Smart Phone Sensors. Additionally, the "ANALYSIS MODULE" is now busy with figuring out the correct diagnosis of the collected samples. The "VERIFY MODULE" checks the computed data within specified disease threshold value. Now the "DIAGNOSIS MODULE" gives the decision whether it is "infected" or "not infected", and forward a copy to the users and the HMS adding the user's current location. Now the HMS prepares and provides the reports to the state authority for taking necessary actions.

The proposed mobile-fog-cloud based disease detection (MFCDD) algorithm automatically takes care of each process with small resources by placing the virtual tools to the actual physical tools by using auto fit virtual tool placemen algorithm (Siddiqui et al., 2016). Thus, it is understood that no one is allowed to interact directly with each other to get this service without the permission of the HMS. In the event of any dispute, HMS will obtain the detailed records of the alleged customers from the USER-HSP mapping chart. Therefore, the HSP is not confused or deceive the users.

Figure 4. Process flow diagram of health preventive measure as a service (HPMaaS) model

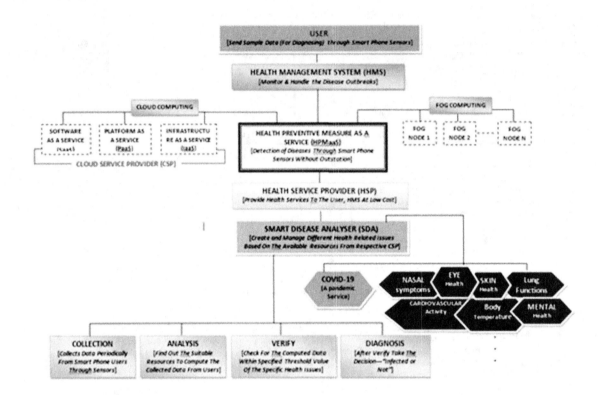

Process Flow Diagram of HPMaaS

Figure 4 represents the processes flow diagram of the model. The working procedure of the HPMaas model is depicted in Figure 4 for better visualization through process flow diagram.

ALGORITHM AND INFORMATION FLOW DIAGRAM

MFCDD (Mobile-Fog-Cloud based Disease Detection) Algorithm

1. USER requests to HMS for diagnosing.
    1.1 HMS tracks the USERS
    1.2 HMS prepares the list of users zone-wise.
    1.3 HMS maintains USER log for future reference.
    1.4 HMS checks for USER's authentication.
    1.5 If authentic
    1.5.1 Services accepted and send an acknowledgement to the USER.
    1.5.2 HMS provides the guidelines to the USER through SMS for diagnosing the disease over Smart Phone.
    1.5.3 Periodic records are sent by the USERS to the HMS over Smart Phone

1.5.4 Move to Step 2

1.6 Else

1.6.1 "Not accepted for services" – message given to the USER

1.6.2 Move to Step 1

2. HMS forwards the request to HSP for diagnosing the problem.

2.1 HSP checks for HMS's endorsement and SLA

2.2 If Authentic –

2.2.1 Services is accepted and send an acknowledgement to HMS

2.2.2 HMS sends the user details to HSP

2.2.3 Move to Step 3

2.3 Else

2.3.1 "Not accepted for services" – message returns to the HMS

2.3.2 Move to Step 2

3. HSP requests to its CSPs' for getting cloud services

3.1 CSP checks the HSP's endorsement and SLA

3.2 If authentic –

3.2.1 Services is accepted and sends an acknowledgement to HSP

3.2.2 Required resources are provided to the HSP

3.2.3 Move to Step 4

3.2.4 SPSA map the PSP to its CSP and maintain a PSP-CSP mapping log.

3.3 Else

3.3.1 "Not accepted for services"—message returns to the SPSA

3.3.2 Go to step 3

4. HSP requests to SDA Module for diagnosis the problem

4.1 Based on the collected data SDA examines the data.

4.2 SDA checks for the specific disease category by its Verify Module.

4.3 If within threshold –

4.3.1 HSP sends "Not infected" message to the USER and the HMS.

4.3.2 Move to step 7

4.4 Else

4.4.1 HSP sends "Not infected" message to the USER and the HMS.

4.4.2 HSP map out the present position of the infected person

4.4.3 HSP trace the location(s) of the contaminated person about last few days

4.4.4 Move to Step 7

5. HMS sends the reports to the Government.

6. Government takes necessary actions.

7. End.

Information Flow Diagram

Figure 5. Information flow diagram of HPMaaS model

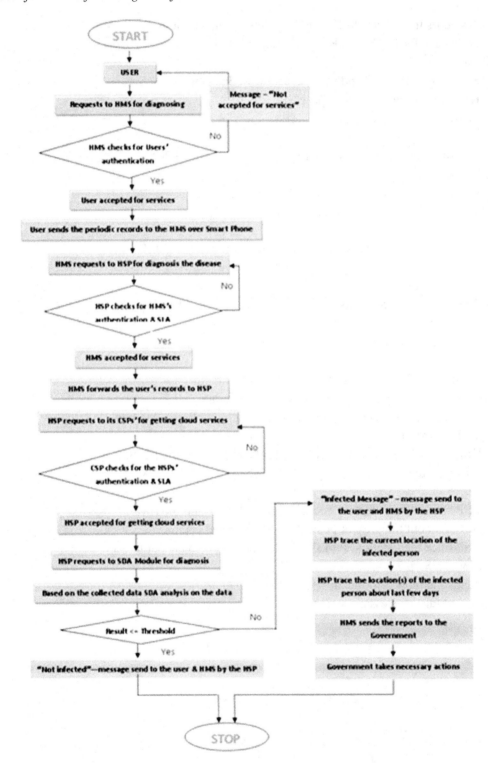

HPMAAS CASE STUDY

Although there have been numerous efforts to develop sensor-based health monitoring systems, each sensor-based device is dedicated to the detection of a certain class of symptom. The suggested approach, however, draws inspiration from earlier efforts with the exception that it can use numerous built-in sensors on a smart phone to simultaneously detect multiple symptoms of an illness. The analysis portion is presented here through some prior efforts to obtain a predicted outcome through cloud computing in order to enhance the suggested framework.

Referring to article (Larson et al., 2011) the detection of nasal symptoms (Sneezing, coughing, blowing the nose) by microphone sensor is shown in Figure 6.

According to preliminary study, it is possible to create an audio-based model of identification that can identify instances involving the nose. The spectrogram of a single audio sample is depicted in Figure 6, with red and blue reflecting values of suitably high and low amplitude. Sneezing and blowing your nose audio events can be distinguished from other audio events including talking, coughing, and quiet. For instance, nose blowing lasts longer and has lower amplitude than coughing. Sneezing also has a distinct period of amplitude that lasts for about 500 ms.

Referring to the output of the article (Larson et al., 2012), Figure 7 and 8 has been demonstrated to detect the lung function by microphone sensor.

Figure 6. Spectrogram image of the acoustic data

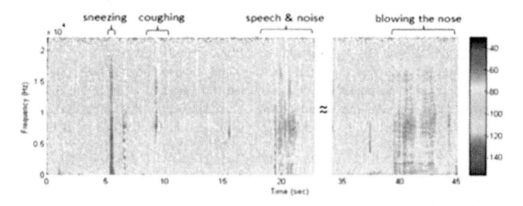

Figure 7. Different flow vs. volume curves

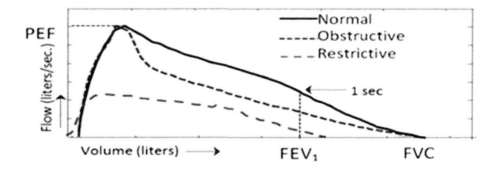

Figure 8. FEV1 Vs. FVC ratio evaluation through mobile phone (a) prior to recording (b) registration of forced exhalation (c) curve of flow volume and approximate FEV1 vs. FVC ratio

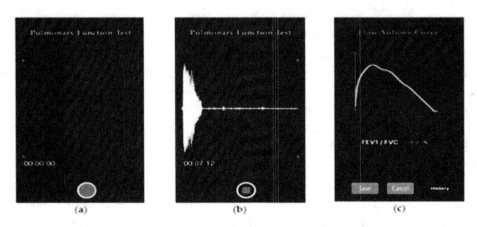

(a)   (b)   (c)

The pulmonologist analyses the downward slope of the flow vs. volume curve from the site of PEF formation, qualitatively examining the flow curve structure depicted in Figure 7. The orange dashed line is indicative of warning lung disease that may be caused by respiratory muscle fatigue or pulmonary fibrosis. The solid line represents normal lung activity, i.e., absence of airflow restriction, while the purple dotted line represents COPD or asthma-like lung dysfunctions, i.e., restriction of airflow due to varying exhaled air time constants in various areas of the lung. Using a smartphone application, Figure 8 determines the FEV1 to FVC ratio.

Referring to the output of the article (Miah et al., 2015), detection of body temperature through camera sensor is presented in Figure 9 and 10 in two different time intervals.

For the system's performance evaluation, a person's body temperature and heart rate are monitored for 20 minutes. The results are presented in Figures 9 and 10, respectively. The actual body temperature (measured using a clinical thermometer) and the sensor-based measurements of that temperature, as well as the actual heart rate (measured using a sphygmomanometer) and the sensor-based measurements of

Figure 9. Actual vs. measured body temperature for 20 minutes

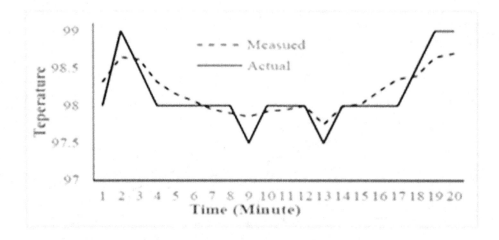

Figure 10. Actual vs. measured heart rate for 20 minutes

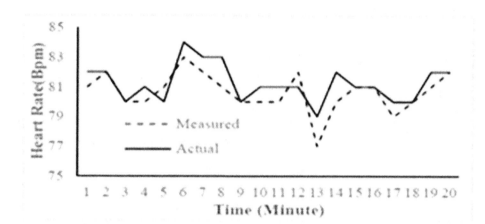

those values, may differ slightly as a result of slight finger movement on the sensor device's surface. As a result, noise affects the analogue value for the related blood flow.

From the narrated case studies, it is understood that the smart phone sensors are capable enough to develop the proposed HPMaas to do the test to detect the disease as suggested in the model.

CONCLUSION

The model's ultimate goal is to present a practical testing instrument with a useful interface that will be used internally and in medical supplies as part of a programme to monitor patient safety. Users can examine their health issues with HPMaaS and report them to the automated system for a fix. The model is a health management system that aids in disease diagnostics and early pandemic disease detection to reduce cross-infection. It will stop any comparisons between users' actual application usage and usage cost records provided by providers as well as any erroneous statements that might be made on either side. The assumption suggested has been proved through case studies.

REFERENCES

Abdulqadir, H. R., Zeebaree, S. R., Shukur, H. M., Sadeeq, M. M., Salim, B. W., Salih, A. A., & Kak, S. F. (2021). A study of moving from cloud computing to fog computing. *Qubahan Academic Journal*, *1*(2), 60–70. doi:10.48161/qaj.v1n2a49

Bailey, E., Fuhrmann, C., Runkle, J., Stevens, S., Brown, M., & Sugg, M. (2020). Wearable sensors for personal temperature exposure assessments: A comparative study. *Environmental Research*, *180*, 108858. doi:10.1016/j.envres.2019.108858 PMID:31708175

Bhambri, P., Rani, S., Gupta, G., & Khang, A. (Eds.). (2022). *Cloud and fog computing platforms for internet of things*. CRC Press. doi:10.1201/9781003213888

Bhardwaj, A., & Krishna, C. R. (2021). Virtualization in cloud computing: Moving from hypervisor to containerization—a survey. *Arabian Journal for Science and Engineering, 46*(9), 8585–8601. doi:10.100713369-021-05553-3

Chan, M., Estève, D., Fourniols, J. Y., Escriba, C., & Campo, E. (2012). Smart wearable systems: Current status and future challenges. *Artificial Intelligence in Medicine, 56*(3), 137–156. doi:10.1016/j.artmed.2012.09.003 PMID:23122689

Dang, L. M., Piran, M. J., Han, D., Min, K., & Moon, H. (2019). A survey on internet of things and cloud computing for healthcare. *Electronics (Basel), 8*(7), 768. doi:10.3390/electronics8070768

El-Sayed, H., Sankar, S., Prasad, M., Puthal, D., Gupta, A., Mohanty, M., & Lin, C. T. (2017). Edge of things: The big picture on the integration of edge, IoT and the cloud in a distributed computing environment. *IEEE Access : Practical Innovations, Open Solutions, 6*, 1706–1717. doi:10.1109/ACCESS.2017.2780087

Haghi Kashani, M., Rahmani, A. M., & Jafari Navimipour, N. (2020). Quality of service-aware approaches in fog computing. *International Journal of Communication Systems, 33*(8), e4340. doi:10.1002/dac.4340

Jain, R., Gupta, M., Nayyar, A., & Sharma, N. (2021). Adoption of fog computing in healthcare 4.0. In *Fog computing for healthcare 4.0 environments* (pp. 3–36). Springer. doi:10.1007/978-3-030-46197-3_1

Karvekar, S. B. (2019). *Smartphone-based human fatigue detection in an industrial environment using gait analysis.* Scholar Works. https://scholarworks.rit.edu/theses/10275/.

Kooistra, J. (2018). *Newzoo's 2018 Global Mobile Market Report: Insights into the World's 3 Billion Smartphone Users.* Newzoo. https://newzoo.com/insights/articles/newzoos-2018-globalmobile-market-report-insights-into-the-worlds-3-billion-smartphone-users/

Kumar, S., Nilsen, W., Pavel, M., & Srivastava, M. (2012). Mobile health: Revolutionizing healthcare through transdisciplinary research. *Computer, 46*(1), 28–35. doi:10.1109/MC.2012.392

Laghari, A. A., Jumani, A. K., & Laghari, R. A. (2021). Review and state of art of fog computing. *Archives of Computational Methods in Engineering, 28*(5), 1–13. doi:10.100711831-020-09517-y

Larson, E. C., Goel, M., Boriello, G., Heltshe, S., Rosenfeld, M., & Patel, S. N. (2012, September). SpiroSmart: using a microphone to measure lung function on a mobile phone. In *Proceedings of the 2012 ACM Conference on ubiquitous computing* (pp. 280-289). ACM. 10.1145/2370216.2370261

Larson, E. C., Lee, T., Liu, S., Rosenfeld, M., & Patel, S. N. (2011, September). Accurate and privacy preserving cough sensing using a low-cost microphone. In *Proceedings of the 13th international conference on Ubiquitous computing* (pp. 375-384). ACM. 10.1145/2030112.2030163

Lawanont, W., Inoue, M., Mongkolnam, P., & Nukoolkit, C. (2018). Neck posture monitoring system based on image detection and smartphone sensors using the prolonged usage classification concept. *IEEJ Transactions on Electrical and Electronic Engineering, 13*(10), 1501–1510. doi:10.1002/tee.22778

Maddah, E., & Beigzadeh, B. (2020). Use of a smartphone thermometer to monitor thermal conductivity changes in diabetic foot ulcers: A pilot study. *Journal of Wound Care*, *29*(1), 61–66. doi:10.12968/jowc.2020.29.1.61 PMID:31930943

Mahmud, R., Kotagiri, R., & Buyya, R. (2018). Fog computing: A taxonomy, survey and future directions. In *Internet of everything* (pp. 103–130). Springer. doi:10.1007/978-981-10-5861-5_5

Mahmud, R., Srirama, S. N., Ramamohanarao, K., & Buyya, R. (2020). Profit-aware application placement for integrated fog–cloud computing environments. *Journal of Parallel and Distributed Computing*, *135*, 177–190. doi:10.1016/j.jpdc.2019.10.001

Miah, M. A., Kabir, M. H., Tanveer, M. S. R., & Akhand, M. A. H. (2015, December). Continuous heart rate and body temperature monitoring system using Arduino UNO and Android device. In *2015 2nd International Conference on Electrical Information and Communication Technologies (EICT)* (pp. 183-188). IEEE.

Mutlag, A. A., Abd Ghani, M. K., Arunkumar, N. A., Mohammed, M. A., & Mohd, O. (2019). Enabling technologies for fog computing in healthcare IoT systems. *Future Generation Computer Systems*, *90*, 62–78. doi:10.1016/j.future.2018.07.049

Nemati, E., Rahman, M. M., Nathan, V., Vatanparvar, K., & Kuang, J. (2019, September). A comprehensive approach for cough type detection. In *2019 IEEE/ACM International Conference on Connected Health: Applications, Systems and Engineering Technologies (CHASE)* (pp. 15-16). IEEE.

Nguyen, H. L., Woon, Y. K., & Ng, W. K. (2015). A survey on data stream clustering and classification. *Knowledge and Information Systems*, *45*(3), 535–569. doi:10.100710115-014-0808-1

Nilashi, M., Ahmadi, H., Manaf, A. A., Rashid, T. A., Samad, S., Shahmoradi, L., & Akbari, E. (2020). Coronary heart disease diagnosis through self-organizing map and fuzzy support vector machine with incremental updates. *International Journal of Fuzzy Systems*, *22*(4), 1376–1388. doi:10.100740815-020-00828-7

Parihar, V. R., Tonge, A. Y., & Ganorkar, P. D. (2017). Heartbeat and temperature monitoring system for remote patients using Arduino. *International Journal of Advanced Engineering Research and Science*, *4*(5), 55–58. doi:10.22161/ijaers.4.5.10

Purswani, J. M., Dicker, A. P., Champ, C. E., Cantor, M., & Ohri, N. (2019, October). Big data from small devices: The future of smartphones in oncology. [). WB Saunders.]. *Seminars in Radiation Oncology*, *29*(4), 338–347. doi:10.1016/j.semradonc.2019.05.008 PMID:31472736

Rao, A. S. S., & Vazquez, J. A. (2020). Identification of COVID-19 can be quicker through artificial intelligence framework using a mobile phone-based survey in the populations when cities/towns are under quarantine. *Infection Control and Hospital Epidemiology*, *41*(7), 1–18. doi:10.1017/ice.2020.61

Roldan Jimenez, C., Bennett, P., Ortiz Garcia, A., & Cuesta Vargas, A. I. (2019). Fatigue detection during sit-to-stand test based on surface electromyography and acceleration: A case study. *Sensors (Basel)*, *19*(19), 4202. doi:10.339019194202 PMID:31569776

Sharma, S., & Sajid, M. (2021). Integrated fog and cloud computing issues and challenges. [IJCAC]. *International Journal of Cloud Applications and Computing*, *11*(4), 174–193. doi:10.4018/IJCAC.2021100110

Siddiqui, S. A., Zhang, Y., Feng, Z., & Kos, A. (2016). A pulse rate estimation algorithm using PPG and smartphone camera. *Journal of Medical Systems*, *40*(5), 1–6. doi:10.100710916-016-0485-6 PMID:27067432

Story, A., Aldridge, R. W., Smith, C. M., Garber, E., Hall, J., Ferenando, G., & Abubakar, I. (2019). Smartphone-enabled video-observed versus directly observed treatment for tuberculosis: A multicentre, analyst-blinded, randomised, controlled superiority trial. *Lancet*, *393*(10177), 1216–1224. doi:10.1016/S0140-6736(18)32993-3 PMID:30799062

Vhaduri, S., Van Kessel, T., Ko, B., Wood, D., Wang, S., & Brunschwiler, T. (2019, June). Nocturnal cough and snore detection in noisy environments using smartphone-microphones. In *2019 IEEE International Conference on Healthcare Informatics (ICHI)* (pp. 1-7). IEEE. 10.1109/ICHI.2019.8904563

Chapter 6
Quality and Performance Measures in Healthcare Systems Using Fog Computing

Riyam Patel

SRM Institute of Science and Technology, India

Aditi Acharjya

SRM Institute of Science and Technology, India

Punyaban Patel

 https://orcid.org/0000-0003-3081-6804

CMR Technical Campus (Autonomous), Hyderabad, India

Borra Sivaiah

CMR College of Engineering and Technology, India

Bibhudatta Sahoo

 https://orcid.org/0000-0001-8273-9850

National Institute of Technology, Rourkela, India

ABSTRACT

Health care organisations must now understand the problems of assessing health care quality and establishing programmes to improve it. The literature covers quality and performance measures in primary, quaternary, public health, and voluntary healthcare. Due to healthcare expansion, reaction time, security, and data volume, latency has become an issue. This systematic study examines fog-based healthcare system approaches. IoT, cloud, and fog computing have created many medical care platforms. Thus, an internet of things and fog computing-based diabetes monitoring system was created to aid diagnosis and prediction. The fog computing-based diabetes monitoring and prediction system includes logistic regression and a decision tree. ML methods can identify if the patient has diabetes. Diabetic patients apply the Donabedian method to improve healthcare quality. This chapter explores, classifies, discusses, and proposes a way to improve Donabedian model, analyses and critique current healthcare metrics, indicators, quality and safety measures, and challenges in measuring health care systems.

DOI: 10.4018/978-1-6684-4466-5.ch006

1. INTRODUCTION

Healthcare is one of the prominent application areas which require real-time and understandable results and the adoption of fog computing to this sector has resulted to a good influence. IoT is rapidly evolving into the healthcare area and it strives to bring simplicity for patients. In the context of rising healthcare expenditures, quality and performance measurement are increasingly integral to accountability which included business planning, annual reporting and contracting. But, recently the accountability has emphasized the achievement of Quality and Performance Measures in Health Care Systems effectively and efficiently. Although the evaluating the health-care sector is difficult and time-consuming, still, it is more common and important to measure the performance of healthcare institutions and society at large. It is difficult for most organizations to assess the quality of anything. Long waiting times (WTs), inefficiency, dissatisfied patients, and burnout among health care workers (HCWs) can all contribute to poor performance. Furthermore, data and accurate information are essential for achieving measurable health improvements. All of these challenges have been met by the healthcare industry by determining quality by measuring specific outcomes of care. To achieve healthcare improvement goals, quality measures must align stakeholder priorities. They must also be evidence-based and unlikely to have negative consequences. The core measure sets should be patient-cantered and aware of socioeconomic determinants of health as a whole. Metrics should be varied, but outcomes and measures that span several aspects of quality performance should be prioritised. Health plans should think outside the box when it comes to gathering performance data (Smith, 2008).

Healthcare performance metrics are data on a specific healthcare-related activity that has been gathered, quantified, and evaluated. Their mission is to find ways to save money and expenses, improve care quality, and increase efficiency in the delivery of care. Substantial resources have been invested on quality and performance measurement system development from the policy level through front-line care delivery. However, because scientific and experiential information about quality and performance measurement spans multiple sources and disciplines, there is no easy way to identify and summarize relevant evidence. Quality Indicators are standardised, evidence-based metrics of health-care quality that may be used to monitor and track clinical performance and outcomes using easily available hospital inpatient administrative data. The measures should not place an undue burden on stakeholders or healthcare professionals. All stakeholders should benefit from the information they supply.

1.1 Background

As needed by the Health Information Technology for Economic and Clinical Health, numerous hospitals have already upgraded their software to comply with the standard. Client-server architecture, a time-honoured technology, is used in the construction of electronic health records. However, information technology has led to the development of procedures that are both more successful and more focused on the needs of patients, and cloud computing has made the process both easier and more cost-effective. Between the cloud and the physical location of the user's devices is where computing occurs in the fog. Trends in cloud computing throughout all industries, including smart homes, factories, and hospitals, for example. The application of fog computing in the creation of intelligent hospitals. A multitude of authors have designed various architectures and suggestions. Numerous researchers have gone through the studies and created a variety of designs to demonstrate the fundamental idea of fog computing in the medical field. The architecture presented fog data, which, in addition to reducing the amount of data, might also make the data more adaptable while simultaneously increasing their level of safety. Between the years 2015 and 2021, sensors based on the body, glucose, skin, and others were utilised in the healthcare industry to detect problems and warn clinicians as soon as possible. Some of these sensors have been used to transport data from healthcare devices to cloud layers for the purpose of processing the patient's health data and identifying early signs of sickness after being used in conjunction with fog computing and Internet of Things technology. Several well-known Internet of Things (IoT)-based healthcare apps are currently operating well.

1.2 Motivation

The purpose of the health care system is to improve the overall human health of a society in order to offer patients a well-organized solution to their problems. It is easier for medical professionals to take into account the requirements of patients when creating healthcare systems and providing services, which ultimately results in an improvement in the level of contentment experienced by patients. As a result, research in the healthcare industry is becoming increasingly more popular. The difficulties in the healthcare system, which include a massive data volume, slow reaction times, significant latency, and insufficient security, are brought to light. Because of this, fog computing, which is a well-known type of distributed architecture, could be helpful in finding solutions to these problems.

The authors specifically conducted a review of the previous research based on a methodology in order to address the following:

- Kind of research might be applicable to fog-based approaches to healthcare
- Most common simulation technologies that are used for fog-based healthcare
- Measurement conditions are utilised while determining the efficacy of fog-based healthcare
- Upcoming trends, unresolved concerns, and challenges associated with healthcare that is based on fog computing

The vast majority of the already available studies either do not examine or evaluate trends, open concerns, or future dimensions of fog-based healthcare systems, or they do not incorporate the standards for conducting a systematic literature review. The motivation of healthcare systems enhances the performance of the Donabedian model as well as the quality metrics.

1.3 Problem Statement

The development of a monitoring system that is based on fog computing is currently under way in order to assist with the forecasting and tracking of diabetes. The proposed monitoring system is composed of three layers: one for the patient information, one for the gateways of fog computing, and one for the cloud. Multiple Internet of Things devices and sensors are utilised in order to collect data on diabetes and monitor the health of individuals. Classifiers have also been developed so that the diabetic infection can be anticipated, which is in addition to the previous point. The suggested logistic and decision tree classifier has been coupled with the fog computing gateway layer in order to alleviate some of the burden that has been placed on the cloud layer. In addition, a cautionary message regarding the present state of health of diabetes patients is generated and shown in the fog layer. It has been observed that the monitoring system that has been proposed is successful in achieving a higher accuracy rate when compared to the other algorithm that is currently being examined. Additionally, it can be shown that the proposed monitoring system is able to efficiently communicate warnings to end users which is a significant advantage.

1.4 Health Care

The intricacy of the medical problems that doctors handle, as well as the abilities and specialisations of the providers, are referred to as levels of care are divided into four categories (Torrey, 2022). These are primary care, secondary care, tertiary care, and quaternary care.

- *Primary care:* Doctors, nurse practitioners, and physician assistants are the major health-care professionals. Illness (a cold, the flu, or another infection), injury (treatment for a broken bone, a painful muscle, a skin rash, or any other acute medical condition), and referral are all included who are coordinating patients care among specialists and other levels.
- *Secondary care*: When a doctor transfers patient care to someone with more particular experience or a specialist in whatever health condition you are facing known as secondary care. Cardiologists (who deal with the heart and blood arteries), Neurologists (who deal with nerve systems), Endocrinologists (who deal with hormone systems, including disorders like diabetes and thyroid disease), and Oncologists (who deal with cancer) are some examples (who is specialise in treating cancers, and many focus on a specific type of cancer). There may be errors at this point owing to a lack of coordination of treatment and the referral of the wrong expert.
- *Tertiary care:* If a patient is hospitalised and requires further specialist treatment, the doctor may send the patient to tertiary care, which involves highly specialised equipment and knowledge. Dialysis, coronary artery bypass surgery, neurosurgery, severe burn treatments, plastic operations, and complex therapies or procedures are only a few examples.
- *Quaternary care:* It is regarded as an additional development of tertiary care. It is, however, far more specialised and unique. It involves experimental treatments, techniques, and specialist operations.

While quality management has proven indispensable in the industrial world, it has yet to find a home in society. The experiences are still quite different, and agreement on the best strategy and equipment is still a long way off. The right to health is a fundamental human right. Everyone wants to have access to adequate and more inexpensive high-quality health care. To address massive unmet needs in individuals and communities, a strong relationship between Mental Health and Psychosocial Support (MHPSS) is required. We all want to find a way to normalise high-value care by using aligned measure sets to promote progress across the board in key quality areas critical to value-based initiatives.

Information is critical for fostering changes in patient care safety and quality. Performance measurement facilitates informed decision-making and safe, high-quality, and reliable care for all stakeholders, including the public, service users, clinicians, and the government, by monitoring, analysing, and communicating the degree to which healthcare organisations meet key goals (Smith, 2008). Accurate performance measurement requires high-quality, consistent data that can be shared across the healthcare industry.

1.5 Fog Computing in Health Care

To overcome the challenges of cloud computing, the Fog computing is introduced. Cisco was the company that first popularised the phrase "fog computing" in the year 2012. The data that is created by different Internet of Things devices is sent to the network's edge, where it is processed by fog computing. The term "fog computing" refers to an extension of "cloud computing" that moves storage, computation, communication, and processing closer to the network's edge in order to decrease the latency of the network. As a result, fog computing is perfect for applications that need a response in very little time or in real time, such as those that are used in the healthcare industry.

The usage of cloud computing in IoT-based healthcare provides data analysis and processing to be carried out in a manner that is significantly quicker and more dependable; yet, cloud computing is experiencing certain possible difficulties (Mukherjee, 2018). IoT-based healthcare systems generate a massive amount of data, which is then processed and analysed at cloud data centres. Sending a massive amount of data to be processed in the cloud ultimately results in issues with latency and network utilisation (Atlam, 2018). Consequently, the utilisation of cloud computing in IoT-based health care systems reduces the efficiency of the systems.

As a result of an increase in the number of patients and the prevalence of chronic diseases, healthcare systems are confronted with huge obstacles. The majority of hospitals determine the value of biometric parameters through manual measurement and then enter that information into the system. Pen and paper are frequently used in the process of measuring the readings from body sensors. In order to conduct an analysis of the patients' health data, the nurses and other members of the clinical team write down the measures on paper. The data from the patient's medical treatment are used to guide the next steps that the medical staff takes. In hospitals, a considerable amount of time is lost due to the manual process. When medical procedures are automated, it can lead to a reduction in the amount of time and money that are wasted. In healthcare systems, it is a requirement to lower costs while at the same time ensuring that patients continue to receive high-quality care (Berwick, 2004). Utilizing fog computing in healthcare systems can make it simpler to manage a patient's data and process the information collected by a network of sensors by providing a level of convenience.

This chapter organized as the Section 1: Introduction, Section 2: Challenges and issues in Fog-based healthcare system, Section 3: Related work, Section 4: Architecture of Health Care System based on Fog Computing, Section 5: Quality in Healthcare System, Section 6: Improvement of outcome measures in Donabedian model for health care, Section 7: Role of Artificial Intelligence (AI) in Health Care System, Section 8: concluded the chapter and the Section 9: presented the future research directions.

2. CHALLENGES AND ISSUES IN FOG-BASED HEALTHCARE

Purchasers, patients, and providers are increasingly using quality monitoring to assess the value of health-care spending. Over the last decade, significant improvements in the science of quality measurement have been made, but many hurdles need to be overcome before quality monitoring can fully fulfil its potential as a cost-cutting tool. Understanding the difficulties of evaluating health-care quality and devising initiatives to enhance it is becoming increasingly crucial for the health-care business. The Internet of Things (IoT) and fog computing will be able to be integrated into healthcare systems, which will allow for the remote monitoring of patients and the efficient observation of patient data. This will be accomplished by reducing latency, network usage, and congestion issues, which will ultimately result in an improvement in healthcare's overall efficiency, quality, and cost. The application of fog computing and the internet of things in the field of healthcare is described in some research as in (Atlam,2018; Saha,2019). The challenges in health care are as follows (McGylnn,1997);

- Reduction in cost of hospitalization of patient.
- Establish the explicit criteria by which health system performance will be judged.
- Handling huge data volume, reducing the response time.
- Enable the improvement of information systems required to support and sustain quality monitoring.
- Develop an accountability framework.
- Identify and balance the competing perspectives of the major participants in the health care delivery system.
- Minimize the conflict between financial and nonfinancial incentives and quality-of-care objectives.
- Select a subset of indicators for routine reporting.

3. RELATED WORK

Many literatures are available in the web, but few of them has been briefly discussed here. Poor data quality has a negative impact on patient care and results. According to a recent literature review, AI models may significantly improve if four specific changes were made: the use of multi-centre datasets, the inclusion of time-varying data, the assessment and evaluation of missing data as well as informative censoring, and the development of clinical utility and usefulness metrics (Goldstein, 2017).

To maximise the value of data, data should comply with the FAIR (findability, accessibility, interoperability, and reusability) principles as a reasonable starting point for minimising data quality issues (Wilkinson, 2016). When and where specific data become available, as well as whether the mechanics of data availability and access are compatible with the model being built, is an often ignored aspect. Simultaneously, we must educate many stakeholders, and model builders must comprehend the datasets from which they learn.

The authors (Frank, 2016) explore at how health-care quality has evolved in comparison to established quality control techniques in other industries, alternative methods for assessing quality, and the current situation of the health-care system. The various types of health care, techniques, functionality, and quality in health care services have all been described (Lillrank, 2015).

Because the field of health is so complex and has so many issues, improving the quality of health care has become a topmost necessity and the primary goal for any health system around the world (Berwick, 2004). Health-care quality performance measurement is becoming increasingly important in order to improve quality, minimise errors, and increase efficiency. The World Health Report highlighted three overall goals for a health-care system: promoting population health, guaranteeing public-responsive health services, and establishing appropriate and fair payment systems (Vaillard, 2005).

According to Veillard (2005), the health-care system has three basic goals: (i) assigning obligations to those who receive health benefits, (ii) developing better-suited politics, and (iii) allowing beneficiaries and other stakeholders to share their knowledge. However, due of the difficulty of assessing care quality, it is a tough notion to grasp. Furthermore, healthcare quality has several aspects and may be understood from various perspectives, including the organisation, configuration, and delivery of health care services, all of which influence the entire health system's performance (Veillard, 2005). Despite the efforts made in terms of research on care quality, significant progress has been made in terms of assessing care quality and applying a variety of quality improvement techniques (Groene et al., 2013).

Similarly, an exhaustive assessment of the research that has been done on assessing and implementing HIS. They go into detail regarding the difficulties that have been encountered as well as the suggestions that have been made for healthcare organisations and assessors. Here, the objective of this study is to provide teams responsible for evaluating complicated HIS with information by identifying the elements that either limit or promote successful HIS adoption and describing appropriate assessment procedures (Sligo, 2017)

In a census of health centres in the United States, Ashley (2018) investigated the parameters that are linked with the utilisation of health information technology (HIT) capabilities, as well as the connection between these HIT capabilities and the quality of treatment provided by the centres. The logistic regressions were used to investigate the features of health centres that are associated with the utilisation of HIT capabilities. On the other hand, the modified linear regressions were used to investigate the correlations between HIT capabilities and the quality of care. By encouraging health centres to make advantage of the possibilities provided by HIT, there may be potential to further improve the quality of treatment provided to patients who are vulnerable.

Likewise, Endeshaw (2021) has read a large number of research papers based on the health care system, and he provides significant consulting services to healthcare companies that are tasked with developing their very own models for evaluating the quality of the services they provide. The Internet of Things devices of today are susceptible to attack and are unable to defend themselves. Further, the fact that fog nodes operate on the edge side are represented, hence lowering lays and improving data protection, consistency, and specificity.

Similarly, a time- and money-saving system for health monitoring that is made up of a fog layer and sensor nodes that are particularly good at conserving energy (Winnie, 2018). This approach reduces the cost of providing medical care while simultaneously improving the standard of such services. The nRF protocol serves as the foundation for these sensor nodes, which are excellent at conserving energy. Decisions are made effectively by the system, and it provides services that require urgent attention. A most important considerations for applications involving data such as medical records is carried out. The utilisation of fog computing helps to increase the data security in the healthcare industry as well (Sood, 2018).

To discover and regulate hypertension attacks at an initial point, Rahmani, (2018), suggested an IoT-Fog based health tracking method. The artificial neural network is used to predict the overall threat of hypertension communities or individuals that are functionally impaired and live isolated. Khan, (2018) proposed a fog computing approach used by healthcare applications to boost various IoT architecture features such as energy consumption, interoperability, performance, and trustworthiness. To explain the effectiveness and usefulness of the system in resolving a medical case study an Early Warning Score (EWS) health monitoring has been introduced.

Depending on the high, intermediate, and low-level IoT layers Gia, (2018), survey and review primary IoT security challenges. This paper outlined security requirements, existing attacks, threats, and these solutions. Khan et al (2018) discuss future transparent open research problems and challenges and characteristics of blockchain-based security solutions. An Intelligent Health Care System has been developed (Tripathy, 2023), which provides health management as a fog service via IoT devices and efficiently organises the data from patients based on the requirements of the user. This system was built in response to a need in the industry. The proposed structure's efficiency in terms of resource utilisation, network throughput, congestion, precision, and runtime is evaluated with the help of FogBus, a cloud framework that is enabled by fog computing.

A survey on healthcare integrated with fog computing and IoT has been carried out to assist researchers in better comprehending the methodologies, technologies, and performance characteristics (Kashyap, 2022). Also, a comparative assessment of previous research that focused on technologies, techniques, and findings to analyse various facets of fog computing in healthcare IoT-based systems has been given.

4. ARCHITECTURE OF HEALTH CARE SYSTEM BASED ON FOG COMPUTING

In this section, the fog computing-based monitoring system (Dev & Malik, 2021) for the prediction and monitoring of diabetes has been explained. The architecture of proposed monitoring system is illustrated in Figure 1. It consists of three layers. These layers are (i) Patient Information Layer, (ii) Fog Computing Gateway Layer and (iii) the Cloud Layer. The Patient Information Layer is responsible to collect the information related to such as health, location, activity, personal, behavioral, environment etc. The various sensors are used to collect the aforementioned information. The gathered information is sent to fog computing gateway layer to process and diagnosis the data. In this layer, logistic regression and decision tree are used to predict the diabetes. Once, the diabetes is predicted, this information is sent to patients through an alert message and preventive action can be taken. The role of cloud layer is to store the processed information and also share this information with doctors, hospitals and family members of patients. The stored information is also used to calculate the impact of the diabetes. Some warning messages can also send to user.

Patient Information Layer: This layer is responsible to collect the data from users according to symptoms of diseases and surrounding environment. This data can be classified as health data, activity data, personal data, behavioural data etc. The data can be collected through different wearable devices and sensors embed in patient's body and surrounding environment. Further, the sensed data are transferred in real time environment through WSNs technologies. For stroke monitoring, the following types of IoT sensors are used to collect the desired information in terms of dataset.

- Health Dataset: Health dataset contains the information regarding the symptoms of diabetes diseases. The symptoms can be Pregnancies, Glucose Blood Pressure, Skin Thickness Insulin, BMI, difficulty in seeing, gradually vision loss etc. Such type of information is collected through health sensor for each individual.
- Environmental Dataset: This dataset contains the information regarding the surrounding environment of individuals. In case of diabetes disease, air pollution, physical activity, smoke, dietary habit, working environment, nature of job can be considered as environmental data.
- Location Dataset: Location dataset consists the information of diabetes affected people including working and residential locations. A RFID tag can be used for close proximity.
- Personal Dataset: This data contains the personal information of each individual. The attributes of this dataset are name, sex, qualification, address, occupation etc. So, all the personal information of each individual is stored in personal dataset.

Fog Computing Gateway Layer: It is intermediately layer between patient information layer and cloud layer. This layer is responsible to process and analyse the real time data collected through different IoT devices and sensors and also predict the patients with stroke infection. If, patient is stroke affected (infectious, positive and recover), then an alert message will generate and sent to corresponding patient. Further, patient data is stored on cloud layer. This layer consists of two components- stroke classification and alert generation.

Cloud Layer: The pre-processed data can be stored on the cloud layer, which is also used for communication purposes. The cloud layer offers an infinite amount of storage space, which may be used to store patient data and can be accessed at any time and from any location. The cloud database can operate in either a non-shareable or shareable mode depending on the user's preferences. The non-shareable mode saves the treatment history, together with the user's personal information, social contact information, and health condition. This mode contains extremely sensitive data and protects it from unauthorised access in order to maintain its privacy. In the shareable mode stores general information such as age, sex, and other details that can be shared with anybody. In addition, the cloud layer permits two distinct categories of authorised individuals to gain access to the aforementioned data. These users are either patients or members of the patient's family, or hospitals or physicians. The patients and their family members have access to the patient's health report, and they provide comments regarding the experience, the patient's current health status, and the treatment they received. patients and can be accessible to hospitals and doctors for the purpose of treatment.

The successful outcome of fog computing is based on the fog devices that are used to process the data. Fog devices must have the potential to process the data at the edge of the network in the early stages. In healthcare systems, there are multiple tasks to be performed by the computing device. Let's assume cloud computing in the healthcare scenario. If the computation and storage requests of all the hospitals are processed on the single centralized cloud server, then it will result in a large end to end delay, a huge network usage, and traffic congestion problems. To resolve these issues, geographically distributed fog nodes could be used. A fog node deployed in a particular area is only responsible to process the requests that are generated by this area. In healthcare systems, the fog node will only process those requests which will be generated by the hospitals of that particular area.

The increase in quality and efficiencies, reducing in the cost of health care, can be possible when the Fog computing is added with the health care system. In addition, the sensors will send the data to the fog nodes so that it can be processed. Clinical staff or medical specialists will quickly be able to gain access to the processed data by using any means of computing. The fog computing architecture offers the ideal distribution of networking, processing, and storage device capabilities. Fog computing refers the cloud computing concepts such as virtualization, hypervisors, and encryption. Fog computing is a modern system that offers minimal processing, memory, and network facilities at the edge of the user's endpoint. The IoT-fog computing-based healthcare architecture is made up of three layers, which are the devices layer, fog layer, and cloud computing layer as shown in Figure 2 (Aladwni, 2019).

IoT devices are on the bottom layer. On the upper layer, IoT nodes are attached to network equipment. The higher layer is capable of transferring health data to the destination layer from the source of generation. A proper balance between these layers is provided by the architecture of fog computing.

- **Sensor Layer:** Patients have sensors and monitors attached to take care of their health. In real-time, these devices can sense and transmit data. These devices are located on the device layer,

Figure 1. Architecture of proposed monitoring system

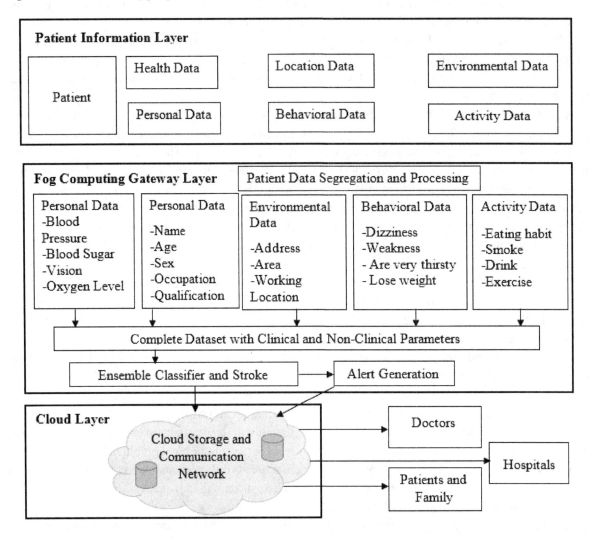

Figure 2. IoT-fog computing-based healthcare architecture

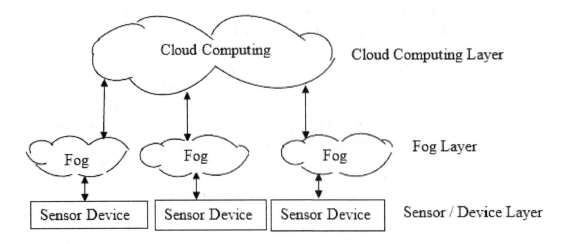

have responsibility for healthcare selection and transmission of healthcare data to the fog layer for accessing via Wi-Fi or mobile network.

- **Fog Computing Layer:** The layer of fog computing extracts medical details from different IoT health tracking devices. This layer is used for IoT health information collection and analysis in real-time. The majority of the difficulties that are linked with cloud computing and the healthcare system are covered by the fog layer that is used in fog computing. Computing in the fog gives the physician / doctors the ability to make informed decisions in the event of an emergency and also assists in the protection of confidential data while reducing the amount of time needed to do so in comparison to using a cloud-based programme.
- **Cloud Computing Layer:** This layer is liable for the storage, preparing, and executing activities that the fog layer is unable to handle and execute. For future actions, patient condition and reports are moved to the cloud layer from the fog layer.

A health fog system was proposed by Ahmad et al. (2018) is three-layer architecture reduces communication costs, where fog computing serves as an intermediate layer between the cloud and end-user. A Smart fog computing architecture was proposed by Greco, (2020), to decrease the latency and network. It is three-layer architecture in which requests can be processed locally and then send to the cloud. Fog computing acts as a middle layer, reduces the drawbacks of IoT health, and enhances the network services. Fog nodes are used in healthcare IoT to reduce latency.

It has been proposed in Alli, (2020) that a multilevel architecture that focuses on addressing health monitoring problems. These health monitoring problems can be static and dynamic monitoring. The authors Abdelmoneem, (2020), proposed an IoT-Fog-Cloud ecosystem. It is an interesting architecture in which IoT devices performs according to users' demand. In this, end devices are at the bottom, the fog layer is the middle layer and the cloud layer is the top layer. This architecture supports localized computation, Fog-edge computing, and remote computing. An architecture proposed that distributes healthcare tasks dynamically between cloud computing and fog computing. Various health problems and a significant percentage of patients will be treated by this architecture (Gia, 2017).

5. QUALITY IN HEALTHCARE SYSTEM

The variety of quality definitions reported in the literature supports the view that quality is a complex concept and emphasises the significance of having a shared understanding of quality before beginning the monitoring process. The process of defining quality includes establishing and maintaining generally accepted performance criteria. According to Ovretveit (2001), "a quality health service delivers a range of services that serve the population's most critical health requirements in a safe and effective manner, without wasting any resources, and while staying in compliance with higher-level rules."

Healthcare quality, according to Donabedian (2003) is a combination of "the science and technology of healthcare, as well as the implementation of that science and technology in actual practise." Providing excellent healthcare entails leveraging available technology and resources to give care that is acknowledged as best practise at the time of delivery. The US Institute of Medicine Ovretveit (2004) offered the most prevalent and widely recognised definition of quality in healthcare: "the degree to which services for individuals and populations maximise the likelihood of desired outcomes and are compatible with current professional knowledge."

Healthcare quality can be defined as doing the right thing for the right patient, at the right time, in the right way to produce the best potential results. The degree to which health services for individuals and populations increase the likelihood of desired health outcomes is referred to as quality of care. It is essential for achieving universal health coverage since it is based on evidence-based professional expertise. Furthermore, the authors have described a performance scale that can theoretically range from poor to excellent, identified that monitoring can include both individual and population perspectives, and that efforts to improve health outcomes must be supported by scientific evidence or expert consensus in the lack of research (Kathleen, 1990).

Good quality healthcare includes characteristics such as accessibility, availability, affordability, acceptability, competency, timeliness, appropriateness, privacy, attentiveness, confidentiality, caring, accuracy, reliability, responsiveness, accountability, comprehensiveness, amenities, continuity, equity, and facilities. Quality metrics are benchmarks for evaluating healthcare practitioners' ability to care for patients and the public (Jazieh, 2020). Important features of care, such as effectiveness, safety, fairness, and timeliness, can be identified using quality metrics. Each quality measure focuses on a distinct component of healthcare delivery, and quality measures and quality measurement taken together create a more complete picture of healthcare quality. Quality measures address many parts of healthcare, including patient safety, clinical processes, health outcomes, efficient use of healthcare resources, patient engagement in their own care, population and public health, patient perceptions of their care, and care coordination.

As a result, overall improvements in the quality and performance in the healthcare environment can assist providers in developing dependable, long-term, and cost-effective healthcare processes, allowing them to achieve their aim of improving care delivery and improving patient outcomes.

5.1 Healthcare Quality Measures

Quality measures are important for any healthcare facility's strategic planning since they show where it excels and where it may improve. Because they show how a hospital should shift its finances and resources, these measurements tend to influence other measures inside organizations. When one begins to measure quality in any organization, it will have enough information to understand the necessity to deliver the greatest possible care to the community. Quality control procedures in healthcare (Jazieh, 2020) are concerned with reducing medical errors and saving patients. These are effectiveness, efficiency and timeliness; safety and security; patient-centred and equitable.

- **Effectiveness, Efficiency & Timeliness:** Effectiveness measures relate to services based on established medical treatments, timeliness measures evaluate the promptness of services, and efficiency measures focus on avoiding waste. Many of these are also frequently included in larger quality improvement.
  - *Readmission Rate*: It can be defined as the percentage of patients readmitted divided by the total number of patients served over a given period of time. A high percentage could indicate care is low quality and ineffective.
  - *Hospital Acquired Conditions (HACs)*: The number of new conditions that patients acquired while in the hospital. It is an unfavourable situation or condition that arises during a patient's stay in a hospital or medical facility. It creates harm to the patient. HACs can range from allergic reactions to medication to pressure ulcers, and they can occur as a direct re-

sult of getting therapy. For example, Methicillin-resistant Staphylococcus aureus (MRSA), Catheter-Associated Urinary Tract Infections (CAUTI), Central-Line-Associated Blood Stream Infections (CLABSI), and Surgical Site Infections for colon surgeries and hysterectomies etc.

- ◦ *Average Minutes Per Surgery (AMPS)*: This metric is typically split by surgical type and refers to standard deviations. High time variations or unusually long procedures could suggest that the surgical process isn't structured in an efficient or logical manner, resulting in a drop in quality.
- ◦ *Average Length of Stay (ALS)*: This metric is typically split by surgical type and refers to standard deviations. High time variations or unusually long procedures could suggest that the surgical process isn't structured in an efficient or logical manner, resulting in a drop in quality.
    - a. *Patient Wait Times by Process Step (TWTPS)*: This metric is divided into sub-measures that track how quickly a hospital's core process steps are completed. For example: arrival to bed, arrival to nurse or physician, arrival to discharge. This metric has a chronological flow, and the findings reveal not only the quality of care but also patient satisfaction ratings.

- **Safety and Security:** Fog computing reduces the amount of data that is transferred back and forth to the cloud, which in turn reduces the amount of latency that is caused as a result of local computation. Since there is a higher probability for security issues when large amounts of data are transferred through networks, fog computing reduces the amount of data that is transferred back and forth to the cloud. The following parameters can be incorporated into Fog computing to provide better health care services.
    - ◦ *Number of Medication Errors (NME)*: The incidence of drug prescription errors called the medication errors. Prescription errors, initial pharmacy dispensation errors, hospitalisation errors, and following outpatient follow-up errors all occurred. If the facility's prescription ordering system is malfunctioning can be rectify through the Fog computing.
    - ◦ *Complication Rate (CR)*: The percentage of patients that suffer difficulties as a result of their care (usually surgical complications). A defined timeframe or division can be used to track it using Fog computing. A high proportion of complications is prevalent in institutions that undertake high-risk procedures on a regular basis; nevertheless, it can also signify poor care quality which can be improved using Fog computing.
    - ◦ *Percentage Leaving Against Medical Advice (PLAMA)*: The percentage of patients who leave the hospital despite doctors' advice, divided by the total number of patients served. A high percentage could indicate that the hospital isn't appropriately serving patients in need of care. In that case, the patients can get medical advice using Fog computing.
    - ◦ *Post-Procedure Death Rate (Post-PDR)*: The number of people who die after receiving treatment. For each procedure, there are estimated death rates (ranging from low to high percentages). The risk level must be taken into account when calculating the post-procedure death rate for accuracy. Track it across the hospital as well as by division and surgical team can be done efficiently using Fog computing.

- **Patient-Centred & Equitable**: This final domain of healthcare quality performance metrics focuses on ensuring that the hospital's services are respectful and responsive to patients' requirements while maintaining a high level of care for all.

    ◦ *Number of Patient Complaints*: The number of complaints patients have made about the care they received. These complaints could be made while receiving therapy or afterward.

    ◦ *Overall Patient Satisfaction*: it is called patients' opinions on the quality of their care. Typically, hospitals solicit feedback from prior patients by mailing or emailing surveys. Low satisfaction can indicate a problem with hospital operations or care quality, whereas good results are frequently used to advertise the hospital and attract contributors.

    ◦ *Doctor-Patient Communication Frequency*: The frequency with which doctors, patients, and procedure lists communicate among themselves. Even when adjusting for therapy kinds, measuring this effectively can be problematic. However, establishing generic benchmarks might reveal whether or not patient needs are being taken into account.

    ◦ *Patient-To-Staff Ratio*: For a given time period, the number of hospital employees divided by the number of patients. This shows whether the facility, or even a specific section, is under-staffed or overstaffed. Understaffing usually results in a drop in quality.

    ◦ *Hours of Valuable Employee Training*: It means that the number of training hours and the associated employee training evaluations. Patient care and quality will likely improve if training hours are high and hospital personnel find the trainings useful.

    ◦ *Occupancy Rate*: The ratio of the number of patients in each room to the total number of rooms in the hospital. Some hospitals have more capacity for overcrowding and can make use of other departments and hospital beds, but others are small and lack those resources. If a facility's occupancy rate is too high for its size, resources will be stretched thin, and service quality will suffer.

    ◦ *Number of Referrals*: It is the number of patients who have been referred to a different facility. If referrals are high, it could mean that patients' requirements aren't being addressed, or it could just be a way to keep track of how many patients are being moved to more specialised facilities.

5.2 Model of Health Care Quality Measures

Avedis (2005) published the first version paradigm for measuring and evaluating healthcare quality. There were three sorts of metrics in total: structural, process, and outcome. Those three broad categories encompass many of the measures used by projects to assess and enhance quality. Balanced measures are an additional component of improvement measurement. Further, the model uses a classification method to assess and compare the quality of health care organisations (Avedis, 2005; Gerard, 2022). Figure 3 shows the classification system which has been named after the physician and researcher who developed it.

Structural Measures: Structural measures (Hayford, 2017) evaluate the capacity or conditions of the physical settings in which providers deliver care as well as the capabilities of those providers. These measures capture a provider's capacity to deliver care, but they do not describe how that care is delivered.

Also, it indicates service provider characteristics such as staff-to-patient ratios and service operation hours. Input measures are what they're called. Consumers can get a sense of a health care provider's capability, systems, and processes by looking at structural measurements. For example:

- The use of electronic medical records or prescription order entry systems by the health-care organisation.
- The percentage or number of board-certified physicians.

- The provider-to-patient ratio.
- Number of nursing care hours per patient-day and the adoption of systems to enable clinicians to prescribe medications electronically.

Process Measures: Process measures seek to measure the underuse, overuse, or misuse of care. Underuse is the failure to deliver recommended health care services. Overuse is the provision of services that are of low value—that is, likely to have little clinical benefit or have a greater likelihood of producing harm than benefits. Misuse is the delivery of the wrong type of care or the inappropriate delivery of care. Most process measures reflect whether recommended care was delivered and thus indicate the presence or absence of underuse. These describe how your systems and processes work together to get the desired result. Process measurements describe what a provider does to maintain or improve a patient's health, whether they are healthy or have been diagnosed with a medical illness. These metrics are usually based on widely established clinical practise guidelines. It can help improve health outcomes by informing customers about the medical care they can expect for a specific condition or disease. For example, the amount of time a patient waits for a senior clinical review, whether a patient obtains particular levels of care or not, whether personnel wash their hands, incident recording and action, and whether patients are made informed of delays while waiting for an appointment. Process measurements make up the majority of health-care quality measures used in public reporting.

Outcome Measures: Outcome measures try to capture the effects of care delivery on a patient's health and show the final result of your improvement work, as well as if it met the goal(s) stated. Some outcome measures often called an "intermediate outcome," which assess the health status of people with chronic conditions, such as blood glucose levels for diabetic patients and blood pressure levels for hypertensive patients. This type of measure helps to identify whether patients with chronic conditions are being managed well and are having their symptoms controlled effectively - without which they are much more likely to develop complications.

The outcome metrics represent the influence of a health-care service or intervention on patients' health. Reduced mortality, duration of stay, hospital acquired infections, adverse occurrences or harm, emergency admissions, and enhanced patient experience are examples of outcome measurements. Although outcome measurements appear to be the "gold standard" for assessing quality, they are the result of a variety of circumstances, many of which are beyond the control of providers. These issues can be accounted for using risk-adjustment methods, which are mathematical models that correct for different features within a population, such as patient health status. The science of risk adjustment, on the other hand, is still developing. Experts agree that new risk-adjustment strategies are required to reduce the reporting of misleading or even erroneous health-care quality data.

Patient safety measures and patient-reported outcomes are two more types of outcome metrics that have lately been created.

- Patient safety measures track the number of problems and adverse events that occur after surgery or other types of therapy. Rates of hospital-acquired infections, postoperative bleeding or bruising, and postoperative respiratory failure are only a few examples.
- Patient-reported outcome measures are intended to capture improvements in health and functional status that may be difficult to evaluate using claims data, such as gains in mobility following knee surgery or reductions in chest discomfort or other symptoms after cardiac treatments.

Figure 3. Donabedian model for healthcare

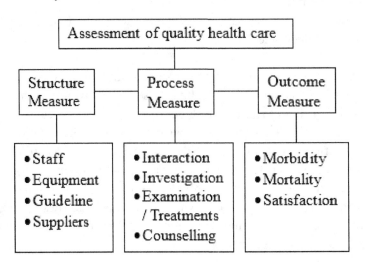

6. IMPROVEMENT OF OUTCOME MEASURES IN DONABEDIAN MODEL

This section highlight the various measures that help improve the measures in Donabedian model. The ML techniques such as the logistic regression and the decision tree are used in this chapter to study the accuracy of the outcome of different attributes (*i.e.*, insulin, glucose, BMI etc.) of diabetic diseases can be improved, so that the outcome measures will be more perfect which can help to physicians for inferring the type of diabetics such as prediabetes, Type-1, Type-2, or gestational diabetes.

6.1 Logistic Regression

Logistic model (Rajendra, 2021) is one of the most important models in the classification and it can be used to predict probability of diabetes. The logistic regression equation is given by

$$log\left(\frac{P_i}{1-P_i}\right) = \delta_0 + \delta_1 x_1 + \ldots + \beta_n x_n \tag{1}$$

Where, P_i is the probability of diabetes for patient i, x is the features of patient sample i, and δ is the coefficients of the logistic regression. The histogram for all features of diabetes data is shown in Figure 4.

The linearity of independent variables and log odds is assumed in logistic regression. Despite this theoretical constraint, the coefficients of a parametric model can reveal things about the relationship between individual characteristics and the likelihood of positive outcomes. The Logistic Regression classification model for the training data of diabetes is shown in Table 1.

The top three most relevant features are "Glucose", "BMI" and "Number of times pregnant" because of the low p-values. Insulin" and "Age" appear not statistically significant. The confusion matrix for the test data is shown in Table 2.

Figure 4. Histogram of all features of diabetes data

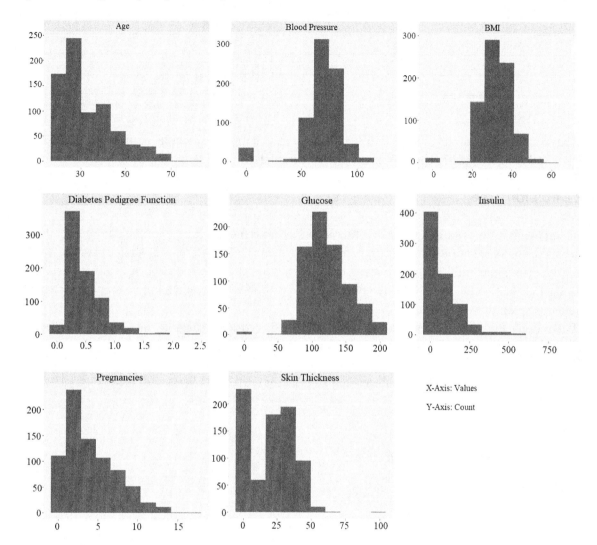

Table 1. Training data of diabetes data set

Features	Estimate	Std. Error	z value	Pr.(>|z|)
Intercept	-8.3461752	0.8157916	-10.231	< 2e-16
Pregnancies	0.1246856	0.0373214	3.341	0.000835
Glucose	0.0315778	0.0042497	7.431	1.08e-13
Blood Pressure	-0.014473	0.006276	-2.306	0.0211
Skin Thickness	-0.001349	0.007795	-0.173	0.8626
Insulin	-0.0013400	0.0009441	-1.419	0.155781
BMI	0.0881521	0.017468	5.440	5.33e-08
Diabetes Pedigree Function	0.9642132	0.3430094	2.811	0.004938
Age	0.0018904	0.0107225	0.176	0.860053

Table 2. Confusion matrix for the test data

Decision	Prediction	
	False	True
0	136	34
1	14	44

The performance of the model evaluated using test data. The accuracy of logistic model is 0.789473684210526 [78%]. The double density plot is as shown in Figure 5.

6.2 Decision Tree

Decision tree is a flow chart like tree structure where nodes represent the test of the attributes and edge indicates the outcome of the test. The decision tree for the diabetes data set is given in Figure 6. The attribute selection measures are used to select the best splitting attribute and majority voting is also used to assign the class for the node if the number tuples are less. The decision trees are easily converted into the classification rules (Karnika, 2019).

If a person's Body Mass Index (BMI) less than 45.4 and his diabetes degree function less than 0.8745, then he is more likely to have diabetes. One of the association rule is given as below:

Person (BMI) ≤ 45.5 and Person (diabetes degree function) < 0.87 → Person (diabetes)

Figure 5: Density plot for diabetes diseases

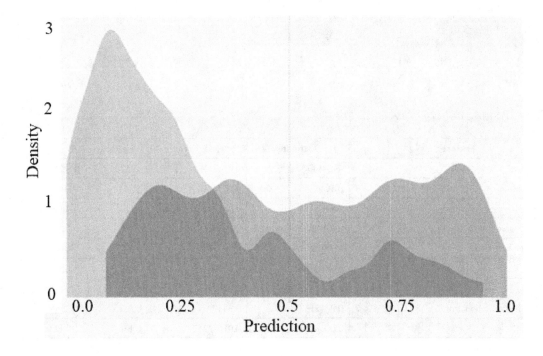

Figure 6: Decision tree for diabetic disease

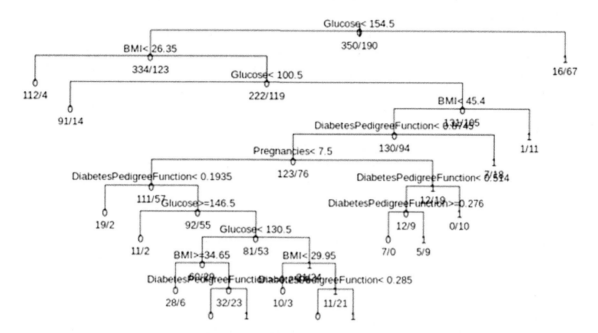

The confusion matrix is as in Table 3. The accuracy of decision tree is 0.745614 *i.e.*, 74.56%. So, the performance of logistic regression and the decision tree algorithms have been compared and found that logistic regression performed better than decision tree.

6.3 Healthcare Performance Measures

Efficiency, effectiveness, yield, productivity, quality, access, and equity are all concepts that are commonly associated with performance (Sicotte, 1998). Several performance measurement frameworks have been developed, based on a triad of the Donabedian model (Structure, Process, and Outputs), the Institute of Medicine, and the World Health Organization domains; all of the frameworks aim to improve the efficiency and effectiveness of their activities (Zaadoud, 2021). Furthermore, quality improvement allows for the revaluing and modifying of strategies, plans, politics, and the associated objectives (Veillard, 2010). For several reasons, it is critical to measure and evaluate the quality of prevention strategies: (i) to better understand their operating mechanisms and potential benefits and risks, (ii) to assess their impact and suitability, and (iii) to assess their effectiveness in reducing health inequalities (Starfield, 2009).

Table 3. Confusion Matrix

DT Prediction	0	1
0	121	29
1	29	49

Healthcare performance measures are gathered, quantified, and analysed data on a specific healthcare-related activity. Their goal is to find ways to reduce costs, improve quality, and increase efficiency in health-care delivery. They're also used to track other actions that an institution wants to - or needs to - track in order to comply with regulatory requirements. These measurement programmes are frequently designed and operated with the active participation of the physicians and hospital workers whose performance is being monitored, as well as government and other third-party bodies, to ensure that the measurements are useful and the data are accurate. Types of healthcare performance measurements based on Fog computing include:

- *Cost of healthcare services:* It processes selected data locally i.e. in Fog layer (shown in Figure 1) instead of sending them to the cloud for processing. Hence, it can save network bandwidth. This leads to lower operational costs.
- *Latency:* It reduces latency requirements and hence quick decisions can be made. It decreased delays compared to a cloud-based application.
- *Confidentiality:* It helps for securing confidential health care data.
- *Efficiency and Quality of patient care:* It allows the doctor to make smart choices during a case of emergencies
- *Care outcomes:* It improves the patient's satisfaction and save life.
- *Disparities in performance:* It improves the inequality in performance.

For a variety of reasons, healthcare performance assessments are critical to healthcare organisations and society in general which can be improve using Fog computing.

6.4 Health Care Performance Indicators

A healthcare Key Performance Indicator (KPI) or metric is a well-defined set of measurable measurements used to quantify a company's overall long-term performance measure which is used to observe, analyse, optimise, and alter a healthcare process to increase patient and provider satisfaction. KPIs are used to determine a company's strategic, financial, and operational accomplishments, particularly when compared to those of other organisations in the same industry (Torrey, 2022).

i. Key performance indicators (KPIs) are indicators that compare a company's performance to a set of aims, objectives, or industry peers.
ii. Financial KPIs include net profit (also known as gross profit margin), revenues minus specific expenses, and the current ratio (liquidity and cash availability).
iii. Per-customer efficiency, customer happiness, and customer retention are common customer-focused KPIs.
iv. Process-focused KPIs are used to track and measure operational performance across the company.
v. In general, firms use business analytics software and reporting tools to measure and track KPIs

7. ROLE OF ARTIFICIAL INTELLIGENCE IN HEALTH CARE SYSTEM

Artificial intelligence (AI) is gradually altering medical practise. Here are several AI applications in medicine that can be utilised in clinical, diagnostic, rehabilitative, surgical, and prognostic treatments, among others. Clinical decision-making and disease diagnostics are two more areas of medicine where AI is having an influence. To detect disease and guide healthcare decisions, AI systems can ingest, analyse, and report massive volumes of data across multiple modalities (Zazieh, 2020). AI applications can deal with the massive amounts of data generated in the medical field and uncover fresh information that would otherwise be lost in the avalanche of medical big data (Berwick, 2004; OECD, 2021). These technologies can also be used to discover new medications for health-care management and patient care (Donabedian, 2003; Ovretveit, 2004).

AI can be defined as the artificial building of a human brain system that can learn natural language and plan, sense, and process it for making decisions with minimum human interaction. ML (Machine Learning) and DL (Deep Learning) are two AI techniques. Figure 7 depicts the classification of AI (Bordoloi, 2022)]. In healthcare data management, data security, medicine, early detection, the AI, ML, and DL are more efficient. AI and machine learning are transforming the healthcare industry, as well as practically every other industry. AI is transforming the way we design cars, improve our energy use, and manage our finances, from the possibilities of deep learning and neural networks in pharmaceutical research to the increasingly sophisticated application of intelligence diagnostic tests and surgical robotics.

This AI-based technology is utilised in the healthcare sector in conjunction with high-tech cameras and sensors to visualise and extract data that may be used for a range of applications in healthcare administration, treatment, and research. Among them are:

- *Computer vision:* It has the ability to analyse patterns and diagnose medical images with far more accuracy, speed, and accuracy, and with far fewer errors. It has the ability to extract information from medical photos that the human eye cannot see. Additionally, because radiologists and MRI technicians are in short supply in the healthcare industry, computer vision can be a viable solution.
- *Smart operating facilities:* Computer vision can help to automate the recording of surgical operations that are repetitive and error-prone. In the United States, approximately 1500 procedures are

Figure 7. Classification and subclasses of AI, ML, and DL

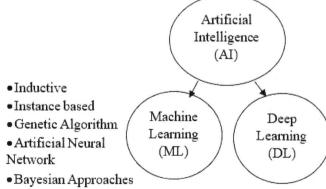

forgotten within the patient each year, and computer vision can track surgical equipment to avoid this problem.

- *Increased workplace safety:* Surveillance systems with computer vision and artificial intelligence can monitor employees for possible disturbances and inform authorities as needed. They can also monitor whether the employees are using the proper safety equipment and procedures.
- *Surgical guidance:* Using cameras enabled by computer vision, computer vision technology is also utilised to advice surgeons during procedures.
- *Better healthcare research:* Computer vision aids in the development and testing of new medicines. When compared to human workers, computer vision systems can conduct faster, more accurate, and unbiased cell counting.
- *Detecting tumours and cancers:* Computer vision systems can aid in the faster and more accurate detection of brain cancers. Additionally, computer vision systems can be educated with data of malignant and healthy tissues using machine learning and deep learning to identify skin and breast cancer more precisely.
- *Virtual nurses:* It is a digital nurse that helps individuals keep track of their patients' health and treatments in between doctor visits. The programme, which specialises on chronic ailments, employs machine learning to assist patients.
- *Reduced patient mix-up:* In the healthcare industry, patient misinterpretation is a regular problem. For both the healthcare provider and the patient, this can be dangerous. This challenge can be solved with a computer vision-based facial recognition system.
- *Managing medical records and other data:* Data management is the most extensively used use of artificial intelligence and digital automation in health care since accumulating and evaluating information is the first step. To enable faster, more consistent access, robots collect, store, re-format, and trace data.
- *Biopharmaceutical development:* BioXcel Therapeutics employs artificial intelligence to find and develop innovative drugs in immuno-oncology and neuroscience. Additionally, AI is used in the company's drug re-innovation effort to find new uses for current drugs or to identify new patients.
- *Health monitoring:* Apple, Garmin, FitBit, Amazfit, Honor and other companies make wearable health trackers that monitor heart rate and activity levels. They can send warnings to the user to encourage them to exercise more, and they can share this information with doctors (and AI systems) for more data on the requirements and habits of patients.

8. CONCLUSION

A systematic review of fog-based healthcare systems, its analysis, applications and challenges were presented in this study. In addition, classification and discussion of different applications were provided. Because of a lack of suitable framework and insufficient understanding of the use of instruments to improve health care quality, measuring health care quality and performance remains difficult. Quality measures are important for any healthcare facility's strategic planning since they show where it excels and where it may improve. Because they show how a hospital should shift its finances and resources, these measurements tend to influence other measures inside organisations. One's will have the information according to you need to give the greatest care to human society once it starts measuring quality of health care organisation. The authors have tried to provide a rigorous systematic review, but it has some limitations that should be taken into consideration.

8.1 Future Research

In recent years, assessing provider quality has become more prevalent, but doing so accurately and presenting the results remains a difficult issue. Although providers have made considerable headway in improving quality, these advancements have been sluggish, and quality issues still exist. As a result, several academics have suggested that new metrics be developed and that existing ones be used more effectively. Researchers are working to develop new quality measures to solve the shortcomings of present ones. Improvements to existing types of measures (for example, process, outcome, and composite measures) and development of new types of measures that encompass the continuum of care, focus more on systems of care, and seek to measure the health of populations rather than individual patients fall into two broad categories.

- **Improvement of Existing Types of Measures:** Historically, measures based on care practises have focused on underuse. Researchers have increasingly concentrated on generating overuse measures as a strategy to improve the health-care system's efficiency and decrease wasteful diagnosis and treatment.
- **Development of New Types of Measures:** In addition, instead of focusing on the performance of particular providers or specific venues, researchers have recommended establishing new types of measurements that assess quality across the continuum of care (for instance, hospitals, nursing homes, or home health). Poor quality is sometimes perceived as a failing of a single provider rather than a systemic problem. This viewpoint could exacerbate the health-care system's fragmentation.

However, there is a growing realisation that health care is often given by teams of physicians, nurses, and other professionals across numerous locations. As a result, evaluating quality across the treatment continuum would place a greater emphasis on the health care team and potentially overcome some of the technical obstacles of measuring individual providers, such as small sample sizes and attribution issues.

REFERENCES

Abdelmoneem, R. M., Benslimane, A., & Shaaban, E. (2020). Mobility-Aware Task Scheduling in Cloud-Fog IoT-Based Healthcare Architectures. *Computer Networks*: .

Avedis, D. (2005). Evaluating the quality of medical care. Milbank *Memorial Fund Q. 1966; 44(3)*, 166-206. *Reprinted in Milbank Q.*, *83*(4), 691–729.

Aladwani, T. (2019). Scheduling IoT Healthcare Tasks in Fog Computing Based on their Importance. *Procedia Computer Science*, *163*, 560–569. doi:10.1016/j.procs.2019.12.138

Alli, A. A., & Muhammad, M. A. (2020). The fog cloud of things: A survey on concepts, architecture, standards, tools, and applications. *Internet of Things*, *9*, 100177. doi:10.1016/j.iot.2020.100177

Kranz, A., Dalton, S., Damberg, C., & Timbie, J. W. (2018). *Using Health IT to Coordinate Care and Improve Quality in Safety-Net Clinics, The Joint Commission.* Elsevier Inc.

Atlam, H., Walters, R., & Wills, G. (2018). Fog Computing and the Internet of Things: A Review, Big Data. *Cognitive Computation, 2*(2), 10–18.

Berwick, D. M. (2004). Lessons from developing nations on improving health care. *BMJ, 328* (7448), 1124–1129. doi:10.1136/bmj.328.7448.1R

Bordoloi, D. (2022). *Deep Learning in Healthcare System for Quality of Service, Journal of care Engineering.* Hindawi. doi:10.1155/2022/8169203

Dev, A. & Malik, S. (2021). IoT and Fog Computing Based Prediction and Monitoring System for Stroke Disease. *Turkish Journal of Computer and Mathematics Education, 12*(12), 3211–3223.

Donabedian, A. (2003). *An Introduction to Quality Assurance in Health Care.* Oxford University Press.

Dwivedi, K., Sharan, H. O., & Vishwakarma, V. (2019). Analysis of Decision Tree for Diabetes Prediction [IJETR]. *International Journal of Engineering and Technical Research, 9*(6). doi:10.31873/IJETR.9.6.2019.64

Endeshaw, B. (2021). Health care service quality measurement models: A review. *Journal of Health Research, Emerald Publishing Limited, 35*(2), 106–117.

Gerard, D. R. (2022). Quality Improvement Using the Donabedian Model. *EMS World.*

Gia, T. N. (2017). Low-cost fog-assisted health-care IoT system with energy efficient sensor nodes. *13th international wireless communications and mobile computing conference.* IEEE.

Gia, T. N. (2018). Fog computing approach for mobility support in internet-ofthings systems. *IEEE Access : Practical Innovations, Open Solutions, 6,* 36064–36082. doi:10.1109/ACCESS.2018.2848119

Goldstein, B. A., Navar, A., Pencina, M. J., & Ioannidis, J. (2017). Opportunities and challenges in developing risk prediction models with electronic health records data: a systematic review. *JAMIA, 24*(1):198-208. . doi:10.1093/jamia/ocw042

Greco, L., Percannella, G., Ritrovato, P., Tortorella, F., & Vento, M. (2020). Trends in IoT based solutions for health care: Moving AI to the Edge. *Pattern Recognition Letters, 135,* 346–353. doi:10.1016/j.patrec.2020.05.016 PMID:32406416

Groene, O., Botje, D., Suñol, R., Lopez, M. A., & Wagner, C. (2013). A systematic review of instruments that assess the implementation of hospital quality management systems. *International Journal for Quality in Health Care, 25*(5), 525–541. doi:10.1093/intqhc/mzt058 PMID:23970437

Hayford, T. B. (2017). Issues and Challenges in Measuring and Improving the Quality of Health Care. *Working Paper Series.* Congressional Budget Office Washington, D.C. doi:10.1377/hlthaff.16.3.7

Jazieh, A. (2020). Quality Measures: Types, Selection, and Application. *Journal of Health Care Quality Assurance 26*(3), 269-78, 201.

Kashyap, V. (2022). A Systematic Survey on Fog and IoT Driven Healthcare: Open Challenges and Research Issues. *Electronics*, 1-25.

Lohr, K. (1990). Health, Health Care, and Quality of Care. In: *Medicare: A Strategy for Quality Assurance. Institute of Medicine. NAP.* https://books.nap.edu/openbook.php?record_id=1547&page=21

Khan, M. A., & Salah, K. (2018). IoT security: Review, blockchain solutions, and open challenges. *Future Generation Computer Systems, 82*, 395–411. doi:10.1016/j.future.2017.11.022

Kilbourne, A. M., Keyser, D., & Pincus, H. A. (2010). Challenges and Opportunities in Measuring the Quality of Mental Health Care. *Canadian Journal of Psychiatry, 55*(9), 549–557. doi:10.1177/070674371005500903 PMID:20840802

Lillrank, P. (2015). Small and big quality in health care. *International Journal of Health Care Quality Assurance, 28*(4), 356–366. doi:10.1108/IJHCQA-05-2014-0068 PMID:25982636

Mukherjee, M., Shu, L., & Wang, D. (2018). Survey of Fog Computing: Fundamental, Network Applications, and Research Challenges. *IEEE Communications Surveys and Tutorials, 20*(3), 1826–1857. doi:10.1109/COMST.2018.2814571

Ovretveit, J. (2004). Formulating a health quality improvement strategy for a developing country. *International Journal of Health Care Quality Assurance, 17*(7), 368–376. doi:10.1108/09526860410563177 PMID:15552392

Rahmani, A. M., Gia, T. N., Negash, B., Anzanpour, A., Azimi, I., Jiang, M., & Liljeberg, P. (2018). Exploiting smart e-Health gateways at the edge of healthcare Internet-of-Things: A fog computing approach. *Future Generation Computer Systems, 78*, 641–658. doi:10.1016/j.future.2017.02.014

Rajendra, P., & Latifi, S. (2021). Prediction of diabetes using logistic regression and ensemble techniques. *Computer Methods and Programs in Biomedicine Update, 1*, 100032. doi:10.1016/j.cmpbup.2021.100032

Sicotte, C. (1998). A Conceptual Framework for the Analysis of Health Care Organizations' Performance. *Sage Journals.* doi:10.1177/095148489801100106

Sligo, J., Gauld, R., Roberts, V., & Villa, L. (2017). A literature review for large-scale health information system project planning, implementation and evaluation. *International Journal of Medical Informatics, 97*, 86–97. doi:10.1016/j.ijmedinf.2016.09.007 PMID:27919399

Starfield, B. (2009). Primary care and equity in health: The importance to effectiveness and equity of responsiveness to peoples' needs. *Humanity & Society, 33*(1–2), 56–76. doi:10.1177/016059760903300105

Tripathy, S. (2023). An Intelligent Health Care System in Fog Platform with Optimized Performance. *Sustainability, MDPI, 15*, 1862, 1-17.

Veillard, J., Champagne, F., Klazinga, N., Kazandjian, V., Arah, O. A., & Guisset, A. L. (2005). A performance assessment framework for hospitals", The WHO regional office for Europe PATH project. *International Journal for Quality in Health Care, 17*(6), 487–496. doi:10.1093/intqhc/mzi072 PMID:16155049

Veillard, J., Garcia-Armesto, S., Kadandale, S., Klazinga, N., & Leatherman, S. (2010). International health system comparisons: From measurement challenge to management tool. Cambridge University Press, 641 672. doi:10.1017/CBO9780511711800.023

Wilkinson, M. D., Dumontier, M., Aalbersberg, I. J., Appleton, G., Axton, M., Baak, A., Blomberg, N., Boiten, J. W., da Silva Santos, L. B., Bourne, P. E., Bouwman, J., Brookes, A. J., Clark, T., Crosas, M., Dillo, I., Dumon, O., Edmunds, S., Evelo, C. T., Finkers, R., & Mons, B. (2016). The FAIR Guiding Principles for scientific data management and stewardship. *Scientific Data*, *3*(1), 160018. doi:10.1038data.2016.18 PMID:26978244

Winnie, Y., Umamaheswari, E. & Ajay. D. M. (2018). Enhancing Data Security in IoT Healthcare Services Using Fog Computing, International *Conference on Recent Trends in Advance Computing*. IEEE.

Yuan, F. & Chung, K. C. (2016). Defining Quality in Health Care and Measuring Quality in Surgery, American Society of Plastic Surgeons. *PRSJ Journal*, 1635-1644. doi:10.1097/PRS.0000000000002028

Zaadoud, B., & Chbab, Y. (2021). The Performance Measurement Frameworks in Health Care: Appropriateness Criteria for Measuring and Evaluating the Quality-of-Care Performance through a Systematic Review. *Management Issues in Healthcare System*, *7*(7), 11–34. doi:10.33844/mihs.2021.60603

Chapter 7
Analytical Approaches to QoS Analysis and Performance Modelling in Fog Computing

Yönal Kirsal

🄳 https://orcid.org/0000-0001-7031-1339

Electrical and Electronics Engineering Department, Faculty of Engineering, European University of Lefke, Lefke, Cyprus

ABSTRACT

This book chapter focuses on the analysis of quality of service (QoS) and performance modelling in the context of fog computing. The chapter proposes analytical frameworks for QoS analysis and performance modelling of fog computing systems. The chapter starts with an introduction to fog computing and the importance of QoS analysis in such systems. The next section presents a literature review of related work and different approaches to QoS analysis in fog computing. The proposed analytical frameworks are then described in detail, including their different components and assumptions. Case studies are also presented to demonstrate the application of the analytical frameworks. The case studies include a scenario of a fog computing system with a specific architecture and different performance metrics and models used for the analysis. The results and analysis of the case studies are then presented. Finally, the chapter concludes with a discussion of the key findings and contributions of the analytical frameworks.

1. INTRODUCTION

Fog computing is a distributed computing paradigm that extends cloud computing capabilities closer to the edge of the network (Das & Inuwa, 2023). It aims to address the limitations of traditional cloud computing in terms of latency, bandwidth constraints, and real-time data processing requirements (Hazra et al., 2023). Fog computing leverages resources available at the edge of the network, such as edge devices, gateways, and edge servers, to enable faster and more efficient processing of data and services (Saad, 2018). In fog computing, data is processed and analysed at the network edge, in close proximity to the devices generating the data. This proximity allows for reduced latency and improved response times,

DOI: 10.4018/978-1-6684-4466-5.ch007

making fog computing suitable for applications that require real-time or near-real-time processing (Das & Inuwa, 2023). By offloading computation and storage tasks from the cloud to the edge, fog computing also helps alleviate network congestion and reduces the amount of data that needs to be transmitted to the cloud (Songhorabadi et al., 2023).

Quality of Service (QoS) refers to the performance characteristics of a system or service that determine its ability to meet specific requirements and expectations of users. In the context of fog computing, QoS analysis involves evaluating and assessing the performance of fog computing systems to ensure that they meet the desired service levels and performance objectives (Liu et al., 2017), (Hussein et al., 2023). Therefore, QoS analysis in fog computing is crucial due to the distributed nature of the infrastructure and the need for efficient modeling and management. It involves measuring and analysing various performance metrics, such as latency, throughput, reliability, availability, and scalability (Umoh et al., 2023). QoS analysis helps in understanding the behavior and performance of fog computing systems, identifying potential bottlenecks or areas for improvement, and making informed decisions for resource allocation, task scheduling, and service provisioning (Shafik et al., 2019), (Sensi et al., 2022).

Benchmarking, simulations, and analytical modeling are essential techniques used in QoS analysis and performance evaluation in fog computing and other computing systems (Kirsal, 2013), (Rodrigues et al. 2022). These techniques help researchers and practitioners understand system behavior, evaluate performance, compare different approaches, and make informed decisions regarding system design, optimization, and resource allocation (Jamil et al. 2022). Benchmarking involves measuring and comparing the performance of computing systems against established standards or reference systems (Dar et al. 2023). It helps in assessing the capabilities of fog computing infrastructure and applications by evaluating key performance indicators (KPIs) such as response time, throughput, resource utilization, and energy efficiency. Benchmarking provides a basis for performance comparison, identifying areas for improvement, and setting performance goals for fog computing systems. However, benchmarking is expensive to apply to such systems (Kirsal, 2013). Benchmarking requires physical setups or access to existing systems, limiting the flexibility and scalability of evaluations. In addition, it involves significant hardware, software, and time investments to set up the test environment, collect measurements, and analyse the data. Moreover, benchmarking may not capture complex system dynamics or interactions, potentially oversimplifying the evaluation of fog computing systems. On the other hand, simulations involve creating computational models that mimic the behavior and characteristics of fog computing systems (Haverkort & Niemegeers, 1996), (Mahmud et al., 2022). These models are used to simulate various scenarios and evaluate system performance under different conditions. Simulations allow researchers to study the impact of different parameters, network topologies, workload patterns, and resource allocation strategies on QoS metrics. By conducting simulations, researchers can explore different "what-if" scenarios, optimize system configurations, and assess the scalability and robustness of fog computing systems objectives (Liu et al., 2015). However, simulations heavily rely on the accuracy and validity of the simulation models. Incorrect assumptions or oversimplifications can lead to inaccurate results (Margariti et al., 2020). One of the main drawbacks is the complexity and scale of simulations, which can require significant computational time, particularly for large-scale fog computing systems (Kirsal, 2018). Analytical modeling involves developing mathematical models and equations that represent the behavior of computing systems. These models capture the relationships between different system components, performance metrics, and parameters. Analytical models can provide insights into the system's performance characteristics, such as response time, throughput, and resource utilization, under varying conditions (Haverkort & Niemegeers, 1996), (Kirsal, 2013), (Shaik et al., 2022). They enable researchers to analyse system behavior, predict performance, and optimize system design and resource allocation. Analytical models can be used to derive closed-form solutions or to develop algorithms and heuristics for efficient system operation (Mas et al. 2022), (Rodrigues et al. 2022).

An analytical approach to QoS analysis in fog computing involves the development of mathematical models using analytical techniques to assess and predict the performance of fog computing systems (Vilaplana et al., 2014), (Ko & Kyung, 2022). These models and techniques enable researchers and practitioners to gain insights into the system's behavior, evaluate different design choices, optimize resource allocation, and make informed decisions to achieve desired QoS levels. By conducting QoS analysis in fog computing, organizations can ensure that their applications and services running on fog infrastructure meet performance expectations, provide a seamless user experience, and effectively utilize the available resources (Iyapparaja et al., 2022). It contributes to the efficient and reliable operation of fog computing systems and facilitates the deployment of a wide range of edge-centric applications, including the Internet of Things (IoT), real-time analytics, smart cities, industrial automation, and autonomous vehicles (Saad, 2018), (Das & Inuwa, 2023).

Analytical modeling holds a significant position in the analysis of fog computing systems (Ko & Kyung, 2022). The conventional performance model often exhibits an optimistic bias as it assumes the system being studied is immune to failures (Goswami et al., 2023). However, in real-world systems, failures are inevitable and have a significant impact on the overall system performance (Hosseini et al., 2023). State space models are commonly employed in practical systems to effectively capture and analyze complex system behavior, enabling the derivation of more accurate and realistic performance and reliability measures (Kirsal, 2013), (Wigren, 2023). A state space model is a representation of the system's configuration of states, serving as a simplified model to describe the behavior of the system under investigation (Kirsal, 2013), (Santos et al., 2021). State space models offer the capability to depict systems where transitions between states are partially independent of one another. Discrete-time Markov chains (DTMC), continuous-time Markov chains (CTMC), Markov reward models (MRM), Semi Markov process (SMP), and Markov regenerative process (MRGP) are well-known state space-based models (Ever, 2007), (Ko & Kyung, 2022), (Mas et al., 2022). DTMCs are mathematical models that represent systems with a discrete set of states and discrete time steps (Kirsal, 2013). The state transitions occur probabilistically, and the system's evolution is represented by a state transition matrix. DTMCs are particularly useful for modeling systems that exhibit discrete events or operate at discrete time intervals (Mansour et al., 2023). On the other hand, CTMCs are similar to DTMCs but model systems where the transitions between states can occur at any point in time (Machida et al., 2023). Instead of discrete time steps, CTMCs use continuous-time parameters to describe the timing and probability of state transitions. CTMCs are well-suited for modeling systems that involve continuous or random processes. Moreover, MRM extends Markov chains by incorporating rewards or costs associated with transitioning between states (Aldağ et al., 2022), (Ma et al., 2023). Rewards can represent various performance metrics, such as latency, throughput, or energy consumption. MRM allows for the evaluation of the long-term expected rewards, providing insights into the overall performance of the system (Kirsal et al., 2021). In addition, SMP is a generalization of Markov chains where the duration of time spent in each state is not fixed but follows a probability distribution (Kharchenko et al., 2022). SMP allows for more flexible modeling of systems with variable state durations, capturing real-world scenarios where transitions may not occur instantaneously. MRGP focuses on the regenerative properties of systems, where the system returns to a particular state or a set of states periodically (Kirsal, 2013). It allows for the analysis of system behavior within each regeneration cycle, providing valuable insights into performance metrics such as steady-state probabilities, mean time to failure, or availability. While each modeling technique has its own strengths and applications, MRM is often considered advantageous due to various reasons. MRM incorporates rewards or costs, enabling a comprehensive analysis of system performance and trade-offs. It provides a quantitative measure of system behavior, allowing for comparisons and optimization. MRM facilitates the evaluation of long-term expected rewards, enabling decision-making based on overall system performance. MRM allows for sensitivity analysis, where the impact of changing system parameters on rewards can be studied. Therefore, due to its many advantages, MRM is employed in this chapter. State space models, however, often encounter a challenge known as the state space explosion problem, characterized by the significant growth in size when dealing with systems comprising numerous components (Ever, 2007; Kirsal, 2013). To address the issue of the state space explosion problem, hierarchical modeling methods can be employed for the evaluation and analysis of QoS in such systems. Hierarchical modeling approaches have been applied in (Ever, 2007) and (Kirsal, 2013) to develop performability models for wireless cellular networks using MRM. MRM is also employed in this chapter to obtain QoS results in fog networks. Therefore, the proposed model in case study 1 used MRM to obtain QoS outputs. Hence, analysis of case study 1 shows that the MRM can be applied to such networks. The experimental results clearly depict that availability issues are important parameters in the performance evaluation of fog networks. Availability and performance models exhibit behavior that can be represented by CTMC. In the context of performability modeling in fog networks using MRM, availability models are employed. Then, the reward rates are derived from the performance measure associated with each state. In order to facilitate the analysis using Markov chains, it is assumed that the failure and repair times utilized in the modeling of performability, follow exponential distributions. The aforementioned QoS modeling techniques are highly effective in obtaining approximate QoS outputs. In particular, queuing theory and Quasi-Birth and Death (QBD) processes are widely employed to model systems with multiple nodes, considering both bounded and unbounded queuing capacities (Kirsal et. al., 2018; Kirsal et. al., 2021; Aldağ et al., 2022). QBD processes are a specialized category of CTMC that can be defined by a probability matrix (Kirsal et. al., 2013). These processes offer a high level of modeling flexibility while also providing efficient solution methods, making them a valuable tool in QoS analysis (Trivedi & Bobbio, 2021). On the other hand, by utilizing a Markovian framework and employing a two-dimensional representation of system states, it becomes feasible to develop an accurate and precise analytical model for QoS modeling of fog networks (Bai et al., 2020). This approach enables an effective and exact representation of the system's behavior and performance characteristics. Various methods can be employed to solve the QBD Markov model and determine the steady-state probabilities of the system. The well-known exact spectral solution (SPX) approach is widely used in the literature in order to get exact QoS results for such systems (Chakka, 1998; Ever, 2007; Kirsal, 2013; Doddapaneni, 2014; Kirsal et. al., 2018; Kirsal et. al., 2021; Aldağ et al., 2022). SPX provides different techniques for obtaining steady-state probabilities and analyzing the behavior of the system. Hence, it is employed in case studies 2 and 3. Therefore, Figures 5 and 6 show the performance results of the fog network employing MRM and SPX for case studies 1 and 2, respectively. Please note that a one-dimensional Markov chain is used in case study 1, but a two-dimensional Markov model is used in case studies 2 and 3. In addition, the two-stage open queueing tandem network is applied in case study 3 to consider dynamic transitions in the integrated fog-edge architecture in order to obtain more realistic QoS outputs. The SPX is also employed in case study 3 to get QoS measurements together with the successive over-relaxation (SOR) method. Figures 7 and 8 show the QoS output results of the fog network for case study 3, considering mobility issues in the proposed model. The SPX results are also validated by the SOR method to show the accuracy and effectiveness of both approaches.

This chapter focuses on the analytical approaches employed in fog computing to analyze and model QoS aspects and performance characteristics. It explores the challenges associated with QoS provisioning in fog computing systems and presents various analytical techniques and models that contribute to addressing these challenges. The chapter also highlights the significant contributions of these approaches, including QoS metrics and models, mobility and management strategies, performance modeling and prediction techniques, fault tolerance and reliability enhancements, and optimization techniques. By understanding and applying these analytical approaches, researchers and practitioners can effectively design, deploy, and manage fog computing architectures with improved QoS. Therefore, the main contributions and objectives of the chapter can be summarized as follows:

- Provide a comprehensive overview of analytical approaches for QoS analysis and performance modeling in fog computing.
- Present analytical models such as the Markov reward model, the exact spectral expansion solution, and successive over-relaxation approaches for QoS evaluation and estimation in fog computing architectures.
- Introduce and discuss QoS metrics and models specific to fog computing environments.
- Discuss different analytical modeling and solution approaches to maximize QoS, considering different system characteristics.
- Analyze mobility and availability enhancements in fog computing to ensure uninterrupted service delivery and improved QoS considering different case studies.
- Provide real-world case studies and examples to illustrate the practical application of analytical approaches.
- Evaluate and validate the proposed models, with different analytical modeling approaches to show the effectiveness of the proposed work.
- Highlight future research directions and emerging trends in the field of QoS analysis and performance modeling in fog computing.

The remainder of this chapter is organized as follows: Section 2 introduces the architecture of fog computing and presents related studies on modeling and performance analysis in fog networks. Section 3 describes the proposed models and the solution approaches. In addition, it presents numerical results and discussions of the case studies. Finally, section 4 provides the conclusions and future work.

2. FOG COMPUTING, ITS ARCHITECTURE, AND QOS ANALYSIS

Fog computing brings computation and storage resources closer to the edge devices and sensors where data is generated (Fantacci & Picano, 2020; Das & Inuwa, 2023). This proximity reduces the latency and bandwidth requirements for data transmission to the cloud. In addition, fog computing encompasses a diverse range of devices, including smartphones, IoT devices, routers, gateways, and edge servers (Saad, 2018). These devices have varying capabilities, processing power, and storage capacities. Fog computing supports horizontal scalability, allowing the addition of more edge devices or fog nodes to accommodate increasing workloads and data processing demands (Hussein et al., 2023). On the other hand, it can handle the mobility of devices and users by dynamically adapting to changes in the network topology and maintaining continuous connectivity. Therefore, QoS analysis plays a crucial role in fog computing (Aldağ et al., 2022), (Battula et al., 2020). It is well-suited for real-time or time-sensitive applications such as industrial automation, autonomous vehicles, healthcare monitoring, and smart cities. QoS analysis ensures that the fog computing infrastructure can meet the stringent latency and response time requirements of these applications (Songhorabadi et al., 2023). Moreover, fog computing involves the efficient allocation of computational resources, storage, and network bandwidth. QoS analysis helps in optimizing resource allocation and management strategies to achieve the desired performance levels, avoid bottlenecks, and ensure the efficient utilization of resources (Liu et al., 2015). Fog computing systems need to scale dynamically to handle varying workloads and traffic patterns. QoS analysis aids in load balancing, where tasks and data are distributed efficiently among fog nodes to prevent overload and maintain performance levels. Thus, fog computing systems must be reliable and resilient to failures or disruptions (Liu et al., 2017). QoS analysis helps in evaluating the system's fault tolerance mechanisms, redundancy strategies, and failover mechanisms to ensure continuous operation and high availability. QoS analysis enables fog computing providers to define and meet service level agreements (SLAs) with customers. It helps in assessing and guaranteeing performance metrics such as response time, reliability, and availability, meeting the agreed-upon service quality levels (D'Oro et al., 2019).

In summary, QoS analysis in fog computing is essential to ensure the efficient and reliable operation of the infrastructure, optimize resource allocation, support real-time applications, and meet service level agreements. It enables organizations to deliver high-performance, low-latency, and reliable services at the network edge, enhancing the overall user experience and enabling innovative edge-centric applications (Santos et al., 2021; Aldağ et al., 2022). The assessment of performance and availability is crucial in modeling and analyzing communication and computing systems (Pereira et al., 2020). State space models are widely employed in practical systems to accurately model and analyse complex systems, enabling the derivation of realistic QoS measures. These models provide a simplified representation of the system's configuration and are utilized as an effective tool for understanding and studying the system (Kirsal et al., 2021; Pereira et al., 2021; Pereira et al., 2022). State space models offer the capability to capture systems where transitions between states can occur partially independently from one another. This allows for a more flexible representation of the dynamics within the system, accommodating dependencies and interactions between different states (Kirsal, 2013).

QoS is crucial in fog computing due to its impact on the overall performance, reliability, and user experience of fog-based applications and services (Songhorabadi et al., 2023). Fog computing aims to provide low-latency, high-bandwidth, and efficient processing at the network edge, which makes QoS a vital consideration (Das & Inuwa, 2023). Fog computing enables real-time and near-real-time applications that require low latency and quick response times. QoS ensures that the fog infrastructure can handle the processing and communication demands of these time-sensitive applications, reducing delays and improving the user experience (Fantacci & Picano, 2020). In addition, fog computing involves data processing and analysis at the network edge, reducing the need to transmit large volumes of raw data to the cloud. QoS mechanisms ensure sufficient bandwidth and throughput to handle the data flow between fog nodes, devices, and the cloud, optimizing data transmission and resource utilization (Hussein et al., 2023). On the other hand, QoS guarantees the reliability and availability of fog computing services. Redundancy, fault tolerance, and load balancing mechanisms are implemented to ensure continuous operation even in the presence of failures or fluctuations in resource availability (Aldağ et al., 2023). QoS parameters help maintain service availability and minimize service disruptions. QoS considerations help manage resources effectively in fog computing environments. QoS parameters such as mean response time, mean queue length, throughput, and availability ensure efficient utilization of fog nodes and resources, allowing for scalability and optimal performance in fog computing (Battula et al., 2020; Mas et al. 2022). By considering and optimizing these QoS parameters, fog computing systems can deliver efficient, reliable, and high-performance services, catering to the specific requirements of diverse applications and users (Rodrigues et al. 2022). Therefore, it is necessary to develop and design appropriate analytical models in order to deliver an improved QoS in fog networks (Aldag et al., 2022).

Queueing theory plays a significant role in analyzing and optimizing the performance of fog networks (Rodrigues et al. 2022; Pereira et al., 2020). It is a mathematical framework for studying the behavior of queues or waiting lines. It involves modeling the arrival and service processes, analyzing queue lengths, waiting times, and system utilization. Queueing theory helps in understanding and optimizing the performance of systems where tasks, requests, or data packets wait in queues before being served, such as fog networks (Pereira et al., 2021; Pereira et al., 2022). In addition, MRMs extend traditional Markov models by associating rewards with different states and transitions. MRM provides a framework for analysing the performance and behavior of systems over time (Kirsal, 2013). In the context of fog networks, MRM can be used to model the availability, reliability, and performance aspects of the network, considering the different rewards associated with system states. MRM enables the evaluation of system performance measures and can help optimize resource allocation and decision-making processes. Moreover, the exact spectral expansion solution is a technique used to analyze Markov models, including Markov chains and MRM (Chakka, 1998). It involves representing the model using eigenvalues and eigenvectors and approximating the behavior of the system using a subset of dominant eigenvalues. SPX provides an efficient and accurate method for analyzing complex Markov models (Ever, 2007). In the context of fog networks, the SPX can be applied to compute steady-state probabilities, expected rewards, and other performance measures.

In order to evaluate the QoS of fault-tolerant load balancers and web servers with mobility issues in fog computing, Aldağ et al., (2022) proposed an analytical model and a solution approach. A two-stage open queueing network was employed. The proposed model is compared to existing ones, showing its effectiveness in evaluating systems with fault-tolerant load balancers, web servers, and mobility issues in fog computing. In Battula et al. (2020), the need for a resource availability model in fog computing, considering its distributed and mobile nature, was emphasized. Existing models did not account for all the characteristics of fog environments. To address this, the study proposed a generic CTMC-based model and demonstrated its applicability by integrating it with resource selection policies. On the other hand, Fantacci and Picano (2020) focused on the performance evaluation and optimization of cloud-fog-edge computing infrastructure. The authors proposed a Markov queueing system model with reneging for the cloud subsystem to consider deadline-based task departures. The paper also presented a resource allocation method to maximize social welfare while meeting QoS requirements. The proposed models and approaches were validated through analytical predictions and simulation results. In addition, Goswami et al. (2023) discussed the significance of IoT and the challenges it faces, such as handling large volumes of data, ensuring QoS and privacy, and managing diverse networking elements. Fog computing was introduced as a paradigm that brings essential networking services closer to edge devices, surpassing cloud computing in scalability, latency reduction, dependability, and security. The study focused on analyzing the fog system as a machine-repair problem, where fog servers are treated as virtual machines (VMs) that may malfunction and numerical analyses are conducted for system evaluation. The complexity of fog computing infrastructure and the need for efficient resource management were highlighted in Iyapparaja et al. (2022). It emphasized the role of fog computing in processing requests locally with nearby resources to minimize latency. The proposed approach, called QTCS (Queuing Theory-Based Cuckoo Search), aimed to optimize resource allocation and improve QoS in fog services. Mas et al. (2022) highlighted the challenge of appropriately sizing components in resource-constrained scenarios where a good QoS was necessary. The proposed model introduced a fog-computing modeling framework based on queuing theory to simulate and adjust system parameters. The results demonstrated the effectiveness of the model in designing optimal fog architectures, identifying bottlenecks, and improving overall performance. Various analytical models were proposed and presented in Pereira et al. 2020, Pereira et al. 2021 and Pereira et al. 2022 for the availability and performance evaluation of fog-edge networks, respectively. However, the existing studies mentioned above lack comprehensive modeling and a solution approach for evaluating QoS in fog computing, particularly in terms of analytical models. These studies have not provided a comprehensive framework or methodology that encompasses all the necessary aspects for accurate QoS evaluation in fog computing environments. Therefore, there is a need for further research and development in this area to propose robust analytical models that can effectively assess and optimize the QoS performance of fog computing systems. Thus, this is the main focus and contribution of this chapter.

Overall, MRM, SPX, and SOR concepts are interconnected and can be used together to analyze and optimize the performance of fog networks. Queueing theory provides a foundation for modeling and understanding queuing behavior, while MRMs enable the evaluation of performance measures in a time-dependent manner. The SPX offers an efficient method to analyze and solve complex Markov models, including those used in fog network performance analysis. By leveraging these techniques, researchers and practitioners can gain insights into the behavior of fog networks, identify performance bottlenecks, and optimize the system to meet desired QoS requirements. Therefore, MRM, SPX, and SOR methods are presented in the following sections.

2.1. Markov Reward Model

A Markov reward model (MRM) is a mathematical framework used to analyse and evaluate the performance and behavior of systems that exhibit stochastic (probabilistic) behavior over time (Trivedi et al., 2002). It combines elements of Markov chains and rewards to model and quantify the expected rewards or costs associated with different states and transitions within a system. In a MRM, a system is represented as a set of states, and transitions between states occur probabilistically according to a set of transition probabilities. Each state is associated with a reward or cost value that represents the desirability or undesirability of being in that state. The rewards can be used to measure performance metrics such as system throughput, mean response time, or mean queue length. State space, transition probabilities, rewards, reward rates, and Markov property are the key components of a MRM (Kirsal, 2013). State space is the set of possible states that the system can occupy. Each state represents a configuration or condition of the system at a given point in time. Transition probabilities are the probabilities associated with transitioning from one state to another. These probabilities capture the stochastic behavior of the system and can be determined through observation, measurement, or domain knowledge. Each state is assigned a reward value, which represents the desirability or undesirability of being in that state. Rewards can be positive, indicating desirable states, or negative, indicating undesirable states or costs. On the other hand, the reward rates capture the long-term expected rewards or costs associated with each state. They represent the average rewards obtained per unit of time spent in a particular state. The Markov property states that the future behavior of the system depends only on the current state and is independent of the past history, given the current state. This property allows the use of transition probabilities to analyze the system's behavior. MRMs can be analyzed using various techniques, such as Markov reward processes or Markov decision processes. These techniques allow for the computation of performance metrics, such as the expected total reward or cost, steady-state probabilities, or optimal policies for decision-making. Overall, a MRM is a powerful tool for analyzing and quantifying the expected rewards or costs associated with different states and transitions within a system exhibiting stochastic behavior over time (Trivedi et al., 2003).

2.2. The Spectral Expansion Solution

The spectral expansion solution is a technique used to solve partial differential equations (PDEs) by representing the solution as a sum of Eigen-functions of a linear operator associated with the PDE. The method involves expanding the solution into a series of basic functions that satisfy the PDE and determining the coefficients of the basic functions by applying the initial or boundary conditions (Chakka, 1998). The basic idea behind the spectral expansion solution is to transform the PDE into an eigenvalue problem for a linear operator, such as a Laplacian or a differential operator. The Eigen-functions of the operator form a complete set of basic functions that can be used to represent the solution of the PDE. The spectral expansion solution has several advantages over other numerical methods for solving PDEs, such as finite difference or finite element methods. One of the main advantages is that it can provide an exact or very accurate solution, depending on the choice of basic functions and the truncation of the series. Another advantage is that the spectral expansion solution can be very efficient for PDEs with periodic or symmetric boundary conditions, as the basis functions can be chosen to match the boundary conditions. However, the spectral expansion solution also has some limitations (Kirsal, 2013), (Kirsal, 2018). One of the main limitations is that it can be computationally expensive, as the number of basic functions needed to accurately represent the solution may be very large. Another limitation is that it may not be well-suited for PDEs with irregular or complex geometries, as it can be difficult to choose a set of basic functions that match the geometry. Applications of the spectral expansion solution include solving PDEs in fluid dynamics, electromagnetism, heat transfer, and quantum mechanics. It has also been used in image and signal processing, where PDEs are used to model noise reduction, image restoration, and feature detection (Kirsal et al., 2021).

2.3. The Solution of a System of Linear Equations

The solution of a system of linear equations refers to finding the values of the variables that satisfy all the equations simultaneously. There are different methods to solve such systems, including:

Gaussian Elimination: This method involves performing row operations on the augmented matrix of the system to reduce it to row-echelon form or reduced row-echelon form. Once in this form, the solution can be obtained by back-substitution. Gaussian elimination is a straightforward and widely used method for solving systems of linear equations (Higham et al., 2011).

Matrix Inversion: If the system can be represented in matrix form as $Ax = b$, where A is the coefficient matrix, x is the vector of variables, and b is the constant vector, then the solution can be obtained by computing the inverse of matrix A (if it exists) and multiplying it with vector b: $x = A^{-1} * b$. However, matrix inversion can be computationally expensive for large systems (Croz et al., 1992).

LU Decomposition: LU decomposition factors the coefficient matrix A into the product of lower (L) and upper (U) triangular matrices. By solving two simpler triangular systems, $L_y = b$ and $U_x = y$, the solution to the original system can be obtained. LU decomposition can be more efficient than direct matrix inversion, especially when solving multiple systems with the same coefficient matrix (Bartels & Golub, 1969).

Iterative Methods: Iterative methods are used when the system is large and sparse, and direct methods may be computationally expensive or impractical. Examples of iterative methods include the Jacobi method, Gauss-Seidel method, and successive over-relaxation (SOR) method. These methods involve iteratively updating the solution until convergence is reached (Evans,1984).

Eigenvalue Decomposition: For certain special cases, such as symmetric positive definite matrices, the eigenvalue decomposition (also known as spectral decomposition) can be used to solve the system. This involves diagonalizing the matrix and using the eigenvectors and eigenvalues to obtain the solution (Hall et al., 2002).

The choice of method depends on the specific characteristics of the system, such as the size, sparsity, and properties of the coefficient matrix. Additionally, numerical stability and computational efficiency are important considerations when selecting a method.

3. ANALYTICAL FRAMEWORK FOR QOS ANALYSIS IN FOG COMPUTING

The proposed analytical framework for QoS analysis in fog computing provides a structured approach to assess and evaluate the QoS aspects of fog computing systems. It aims to analyze the performance characteristics, and optimization strategies within fog computing environments. The framework combines mathematical modeling, performance metrics, and analysis techniques to gain insights into system behavior and make informed decisions. The general architecture of the fog network considered in this chapter is shown in Figure 1.

The concept of fog network computing aims to enhance connectivity between the server core and remote application users on both ends. This architecture enables efficient mobility support and reduces the need for high bandwidth usage by aggregating tasks at specific points instead of routing them directly through cloud channels. As a result, this fog network offers faster processing, supports mobility with location awareness, and achieves minimal latency. Consequently, there has been increased interest in designing and modeling cloud-fog-edge computing architectures to improve the QoS provided. Thus, the design and modeling of such an architecture are necessary for improving QoS. Thus, in this chapter, the analytical models and the solution approaches are presented and employed to obtain better QoS for such environments in terms of performance metrics.

3.1. Case Study on Application of the MRM for the Proposed Fog Network

The modeling approach only considers the fog network in the proposed architecture for QoS evaluation. A fog network considers F identical nodes with a queuing capacity of QC_F. The notations used in the chapter for the proposed models and all case studies are given in Table 1. The failure and repair behaviors of the fog nodes are also taken into account in order to produce more realistic results. However, stand-alone solution approaches cannot be applicable to this type of formation. Thus, MRM is applied to solve this proposed network in case study 1.

Figure 1. The fog network architecture

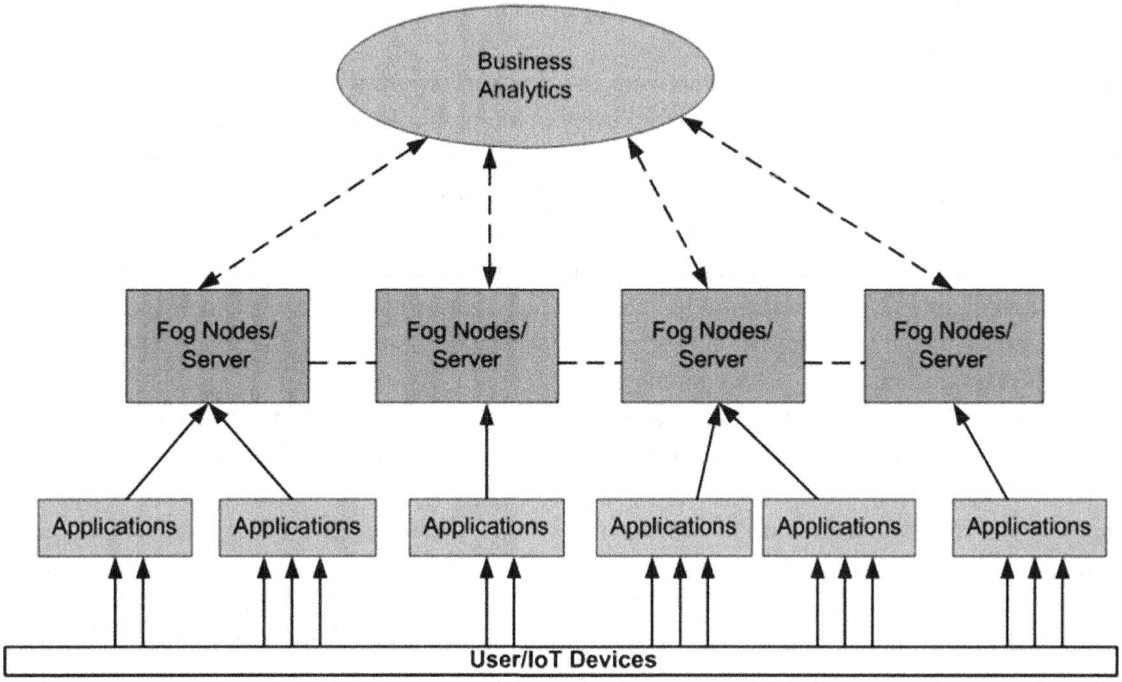

Table 1. Summary of symbols

Symbol	Definition
F	Number of nodes in the fog network
E	Number of nodes in the edge network
QC_F	Queue size of the fog network
QC_E	Queue size of the edge network
L_F	System capacity of the fog network LF = F+ QC_F
L_E	System capacity of the fog network LE = E+ QC_E
λ_F	The mean arrival rate of tasks in the fog network
λ_E	The mean arrival rate of tasks in the edge network
μ_F	The mean service rate of tasks in the fog network
μ_E	The mean service rate of tasks in the edge network
ρ	Traffic intensity (λ_F/μ_F)
θ_F	The mobility rate in a fog network
θ_E	The mobility rate in an edge network
ξ_F	The failure rate of fog nodes
η_F	The repair rate of fog nodes

The proposed system can accommodate a maximum number of tasks equal to the sum of the tasks allocated to the nodes in a fully operational state and the capacity of the task queue. Thus, the maximum number of tasks in the fog network can be written as L_F where $L_F = F + QC_F$. Figure 2 provides the model considered for only the fog network of the queuing system, which is utilized to represent and assess the QoS evaluation of the fog network.

Incoming tasks are received by the network in a Poisson stream and are then added to the queue. The arrival rates represent tasks coming from users in the proposed network. The average arrival rate can be denoted as λ_F. Tasks can be allocated to any available or idle nodes in the fog network. However, if a node is experiencing a failure or is already occupied, incoming tasks are placed into a queue. In addition, μ_F is the service rate of the fog nodes in the proposed model. The mean service rate is also exponentially distributed. On the other hand, θ_F is assumed to be the mobility rate in the network. In the proposed model, mobility rate refers to the rates at which mobile users move between different queues or service nodes within the network. In other words, this rate is commonly referred to as the transition rate, and it plays a crucial role in determining the

behavior and performance of the proposed architecture. On the other hand, ξ_F is the failure rate of fog nodes. If failures occur in a fog node, nodes are repaired at a mean repair rate of η_F. The concurrent execution of repairs may be limited, as indicated by the presence of R repairmen (where $R \leq F$), each capable of working on a maximum of one repair at a time. Consequently, an inoperative node period encompasses the potential wait time for a repairman. If there are tasks awaiting service, no functional node can remain idle, and if there are failed nodes requiring repair, no repairman can remain idle. All random variables related to inter-arrival times, service times, channel operability, and repair durations are independent of one another. Figure 3 illustrates the patterns of node failures and repairs within F nodes in the fog network. The analysis assumes the presence of a single repair facility responsible for all the nodes. However, the models presented can be readily expanded to accommodate systems with multiple repair facilities.

Hence, equation (1) can be derived and used by considering q_i as the steady-state probabilities, representing the probability of having i operative nodes. Since each operative state is attained through either node failures or repairs, the equation is obtained.

Figure 2. The model considered for the fog network with failure and repairs

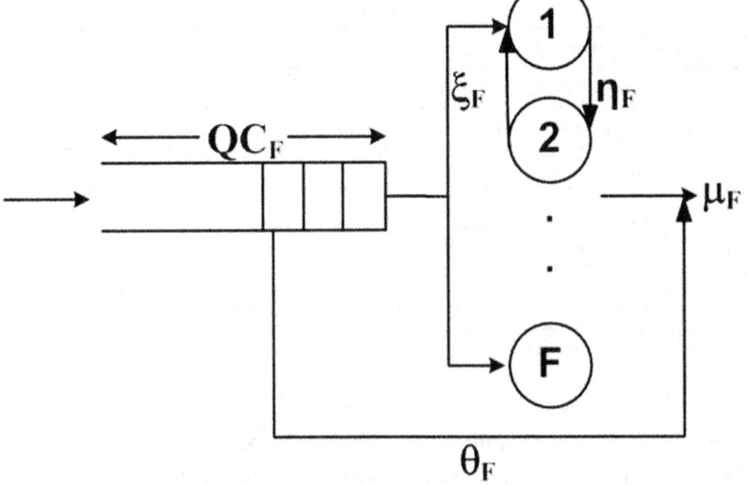

Figure 3. The state transition diagram for the availability model of the system

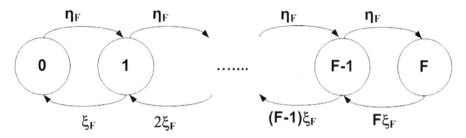

$$q_i = \binom{F}{i}\left(\frac{\eta_F}{\xi_F + \eta_F}\right)^i \left(\frac{\xi_F}{\xi_F + \eta_F}\right)^{F-i}, \; i = 0,1,...,F \tag{1}$$

Alternatively, the state i (where i = 0, 1, 2, ..., L_F) can be defined as the number of tasks present in the fog network at time t. Figure 4 provides the state transition diagram for the performance model of the system (Kirsal, 2013).

Under the assumption of a steady-state system, the state probabilities p_i can be derived (Kirsal, 2013). Equation (2) presents the corresponding values of these probabilities, where $\rho = \lambda_F/\mu_F$

$$p_i = \begin{cases} \dfrac{\rho^i}{i!} p_0, \; 0 \le i \le F \\[2em] \dfrac{\dfrac{\rho^F}{F!}\lambda^{i-F} p_0}{\prod_{j=F+1}^{i}\left[F\mu_F + (j-F)\theta_F\right]}, \; F \le i \le F + QC_F \end{cases} \tag{2}$$

In equation (2), p_i represents the probability of having i tasks in the fog network. Specifically, p_0 can be defined in equation (3) in the following manner:

$$p_0 = \left[\sum_{i=0}^{F}\frac{\rho^i}{i!} + \sum_{i=F+1}^{F+QC_F}\frac{\dfrac{\rho^F}{F!}\lambda^{i-F}}{\prod_{j=F+1}^{i}\left[F\mu_F + (j-F)\theta_F\right]}\right]^{-1} \tag{3}$$

Figure 4. The state transition diagram for the performance model of the system

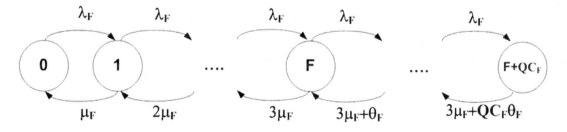

133

The calculation of the average number of tasks in the system's mean queue length (MQL) can be determined by evaluating the expression $MQL = \sum_{i=0}^{F+QC_F} iP_i$ that gives

$$MQL = \left[\sum_{i=0}^{F} i\frac{\rho^i}{i!} + \sum_{i=F+1}^{F+QC_F} \frac{i\frac{\rho^F}{F!}\lambda^{i-F}}{\prod_{j=F+1}^{i}\left[F\mu_F + \left(j-F\right)\theta_F\right]} \right] P_0 \tag{4}$$

By considering that the time between failures and repair times follow exponential distributions, Equation (4) provides the MQL assuming all tasks are operative. However, to account for the fact that only i nodes are operative at any given time, the MQL can now be denoted as MQL_i, where i represents the number of operative nodes. To obtain the overall MQL_F, a Markov reward model can be employed as follows: $MQL_F = \sum_{i=0}^{F} q_i MQL_i$. Similarly, the various QoS outputs can be easily obtained. The results of case study 1 are represented together with the results of case study 2 in the next section to show the capability of both solution approaches.

3.2 Case Study on Application of the Exact Spectral Expansion for the Proposed Fog Network

On the other hand, the exact spectral expansion approach can also be used to resolve case study 1 in such a fog environment. Assume that, at time t, the state of the system can be characterized by two random variables: I(t) and J(t), which represent the node's configuration (also referred to as the operative state of the nodes in the fog network) and the number of tasks present, respectively. The node configuration, reflected by the range of values of I(t), indicates the availability of nodes in the system.

Consider a scenario where there are F+1 possible node configurations denoted by the values I(t) = 0, 1, ..., F. These F+1 configurations encompass the feasible operative states within the model. To ensure the irreducibility of the Markov process I(t), t ≥ 0, the model assumptions are imposed. In this context, J(t) (where J(t) ≤ L_F) represents the total number of tasks in the system at time t, including those being serviced. The system can be effectively modelled by Z = {[I(t), J(t)]; t ≥ 0}, which constitutes an irreducible Markov process on a lattice strip. This process, known as a QBD process, defines the state space as {0, 1, ..., F} x {0, 1, ..., L_F}. The operative states, representing the availability model, can be depicted horizontally, while the number of tasks can be represented vertically in a lattice strip, forming the performance model.

The exact spectral expansion solution considers three matrices as A, B, and C for the solution. In this context, matrix A represents the instantaneous transition rates from state (i, j) to state (k, j) in model Z, with zeros on the main diagonal. These transitions exclusively involve lateral movements within the model. Matrices B and C, on the other hand, correspond to the transition matrices for one-step upward and one-step downward transitions, respectively. Notably, the transition rate matrices are independent of j when j is greater than or equal to the threshold value M, where M is an integer. However, when considering the proposed fog network, the transition rate matrices invariably depend on the value of j.

Further details of the exact spectral expansion solution can be found in (Ever, 2007; Kirsal, 2013; Chakka, 1998). The process Z evolves through instantaneous transitions as follows:

A_j (i, k): The transition rate A_j (i, k) corresponds to the purely lateral transition from the state (i, j) to the state (k, j) within the model, where (i=0, 1, …, F; k=0, 1, …, F; i ≠ k; j=0, 1, …, L_F), This transition is triggered by a change in the operative state of the nodes, such as a failure followed by a repair.

B_j(i, k): The transition rate B_j(i, k) corresponds to the one-step upward transition from the state (i, j) to the state (k, j+1) within the model, where i=0, 1, …, F; k=0, 1, …, F; i ≠ k; j=0, 1, …, L_F. This transition is triggered by the arrival of tasks from users in the fog network.

C_j(i, k): The transition rate C_j(i, k) represents the one-step downward transition from the state (i, j) to the state (k, j-1) within the model, where i=0, 1, …, F; k=0, 1, …, F; i ≠ k; j=0, 1, …, L_F. This transition occurs when the serviced tasks depart from the system. Therefore, matrix A's elements depend on the parameters F, ξ_F, and η_F. In a system with F nodes, the transition matrices have dimensions of (F+1)×(F+1). The state transition matrices, namely A, A_j, B, and B_j, can be expressed as follows:

$$A = A_j = \begin{bmatrix} 0 & \eta_F & 0 & 0 & 0 & 0 & 0 & 0 \\ \xi_F & 0 & \eta_F & 0 & 0 & 0 & 0 & 0 \\ 0 & 2\xi_F & 0 & \eta_F & 0 & 0 & 0 & 0 \\ 0 & 0 & 3\xi_F & 0 & \ddots & 0 & 0 & 0 \\ 0 & 0 & 0 & \ddots & 0 & \eta_F & 0 & 0 \\ 0 & 0 & 0 & 0 & (F-2)\xi_F & 0 & \eta_F & 0 \\ 0 & 0 & 0 & 0 & 0 & (F-1)\xi_F & 0 & \eta_F \\ 0 & 0 & 0 & 0 & 0 & 0 & F\xi_F & 0 \end{bmatrix}$$

$$B = B_j = \begin{bmatrix} \lambda_F & 0 & 0 & 0 & 0 & 0 & 0 & 0 \\ 0 & \lambda_F & 0 & 0 & 0 & 0 & 0 & 0 \\ 0 & 0 & \lambda_F & 0 & 0 & 0 & 0 & 0 \\ 0 & 0 & 0 & \ddots & 0 & 0 & 0 & 0 \\ 0 & 0 & 0 & 0 & \lambda_F & 0 & 0 & 0 \\ 0 & 0 & 0 & 0 & 0 & \lambda_F & 0 & 0 \\ 0 & 0 & 0 & 0 & 0 & 0 & \lambda_F & 0 \\ 0 & 0 & 0 & 0 & 0 & 0 & 0 & \lambda_F \end{bmatrix}$$

The elements of matrices C and C_j are influenced by the parameters F, μ_F, and θ_F. As illustrated in Figure 4 above, it is evident that the C matrix is dependent on the number of tasks for j=0, 1, …, L_F.

Consequently, the threshold value M is set as M= L_F. Each task is assigned a node in scenarios where the number of tasks in the system is lower than the number of available nodes. Hence, the downward transition rate is determined as the minimum value between the number of tasks and the number of available nodes. Alternatively, in situations where the number of tasks exceeds the available nodes in the system, all of the available nodes are allocated to incoming tasks. The matrix C, along with the C_j matrices are defined as follows to accommodate the two distinct regions: Top of FormBottom of Form

$$
C = \begin{bmatrix}
0 & 0 & 0 & 0 & 0 & 0 \\
0 & \mu_F + QC_F\theta_F & 0 & 0 & 0 & 0 \\
0 & 0 & 2\mu_F + QC_F\theta_F & 0 & 0 & 0 \\
0 & 0 & 0 & \ddots & 0 & 0 \\
0 & 0 & 0 & 0 & (F-1)\mu_F + QC_F\theta_F & 0 \\
0 & 0 & 0 & 0 & 0 & F\mu_F + QC_F\theta_F
\end{bmatrix}
$$

$$
C_j = \begin{bmatrix}
0 & 0 & 0 & 0 & 0 & 0 \\
0 & \mu_F + (j-F)\theta_F & 0 & 0 & 0 & 0 \\
0 & 0 & 2\mu_F + (j-F)\theta_F & 0 & 0 & 0 \\
0 & 0 & 0 & \ddots & 0 & 0 \\
0 & 0 & 0 & 0 & (F-1)\mu_F + (j-F)\theta_F & 0 \\
0 & 0 & 0 & 0 & 0 & F\mu_F + (j-F)\theta_F
\end{bmatrix} \text{ for } j > F
$$

$$
C = \begin{bmatrix}
0 & 0 & 0 & 0 & 0 & 0 \\
0 & \mu_F & 0 & 0 & 0 & 0 \\
0 & 0 & 2\mu_F & 0 & 0 & 0 \\
0 & 0 & 0 & \ddots & 0 & 0 \\
0 & 0 & 0 & 0 & (F-1)\mu_F & 0 \\
0 & 0 & 0 & 0 & 0 & F\mu_F
\end{bmatrix} \text{ for } j \le F
$$

The system can be solved to determine the steady-state probabilities, $P_{i,j}$, by employing the steady-state solution outlined in the subsequent section.

3.3 The Steady-State Solution

The solution is provided for a bounded queue condition, where $F \le L_F$. The spectral expansion solution is applied, although the balance equations specified for $(M-1) \le j \le (L_F - 2)$ are excluded due to the threshold value being defined as M= L_F. By following the spectral expansion solution, the steady-state probabilities of the considered system can be represented as:

$$
P_{i,j} = \lim_{t \to \infty} P(I(t) = i, J(t) = j); 0 \le i << L_F + 1, 0 \le j << L_F + 1
$$

Specific diagonal matrices can be defined with dimensions of (L_F+1) x (L_F+1), as follows:

$$D_j^A(i,i)\sum_{k=0}^{L_F}A_j(i,k); \ D^A(i,i)\sum_{k=0}^{L_F}A(i,k);$$

$$D_j^B(i,i)\sum_{k=0}^{L_F}B_j(i,k); \ D^B(i,i)\sum_{k=0}^{L_F}B(i,k);$$

$$D_j^C(i,i)\sum_{k=0}^{L_F}C_j(i,k); \ D^C(i,i)\sum_{k=0}^{L_F}C(i,k);$$

and $Q_0=B$, $Q_1=A-D^A-D^B-D^C$, $Q_2=C$. Hence, the state probabilities in a row, represented by the row vectors $\mathbf{v}_j$, can be defined as $\mathbf{v}_j = (p_{0,j}, p_{1,j}, \dots, p_{N,j})$; $j=0,1,2\dots,L_F$. The steady-state balance equations can now be written as:

$$v_0\left[D_0^A + D_0^B\right] = v_0 A_0 + v_1 C_1 \tag{5}$$

$$v_j\left[D_j^A + D_j^B + D_j^C\right] = v_{j-1} B_{j-1} + v_j A_j + v_{j+1} C_{j+1}; 1 \le j \le M-1 \tag{6}$$

$$v_j\left[D^A + D^B + D^C\right] = v_{j-1} B + v_j A + v_{j+1} C; M \le j \le L_F \tag{7}$$

$$v_L\left[D^A + D^C\right] = v_{L-1} B + v_L A \tag{8}$$

Thus, the normalizing equation is defined as: $\sum_{j=0}^{L} v_j e = \sum_{j=0}^{L_F}\sum_{i=0}^{L_F} P_{i,j} = 1.0$. The characteristic matrix polynomials that can be represented as: $Q(\lambda) = Q_0 + Q_1\lambda + Q_2\lambda^2$, $\bar{Q}(\beta) = Q_2 + Q_1\beta + Q_0\beta^2$ where $\psi Q(\lambda) = 0$, $|Q(\lambda)| = 0$, $\phi\bar{Q}(\beta) = 0$; $|\bar{Q}(\beta)| = 0$. λ and ψ are eigenvalues and left-eigenvectors of $Q(\lambda)$, while β and φ are eigenvalues and left-eigenvectors of $|\bar{Q}(\beta)|$. It should be noted that ψ and φ are row vectors. $\psi = \psi_0, \psi_1, \dots, \psi_N$, $\lambda = \lambda_0, \lambda_1, \dots, \lambda_N$, $\phi = \phi_0, \phi_1, \dots, \phi_N$, $\beta = \beta_0, \beta_1, \dots, \beta_N$., Furthermore, $v_j = \sum_{k=0}^{N}\left(a_k\psi_k\lambda_k^{j-M+1} + b_k\phi_k\beta_k^{L-j}\right)$, $M-1 \le j \le L_F$ and in the state probability form,

$$P_{i,j} = \sum_{k=0}^{F}\left(a_k\psi_k\lambda_k^{j-M+1} + b_k\phi_k\beta_k^{L-j}\right), \ M-1 \le j \le L_F \tag{9}$$

Among the eigenvalues, λ_k ($k=0,1,\dots,F$) and β_k ($k=0,1,\dots,F$) there are $F+1$ eigenvalues each that lie strictly within the unit circle. Additionally, the constants a_k and b_k ($k=0,1,\dots,F$) can take on arbitrary values, whether scalar or complex-conjugate. The remaining v_j vectors, along with the values of a_k and b_k can be determined through the methodology outlined in (Chakka, 1998). Based on the steady-state probabilities $P_{i,j}$, various QoS outputs such as mean queue length (MQL_F), throughput ($THRP_F$), and mean response time (MRT_F) of the fog network can be computed as follows:

$$MQL_F = \sum_{j=0}^{L_F} j \sum_{i=0}^{F} P_{i,j} \tag{10}$$

$$THRP_F = \sum_{i=0}^{F} \mu_i \sum_{j=0}^{L_F} P_{i,j} \tag{11}$$

$$MRT_F = \frac{MQL_F}{THRP_F} \tag{12}$$

3.4 Numerical Results and Discussions of Case Studies 1 and 2

This section presents the numerical results of the QoS evaluation for a fog network employing both the exact spectral expansion solution (SPX) and the MRM approach. The proposed model and evaluation take into account both mobility and availability issues. The mean queue length and throughput results of case studies 1 and 2 are presented in Figures 5 and 6, respectively. The MRM and SPX model results are presented in both figures in order to show the capability and effectiveness of the proposed work. The analysis considers assumptions and parameters from the related literature and various other models (Fantacci & Picano, 2020), (Kirsal, 2013), (Kirsal et al., 2021), (Pereira et al., 2020), (Pereira et al., 2021), (Pereira et al., 2022) unless specified otherwise. The following values were used: $F = 10$ (number of nodes in the fog network), $L_F = 100$ (maximum number of tasks in the fog network), $Q_F = 90$ (capacity of the fog queue), $\mu_F = 10$ tasks/sec (service rate of the fog nodes), $\eta_F = 0.5$ (repair rate of the fog nodes), $\theta_F = 0.4$ (mobility rate of the fog nodes). The arrival rate per user, λ_F, varies from 10 tasks per second. Additionally, some parameters were varied during the analysis. For example, the failure rate, ξ_F varied between 0.01 and 0.05.

Figures 5 and 6 show the MQL and THRP results as a function of the mean arrival rate in the fog network for SPX and MRM approaches, respectively. As clearly seen, failure rates and mobility affect system performance significantly. MQL results decrease as the failure rate increases, as shown in Figure 5. Since the fog nodes fail frequently, the tasks cannot be served by the system. Consequently, it is observed that the system reaches its capacity rapidly, resulting in a corresponding increase in the MQL. Similar observations and discussions can be applied to the THRP depicted in Figure 6, which represents a comparable system. The insights and findings discussed earlier in this paper are applicable and provide valuable understanding in interpreting and analyzing these results.

The results show that the comparison between the SPX and MRM approaches reveals that the MRM approach provides accurate approximations, as supported by the SPX solution. The discrepancy between these two approaches is found to be less than 1% for both experiments. This indicates the effectiveness and reliability of both approaches in accurately estimating fog network performance.

3.5 Case Study on the Exact Spectral Expansion for the Integrated Edge-Fog Architecture

In this case study, the proposed network is different from the previous cases. In order to find more realistic outputs, the integrated edge-fog architecture is taken into account for QoS analysis. Using individual networks in isolation or neglecting the relationship between nearest-neighbour transitions may not yield realistic QoS results for fog computing systems. To overcome this limitation, a network of queues can

Figure 5. Mean queue length results of fog network with different failures rates

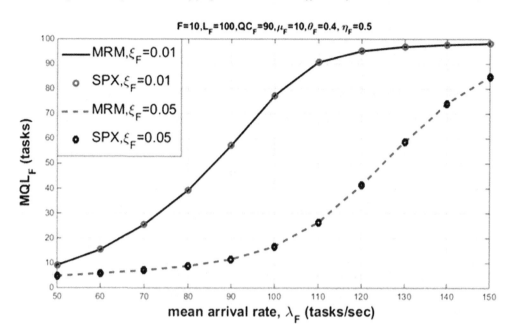

Figure 6. Throughput results of fog network with different failures rates

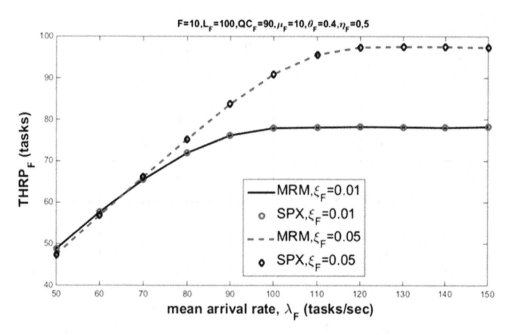

be employed to achieve more accurate QoS outcomes instead of relying on a product-form solution or considering only the fog network. Therefore, an integrated edge-fog network is considered, which consists of a two-stage open queuing tandem network, as depicted in Figure 7. The proposed queuing model, illustrated in Figure 7, is specifically designed for analysing the QoS of an integrated edge-fog

Figure 7. The proposed model considered for the integrated edge-fog architecture

Edge-Fog System

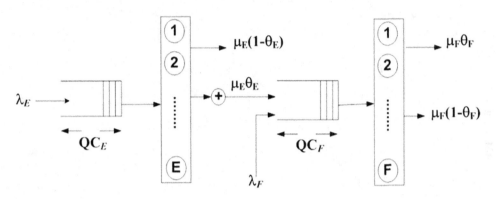

computing system. Furthermore, when evaluating system performance in an integrated model, it is essential to account for mobility-related factors and incorporate realistic behaviors that are characteristic of such environments.

In other words, the two-stage open queuing model serves as a mathematical tool for analysing and optimizing queuing systems. Consequently, the depicted model in Figure 7 proves valuable in scenarios where the queuing process involves two separate networks, such as an edge network and a fog network region. The two-stage open queuing model comprises the edge network in the first stage and the fog network in the second stage. Upon arrival at the edge network, users are served if all nodes are accessible; otherwise, they join a queue until a node becomes available. Additionally, mobile users have the option to transition to the fog network, either without receiving service or after receiving service. It should be noted that the proposed model assumes a Poisson arrival process for users at the edge network and an exponential distribution for service times. Similarly, in the fog network stage, users are served by one or more available nodes, and mobile users can potentially move to other existing networks without receiving service or after receiving service. The edge network consists of E nodes, while the fog network has F nodes in the proposed edge-fog computing architecture. The edge network's queue capacity is denoted as QC_E, and the fog network's queue capacity is denoted as QC_F as shown in Figure 7. When a task requests service and finds all nodes occupied within a network, it will join the corresponding network's queue or hand over to available nodes in a different network. Once an idle node becomes available, a task from the queue will be selected for service based on the first-come-first-serve (FCFS) principle. Additionally, after completing service at a node, the task may move to another network for further processing. Top of FormBottom of Form Each node follows an independent and identically distributed exponential service time distribution, with mean values of $1/\mu_E$ and $1/\mu_F$ for the edge and fog networks, respectively. The arrival rates for the edge and fog networks are represented as λ_E and λ_F, respectively. The arrival process in the edge and fog networks is modelled as a Poisson process. The mobility rates, denoted as θ_E and θ_F, represent the rates at which mobile users transition between different queues or service nodes within the network. These rates, also known as transition rates, are fundamental in determining the behavior and performance of the proposed architecture. The transition probability, θ_E, represents the probability that a mobile user in the edge network will move to the fog network in the next time interval. Conversely, the mobile user can either move to a different network or complete the service at a rate of $(1-\theta_E)$, as depicted in Figure 7. Consequently, the output of the edge network, denoted as $\mu_E\theta_E$, serves as the input for the fog network. Similarly, in the fog network, users may be routed to the cloud network with a probability of θ_F, or they may leave the system due to mobility with a probability of $(1\text{-}\theta_F)$. Likewise, the output of the fog network, labelled $\mu_F\theta_F$, serves the users in the fog network. Therefore, the proposed model facilitates the creation of dynamic models that effectively capture the system's dynamic behavior, taking into account real-world workload patterns and resource characteristics.

Thus, Figure 8 illustrates the transitions of inter-arrival, service, and mobility rates. The depicted model can be described using a two-dimensional CTMC. The number of tasks within the edge network is represented by the variable "x," while the number of tasks present in the fog network is denoted by the variable "y." Therefore, the exact spectral expansion solution approach can also be applied in a two-stage open queuing model. Thus, the transition matrices of the proposed edge-fog network are of size $(L_E +1)$ x $(L_F +1)$. As explained in case study 2, the transition matrices can be obtained as follows:

$$A = A_j = \begin{bmatrix} 0 & \lambda_E & 0 & 0 & 0 & 0 & 0 & 0 \\ \mu_E & 0 & \lambda_E & 0 & 0 & 0 & 0 & 0 \\ 0 & 2\mu_E & 0 & \lambda_E & 0 & 0 & 0 & 0 \\ 0 & 0 & 3\mu_E & 0 & \ddots & 0 & 0 & 0 \\ 0 & 0 & 0 & \ddots & 0 & \lambda_E & 0 & 0 \\ 0 & 0 & 0 & 0 & E\mu_E & 0 & \lambda_E & 0 \\ 0 & 0 & 0 & 0 & 0 & E\mu_E\left(1-\theta_E\right)+\mu_E\left(1-\theta_E\right) & 0 & \lambda_E \\ 0 & 0 & 0 & 0 & 0 & 0 & E\mu_E\left(1-\theta_E\right)+QC_E\mu_E\left(1-\theta_E\right) & 0 \end{bmatrix}$$

$$B = B_j = \begin{bmatrix} \lambda_F & 0 & 0 & 0 & 0 & 0 & 0 & 0 \\ \mu_E\theta_E & \lambda_F & 0 & 0 & 0 & 0 & 0 & 0 \\ 0 & \ddots & \lambda_F & 0 & 0 & 0 & 0 & 0 \\ 0 & 0 & \ddots & \lambda_F & 0 & 0 & 0 & 0 \\ 0 & 0 & 0 & E\mu_E\theta_E+\mu_E\theta_E & \ddots & 0 & 0 & 0 \\ 0 & 0 & 0 & 0 & \ddots & \lambda_F & 0 & 0 \\ 0 & 0 & 0 & 0 & 0 & \ddots & \lambda_F & 0 \\ 0 & 0 & 0 & 0 & 0 & 0 & E\mu_E\theta_E+QC_E\mu_E\theta_E & \lambda_F \end{bmatrix}$$

$$C = \begin{bmatrix} 0 & F\mu_F\theta_F+QC_F\mu_F\theta_F & 0 & 0 & 0 & 0 \\ 0 & F\mu_F(1-\theta_F)+QC_F\mu_F(1-\theta_F) & F\mu_F\theta_F+QC_F\mu_F\theta_F & 0 & 0 & 0 \\ 0 & 0 & \ddots & \ddots & 0 & 0 \\ 0 & 0 & 0 & \ddots & F\mu_F\theta_F+QC_F\mu_F\theta_F & 0 \\ 0 & 0 & 0 & 0 & \ddots & F\mu_F\theta_F+QC_F\mu_F\theta_F \\ 0 & 0 & 0 & 0 & 0 & F\mu_F(1-\theta_F)+QC_F\mu_F(1-\theta_F) \end{bmatrix}$$

$$C_j = \begin{bmatrix} \mu_F & \mu_F\theta_F & 0 & 0 & 0 & 0 \\ 0 & 2\mu_F & 2\mu_F\theta_F & 0 & 0 & 0 \\ 0 & 0 & 3\mu_F & \ddots & 0 & 0 \\ 0 & 0 & 0 & \ddots & \left(F-1\right)\mu_F\theta_F & 0 \\ 0 & 0 & 0 & 0 & \left(F-1\right)\mu_F & F\mu_F\theta_F \\ 0 & 0 & 0 & 0 & 0 & F\mu_F \end{bmatrix} \text{for } j \leq F$$

Figure 8. The state transition diagram of the integrated edge-fog system

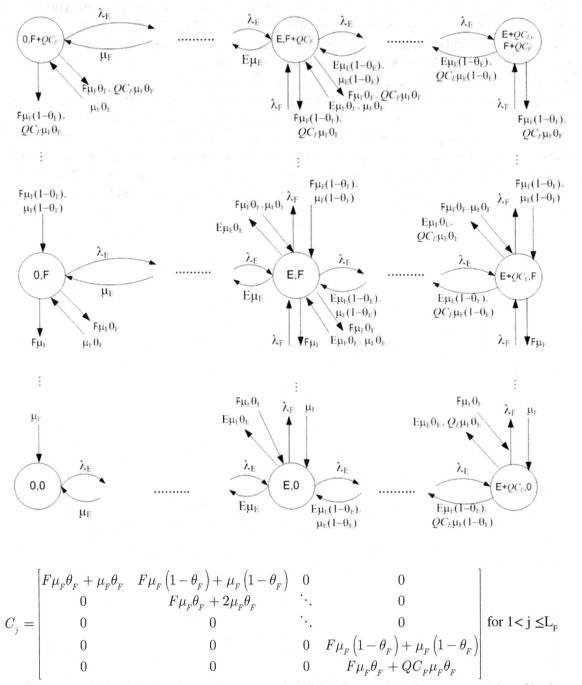

$$C_j = \begin{bmatrix} F\mu_F\theta_F + \mu_F\theta_F & F\mu_F\left(1-\theta_F\right) + \mu_F\left(1-\theta_F\right) & 0 & 0 \\ 0 & F\mu_F\theta_F + 2\mu_F\theta_F & \ddots & 0 \\ 0 & 0 & \ddots & 0 \\ 0 & 0 & 0 & F\mu_F\left(1-\theta_F\right) + \mu_F\left(1-\theta_F\right) \\ 0 & 0 & 0 & F\mu_F\theta_F + QC_F\mu_F\theta_F \end{bmatrix} \text{ for } 1 < j \le L_F$$

Consequently, by deriving the steady-state probabilities, $P_{i,j}$s, and performance metrics of both networks, they can be computed. Specifically, the MQL_E /MQL_F, $THRP_E$ / $THRP_F$ and MRT_E /MRT_F of both edge and fog networks can be evaluated as follows:

$$MQL_E = \sum_{i=0}^{L_E} i \sum_{j=0}^{L_F} P_{i,j} \ \text{ and } \ MQL_F = \sum_{j=0}^{L_F} j \sum_{i=0}^{L_E} P_{i,j} \tag{13}$$

$$THRP_E = \sum_{i=0}^{L_E}\mu_i\sum_{j=0}^{L_F}P_{i,j} \ \ and \ \ THRP_F = \sum_{j=0}^{L_F}\mu_j\sum_{i=0}^{L_E}P_{i,j} \tag{14}$$

$$MRT_E = \frac{MQL_E}{THRP_E} \ and \ MRT_F = \frac{MQL_F}{THRP_F} \tag{15}$$

3.5.1 Successive Over Relaxation Method

On the other hand, the state probabilities $P_{i,j}$s could be determined using the successive over-relaxation (SOR) method, which involves solving a system of balance equations. The SOR method can be employed when the proposed solution approach has a large number of states. In addition, the exact spectral expansion solution encounters the state explosion problem. Thus, the SOR method is also presented. The proposed model is implemented using MATLAB for solving the system. By properly deriving the balance equations, the system's state probabilities can be obtained as a solution to a set of linear equations of the form Ax=B, as depicted in equation

$$\begin{pmatrix} A_{0,0} & A_{0,1} & \cdots & A_{0,L_F*L_E} \\ A_{1,0} & A_{1,1} & \cdots & A_{1,L_F*L_E} \\ \vdots & \vdots & \vdots & \vdots \\ A_{L_F*L_E,0} & A_{L_F*L_E,1} & \cdots & A_{L_F*L_E,L_F*L_E} \end{pmatrix} \begin{pmatrix} X_0 \\ X_1 \\ \vdots \\ X_{L_F*L_E} \end{pmatrix} = \begin{pmatrix} B_0 \\ B_1 \\ \vdots \\ B_{L_F*L_E} \end{pmatrix} \tag{16}$$

In the proposed system, matrix A has dimensions of L_FxL_E. The unknown state probabilities, P_i (i=0, 1,..., L_FxL_E), are represented as a column vector of X. Matrix B consists of the scalars corresponding to the balance equations. A is a symmetric matrix with real, positive diagonal elements. MATLAB attempts to perform a Cholesky factorization on A (Kirsal, 2013). If the Cholesky factorization fails, MATLAB employs an asymmetric, indefinite factorization method. The vector B_i is denoted, where B={0,0,...,0,1}. The system solution is obtained by solving the equation A_ixP_i=B_i for i=0,1, ..., L_FxL_E. The transition rates and the equilibrium balance equations are utilized in MATLAB for this purpose.

i=0 and j=0

$$P_{i,j} = \frac{\mu_E P_{i+1,j} + \mu_F P_{i,j+1}}{\lambda_E} \tag{17}$$

i=0 and 0< j ≤ F;

$$P_{i,j} = \frac{(i+1)\mu_E P_{i+1,j} + (i+1)\mu_E\theta_E P_{i+1,j-1} + j\mu_F(1-\theta_F)P_{i,j-1} + \mu_F(1-\theta_F)P_{i,j+1}}{\lambda_E + j\mu_F\theta_F + j\mu_F} \tag{18}$$

i=0 and F<j<F+QC$_F$;

$$P_{i,j} = \frac{(i+1)\mu_E P_{i+1,j} + (i+1)\mu_E\theta_E P_{i+1,j-1} + j\mu_F(1-\theta_F)P_{i,j-1} + \mu_F(1-\theta_F)P_{i,j+1}}{\lambda_E + F\mu_F\theta_F + j\mu_F\theta_F + F\mu_F(1-\theta_F) + j\mu_F(1-\theta_F)} \tag{19}$$

i=0 and j= F+QC$_F$;

$$P_{i,j} = \frac{(i+1)\mu_E P_{i+1,j} + (i+1)\mu_E \theta_E P_{i+1,j-1}}{\lambda_E + F\mu_F\theta_F + QC_F\mu_F\theta_F + F\mu_F(1-\theta_F) + QC_F\mu_F\theta_F} \tag{20}$$

0≤i≤E and j=0;

$$P_{i,j} = \frac{\left[(i+1)\mu_E(1-\theta_E) + \mu_E(1-\theta_E)\right]P_{i+1,j} + \lambda_E P_{i-1,j} + (i+1)\mu_F\theta_F + (j+1)\mu_F P_{i,j+1}}{\lambda_E + i\mu_E + i\mu_E\theta_E + \lambda_F} \tag{21}$$

i=E and j=F

$$P_{i,j} = \frac{\left[(i+1)\mu_E(1-\theta_E) + \mu_E(1-\theta_E)\right]P_{i+1,j} + \left[E\mu_E\theta_E + \mu_E\theta_E\right]P_{i+1,j-1} + \lambda_E P_{i-1,j} + F\mu_F\theta_F + \mu_F\theta_F P_{i-1,j+1} + F\mu_F(1-\theta_F) + \mu_F(1-\theta_F)P_{i-1,j+1}}{\lambda_E + F\mu_F\theta_F + F\mu_F + i\mu_E + E\mu_E\theta_E + \lambda_F} \tag{22}$$

i=E and j=F+QC$_F$;

$$P_{i,j} = \frac{\left[E\mu_E(1-\theta_E) + \mu_E(1-\theta_E)\right]P_{i+1,j} + \left[E\mu_E\theta_E + \mu_E\theta_E\right]P_{i+1,j-1} + \lambda_F P_{i,j-1} + \lambda_E P_{i-1,j}}{\lambda_E + F\mu_F\theta_F + QC_F\mu_F\theta_F + F\mu_F(1-\theta_F) + QC_F F\mu_F\theta_F + E\mu_E} \tag{23}$$

i= E+QC$_E$ and j=0;

$$P_{i,j} = \frac{\lambda_E P_{i-1,j} + F\mu_F\theta_F + (j+1)\mu_F P_{i,j+1}}{E\mu_E(1-\theta_E) + QC_E\mu_E(1-\theta_E) + E\mu_E\theta_E + QC_E\mu_E\theta_E + \lambda_F} \tag{24}$$

i= E+QC$_E$ and j=F;

$$P_{i,j} = \frac{\lambda_F P_{i,j-1} + \lambda_E P_{i-1,j} + F\mu_F\theta_F + (j+1)\theta_F\mu_F P_{i,j+1} + F\mu_F(1-\theta_F) + \mu_F(1-\theta_F)P_{i,j+1}}{F\mu_F + E\mu_E(1-\theta_E) + QC_E\mu_E(1-\theta_E) + E\mu_E\theta_E + QC_E\mu_E\theta_E + \lambda_F} \tag{25}$$

i= E+QC$_E$ and j=F+ QC$_F$;

$$P_{i,j} = \frac{\lambda_F P_{i,j-1} + \lambda_E P_{i-1,j}}{F\mu_F(1-\theta_F) + QC_F\mu_F\theta_F + E\mu_E(1-\theta_E) + QC_E\mu_E(1-\theta_E)} \tag{26}$$

When all the steady-state probabilities, P$_{i,j}$s, are obtained, various QoS measurements could be easily computed.

3.6 Numerical Results and Discussions of Third Case Study

This section presents the numerical results of the QoS evaluation for the integrated fog-edge computing systems. The proposed models and evaluation take into account mobility considerations within integrated queuing systems. The analysis considers assumptions and parameters from the related literature and various other models (Fantacci & Picano, 2020), (Kirsal, 2013), (Kirsal, 2021), (Pereira, 2020), (Pereira, 2021), (Pereira, 2022) unless specified otherwise. Please note that the results section only focuses on the fog network results. Moreover, the proposed model can also be utilized to obtain performance results for the edge network. The following values were used: E=10 (number of nodes in the edge network), $L_E = 70$ (maximum number of tasks in the edge network), $QC_E = 60$ (capacity of the edge queue), $\mu_E = 10$ tasks/sec (service rate of the edge nodes), F = 10 (number of nodes in the fog network), $L_F = 50$ (maximum number of tasks in the fog network), $QC_F = 40$ (capacity of the fog queue), $\mu_F = 5$ tasks/sec (service rate of the fog nodes). The arrival rate per user, λ_E, varies from 10 tasks per second. Additionally, some parameters are varied during the analysis. For example, the mobility rates θ_E and θ_F varied between 0.1 and 0.9. The SPX results are presented in all figures for case study 3; however, the SOR method results are also shown for validation purposes. All figures show both SPX and SOR solution approaches. Hence, the proposed analytical model's results are promising and demonstrate its accuracy and effectiveness.

The analysis of QoS and mobility from the edge-to-fog networks is depicted in Figures 9 to 11. MQL_F, $THRP_F$, and MRT_F results are given in Figures 9, 10, and 11, respectively.

As the mobility rate θ_E increases, there is a migration of tasks from the edge network to the fog network, resulting in an increase in the number of tasks and throughput in the fog network. This migration improves the performance of both the edge and fog networks. However, the increased migration also leads to a higher workload in the fog network, as shown in Figure 9. The throughput of the fog network exhibits an increasing trend with higher mobility rates, but eventually stabilizes at a certain point, as depicted in Figure 10. This stabilization occurs because the service rate of the fog network reaches its limit and can no longer handle additional tasks beyond a certain point. Thus keeping the throughput constant, dependent on the arrival rate (λ_E). Furthermore, MRT_F experiences a notable increase, particularly when the mobility rates from the edge network are high. This trend is evident in Figure 11, which clearly illustrates the impact of mobility on the MRT_F.

Overall, both the approximate SOR and the exact solution approach employed in this study yielded similar results, demonstrating their effectiveness for evaluating the QoS of fog networks and edge net-

Figure 9. Mean queue length results of fog network with different edge network mobility rates

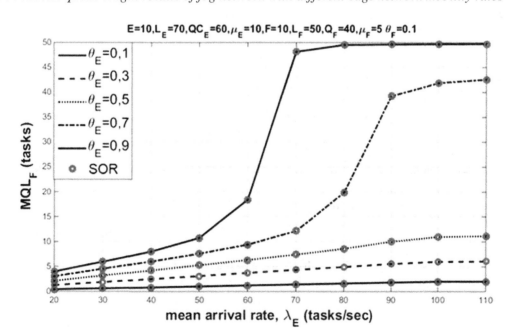

Figure 10. Throughput results of fog network with different edge network mobility rates

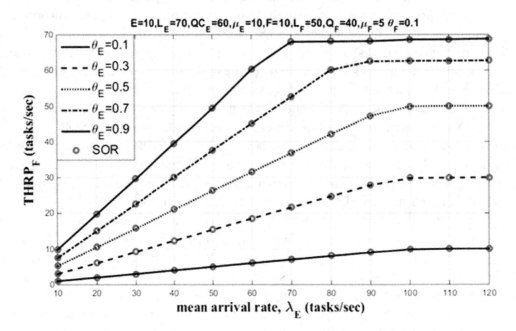

Figure 11. Mean response time results of fog network with different edge network mobility rates

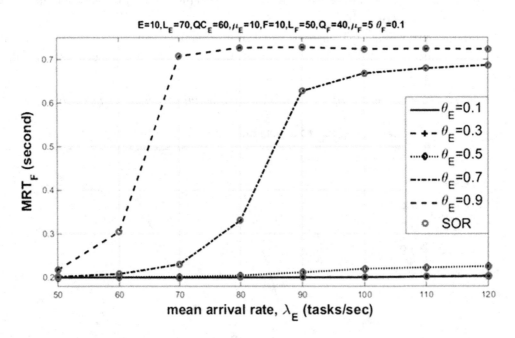

works. These approaches serve as valuable tools for making crucial decisions regarding system design and optimizing mobility and queuing parameters.

4. CONCLUSION

In conclusion, this book chapter offers a comprehensive examination of QoS and performance modeling in the context of fog computing. It presents analytical frameworks specifically designed for QoS analysis and performance evaluation of fog computing systems. The proposed analytical frameworks are described in detail, encompassing different components and assumptions essential for evaluating and analysing the QoS of fog computing systems. Various case studies have presented well-known solution approaches. The Markov reward model, exact spectral expansion and successive over-relaxation techniques were employed to the proposed models. Through case studies, the chapter demonstrates the application of these frameworks, illustrating a scenario of a fog computing system with a specific architecture and employing diverse performance metrics and models for analysis. The experimental results presented in this study provide clear evidence of the effectiveness and capability of both the analytical models and solution approaches in capturing and evaluating QoS measurements. These findings validate the practical utility and performance of the proposed models and solutions. The results and analysis of the case studies contribute valuable insights into the performance and QoS characteristics of fog computing systems. The chapter concludes by highlighting the key findings and contributions of the analytical frameworks while also discussing potential areas for improvement and future research directions. By providing a comprehensive analysis and modeling approach for QoS in fog computing, this book chapter offers valuable knowledge and guidance to researchers and practitioners engaged in the field. It equips them with the necessary tools and insights to enhance the performance, reliability, and overall QoS of fog computing systems, thus advancing the development and deployment of efficient and robust fog computing solutions.

The future direction of such work might involve enhancing existing models, incorporating machine learning techniques, addressing hybrid fog-cloud architectures, considering security and privacy concerns, and validating the proposed approaches through real-world deployments and simulations. These advancements will contribute to the development of more robust and efficient fog computing systems with improved QoS and performance capabilities.

REFERENCES

Aldağ, M., Kırsal, Y., & Ülker, S. (2022). An analytical modeling and QoS evaluation of fault-tolerant load balancer and web servers in fog computing. *The Journal of Supercomputing*, *78*(10), 12136–12158. doi:10.100711227-022-04345-2

Bai, J., Chang, X., Ning, G., Zhang, Z., & Trivedi, K. S. (2020). Service availability analysis in a virtualized system: A Markov regenerative model approach. *IEEE Transactions on Cloud Computing*, *10*(3), 2118–2130. doi:10.1109/TCC.2020.3028648

Bartels, R. H., & Golub, G. H. (1969). The simplex method of linear programming using LU decomposition. *Communications of the ACM*, *12*(5), 266–268. doi:10.1145/362946.362974

Battula, S. K., O'Reilly, M. M., Garg, S., & Montgomery, J. (2020). A generic stochastic model for resource availability in fog computing environments. *IEEE Transactions on Parallel and Distributed Systems*, *32*(4), 960–974. doi:10.1109/TPDS.2020.3037247

Chakka, R. (1998). Spectral expansion solution for some finite capacity queues. *Annals of Operations Research*, 79(0), 27–44. doi:10.1023/A:1018974722301

Croz, J. J. D., & Higham, N. J. (1992). Stability of methods for matrix inversion. *IMA Journal of Numerical Analysis*, 12(1), 1–19. doi:10.1093/imanum/12.1.1

D'Oro, E. C., Colombo, S., Gribaudo, M., Iacono, M., Manca, D., & Piazzolla, P. (2019). Modeling and evaluating a complex edge computing based systems: An emergency management support system case study. *Internet of Things*, 6, 100054. doi:10.1016/j.iot.2019.100054

Dar, F., Liyanage, M., Radeta, M., Yin, Z., Zuniga, A., Kosta, S., Tarkoma, S., Nurmi, P., & Flores, H. (2023). Upscaling Fog Computing in Oceans for Underwater Pervasive Data Science using Low-Cost Micro-Clouds. *ACM Transactions on Internet of Things*, 4(2), 1–29. doi:10.1145/3575801

De Sensi, D., De Matteis, T., Taranov, K., Di Girolamo, S., Rahn, T., & Hoefler, T. (2022). Noise in the Clouds: Influence of Network Performance Variability on Application Scalability. *Proceedings of the ACM on Measurement and Analysis of Computing Systems, 6*(3), 1-27.

Doddapaneni, K. (2014). *Energy-aware performance evaluation of WSNs* [Doctoral dissertation, Middlesex University].

Evans, D. J. (1984). Parallel SOR iterative methods. *Parallel Computing*, 1(1), 3–18. doi:10.1016/S0167-8191(84)90380-6

Ever, E. (2007). *Performability modeling of homogenous and heterogeneous multiserver systems with breakdowns and repairs* [Doctoral dissertation, Middlesex University].

Fantacci, R., & Picano, B. (2020). Performance analysis of a delay constrained data offloading scheme in an integrated cloud-fog-edge computing system. *IEEE Transactions on Vehicular Technology*, 69(10), 12004–12014. doi:10.1109/TVT.2020.3008926

Goswami, V., Sharma, B., Patra, S. S., Chowdhury, S., Barik, R. K., & Dhaou, I. B. (2023, January). IoT-Fog Computing Sustainable System for Smart Cities: A Queueing-based Approach. In *2023 1st International Conference on Advanced Innovations in Smart Cities (ICAISC)* (pp. 1-6). IEEE. 10.1109/ICAISC56366.2023.10085238

Hall, P., Marshall, D., & Martin, R. (2002). Adding and subtracting eigenspaces with eigenvalue decomposition and singular value decomposition. *Image and Vision Computing*, 20(13-14), 1009–1016. doi:10.1016/S0262-8856(02)00114-2

Haverkort, B. R., & Niemegeers, I. G. (1996). Performability modeling tools and techniques. *Performance Evaluation*, 25(1), 17–40. doi:10.1016/0166-5316(94)00038-7

Hazra, A., Rana, P., Adhikari, M., & Amgoth, T. (2023). Fog computing for next-generation internet of things: Fundamental, state-of-the-art and research challenges. *Computer Science Review*, 48, 100549. doi:10.1016/j.cosrev.2023.100549

Higham, N. J. (2011). Gaussian elimination. *Wiley Interdisciplinary Reviews: Computational Statistics*, 3(3), 230–238. doi:10.1002/wics.164

Hosseini, E., Nickray, M., & Ghanbari, S. (2023). Energy-efficient scheduling based on task prioritization in mobile fog computing. *Computing*, *105*(1), 187–215. doi:10.100700607-022-01108-y

Hussein, W. N., Hussain, H. N., Hussain, H. N., & Mallah, A. Q. (2023). A deployment model for IoT devices based on fog computing for data management and analysis. *Wireless Personal Communications*, 1–13. doi:10.100711277-023-10168-y

Iyapparaja, M., Alshammari, N. K., Kumar, M. S., Krishnan, S., & Chowdhary, C. L. (2022). Efficient Resource Allocation in Fog Computing Using QTCS Model. *Computers, Materials & Continua*, *70*(2), 2225–2239. doi:10.32604/cmc.2022.015707

Jamil, B., Ijaz, H., Shojafar, M., Munir, K., & Buyya, R. (2022). Resource allocation and task scheduling in fog computing and internet of everything environments: A taxonomy, review, and future directions. *ACM Computing Surveys*, *54*(11s), 1–38. doi:10.1145/3513002

Kharchenko, V., Ponochovnyi, Y., Ivanchenko, O., Fesenko, H., & Illiashenko, O. (2022). Combining Markov and Semi-Markov Modeling for Assessing Availability and Cybersecurity of Cloud and IoT Systems. *Cryptography*, *6*(3), 44. doi:10.3390/cryptography6030044

Kirsal, Y. (2013). *Modeling and performance evaluation of wireless and mobile communication systems in heterogeneous environments* [Doctoral dissertation, Middlesex university].

Kirsal, Y. (2018). Analytical modeling and optimization analysis of large-scale communication systems and networks with repairmen policy. *Computing*, *100*(5), 503–527. doi:10.100700607-017-0580-7

Kirsal, Y., Ever, Y. K., Mapp, G., & Raza, M. (2021). 3D Analytical Modeling and Iterative Solution for High Performance Computing Clusters. *IEEE Transactions on Cloud Computing*, *10*(4), 2238–2251. doi:10.1109/TCC.2021.3055119

Ko, H., & Kyung, Y. (2022). Performance Analysis and Optimization of Delayed Offloading System with Opportunistic Fog Node. *IEEE Transactions on Vehicular Technology*, *71*(9), 10203–10208. doi:10.1109/TVT.2022.3179658

Liu, B., Chang, X., Liu, B., & Chen, Z. (2017). Performance analysis model for fog services under multiple resource types. In *2017 International Conference on Dependable Systems and Their Applications (DSA)* (pp. 110-117). IEEE. 10.1109/DSA.2017.26

Liu, X., Li, S., & Tong, W. (2015). A queuing model considering resources sharing for cloud service performance. *The Journal of Supercomputing*, *71*(11), 4042–4055. doi:10.100711227-015-1503-z

Ma, X., Li, Y., & Gao, Y. (2023). Decision model of intrusion response based on markov game in fog computing environment. *Wireless Networks*, 1–10. doi:10.100711276-023-03382-w

Machida, F., Zhang, Q., & Andrade, E. (2023). Performability analysis of adaptive drone computation offloading with fog computing. *Future Generation Computer Systems*, *145*, 121–135. doi:10.1016/j.future.2023.03.027

Mahmud, R., Pallewatta, S., Goudarzi, M., & Buyya, R. (2022). iFogSim2: An extended iFogSim simulator for mobility, clustering, and microservice management in edge and fog computing environments. *Journal of Systems and Software*, *190*, 111351. doi:10.1016/j.jss.2022.111351

Mansour, K. (2023). A two dimensional Markov chain model for aggregation-enabled 802.11 networks. *International Journal of Ad Hoc and Ubiquitous Computing*, *42*(4), 269–280. doi:10.1504/IJAHUC.2023.130467

Margariti, S. V., Dimakopoulos, V. V., & Tsoumanis, G. (2020). Modeling and simulation tools for fog computing—A comprehensive survey from a cost perspective. *Future Internet*, *12*(5), 89. doi:10.3390/fi12050089

Mas, L., Vilaplana, J., Mateo, J., & Solsona, F. (2022). A queuing theory model for fog computing. *The Journal of Supercomputing*, *78*(8), 11138–11155. doi:10.100711227-022-04328-3

Pereira, P., Araujo, J., Melo, C., Santos, V., & Maciel, P. (2021). Analytical models for availability evaluation of edge and fog computing nodes. *The Journal of Supercomputing*, *77*(9), 9905–9933. doi:10.100711227-021-03672-0

Pereira, P., Araujo, J., Torquato, M., Dantas, J., Melo, C., & Maciel, P. (2020). Stochastic performance model for web server capacity planning in fog computing. *The Journal of Supercomputing*, *76*(12), 9533–9557. doi:10.100711227-020-03218-w

Pereira, P., Melo, C., Araujo, J., Dantas, J., Santos, V., & Maciel, P. (2022). Availability model for edge-fog-cloud continuum: An evaluation of an end-to-end infrastructure of intelligent traffic management service. *The Journal of Supercomputing*, *78*(3), 1–28. doi:10.100711227-021-04033-7

Rodrigues, L., Rodrigues, J. J., Serra, A. D. B., & Silva, F. A. (2022). A queueing-based model performance evaluation for internet of people supported by fog computing. *Future Internet*, *14*(1), 23. doi:10.3390/fi14010023

Saad, M. (2018). Fog computing and its role in the internet of things: Concept, security and privacy issues. *International Journal of Computer Applications*, *180*(32), 7–9. doi:10.5120/ijca2018916829

Santos, L., Cunha, B., Fé, I., Vieira, M., & Silva, F. A. (2021). Data processing on edge and cloud: A performability evaluation and sensitivity analysis. *Journal of Network and Systems Management*, *29*(3), 27. doi:10.100710922-021-09592-x

Shafik, W., Matinkhah, S. M., & Ghasemazade, M. (2019). Fog-mobile edge performance evaluation and analysis on internet of things. *Journal of Advance Research in Mobile Computing*, *1*(3), 1–17.

Shaik, S., Hall, J., Johnson, C., Wang, Q., Sharp, R., & Baskiyar, S. (2022). PFogSim: A simulator for evaluation of mobile and hierarchical fog computing. *Sustainable Computing: Informatics and Systems*, *35*, 100736. doi:10.1016/j.suscom.2022.100736

Songhorabadi, M., Rahimi, M., MoghadamFarid, A. M., & Haghi Kashani, M. (2023). Fog computing approaches in IoT-enabled smart cities. *Journal of Network and Computer Applications*, *211*, 103557. doi:10.1016/j.jnca.2022.103557

Trivedi, K., & Bobbio, A. (2021). Reliability and Availability Analysis in Practice. Handbook of Advanced Performability Engineering, 501-522.

Trivedi, K. S., Dharmaraja, S., & Ma, X. (2002). Analytic modeling of handoffs in wireless cellular networks. *Information Sciences*, *148*(1-4), 155–166. doi:10.1016/S0020-0255(02)00292-X

Trivedi, K. S., Ma, X., & Dharmaraja, S. (2003). Performability modeling of wireless communication systems. *International Journal of Communication Systems*, *16*(6), 561–577. doi:10.1002/dac.605

Umoh, V., Ekpe, U., Davidson, I., & Akpan, J. (2023). Mobile Broadband Adoption, Performance Measurements and Methodology: A Review. *Electronics (Basel)*, *12*(7), 1630. doi:10.3390/electronics12071630

Vilaplana, J., Solsona, F., Teixidó, I., Mateo, J., Abella, F., & Rius, J. (2014). A queuing theory model for cloud computing. *The Journal of Supercomputing*, *69*(1), 492–507. doi:10.100711227-014-1177-y

Wigren, T. (2023). Recursive identification of a nonlinear state space model. *International Journal of Adaptive Control and Signal Processing*, *37*(2), 447–473. doi:10.1002/acs.3531

Chapter 8
Fog Computing for Spatial Data Infrastructure: Challenges and Opportunities

Munir Ahmad
https://orcid.org/0000-0003-4836-6151
Survey of Pakistan, Pakistan

Asmat Ali
https://orcid.org/0000-0002-8804-2285
Survey of Pakistan, Pakistan

Malik Sikander Hayat Khiyal
Preston University Kohat, Islamabad, Pakistan

ABSTRACT

Fog computing is a promising approach to address the challenges faced by traditional spatial data infrastructure when processing large-scale and real-time data. This chapter examined the opportunities and challenges of using fog computing in SDI through the service dominant logic framework. The study showed that fog computing can improve SDI by providing real-time data processing, improved data security and privacy, and increased accessibility of geospatial data. However, challenges such as data quality and interoperability, collaboration, technical infrastructure, and governance policies need to be addressed. The chapter suggested ways to improve the value co-creation process between fog computing and SDI users, including collaboration and partnership, investment in technical infrastructure, and capacity building initiatives. Future research can investigate the practical implementation and evaluation of fog computing in SDI applications.

1. INTRODUCTION

Spatial data infrastructures (SDIs) have transformed the way spatial data is utilized by enabling sharing, discovery, and use of spatial data across various sectors such as government, academia, industry, and the

DOI: 10.4018/978-1-6684-4466-5.ch008

general public. SDIs have revolutionized the utilization of spatial data by promoting seamless sharing and integration of spatial data (Hendriks et al., 2012). However, SDIs are facing new difficulties in data processing and analysis due to the exponential growth of spatial data from numerous sources, including remote sensing, social media, and the Internet of Things (IoT). The sheer amount and variety of data are too much for traditional methods of data processing and analysis to handle, especially when real-time processing is needed. To increase the efficiency and effectiveness of SDIs, there is a rising demand for creative strategies like fog computing (Das et al., 2021).

Fog computing, a distributed computing paradigm that extends cloud computing to the edge of the network, has emerged as a promising solution for addressing these challenges. Fog computing can provide low-latency and high-bandwidth communication, as well as processing and storage capabilities, to support real-time and location-based applications. The fog nodes, located closer to the data sources, can filter and preprocess the data before sending it to the cloud for further analysis, reducing network traffic and processing time. Therefore, there is a growing interest in exploring the opportunities and challenges of using fog computing in SDIs (Barik, Dubey, et al., 2017; Barik et al., 2019).

In this context, this chapter investigated the potential of fog computing for supporting SDIs and addressing their challenges. We applied the Service-Dominant Logic (SDL) framework (Font et al., 2021; Zhang & Berghäll, 2021) to investigate the potential of fog computing for supporting SDIs and addressing their challenges. Specifically, we aimed to answer the following research questions: (1) What are the key opportunities and challenges of using fog computing in SDIs? (2) How can the SDL framework be used to establish the relationship between fog computing and SDIs? By addressing these questions, we provided insights into the potential benefits and limitations of fog computing in the context of SDI, as well as how the SDL framework can be leveraged to create value for SDI stakeholders.

The objectives of this chapter are twofold: (1) to identify the opportunities and challenges of using fog computing in SDIs, and (2) to establish a theoretical framework for understanding the relationship between fog computing and SDIs using the SDL framework. To achieve these objectives, the chapter reviewed the relevant literature on fog computing and SDIs and applied the SDL framework to analyze the potential benefits and limitations of fog computing for SDIs. The chapter focused on identifying the key opportunities and challenges of using fog computing in SDI, as well as the theoretical and practical implications of this integration. By doing so, the chapter contributes to a better understanding of the potential of fog computing for supporting SDIs and addressing their challenges

The structure of this chapter is organized into several sections. Firstly, in Section 2, the fundamental concepts of spatial data infrastructure are introduced. Fog computing are introduced in section 3 as a background to the study. In Section 4, the methodology employed in this study is described, outlining the steps taken to identify the opportunities and challenges of using fog computing in SDIs and establishing the theoretical framework for understanding the relationship between fog computing and SDIs using the SDL framework. In Section 5, the results of the study are presented, which include the identified opportunities and challenges of using fog computing in SDIs. Section 6 provides discussions on the results, analyzing the theoretical and practical implications of this integration. Finally, in section 7 of the chapter, the conclusion is presented, summarizing the main findings of the study and outlining potential directions for future research in this area.

2. THEORETICAL BACKGROUND

This section presents a detailed description of two fundamental concepts: fog computing and spatial data infrastructure to provide a comprehensive comprehension of the research topic. The basic definitions, characteristics, and architecture will be covered in the discussion, along with the applications in many fields.

2.1 Spatial Data Infrastructure

The notion of Spatial Data Infrastructure (SDI) is now well-known in the fields of geographic information systems and spatial data management. Its origins can be found in the concept of the National Spatial Data Infrastructure, which was first presented in 1991 at the Canadian Conference on Geographic Information Systems (McLaughlin, 1991). This concept was further developed in Executive Order 12906 signed by President Clinton the following year, entitled 'Coordinating Geographic Data Acquisition and Access: The National Spatial Data Infrastructure'. The order greatly raised awareness of the need for government initiatives to promote geospatial data collection, management, and utilization, not just among Federal agencies in the United States but also at the national and worldwide levels (Masser, 2005).

SDI is the fundamental physical and organizational structure required to support the efficient and effective use of spatial data (Rajabifard et al., 2006). To effectively utilize spatial data produced by others, and fully realize its potential, an SDI requires the ability to envision and comprehend its applications, beyond just the technical aspects and data models (Ahmad et al., 2022; Ali et al., 2021). Many governments at the local, national, and international levels have initiated SDI projects to facilitate the sharing and integration of spatial data for various purposes (Crompvoets et al., 2004; Masser, 2005; Rajabifard et al., 2006). The initial purpose of national and regional spatial data infrastructures was to establish centralized databases of geospatial data that predominantly originated from authoritative sources. (Groot & McLaughlin, 2000; Jacoby et al., 2002; Masser, 1999).

Characteristic of SDI: One crucial aspect of SDI is its interoperability, which allows spatial data to be exchanged and utilized across different applications, platforms, and organizations, regardless of their source, structure, or format. This interoperability is achieved through the implementation of standardized protocols and specifications, such as those established by the Open Geospatial Consortium (OGC) and the International Organization for Standardization (ISO). These common standards facilitate the integration of different datasets and enable seamless data sharing and collaboration among stakeholders of SDI (Chaturvedi et al., 2019; Corti et al., 2019). Interoperability in SDIs is crucial as it allows spatial data to be seamlessly shared and integrated with other data sources. This capability facilitates the execution of sophisticated spatial analyses and the creation of integrated solutions that leverage data from multiple sources. Consistency is another crucial attribute of SDI, which pertains to the precision, standardization, and currency of spatial data. To achieve consistency, standardized data models, quality assurance processes, and metadata are utilized, which guarantee that spatial data is dependable, equivalent, and fit for purpose (Lutz et al., 2009; Masser, 2009). The provision of reliable and consistent spatial data by SDI facilitates accurate spatial analysis, modeling, and visualization, which ultimately aids in effective decision-making by the users.

Another important feature of SDI is its accessibility, which pertains to the simplicity with which spatial data can be accessed, discovered, and retrieved by users. To achieve this, web-based portals, databases, and services have been developed, providing users with an array of tools and functionalities for searching, querying, and downloading spatial data. These web-based interfaces make it simple for users to locate and obtain the spatial data they require, contributing to a broad spectrum of applications and use cases (Giuliani et al., 2017; Vancauwenberghe & van Loenen, 2018). SDI is also characterized by security, which is vital to protect spatial data from unauthorized access, use, and modification. To achieve this, various mechanisms are used such as encryption, authentication, and authorization. These measures ensure that data breaches are prevented and data privacy is maintained (Chaturvedi et al., 2019; Masser, 2009). By enabling secure access to spatial data, SDI enables organizations to share data confidently, promoting collaboration and innovation.

Benefits of SDI: SDI offers a significant advantage of better decision-making, as it provides access to precise and timely spatial data. By utilizing SDI, decision-makers across diverse fields such as public health, land management, and transportation can make well-informed decisions. Access to spatial data through SDI helps decision-makers uncover patterns, relationships, and trends that might not have been noticeable otherwise, resulting in informed decisions with positive outcomes (Boerboom, 2010). In situations such as disaster management, SDI can offer decision-makers precise and timely data on the areas, people, and critical infrastructure affected by the disaster. This data can be used to make informed decisions that enable effective response and recovery efforts (Manfré et al., 2012).

SDI can help organizations save a considerable amount of money. SDI offers a significant cost-saving advantage by avoiding the duplication of efforts and resources required for data collection, maintenance, and dissemination (Bishop et al., 2000). This reduction is achieved by sharing spatial data through web-based portals and services, which minimizes the need for costly data acquisition and maintenance while also eliminating the expenses associated with managing multiple data sources (Borzacchiello & Craglia, 2013). These cost savings free up resources for other activities, such as data analysis and decision-making, which can lead to further benefits for organizations that utilize SDI.

SDI also provides greater efficiency. It can streamline data management and sharing procedures, reducing administrative burdens and allowing for faster and more effective data processing (Borzacchiello & Craglia, 2013). By utilizing standardized data models and metadata, SDI can automate data discovery, validation, and integration, resulting in a reduction in time and effort spent on managing spatial data (Crompvoets et al., 2011). This heightened efficiency assists organizations in operating more efficiently and responding more quickly to changing conditions and requirements.

SDI enables enhanced cooperation among different entities including governmental institutions, private sector entities, and the public. By providing a shared platform for data exchange and cooperation, SDI can advance transparency and responsibility while also promoting public involvement and interaction (Bishop et al., 2000; Crompvoets et al., 2011). SDI allows citizens to contribute to the collection and analysis of spatial data, for example, through participatory mapping and crowdsourcing, which supports decision-making and policy development.

2.2 SDI Architecture

The architecture of SDI comprises several components that work together to enable the sharing and management of spatial data. The various SDI components share several key characteristics. According to their objectives, concepts, and priorities, numerous scholars and organizations have developed their own NSDI elements. As shown in Figure 1, the authors in (Rajabifard, Feeney, et al., 2002) proposed five components of SDI: policy, access network, standards, people, and data.

Figure 1. Components of SDI
Rajabifard, Feeney, et al., 2002)

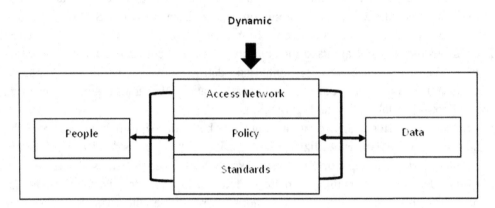

In Figure 1, the dynamic technological elements of SDI, such as access networks, regulations, and standards, influence the fundamental association between the other two segments, i.e., geographic data and individuals. The dynamic nature of the model indicates that an inclusive SDI involves crucial concerns of interoperability, regulations, and networks instead of merely comprising spatial data and individuals (Rajabifard, Feeney, et al., 2002). The GSDI Cookbook provided a more in-depth analysis of the components of an SDI (GSDI, 2004). It focused on aspects such as metadata, catalogues, and web applications, providing a more comprehensive view of an SDI's elements, as depicted in Figure 2.

As the concept and evolution of the SDI framework have progressed, the significance of several other elements has emerged. Capacity building, spatial data sharing, partnerships, and governance have been recognized as having a significant impact on the effectiveness and success of SDIs (Mohammadi, 2008).

To implement SDI, various standards and technologies are used to ensure interoperability and consistency across different systems and platforms as described in Table 2.

Table 2 illustrates the important technologies and standards utilized in SDI, such as OGC standards, INSPIRE, ISO standards, and web services. These technologies and standards play a crucial role in en-

Figure 2. Elements of SDI
(GSDI, 2004)

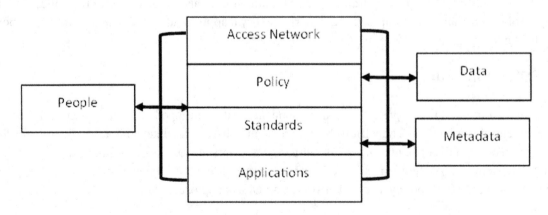

Table 1. SDI Components adopted from (Mohammadi, 2008).

Component	Description
Data	SDI collects spatial data that is integrated and continuous, and this data provides a jurisdiction with reference and context information. The collection of base data that is necessary and frequently used is referred to as framework data. Framework data is commonly utilized in fields such as transportation, hydrography, cadastral, geodetic control, orthoimagery, elevation and bathymetry, and governmental units.
Institutional Arrangements	Tools have been created to allow key stakeholders to work together and participate in the design and implementation of SDI. These tools can take the form of informal negotiations or formal agreements such as laws, policies, rules, or written agreements.
People	Includes data managers, data providers, data consumers, and data owners from the public, private, small, and large business sectors.
Policies	Strategic policies outline the objectives and directions of organizations for promoting the creation or utilization of SDI, while operational policies address issues related to the lifespan of spatial data and facilitate access to and utilization of spatial data.
Standards	Spatial standards are technical documents that describe interfaces or encodings designed to address specific interoperability problems. The more standards there are for organizing and presenting information, the easier it is for electronic devices and people to access, exchange, and use that information.
Technologies	The technological architecture of an SDI comprises a network of physical servers that provide data and Web services. Users can access data and services via the Internet to create and analyze spatial data to make informed decisions.
Metadata	Metadata is a systematic summary of information describing data and is critical to record, protect, and maintain an agency's geographic data assets.
Partnership	To establish an effective SDI, a well-coordinated partnership of federal, state, local, and academic organizations, as well as a variety of private sector and other business information producers and users, is necessary.
Data Sharing	Spatial Data Sharing (SDS) refers to the process of exchanging access to spatial data between individuals, organizations, or divisions of organizations.
Governance	In addition to establishing the framework for SDI coordination, it is important to prioritize the development of suitable SDI governance institutions that are both understood and embraced.
Capacity Building	In less developed countries where the success of SDI programs often depends on a small number of people with the necessary GI management skills, capacity building is critical.

Table 2. Key standards and technologies used in SDI

Standard/Technology	Description
OGC Standards	The Open Geospatial Consortium (OGC) standards consist of a set of specifications that ensure interoperability among spatial data and services. These specifications cover areas such as data encoding (e.g., GeoJSON, GML), web services (e.g., WMS, WFS), and metadata (e.g., ISO 19115).
ISO standards	International Organization for Standardization (ISO) has published guidelines for creating, managing, and sharing spatial data and metadata. These guidelines cover areas such as data quality (e.g., ISO 19157), metadata (e.g., ISO 19115), and geographic information (e.g., ISO 19101).
Web-based technologies	Web-based technologies, such as HTML, CSS, JavaScript, and RESTful APIs, are widely used to access and interact with spatial data and services over the internet. These technologies allow for the creation of web-based mapping applications, data portals, and other spatial applications.
Spatial databases	Spatial databases are specialized databases that are designed to store and manage spatial data. These databases provide advanced capabilities for spatial queries, indexing, and analysis. Examples of spatial databases include PostgreSQL/PostGIS and Oracle Spatial.
Data management systems	Data management systems are software tools that facilitate the creation, management, and dissemination of spatial data and metadata. These systems offer features such as data ingestion, validation, transformation, and publishing. Examples of data management systems include GeoServer and ArcGIS Server.

abling the exchange of spatial data and metadata across diverse platforms and systems. INSPIRE offers guidelines and standards for unifying spatial data across the European Union member states, while ISO standards provide a common framework for managing and exchanging spatial data. In addition, web services allow for the sharing and accessing of spatial data over the internet.

2.3 Applications of SDI

SDI has found widespread application in environmental monitoring, where it has been utilized to keep track of various environmental parameters, such as air and water quality, land use, and vegetation cover. For example, SDI has been employed to monitor and manage water resources, leading to improved water quality, reduced pollution, and enhanced water use efficiency (Ajmi et al., 2014; Higgins et al., 2016). Moreover, SDI has been employed to monitor and simulate climate change and its impacts on the environment, such as shifts in sea levels, temperature, and precipitation patterns (Bernard & Ostländer, 2008).

SDI has found numerous applications in the field of urban planning, particularly in the collection and management of spatial data related to urban infrastructure, such as buildings, roads, and utilities. This data can support a range of planning and management activities, including the development of smart cities, which aim to enhance the efficiency and sustainability of urban systems such as energy, transportation, and waste management (Bhattacharya & Painho, 2017; Chaturvedi et al., 2019). Additionally, SDI has been utilized in urban design and redevelopment, aiding in identifying development opportunities, evaluating proposals, and monitoring urban growth and change.

SDI has found application in disaster management as well, where it has been utilized to collect and administer spatial data that pertains to disaster risks like exposure, vulnerabilities, and hazards. This information can then be employed for risk evaluation, preparedness, and response. For example, SDI has been used in the handling of natural disasters, such as earthquakes and floods, where it has assisted in the forecast of potential disaster impacts, identification of vulnerable areas and populations, and the allocation of emergency resources (Molina & Bayarri, 2011; Rajabifard, Mansourian, et al., 2002; Rosario Michel et al., 2023). SDI has also been used in the management of human-made disasters, such as terrorist attacks and industrial accidents, where it has been used to facilitate emergency response and recovery efforts (Hashmi et al., 2021).

SDI has also found application in the domain of transportation, primarily aimed at collecting and managing spatial data of transportation infrastructure and traffic movements. In transportation planning, design, and management, SDI has played a key role in developing efficient, safe, and sustainable transportation systems. The use of SDI in planning public transportation systems like bus and rail systems has facilitated route planning, optimization of schedules, and better passenger management (Vidal-Filho et al., 2021). SDI has found application in agriculture, wherein it is utilized for gathering and organizing spatial data associated with weather patterns, soil properties, and crop productivity. Such data can facilitate precision agriculture, natural resource management, and land use planning. For instance, SDI has been utilized in precision agriculture to detect crop stress, nutrient deficiencies, and disease outbreaks, thus enabling farmers to maximize yields and minimize the use of fertilizers and pesticides (Bordogna et al., 2016).

SDI is an important tool for enabling the effective sharing, management, and utilization of spatial data across a wide range of domains, applications, and organizations. SDI offers numerous advantages, including enhanced decision-making, cost-effectiveness, improved efficiency, and better collaboration. The architecture of SDI consists of multiple layers, such as the data, service, catalogue, and user interface layers, and its critical components include spatial data, metadata, data management systems, web-based services, and metadata catalogues. SDI has various applications in fields like environmental monitoring, urban planning, disaster management, transportation, and agriculture. To ensure the consistency, interoperability, and accuracy of spatial data, SDI relies on different standards and technologies, including OGC and ISO standards as well as web-based technologies.

3. FOG COMPUTING

Fog computing is a decentralized computing infrastructure that combines the advantages of cloud computing and edge devices. Fog computing provides several functionalities, including reduced latency, high bandwidth, mobility support, multi-tenancy, and high-quality services, among others, to facilitate modern computing systems. Fog computing extends the capabilities of cloud computing by bringing data processing closer to the network's edge, enabling the deployment of real-time applications with low latency, high bandwidth, and high availability. This technology has several characteristics, benefits, architecture, components, and applications in real-world scenarios, making it an essential computing paradigm in various domains.

3.1 Characteristics of Fog Computing

As a distributed computing infrastructure, fog computing stands apart from other paradigms in computing because of its distinctive qualities. Because of these qualities, it may satisfy the requirements of many applications in various sectors. The first attribute is the capacity to extend cloud computing capabilities to the edge of the network, which implies that fog computing enables the deployment of cloud services closer to the users and devices at the edge of the network (Bonomi et al., 2012).

Low latency, high bandwidth, and high availability are the second characteristic of fog computing. This is accomplished by minimizing the distance that data needs to travel between devices and the cloud by moving data processing closer to the network's edge. As a result, data transmission latency is decreased, data communication capacity is enhanced, and cloud services are more readily available. A real-time application's ability to be deployed with low latency and high bandwidth constitutes fog computing's third attribute. Applications like industrial automation, smart cities, and autonomous vehicles, which demand quick data processing, should pay particular attention to this. The time it takes for data to be transported to the cloud for processing and analysis is decreased because of fog computing, which enables real-time data processing at the network's edge (Nguyen et al., 2020).

The capacity to offer a flexible and scalable infrastructure that can be easily customized to meet the needs of various applications is another property of fog computing (Jeyashree & Padmavathi, 2023). This is accomplished by installing fog nodes that can be set up to carry out particular tasks according to the needs of the application. Fog computing offers a scalable, modular architecture that can be quickly modified to meet the varying requirements of many applications. Data privacy and confidentiality are guaranteed by the extremely secure infrastructure offered by fog computing (Ometov et al., 2022). The protection of data exchanged between devices and the cloud is accomplished by offering end-to-end encryption and other security measures. The deployment of crucial applications in numerous industries, including healthcare, banking, and defence, is made possible by the security aspects of fog computing.

3.2 Benefits of Fog Computing

Fog computing has several advantages that make it a popular choice for many applications. According to the studies (Hu et al., 2017; Mouradian et al., 2018), the following are the key benefits of fog computing:

1. Low latency and high bandwidth: By moving the processing closer to the network's edge, fog computing decreases latency and boosts bandwidth. This makes it possible to deploy real-time apps with quick responses.
2. Reduced network congestion: By processing data closer to the network's edge, fog computing decreases network congestion by lowering the volume of data that must be transported across the network. As a result, network performance is enhanced.
3. Enhanced data privacy and security: End-to-end encryption and other security measures are provided by fog computing to safeguard data privacy and confidentiality. By doing this, it is made sure that the data is safe and that no one else may access it.
4. Cost savings: Fog computing lowers the burden on the cloud, which lowers the cost of cloud computing by shifting processing to the network's edge.
5. Scalability and flexibility: The infrastructure offered by fog computing is both scalable and versatile, allowing it to be easily tailored to meet the needs of various applications. According to the requirements of the application, fog nodes can be quickly added or withdrawn, guaranteeing that the system will continue to be scalable.
6. Energy efficiency: By processing data closer to the network's edge, fog computing lowers energy consumption. This increases the system's overall energy efficiency and lowers the amount of energy needed to transfer data over the network.

3.3 The Architecture of Fog Computing

Fog computing is an innovative distributed computing paradigm that expands the capabilities of cloud computing to the network's edge. The architecture of fog computing consists of multiple layers, namely the cloud layer, the fog layer, and the edge layer. The cloud layer serves as the backbone infrastructure for fog computing, encompassing resources such as storage, computation, and networking. The fog layer acts as a middleware layer that links the cloud layer to the edge layer. The edge layer constitutes the frontend infrastructure for fog computing, comprising sensors, actuators, and mobile devices. The fog layer and the edge layer collaborate to provide low latency, high bandwidth, and high availability by processing data closer to the network's edge

In fog computing, the cloud layer is made up of cloud servers that offer the supporting infrastructure for resources such as networking, storage, and computing. The middleware layer for fog computing, including data processing, analytics, and storage, is provided by the fog layer, which is made up of fog nodes. To decrease network congestion and the amount of data that needs to be transferred across the network, fog nodes process and analyze data locally. Additionally, fog nodes are capable of data aggregation and filtering, which significantly reduces the amount of data that the cloud servers must process.

The frontend interface for fog computing is provided by the edge layer, which is made up of sensors, actuators, and mobile devices. Fog computing requires input and output from sensors and actuators to collect data from the environment and operate physical objects. The frontend interface for using cloud services and processing data locally is provided by mobile devices. Devices can communicate with one another and with cloud servers thanks to gateways, which offer communication between the edge layer and the fog layer. Figure 3 depicts the layers of fog computing architecture, such as the cloud layer, fog layer, and edge layer.

3.4 Applications of Fog Computing

Fog computing has found a diverse range of applications in various industries, and its potential has been recognized by many as can be seen in Figure 4. In the healthcare industry, fog computing can offer real-time analysis of medical data, remote patient monitoring, and personalized medicine. This can aid medical professionals in tracking patients' health statuses and providing timely interventions, even in remote regions, which can save lives. Furthermore, fog computing can analyze significant amounts of

Figure 3. Architecture of fog computing

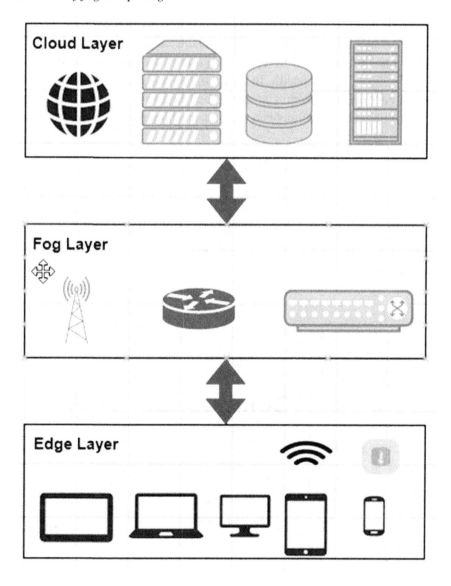

data generated by medical devices, such as wearables and electronic health records, to identify trends and patterns and support medical decision-making processes. A study (Sood & Singh, 2018) showcased the feasibility of real-time monitoring of electroencephalogram (EEG) signals using fog computing, which can improve the diagnosis and treatment of neurological disorders.

Fog computing has several applications in the transportation industry, including real-time traffic analysis, intelligent transportation systems, and vehicle-to-vehicle communication. The utilization of fog computing can allow for the real-time monitoring and management of traffic, leading to reduced congestion, fuel conservation, and lower emissions. Vehicle-to-vehicle communication can also improve road safety by issuing real-time alerts and warnings to drivers. Recent studies (de Mendonça Junior et al., 2021; Thakur & Malekian, 2019) have demonstrated the use of fog computing for real-time traffic prediction, enabling drivers to choose optimal routes and avoid traffic jams.

Fog computing has multiple applications in the smart cities' domain, including public safety, energy management, and environmental monitoring. Through the utilization of fog computing, real-time monitoring of various city aspects such as traffic flow, air quality, and energy consumption can be made possible. This can aid city officials in making informed decisions based on data to enhance citizens' quality of life. The research (Popović et al., 2022; Tang et al., 2017) conducted illustrated that fog computing has the potential to monitor air quality in smart cities, providing immediate data to residents and allowing them to take precautions to safeguard their health. In addition, fog computing has numerous applications in industrial automation, such as predictive maintenance, real-time monitoring, and process optimization. By utilizing fog computing, manufacturers can monitor machine performance in real time, anticipate

Figure 4. Applications of fog computing

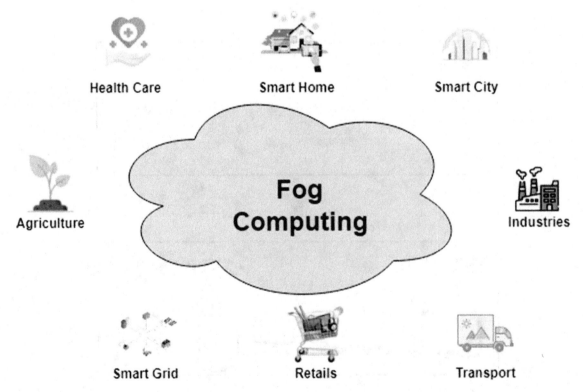

potential issues before they arise, and streamline production to reduce waste and increase efficiency. The application of fog computing was demonstrated in (Qi & Tao, 2019) for monitoring and controlling a manufacturing process in real-time, leading to a decrease in downtime and an increase in productivity. Table 3 depicts some of the Applications of Fog Computing in Real-World Scenarios.

By delivering low latency, high bandwidth, and high availability computing infrastructure at the edge of the network, fog computing has the potential to revolutionize several sectors. Fog computing applications are still developing, and more study is required to fully understand their potential. Compared to other computing paradigms like cloud computing and conventional distributed computing, it offers some advantages. It offers high bandwidth and low latency, allowing the development of real-time applications with quick responses. Because less data needs to be transmitted over the network, it relieves network congestion by processing data closer to the network's edge. End-to-end encryption and other security measures are offered to safeguard data privacy and confidentiality, which enhances data privacy and security. By shifting computation to the network's edge, it lessens the burden on the cloud, lowering the cost of cloud computing. Last, but not least, it offers a scalable, adaptable architecture that can be quickly changed to accommodate various application needs.

3.5 Review on Fog Computing for SDI

This section aims to provide a thorough understanding of the research topic by reviewing the existing literature on fog computing and its relation to spatial data infrastructure.

Both SDI and fog computing have various applications across multiple domains. In the health sector, researchers have investigated the potential of combining SDI and fog computing to tackle the challenges presented by the COVID-19 pandemic. The study (Ghosh & Mukherjee, 2022) proposed a framework that utilizes SDI for managing, storing, analyzing, and sharing spatiotemporal information, a hierarchical Cloud-Fog-Edge architecture for diagnosing and monitoring patients' mobility and health parameters, and efficient data-driven techniques for assisting users during emergencies. The framework utilizes health sensors, movement sensors, and smartphones to collect health-related parameters and mobility traces of users, resulting in the accurate detection of suspected infected individuals and the reduction of delays in healthcare services. Another study (Ghosh et al., 2022) proposed a spatiotemporal knowledge mining framework called STOPPAGE, which incorporates data from various sources such as human mobility and transport statistics through the fog/edge-based architecture to combat pandemics. The framework includes a pandemic-knowledge graph to identify correlations between mobility and disease spread, a deep learning architecture to predict hotspot zones, and support for home-health monitoring. Experimental evaluations on real-life COVID-19 datasets in India demonstrated that STOPPAGE outperforms existing methods. In a study (Barik et al., 2019) a framework called GeoFog4Health was introduced,

Table 3. Applications of fog computing in real-world scenarios

Industry	Application of fog computing
Healthcare	Remote patient monitoring, real-time analysis of medical data, personalized medicine
Transportation	Real-time traffic analysis, intelligent transportation
Smart Cities	Energy management, public safety, waste management
Industrial Automation	Predictive maintenance, real-time monitoring of production processes, asset tracking

which uses embedded computers at the network edge to analyze geo-health big data with reduced latency and increased throughput. The framework includes lossless data compression and overlay analysis of geospatial data and was evaluated using a case study on Malaria vector-borne disease-positive maps of Maharastra state in India, demonstrating its effectiveness in analyzing data from various sensing frameworks while achieving energy savings, cost analysis, and scalability. Another study (Ashok Sasane et al., 2019) proposed the use of Cloud-based SDI and Open-Source GIS software to create a geospatial health database for positive malaria cases and deaths from 2001 to 2014, utilizing climate change-related data.

In Barik, Lenka, et al., (2017), an SDI framework based on fog computing and a Raspberry Pi microprocessor was introduced for mineral resources management in India. The study utilized open-source GIS software to reduce the amount of data transferred from the fog node to the cloud. Another study,(Roy et al., 2022), proposed a geospatial cloud computing model called GeoCloud4EduNet, which aims to address big data problems in educational information infrastructure. The model is designed to connect aspiring students with the right faculty in their domain by mapping colleges and their faculties to their research works. The study (Rabindra, 2017) proposed CloudGanga, a cloud computing-based SDI for managing geospatial data related to rivers. The study used open-source software, machine learning techniques, and a QGIS plugin linked to a cloud computing environment to provide comprehensive information to decision-makers, planners, and researchers. In another study (Barik, Muruga Perumal, et al., 2018), a cloud SDI model was proposed to facilitate better mapping and visualization of potential renewable energy sites by sharing information related to factors associated with wind, small hydropower, biomass power, and solar energy potential.

A study (Fu et al., 2020) examined the literature on fog computing in the health management field and concluded that despite its advantages such as real-time processing, low latency, and high bandwidth, security concerns still need to be addressed. In another study (Bhusan Dash et al., 2023), fog computing was utilized to develop a secure and dependable SDI for accessing and sharing spatial data. The study employed a deterministic multi-server system that used virtual machines (VMs) as Service Providers to manage user access for data storage and retrieval. The research also introduced a recurring approach based on steady-state possibilities and provided numerical examples to demonstrate the effectiveness of the proposed SDI model. In (Saber et al., 2022), the GSDFog framework is proposed as a solution to improve the processing and analysis of large geospatial data. The framework was tested using tourism-related data and was found to perform better than the traditional QGIS application in terms of request handling, response time, and CPU utilization. Meanwhile, (Tripathi et al., 2020) proposed cloud-enabled SDI architecture to address various challenges related to spatial data handling, processing, sharing, and management. The study also compared the NSDIs of different countries and discussed the service-oriented architecture of the proposed cloud-enabled SDI. From the analysis of the above literature, a typical architecture for fog computing-based SDI is presented below in Figure 5.

4. METHODOLOGY

The chapter's methodology adopts the service-dominant logic framework (Font et al., 2021; Zhang & Berghäll, 2021) to investigate the connection between SDI and fog computing. SDL is a theoretical framework that emphasizes the importance of services in the economy and value creation. According to SDL, services are not just economic activities but also represent the fundamental basis for economic exchange and value creation. SDL is a concept that emphasizes the idea that value is not created solely

Figure 5. Fog computing SDI architecture

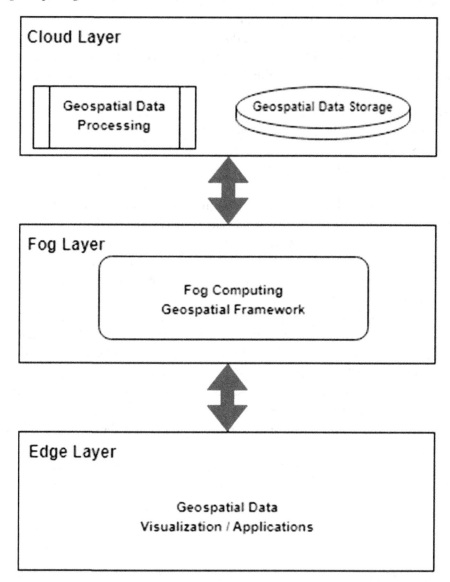

by the service provider or the service user, but through their collaboration. The emphasis is placed on comprehending the service relationship and the process of value co-creation rather than on the product or service itself.

In the context of fog computing and SDI, the SDL framework can be a beneficial tool to comprehend how fog computing and SDI can collaboratively create value for organizations and users. One instance of how fog computing and SDI can work in synergy is by allowing the delivery of computing services closer to the network's edge using fog computing, while SDI enables the sharing and exchange of geospatial data. This combined approach has the potential to offer new services that benefit both users and organizations by adding value to the market.

SDL views service as the fundamental basis of exchange and value creation. It posits that all economic actors involved in fog computing and SDI, including individuals, organizations, and governments, are both service providers and service recipients and that the provision of service is the primary means of exchanging value in this context. A literature review approach is used to apply the SDL framework to the context of SDI and fog computing to highlight the opportunities and challenges of using fog computing in SDI.

To apply SDL to develop a relationship between the usefulness of fog computing for SDI, we focused on the value co-creation process between the service provider (in this case, fog computing technology) and the service user (in this case, SDI users).

The steps involved in our methodology are:

1. Identification of potential benefits of fog computing for SDI users. For example, fog computing can enable real-time processing of geospatial data, which can be particularly useful in emergency response situations or for monitoring natural disasters.
2. Translation of benefits into value for SDI users. For example, real-time processing of geospatial data can enable faster decision-making, which can lead to improved emergency response times and reduced damage from natural disasters.
3. Identification of the key challenges that influence the value co-creation process between fog computing and SDI users. These challenges may include the availability of fog computing resources, the compatibility between fog computing and SDI technologies, and the level of trust between fog computing providers and SDI users.
4. Improvements in the value co-creation process between fog computing and SDI users. For example, fog computing providers could work to improve the availability and accessibility of fog computing resources for SDI users, while SDI users could work to improve the compatibility between their systems and fog computing technologies.
5. Evaluation of the potential impact of fog computing on SDI users, taking into account the value co-creation process and the potential benefits and challenges identified in steps 1-4.

5. RESULTS

The proposed methodology has been implemented, and the subsequent paragraphs present a detailed account of the obtained results. The outcomes obtained through the proposed methodology are thoroughly explained in the following sections. The first step involves the identification of the benefits of fog computing. Resultantly, the potential benefits of fog computing for SDI users are furnished below.

*   Real-time processing of geospatial data (Barik et al., 2020; Chemodanov et al., 2020; D. S. Silva & Holanda, 2022)
*   Reduced latency in geospatial data analysis (Sadri et al., 2022; D. S. Silva & Holanda, 2022)
*   Improved data security and privacy (Bonomi et al., 2014; Kumar et al., 2022; Ometov et al., 2022)
*   Scalability of computing resources (Barik et al., 2020; Bonomi et al., 2014)
*   Increased availability and accessibility of geospatial data (Arifin et al., 2023; Kamruzzaman et al., 2022)

These benefits comprise the processing of geospatial data in real-time, quicker analysis of geospatial data, enhanced security and privacy of data, augmented availability and accessibility of geospatial data, as well as the ability to scale computing resources. In the second stage, the benefits identified in the first stage are translated into value for SDI users. This step also involves linking the benefits with the components of SDI. In Table 4, the connection between the benefits of fog computing, the components of SDI, and the value for SDI users are displayed.

Table 4 indicates that fog computing has the potential to support various components of SDI, such as data, technology, governance, partnership, and capacity building. By providing real-time processing and reduced latency in data processing and analysis, fog computing can enhance the value of geospatial data. Furthermore, the improved data security and privacy provided by fog computing can be linked with governance in terms of developing policies and practices to secure sensitive geospatial data. The increased availability and accessibility of geospatial data provided by fog computing can be linked with partnerships among stakeholders for sharing and disseminating geospatial data. Lastly, the scalability of computing resources provided by fog computing can be linked with technology and capacity building, in terms of developing skills and knowledge for managing complex systems.

In the third step, the focus was on identifying the main obstacles that can affect the process of creating value between fog computing and SDI users. As a result, Table 5 presents the key challenges that can impact the value co-creation process between fog computing and SDI users.

Table 5 displays that understanding the needs and requirements of users, promoting collaboration and partnerships among stakeholders, ensuring data quality and interoperability, having appropriate technical infrastructure and capabilities, and establishing clear policy and governance frameworks are critical challenges that affect the process of value co-creation between fog computing and SDI users. These factors are vital for achieving the maximum benefits of fog computing and SDI for geospatial data analysis, processing, and distribution, and should be addressed with careful consideration.

The fourth step suggests improving the co-creation process between fog computing and SDI users. Here are some factors that can be used to enhance this process:

1. Collaboration and partnerships
2. Data quality and interoperability

Table 4. Benefits of fog computing, components of SDI, and value for SDI users

Benefits of Fog Computing	Components of SDI	Value for SDI Users
Real-time data processing and analysis	Data	Improved decision-making based on up-to-date and accurate information
Reduced latency in geospatial data analysis	Technology (geospatial data transmission and analysis)	Improved efficiency and faster response time for time-sensitive applications
Improved data security and privacy	Governance (data security and privacy policies and practices)	Increased protection and privacy of sensitive geospatial data
Increased availability and accessibility of geospatial data	Partnership (data sharing and dissemination among stakeholders)	Enhanced access to and utilization of geospatial data
Scalability of computing resources	Technology (scalable computing resources for data processing and analysis) Capacity building (skills and knowledge development for managing complex systems)	Ability to handle large volumes of data and increased processing power

Table 5. Challenges of fog computing

Challenges	Description
User needs and requirements	To deliver value through fog computing and SDI, it is crucial to understand user needs and requirements (Javadzadeh & Rahmani, 2020).
Collaboration and partnership	Collaborative efforts and partnerships among stakeholders are essential to co-create value between fog computing and SDI users (de Moura Costa et al., 2020; Gomes et al., 2021; Mouradian et al., 2018).
Data quality and interoperability	The realization of the potential benefits of fog computing and SDI requires high-quality and interoperable geospatial data (Barik et al., 2019; Indrajit et al., 2021).
Technical infrastructure and capabilities	Technical infrastructure and capabilities, such as hardware, software, and network resources, play a crucial role in enabling the effective use of fog computing and SDI (Chen et al., 2017; Mouradian et al., 2018).
Policy and governance	Clear policies and governance frameworks are necessary to facilitate value co-creation between fog computing and SDI users while ensuring data security, privacy, and ethical use (de Moura Costa et al., 2020; Gomes et al., 2021; Indrajit et al., 2021).

3.   Technical infrastructure and capabilities
4.   Policies and governance frameworks
5.   Capacity building and training

Considering these factors, fog computing providers and SDI users can collaborate to improve the efficiency of geospatial data processing, analysis, and dissemination. Table 6 provides a summary of how the value co-creation process between fog computing and SDI users can be improved.

Table 6 outlines five ways to improve the value co-creation process between fog computing and SDI users. The first point highlights the need for collaboration and partnership between the two parties to identify common goals and establish effective communication channels. The second point emphasizes the improvement of geospatial data quality and interoperability through standardized data formats, metadata, and data models. The third point highlights the importance of investment in technical infra-

Table 6. Improvement factors

Improvement Factors	Details
Strengthening collaboration and partnerships	To improve the value co-creation process, fog computing providers and SDI users can work collaboratively to identify common goals and objectives, and establish effective communication channels for collaboration and partnership (Barik et al., 2019; Ghosh & Mukherjee, 2022).
Enhancing data quality and interoperability	To improve the compatibility between fog computing and SDI systems, efforts can be made to improve the quality and interoperability of geospatial data, including the use of standardized data formats, metadata, and data models (Badidi et al., 2020; Barik, Dubey, et al., 2018).
Investing in technical infrastructure and capabilities	To enhance the availability and accessibility of fog computing resources for SDI users, investment in technical infrastructure and capabilities, such as hardware, software, and network resources, can be made (Barik, Dubey, et al., 2018; Bhusan Dash et al., 2023; T. P. Da Silva et al., 2022).
Developing policies and governance frameworks	To ensure the ethical use of geospatial data and facilitate the co-creation of value between fog computing and SDI users, clear policies and governance frameworks can be developed (Barik et al., 2019; Ghosh & Mukherjee, 2022; Saber et al., 2022).
Encouraging capacity building and training	To improve the skills and knowledge of fog computing providers and SDI users, training and capacity-building initiatives can be promoted, enabling them to make better use of fog computing technologies for geospatial data processing, analysis, and dissemination (T. P. Da Silva et al., 2022; Perera et al., 2017).

structure and capabilities such as hardware, software, and network resources to enhance the availability and accessibility of fog computing resources for SDI users. The fourth point suggests the development of clear policies and governance frameworks to ensure the ethical use of geospatial data and facilitate the co-creation of value between fog computing and SDI users. The final point emphasizes the need for capacity building and training initiatives to enhance the skills and knowledge of fog computing providers and SDI users, enabling them to make better use of fog computing technologies for geospatial data processing, analysis, and dissemination.

The final step discusses how fog computing impacts SDI users based on its possible advantages and value for SDI users. Table 7 summarizes the probable impacts, opportunities, and utility of fog computing for SDI users.

Table 7 summarizes the benefits of fog computing for SDI users, the value derived from these benefits, and the potential impacts. Fog computing provides real-time data processing and analysis, reduced latency in geospatial data analysis, improved data security and privacy, increased availability and accessibility of geospatial data, and scalability of computing resources. These benefits translate into improved decision-making based on up-to-date and accurate information, improved efficiency and faster response time for time-sensitive applications, increased protection and privacy of sensitive geospatial data, enhanced access to and utilization of geospatial data, and ability to handle large volumes of data and increased processing power. The potential impacts of these benefits include better resource management, cost savings, improved service delivery, improved public safety, and better urban planning. Fog computing offers significant potential for enhancing the value co-creation process between fog computing and SDI users by providing a range of benefits that can improve decision-making, increase efficiency, and enhance the overall effectiveness of geospatial data processing, analysis, and dissemination.

6. DISCUSSION

Through the application of SDL to the relationship between fog computing and SDI, we gained a more profound comprehension of how these technologies can work together to create value for users. The findings of the study revealed some significant advantages of fog computing for SDI. One of these benefits is the ability to process geospatial data in real time, which provides users with quicker and more

Table 7. Potential impacts

Benefits of Fog Computing for SDI Users	Value for SDI Users	Potential Impact
Real-time data processing and analysis	Improved decision-making based on up-to-date and accurate information	Improved situational awareness and decision-making capabilities
Reduced latency in geospatial data analysis	Improved efficiency and faster response time for time-sensitive applications	Improved collaboration and knowledge sharing for more timely and responsive services
Improved data security and privacy	Increased protection and privacy of sensitive geospatial data	Better protection and management of sensitive data
Increased availability and accessibility of geospatial data	Enhanced access to and utilization of geospatial data	Improved data sharing and collaboration
Scalability of computing resources	Ability to handle large volumes of data and increased processing power	Ability to handle large and complex data sets

precise insights into the data. By reducing the latency in geospatial data analysis, users can make better-informed decisions promptly. Another benefit is improved data security and privacy, as fog computing provides end-to-end encryption and other security measures that ensure the confidentiality and privacy of geospatial data. Moreover, fog computing can enhance the availability and accessibility of geospatial data by processing data closer to the edge of the network, which reduces the amount of data that needs to be transmitted over the network. Additionally, the scalability of fog computing resources enables SDI users to customize their infrastructure to fulfill various application requirements, allowing them to handle different data processing tasks effectively.

The study results also indicated the value of fog computing benefits for SDI users, as it can significantly impact various components of the SDI. One of the most significant benefits of fog computing is its ability to provide real-time data processing and analysis, reducing the latency of data processing, and leading to improved decision-making based on accurate and up-to-date information. This technology allows SDI users to analyze geospatial data in real time and gain insights that were not possible before. The quick and precise data processing can result in improved efficiency and faster response time for time-sensitive applications. Another critical benefit of fog computing is its improved data security and privacy features, which protect the confidentiality and privacy of geospatial data through end-to-end encryption and other security measures. Fog computing can be linked with governance by developing policies and practices to secure sensitive geospatial data, building trust among stakeholders, and ensuring the ethical use of geospatial data. By establishing clear policies and governance frameworks, SDI users can facilitate the co-creation of value between fog computing and SDI users.

Another advantage of fog computing is that it can boost the accessibility and availability of geospatial data by processing data closer to the edge of the network. This, in turn, decreases the amount of data that must be transmitted over the network, leading to better utilization and access to geospatial data. SDI users and fog computing providers can collaborate to develop common goals, objectives, and communication channels for partnership and teamwork. This can lead to more efficient delivery of services, better resource utilization, and improved decision-making. By providing better data security and privacy, increasing the availability and accessibility of geospatial data, and providing scalability of computing resources, fog computing has the potential to offer significant benefits to SDI users. By leveraging this technology, SDI users can enhance the value of geospatial data, improve decision-making, and manage complex systems more effectively. To reap the full benefits of fog computing, SDI users can collaborate with fog computing providers to improve the quality and interoperability of geospatial data, invest in technical infrastructure and capabilities, develop governance frameworks and policies, and encourage capacity building and training initiatives.

The study revealed several challenges that affect the advantages of using fog computing. One such challenge is the need for fog computing providers to understand the specific needs and requirements of SDI users so that they can design and develop systems that fully utilize the potential benefits of real-time data processing and enhanced data security and privacy. Additionally, fostering collaboration and partnerships among stakeholders is crucial to realize the benefits of fog computing. Through effective communication and collaboration, fog computing providers and SDI users can identify common objectives and goals, leading to the co-creation of value from geospatial data.

Ensuring the quality and interoperability of geospatial data is crucial for the increased availability and accessibility of data provided by fog computing. Improving the quality and interoperability of geospatial data can enable SDI users to make better use of fog computing technologies, resulting in improved decision-making, efficiency, and faster response times. Having appropriate technical infrastructure and capabilities, such as hardware, software, and network resources, is also essential for fog computing to offer scalability of computing resources. By investing in these resources, SDI users can manage large volumes of data and increase processing power. Furthermore, clear policy and governance frameworks are critical for the ethical use of geospatial data and the co-creation of value between fog computing and SDI users. Such frameworks can ensure the protection and privacy of sensitive geospatial data while enabling enhanced access to and utilization of geospatial data.

The findings proposed suggestions for enhancing the collaborative process of value creation between fog computing and SDI users. The first suggestion emphasizes the significance of collaboration and partnership to identify common objectives and effective communication channels for cooperation and engagement. This is especially important as the successful deployment of fog computing depends on the involvement of all stakeholders. The second recommendation stresses the need to improve geospatial data quality and interoperability, which is vital for ensuring compatibility between fog computing and SDI systems. By utilizing standardized data formats, metadata, and data models, geospatial data can be better integrated and used in fog computing systems. The third recommendation highlights the importance of investing in technical infrastructure and capabilities, such as hardware, software, and network resources, to enhance the availability and accessibility of fog computing resources for SDI users. Through these investments, SDI users can access the necessary resources and tools for effective management, processing, and analysis of geospatial data.

The fourth recommendation proposes the creation of explicit policies and governance frameworks to ensure that the use of geospatial data is ethical and to promote value co-creation between fog computing and SDI users. This suggestion is critical to guarantee that the use of geospatial data adheres to ethical principles and facilitates an atmosphere that encourages value co-creation between fog computing and SDI users. The final recommendation underscores the importance of capacity building and training programs to enhance the expertise and knowledge of both fog computing providers and SDI users, which will allow them to leverage fog computing technologies for geospatial data processing, analysis, and dissemination more effectively. This recommendation is critical to ensure that all stakeholders possess the required skills and knowledge to utilize fog computing technologies to their fullest potential, thus contributing to the value co-creation process between fog computing and SDI users.

The SDL framework analysis revealed the potential impacts of fog computing for SDI users and the value that could be derived from it. Real-time data processing and analysis have the potential to provide SDI users with accurate and timely information, leading to improved decision-making. Furthermore, faster response times can be achieved by reducing latency in geospatial data analysis, improving the efficiency of time-sensitive applications. Improved data security and privacy can also protect sensitive geospatial data from data breaches and unauthorized access. Moreover, fog computing can enhance the availability and accessibility of geospatial data, allowing for better utilization of the data. The scalability of computing resources can support users in handling larger volumes of data and increased processing power, which can lead to better resource management and cost savings.

The benefits of fog computing for SDI users have the potential to create various impacts, such as improving service delivery, public safety, and urban planning. The ability to make decisions based on real-time data can improve service delivery, and faster response times can enhance public safety. The increased availability and accessibility of geospatial data can facilitate more efficient and sustainable development, resulting in better urban planning. The use of fog computing can lead to better decision-making, increase efficiency, and improve the overall effectiveness of geospatial data processing, analysis, and dissemination, thereby enhancing the value co-creation process between fog computing and SDI users. These benefits have significant and diverse potential impacts, highlighting the potential of fog computing to revolutionize the management and utilization of geospatial data.

7. CONCLUSION

This chapter evaluated the opportunities and challenges of using fog computing in SDI, using the service-dominant logic framework. SDL emphasized the co-creation of value between the service provider (fog computing) and the service user (SDI) by focusing on the delivery of outcomes that fulfill the needs and preferences of the users. The results of the study showed that fog computing can enhance the performance and efficiency of SDI by providing real-time geospatial data processing, quicker analysis of geospatial data, enhanced security and privacy of data, augmented availability and accessibility of geospatial data, as well as the ability to scale computing resources. Faster and more accurate data processing can benefit various domains such as environmental monitoring, urban planning, disaster management, transportation, and agriculture. Despite the opportunities, several challenges need to be addressed when using fog computing in SDI. The challenges include understanding user needs, promoting collaboration, ensuring data quality and interoperability, having the right technical infrastructure, and establishing clear governance policies.

This chapter also outlined ways to improve the value co-creation process between fog computing and SDI users. These include collaboration and partnership, improving geospatial data quality and interoperability, investing in technical infrastructure and capabilities, developing clear policies and governance frameworks, and providing capacity-building and training initiatives. These measures aim to enhance communication, standardization, accessibility, ethics, and skills development in the use of fog computing technologies for geospatial data. Fog computing offers benefits such as real-time data processing and improved data security for SDI users, resulting in improved decision-making and increased efficiency. This can also lead to better resource management, cost savings, and improved service delivery. The potential impacts include improved public safety and urban planning. Fog computing has the potential to enhance the value co-creation process between fog computing and SDI users by improving the overall effectiveness of geospatial data processing, analysis, and dissemination

In terms of limitations, this study has focused on the conceptual and theoretical aspects of the relationship between fog computing and SDI. The study has not included any empirical evaluation of the proposed framework. Future research can investigate the practical implementation and evaluation of fog computing in SDI, including the development of interoperable and standardized platforms, and the assessment of the performance and effectiveness of fog computing in different SDI applications.

REFERENCES

Ahmad, M., Khayal, M. S. H., & Tahir, A. (2022). Analysis of Factors Affecting Adoption of Volunteered Geographic Information in the Context of National Spatial Data Infrastructure. ISPRS International Journal of Geo-Information, 11(2). https://doi.org/10.3390/ijgi11020120

Ajmi, M., Hamza, M. H., Labiadh, M., Yermani, M., Khatra, N. Ben, Al-Thubaiti, A. S., Moharrem, I. A., & Arrim, A. El (2014). Setting up a Spatial Data Infrastructure (SDI) for the ROSELT/OSS Network. *Journal of Geographic Information System, 06*(02), 150–161. doi:10.4236/jgis.2014.62016

Ali, A., Imran, M., Jabeen, M., Ali, Z., & Mahmood, S. A. (2021). Factors influencing integrated information management: Spatial data infrastructure in Pakistan. Information Development. https://doi.org/10.1177/02666669211048483

Arifin, S., Silalahi, F. E. S., Prayitno, M., Majid, N. K., Amhar, F., & Gularso, H. (2023). Geospatial Big Data Management Testing Using Open Source Technology. *Mechanisms and Machine Science, 121,* 29–42. doi:10.1007/978-3-031-09909-0_3

Ashok Sasane, S., Jadhav, A. S., Barik, R. K., Krishnakumar, G., & Raghavswamy, V. (2019). Application of spatial technology in Malaria information infrastructure mapping with climate change perspective in Maharashtra, India. *Mausam (New Delhi), 70*(4), 787–806. doi:10.54302/mausam.v70i4.264

Badidi, E., Mahrez, Z., & Sabir, E. (2020). Fog computing for smart cities' big data management and analytics: A review. In Future Internet, 12(11). doi:10.3390/fi12110190

Barik, R. K., Dubey, H., Mankodiya, K., Sasane, S. A., & Misra, C. (2019). GeoFog4Health: A fog-based SDI framework for geospatial health big data analysis. *Journal of Ambient Intelligence and Humanized Computing, 10*(2), 551–567. doi:10.100712652-018-0702-x

Barik, R. K., Dubey, H., Misra, C., Borthakur, D., Constant, N., Sasane, S. A., Lenka, R. K., Mishra, B. S. P., Das, H., & Mankodiya, K. (2018). Fog Assisted Cloud Computing in Era of Big Data and Internet-of-Things: Systems, Architectures, and Applications. In Studies in Big Data, 39. doi:10.1007/978-3-319-73676-1_14

Barik, R. K., Dubey, H., Samaddar, A. B., Gupta, R. D., & Ray, P. K. (2017). FogGIS: Fog Computing for geospatial big data analytics. *2016 IEEE Uttar Pradesh Section International Conference on Electrical, Computer and Electronics Engineering, UPCON 2016.* IEEE. 10.1109/UPCON.2016.7894725

Barik, R. K., Lenka, R. K., Simha, N. V. R., Dubey, H., & Mankodiya, K. (2017). *Fog computing based SDI framework for mineral resources information infrastructure management in India.* In arXiv.

Barik, R. K., Muruga Perumal, K., Ajay-D-Vimal Raj, P., & Rajasekar, S. (2018). Development and implementation of renewable energy potential geospatial database mapping in India for cloud SDI using open source GIS. *Lecture Notes in Electrical Engineering, 435,* 419–428. doi:10.1007/978-981-10-4286-7_41

Barik, R. K., Priyadarshini, R., Lenka, R. K., Dubey, H., & Mankodiya, K. (2020). Fog computing architecture for scalable processing of geospatial big data. *International Journal of Applied Geospatial Research, 11*(1), 1–20. doi:10.4018/IJAGR.2020010101

Bernard, L., & Ostländer, N. (2008). Assessing climate change vulnerability in the arctic using geographic information services in spatial data infrastructures. *Climatic Change, 87*(1–2), 263–281. Advance online publication. doi:10.100710584-007-9346-0

Bhattacharya, D., & Painho, M. (2017). Smart cities intelligence system (SMACISYS) integrating sensor web with spatial data infrastructures (sensdi). isprs. *Annals of the Photogrammetry, Remote Sensing and Spatial Information Sciences, 4*(4W3). doi:10.5194/isprs-annals-IV-4-W3-21-2017

Bhusan Dash, B., Shekhar Patra, S., Nanda, S., Rani Jena, J., Rout, S., & Kumar Barik, R. (2023). *SFA4SDI: A Secure Fog Architecture for Spatial Data Infrastructure.* IEEE. doi:10.1109/iSSSC56467.2022.10051572

Bishop, I. D., Escobar, F. J., Karuppannan, S., Williamson, I. P., Yates, P. M., Suwarnarat, K., & Yaqub, H. W. (2000). Spatial data infrastructures for cities in developing countries. Lessons from the Bangkok experience. *Cities (London, England), 17*(2), 85–96. doi:10.1016/S0264-2751(00)00004-4

Boerboom, I. (2010). *Integrating spatial planning and decision support system infrastructure and spatial data infrastructure.* GSDI 12 World Conference, Singapore. http://www.gsdi.org/gsdiconf/gsdi12/papers/82.pdf

Bonomi, F., Milito, R., Natarajan, P., & Zhu, J. (2014). Fog computing: A platform for internet of things and analytics. *Studies in Computational Intelligence, 546,* 169–186. Advance online publication. doi:10.1007/978-3-319-05029-4_7

Bonomi, F., Milito, R., Zhu, J., & Addepalli, S. (2012). Fog computing and its role in the internet of things. *MCC'12 - Proceedings of the 1st ACM Mobile Cloud Computing Workshop.* ACM. 10.1145/2342509.2342513

Bordogna, G., Kliment, T., Frigerio, L., Brivio, P. A., Crema, A., Stroppiana, D., Boschetti, M., & Sterlacchini, S. (2016). A spatial data infrastructure integrating multisource heterogeneous geospatial data and time series: A study case in agriculture. *ISPRS International Journal of Geo-Information, 5*(5), 73. doi:10.3390/ijgi5050073

Borzacchiello, M. T., & Craglia, M. (2013). Estimating benefits of spatial data infrastructures: A case study on e-Cadastres. *Computers, Environment and Urban Systems, 41,* 276–288. doi:10.1016/j.compenvurbsys.2012.05.004

Chaturvedi, K., Matheus, A., Nguyen, S. H., & Kolbe, T. H. (2019). Securing Spatial Data Infrastructures for Distributed Smart City applications and services. *Future Generation Computer Systems, 101,* 723–736. doi:10.1016/j.future.2019.07.002

Chemodanov, D., Calyam, P., & Palaniappan, K. (2020). Fog computing to enable geospatial video analytics for disaster-incident situational awareness. In *Fog Computing.* Theory and Practice. doi:10.1002/9781119551713.ch19

Chen, N., Chen, Y., Ye, X., Ling, H., Song, S., & Huang, C. T. (2017; Vol. 22). Smart City Surveillance in Fog Computing. In Studies in Big Data. doi:10.1007/978-3-319-45145-9_9

Corti, P., Bartoli, F., Fabiani, A., Giovando, C., Kralidis, A. T., & Tzotsos, A. (2019). GeoNode: An open source framework to build spatial data infrastructures. *PeerJ, 7.*

Crompvoets, J., Bregt, A., Rajabifard, A., & Williamson, I. (2004). Assessing the worldwide developments of national spatial data clearinghouses. *International Journal of Geographical Information Science, 18*(7), 665–689. doi:10.1080/13658810410001702030

Crompvoets, J., Vancauwenberghe, G., Bouckaert, G., & Vandenbroucke, D. (2011). Practices to develop spatial data infrastructures: Exploring the contribution to e-government. In *Practical Studies in E-Government*. Best Practices from Around the World. doi:10.1007/978-1-4419-7533-1_13

Da Silva, T. P., Batista, T., Lopes, F., Neto, A. R., Delicato, F. C., Pires, P. F., & Da Rocha, A. R. (2022). Fog Computing Platforms for Smart City Applications: A Survey. *ACM Transactions on Internet Technology*, *22*(4), 1–32. doi:10.1145/3488585

Das, J., Ghosh, S. K., & Buyya, R. (2021). Geospatial Edge-Fog Computing: A Systematic Review, Taxonomy, and Future Directions. In Mobile Edge Computing. doi:10.1007/978-3-030-69893-5_3

de Mendonça, F. F. Junior, Lopes Dias, K., d'Orey, P. M., & Kokkinogenis, Z. (2021). FogWise: On the limits of the coexistence of heterogeneous applications on Fog computing and Internet of Vehicles. *Transactions on Emerging Telecommunications Technologies*, *32*(1). doi:10.1002/ett.4145

de Moura Costa, H. J., da Costa, C. A., da Rosa Righi, R., & Antunes, R. S. (2020). Fog computing in health: A systematic literature review. In Health and Technology, 10(5). doi:10.100712553-020-00431-8

Font, X., English, R., Gkritzali, A., & Tian, W. (2021). Value co-creation in sustainable tourism: A service-dominant logic approach. *Tourism Management*, *82*, 104200. doi:10.1016/j.tourman.2020.104200

Fu, C., Lv, Q., & Badrnejad, R. G. (2020). Fog computing in health management processing systems. In Kybernetes, 49(12). doi:10.1108/K-09-2019-0621

Ghosh, S., & Mukherjee, A. (2022). STROVE: Spatial data infrastructure enabled cloud–fog–edge computing framework for combating COVID-19 pandemic. *Innovations in Systems and Software Engineering*. doi:10.100711334-022-00458-2 PMID:35677629

Ghosh, S., Mukherjee, A., Ghosh, S. K., & Buyya, R. (2022). STOPPAGE: Spatio-temporal data driven cloud-fog-edge computing framework for pandemic monitoring and management. *Software, Practice & Experience*, *52*(12), 2700–2726. doi:10.1002pe.3144

Giuliani, G., Lacroix, P., Guigoz, Y., Roncella, R., Bigagli, L., Santoro, M., Mazzetti, P., Nativi, S., Ray, N., & Lehmann, A. (2017). Bringing GEOSS Services into Practice: A Capacity Building Resource on Spatial Data Infrastructures (SDI). *Transactions in GIS*, *21*(4), 811–824. doi:10.1111/tgis.12209

Gomes, E., Costa, F., De Rolt, C., Plentz, P., & Dantas, M. (2021). A Survey from Real-Time to Near Real-Time Applications in Fog Computing Environments. In Telecom, 2(4). doi:10.3390/telecom2040028

Groot, R., & McLaughlin, J. (2000). Geospatial data infrastructure : concepts, cases and good practice. In R. Groot & J. McLaughlin (Eds.), *GeoSpatial Data Infrastructure: Concepts, Cases and Good Practice*. Oxford University Press. https://research.utwente.nl/en/publications/geospatial-data-infrastructure-concepts-cases-and-good-practice

GSDI. (2004). Developing Spatial Data Infrastructures: The SDI Cookbook. In GSDI/Nebert.

Hashmi, A., Ahmad, M. A., & Nawaz, M. A. (2021). The Role of Coordination, Decision Making and Spatial Data Infrastructure on the Disaster Management in Pakistan: Moderating Role of Information System. *Review of Applied Management and Social Sciences*, *4*(1), 79–91. doi:10.47067/ramss.v4i1.100

Hendriks, P. H. J., Dessers, E., & van Hootegem, G. (2012). Reconsidering the definition of a spatial data infrastructure. In International Journal of Geographical Information Science, 26(8), 1479–1494. doi:10.1080/13658816.2011.639301

Higgins, C. I., Williams, J., Leibovici, D. G., Simonis, I., Davis, M. J., Muldoon, C., van Genuchten, P., O'Hare, G., & Wiemann, S. (2016). Citizen OBservatory WEB (COBWEB): A Generic Infrastructure Platform to Facilitate the Collection of Citizen Science data for Environmental Monitoring. *International Journal of Spatial Data Infrastructures Research*, *11*. doi:10.2902/1725-0463.2016.11.art3

Hu, P., Dhelim, S., Ning, H., & Qiu, T. (2017). Survey on fog computing: architecture, key technologies, applications and open issues. In Journal of Network and Computer Applications, 98). doi:10.1016/j.jnca.2017.09.002

Indrajit, A., van Loenen, B., Suprajaka, Jaya, V. E., Ploeger, H., Lemmen, C., & van Oosterom, P. (2021). Implementation of the spatial plan information package for improving ease of doing business in Indonesian cities. *Land Use Policy*, *105*, 105338. doi:10.1016/j.landusepol.2021.105338

Jacoby, S., Smith, J., Ting, L., & Williamson, I. (2002). Developing a common spatial data infrastructure between state and local government - An Australian case study. *International Journal of Geographical Information Science*, *16*(4), 305–322. doi:10.1080/13658810110096001

Javadzadeh, G., & Rahmani, A. M. (2020). Fog Computing Applications in Smart Cities: A Systematic Survey. *Wireless Networks*, *26*(2), 1433–1457. doi:10.100711276-019-02208-y

Jeyashree, G., & Padmavathi, S. (2023). A Fog Cluster-Based Framework for Personalized Healthcare Monitoring. In Research Advances in Network Technologies. doi:10.1201/9781003320333-7

Kamruzzaman, M. M., Yan, B., Sarker, M. N. I., Alruwaili, O., Wu, M., & Alrashdi, I. (2022). Blockchain and Fog Computing in IoT-Driven Healthcare Services for Smart Cities. *Journal of Healthcare Engineering*, *2022*, 1–13. doi:10.1155/2022/9957888 PMID:35126961

Kumar, A., Upadhyay, A., Mishra, N., Nath, S., Yadav, K. R., & Sharma, G. (2022; Vol. 1030). Privacy and Security Concerns in Edge Computing-Based Smart Cities. In Studies in Computational Intelligence. doi:10.1007/978-3-030-96737-6_5

Lutz, M., Sprado, J., Klien, E., Schubert, C., & Christ, I. (2009). Overcoming semantic heterogeneity in spatial data infrastructures. *Computers & Geosciences*, *35*(4), 739–752. doi:10.1016/j.cageo.2007.09.017

Manfré, L., Hirata, E., Silva, J. B., Shinohara, E. J., Giannotti, M., Larocca, A. P. C., & Quintanilha, J. (2012). An Analysis of Geospatial Technologies for Risk and Natural Disaster Management. *ISPRS International Journal of Geo-Information*, *1*(2), 166–185. doi:10.3390/ijgi1020166

Masser, I. (1999). All shapes and sizes: The first generation of national spatial data infrastructures. *International Journal of Geographical Information Science*, *13*(1), 67–84. doi:10.1080/136588199241463

Masser, I. (2005). GIS worlds: creating spatial data infrastructures, 338). ESRI press Redlands, CA.

Masser, I. (2009). Changing notions of a spatial data infrastructure. *SDI Convergence*, 219–228. http://drupal.gsdi.org/gsdiconf/gsdi11/SDICnvrgncBook.pdf#page=228

McLaughlin, J. D. (1991). Towards national spatial data infrastructure. *Proceedings of the Canadian Conference on GIS*, (pp. 1–5). IEEE.

Mohammadi, H. (2008). The Integration of multi-source spatial datasets in the context of SDI initiatives. [PhD thesis. Department of Geomatics. The University of Melbourne].

Molina, M., & Bayarri, S. (2011). A multinational SDI-based system to facilitate disaster risk management in the Andean Community. *Computers & Geosciences*, *37*(9), 1501–1510. Advance online publication. doi:10.1016/j.cageo.2011.01.015

Mouradian, C., Naboulsi, D., Yangui, S., Glitho, R. H., Morrow, M. J., & Polakos, P. A. (2018). A Comprehensive Survey on Fog Computing: State-of-the-Art and Research Challenges. In IEEE Communications Surveys and Tutorials, 20(1). doi:10.1109/COMST.2017.2771153

Nguyen, N. D., Phan, L. A., Park, D. H., Kim, S., & Kim, T. (2020). ElasticFog: Elastic resource provisioning in container-based fog computing. *IEEE Access : Practical Innovations, Open Solutions*, *8*, 183879–183890. doi:10.1109/ACCESS.2020.3029583

Ometov, A., Molua, O. L., Komarov, M., & Nurmi, J. (2022). A Survey of Security in Cloud, Edge, and Fog Computing. In Sensors, 22(3). doi:10.339022030927

Perera, C., Qin, Y., Estrella, J. C., Reiff-Marganiec, S., & Vasilakos, A. V. (2017). Fog computing for sustainable smart cities: A survey. *ACM Computing Surveys*, *50*(3), 1–43. doi:10.1145/3057266

Popović, I., Radovanovic, I., Vajs, I., Drajic, D., & Gligorić, N. (2022). Building Low-Cost Sensing Infrastructure for Air Quality Monitoring in Urban Areas Based on Fog Computing. *Sensors (Basel)*, *22*(3), 1026. doi:10.339022031026 PMID:35161775

Qi, Q., & Tao, F. (2019). A Smart Manufacturing Service System Based on Edge Computing, Fog Computing, and Cloud Computing. *IEEE Access : Practical Innovations, Open Solutions*, *7*, 86769–86777. doi:10.1109/ACCESS.2019.2923610

Quy, V. K., Van Hau, N., Van Anh, D., & Ngoc, L. A. (2022). Smart healthcare IoT applications based on fog computing: Architecture, applications and challenges. *Complex & Intelligent Systems*, *8*(5), 3805–3815. doi:10.100740747-021-00582-9 PMID:34804767

Rabindra, B. (2017). CloudGanga: Cloud computing based SDI model for ganga river basin management in India. *International Journal of Agricultural and Environmental Information Systems*, *8*(4), 54–71. doi:10.4018/IJAEIS.2017100104

Rajabifard, A., Binns, A., Masser, I., & Williamson, I. (2006). The role of sub-national government and the private sector in future spatial data infrastructures. *International Journal of Geographical Information Science*, *20*(7), 727–741. doi:10.1080/13658810500432224

Rajabifard, A., Feeney, M. E. F., & Williamson, I. P. (2002). Future directions for SDI development. *International Journal of Applied Earth Observation and Geoinformation*, *4*(1), 11–22. doi:10.1016/S0303-2434(02)00002-8

Rajabifard, A., Mansourian, A., Javad, M., Zoej, V., & Williamson, I. (2002). Developing Spatial Data Infrastructure to Facilitate Disaster Management. *Management*.

Rosario Michel, G., Gonzalez-Campos, M. E., Manzano Aybar, F., Jiménez Durán, T., & Crompvoets, J. (2023). Identifying critical factors to enhance SDI performance for facilitating disaster risk management in small island developing states. *Survey Review*, *55*(389), 114–126. doi:10.1080/00396265.2021.2024969

Roy, C., Maheshwari, E., Pandey, M., Rautaray, S. S., & Barik, R. K. (2022). *GeoCloud4EduNet: Geospatial Cloud Computing Model for Visualization and Analysis of Educational Information Network*. doi:10.1007/978-981-19-0475-2_2

Saber, W., Eisa, R., & Attia, R. (2022). *Efficient Geospatial Data Analysis Framework in Fog Environment*. IEEE. doi:10.1109/ACCESS.2022.3231787

Sadri, A. A., Rahmani, A. M., Saberikamarposhti, M., & Hosseinzadeh, M. (2022). Data reduction in fog computing and internet of things: A systematic literature survey. *Internet of Things (Netherlands)*, *20*, 100629. Advance online publication. doi:10.1016/j.iot.2022.100629

Silva, D. S., & Holanda, M. (2022). Applications of geospatial big data in the Internet of Things. In Transactions in GIS, 26(1). doi:10.1111/tgis.12846

Sood, S. K., & Singh, K. D. (2018). An Optical-Fog assisted EEG-based virtual reality framework for enhancing E-learning through educational games. *Computer Applications in Engineering Education*, *26*(5), 1565–1576. doi:10.1002/cae.21965

Tang, B., Chen, Z., Hefferman, G., Pei, S., Wei, T., He, H., & Yang, Q. (2017). Incorporating Intelligence in Fog Computing for Big Data Analysis in Smart Cities. *IEEE Transactions on Industrial Informatics*, *13*(5), 2140–2150. doi:10.1109/TII.2017.2679740

Thakur, A., & Malekian, R. (2019). Fog Computing for Detecting Vehicular Congestion, an Internet of Vehicles Based Approach: A Review. *IEEE Intelligent Transportation Systems Magazine*, *11*(2), 8–16. doi:10.1109/MITS.2019.2903551

Tripathi, A. K., Agrawal, S., & Gupta, R. D. (2020). Cloud enabled SDI architecture: a review. In Earth Science Informatics, 13(2). doi:10.100712145-020-00446-9

Vancauwenberghe, G., & van Loenen, B. (2018). *Exploring the Emergence of Open Spatial Data Infrastructures: Analysis of Recent Developments and Trends in Europe*. Springer. doi:10.1007/978-3-319-59442-2_2

Vidal-Filho, J. N., Times, V. C., Lisboa-Filho, J., & Renso, C. (2021). Towards the Semantic Enrichment of Trajectories Using Spatial Data Infrastructures. *ISPRS International Journal of Geo-Information*, *10*(12), 825. doi:10.3390/ijgi10120825

Zhang, M., & Berghäll, S. (2021). E-commerce in agri-food sector: A systematic literature review based on service-dominant logic. In Journal of Theoretical and Applied Electronic Commerce Research, 16(7). doi:10.3390/jtaer16070182

Section 3
Multi–Disciplinary Applications of Fog Computing

Chapter 9
Application of Fog Computing in the Retail Industry for Transition to Retail 4.0:
An Overview

Sreekumar

iD https://orcid.org/0000-0002-6534-896X

Rourkela Institute of Management Studies, India

Swati Das

Rourkela Institute of Management Studies, India

Rema Gopalan

CMR Institute of Technology, India

Bikash Ranjan Debata

Kirloskar Institute of Management, India

ABSTRACT

Retail industry plays an important role in global economic scenario and contributes around 27 percent of world economy. The use of information technology enhances customer self-awareness, and it is a proven fact that consumers who enjoy their shopping experience end up buying more and more things. Retail is one of the sectors that has seen significant change since the introduction of Industry 4.0 technologies like cloud computing, IoT, fog computing, artificial intelligence, etc. This change can be seen in supermarkets like Amazon Go store, Alibaba Hema store, IKEA, and many more. The study focuses on various technological advancement including application of fog computing for giving the Indian retail industry a competitive advantage. The study also observes that store organizations that emphasize store design and adoption of technological innovations to simplify the purchasing process have been very successful in creating loyal customers for their stores.

DOI: 10.4018/978-1-6684-4466-5.ch009

1. INTRODUCTION

Retail industry plays an important role in global economic scenario and contributes around 27 percent of world economy. As per retail reports, in United States the retail industry accounts for around 22 percent of its GDP and in India the figure is over 10 percent. The retail experience today is vastly different from 10 years ago when entering a store was the only option. The adoption of technological advances in retail has opened up a world of new opportunities. Manufacturing innovation has led to the automation of traditional manufacturing and industrial processes. It is a proven fact that the use of information technology raises consumers' self-awareness and that customers who enjoy shopping are buying more and more. Retail is one of the sectors that has seen significant change since the introduction of Industry 4.0 technologies like Cloud Computing, IoT, Fog Computing, AI etc. This change can be seen in supermarkets such as Amazon GoStore, Alibaba Hema Store, IKEA etc.

This study focuses on how shopping behavior in the digital world creates challenges for retailers. The retailers are forced to revamp their current business models by applying digital technology to transform their offerings and customer experiences. In the past, retailers have attempted to create customer categories without relying on statistics and historical data, today they have to depend on flexible information related to customer perceptions to craft strategies. For this reason, retailers must use digital data and digital information to connect customers across multiple technologies and multiple sensory domains. Customer touchpoints are now in digital signage, Bluetooth beacons and customer smartphones. At its core is a digital platform that serves as a visual link between the customer touchpoints and the many front and back programs that own all the data and information. In fact, we need to know our customers' needs and desires just in case.

The Internet of Things (IoT) is aiming to connect billions of smart things to the Internet, which could provide a promising future for smart cities. These devices are expected to generate large amounts of data, especially when gathering information so that appropriate actions can be taken, and send the data to the cloud for further processing. However, actually hearing all the possible data objects captured by an intelligent object and sending the complete captured data to the cloud is not very helpful. In addition, such an approach could also lead to the loss of resources (e.g., network, storage, etc.). The Fog (Edge) computing paradigm has been proposed to address vulnerabilities by pushing data acquisition processes using data analysis at the edges. However, peripheral devices have limited calculation capabilities. Because of the strengths and weaknesses inherited, Cloud computing or Fog computing paradigm deals with these challenges alone. Therefore, both paradigms need to work together to build a sustainable IoT infrastructure for smart cities. With advances in the Internet of Things (IoT) technology, as well as a reduction in its cost and maintenance, researchers are looking for ways to harness this technology to make cities smarter (Aliyu et al., 2023). In this study we review the existing ways to deal with challenges in the Fog computer domain. Specifically, we describe a few encouraging aspects of Fog computing usage, identify ten key features and common features of Fog computing. Based on our study, we have also identified a number of major functions that Fog computer platforms should support and a few open-to-use challenges, in order to illuminate future research guidelines on recognizing Fog computing for smart and sustainable retail business. Fog computing brings cloud services closer to the edge, enabling faster response times and reduced latency for applications and services. This is particularly advantageous for real-time and latency-sensitive applications, such as IoT, augmented reality, and autonomous vehicles (Vina Gautam et. al, 2023).

In this study we discuss about the impact of IoT and fog computing on Indian retail industry. The study also focuses on various technological advancement including application of Fog computing for giving the Indian retail industry a competitive advantage. The study also observes that store organizations that emphasize store design and adoption of technological innovations to simplify the purchasing process have been very successful in creating loyal customers for their stores. However, India is still lacking in the adoption of IT systems in the retail sector and greater efforts are needed in this regard.

2. GLOBAL RETAIL SCENARIO

The continuous evolution of the retailing landscape forces retailers to operate in a highly dynamic and competitive customer-driven market. They are required to constantly adapt to the changing expectations of consumers in order to keep them coming back. The retail industry has witnessed several changes during the period of 2019-2022, with changing economic conditions across the world. The global economy, which slowed in 2019, crashed in 2020 due to the COVID-19 outbreak, resulting in a challenging forecast period for the retail industry (OECD, 2020). According to Modor Intelligence retail report, the retail industry is expected to show slow recovery during the initial forecast period, yet the customer necessity for the majority of products is anticipated to drive the market once the situation settles down.

As per the retail reports, the global retail industry is mature and highly competitive in the developed economies of Europe and North America. On the other hand, the developing economies of Asia-Pacific, the Middle East, and Latin America have been instrumental in driving the market growth. Countries, such as Singapore, Malaysia, and Thailand, are popular shopping destinations in the Asia-Pacific region, with visitors contributing substantially to the retail sectors in the respective markets. According to AT Kearney (2021) report, consumer spending world's centre of gravity is shifting away from the US and developed European markets. The report also highlights that the pace of that development is directly linked to the innovation, penetration, and acceptance of consumer and retail technologies, from simple mobile phone connectivity to sophisticated and secure electronic payment systems. Consumer spending, which typically accounts for more than two-thirds of the GDP, has been a key indicator of the health of the retail market. Moreover, the increasing strength of online shopping has been a major driver (especially during the COVID-19 crisis). Apart from this, the growing smartphone penetration across countries is driving the e-commerce channel. Also, IoT, augmented reality, and other disruptive technologies are reshaping the retail industry. According to a study by Ernst and Young, retail business leaders see digitalization as the driving tool in returning to growth in the post Covid-19 era. From Industrial Age, department stores to today's multi-channel, ubiquitous environments, the evolution of retail business continues to change dramatically.

2.1. Indian Retail Industry

As per Kearney Research, India's retail industry is projected to grow at a slower pace of nine percent over 2019-2030, from 779 billion US dollars in 2019 to 1,407 billion US dollars by 2026 and more than 1.8 trillion US dollars by 2030. According to the Retailers Association of India (RAI), the retail industry achieved ninety three percent of pre-COVID sales in February 2021; consumer durables and quick service restaurants (QSR) increased by 15 percent and 18 percent respectively.Indian retail industry has emerged as one of the most dynamic and fast-paced industries due to the entry of several new players.

The technology adoption was treading slowly in the Indian retail world until 2020. However, the CO-VID-19 pandemic-induced crisis catapulted technology adoption in the Indian retail market unlike ever before, and today, retail leadership are talking about integrating the latest technologies to enhance their customer's online shopping experience. The past two years have seen the rise of new customer segments, and new capital has been unlocked to target and convert them into loyal customers. Most of the strategies crafted by the retailers are targeted for online platforms. The merging of offline and online platforms has never been this obvious as we see the impact of Artificial Intelligence shape customer experience like never before. From creating virtual (called synthetic) models to automate image generation, to creating world-class content using AI, merchants are tapping into new customer cohorts through targeted media. Technology is playing a pivotal role in formalization of retail-both online and offline channels are boosting their technology, and closely collaborating with each other, to drive efficiencies, increase market access, and create compelling value propositions for consumers (NASSCOM, 2021). The following section discusses the evolution of retail industry from Retail 1.0 to Retail 4.0 and specifically in the Indian retail context.

2.2. Revolution of the Retail Industry

Through the ages, the retail industry had developed in a strong correlation with transportation, technology developments and culture. As a result of industrial revolution, the retail industry also experienced a four times revolution. The retail industry's revolution can be divided into three areas; namely Retail 1.0, Retail 2.0, Retail 3.0, and Retail 4.0. For India's retail journey from Retail 1.0 to 3.0, the sector evolved from being a near-complete neighborhood *kirana* market to becoming a global, multi-channel retail market with cross-border trade, product diversification and rapid technology advancement.

Retail 1.0: According to Susan (2020), the first retail disruption, or Retail 1.0, also known as mechanization, began in the mid-eighteenth century and ended in the mid-nineteenth century as electrification and mass production was introduced and the second industrial revolution happened.In the grocery business, Piggly Wiggly was arguably the earliest and most influential innovator, offering the first true self-service grocery store—at least in America. Before the late 1800s, neighborhood merchants dominated retail, providing comprehensive services to clients, such as credit, repairs, and one-on-one assistance to explain the details and advantages of products to customers (Har Loh Li et al., 2022). Individuals were required to carry cash, and merchants were required to physically deposit cash and checks to keep the wheels of commerce turning. Nonetheless, technological advancements during the industrial revolution resulted in a significant rise in the availability of affordable, high-quality goods (Lumen Learning, 2020). Department stores such as Bloomingdales, Sears and Macy's have started to appear in Chicago and New York City as more prosperous Americans develop broader preferences.

In India, while dominated by traditional retail, Retail 1.0 saw emergence of pure-play modern retail, in metro cities in 1990s. The consumer preference started shifting from need-based shopping to premium shopping experience, and first signs of modernization in operations (backend) and formalization of value chain appeared.

Retail 2.0: Modern retail evolved in Retail 2.0 with emergence of hyper-marts, super-marts, and cash and carry stores formats, coupled with geographical expansion from Metros to Tier 1 cities. The key consideration for consumer transitioned from premium shopping experience to convenience; and technology accelerated the modernization in operations (backend). Players started leveraging technology for information dissemination through websites. The focus of the retailers shifted to superior and consistent customer experience with greater product assortment.

Retail 3.0: Retail 3.0 began with the creation of the Internet, which permitted the global production, marketing, and consumption of products and services and the global utilize of digital technologies (Reagan and Singh, 2020). In India, Retail 3.0 was marked with a rapid growth phase, and an increased realization by all retail participants of the need to embrace digital technologies in order to remain relevant to an increasingly digital consumer. Personalization became the key consideration for customer, and retail growth story started moving beyond top 500 cities in India.

Retail 4.0: Emergence of Industry 4.0 has led to a steep shift towards the adoption of digitisation. Advanced technologies have revolutionized the retail industry bringing forth its new avatar - Retail 4.0. From automation of the operational process to churning of digital data encompassing buyer's journey that is proving instrumental in retail business strategies, retail industry underwent a renaissance of sorts. The term Retail 4.0 has appeared to explain an abundance of trends and developments in the global retail sector. Often referred to as "intelligent digital," it focuses on bringing innovation to customer experience and reconsidering the role of the store in merchant-customer relationships. Retail 4.0 is the fourth retail industry transformation, leveraging Industry 4.0 technologies, namely Artificial Intelligence (AI), Internet of Things (IoT), Cloud Computing, Big Data Analytics (BDA) and Augmented Reality (AR), to meet the customers' needs.

3. TECHNOLOGY AS AN ENABLER TO RETAIL INDUSTRY

In the recent market conditions, only retailers who seek innovation and differentiation can survive, and this innovation is only possible through the best of technology. Technology is the solution to all the problems of the digital age.Digital innvation occurs when a process, content, or object is transformed from the visual space to the digital realm (Fichman et al., 2014; Yu et al., 2010).Industry 4.0 delivers four major new capabilities: the Internet of Things (IoT), robotics and automation, 3D printing, and augmented reality. All these new methods come with a range of many technologies such as beacons, body scanners, POS, EDI technologies and more. All these technologies influence the perception of stores. New retail solutions such as automated checkout systems, personal shopping assistants, and omni channel services are fundamentally transforming traditional retail stores into "smart" stores that can "meet their customer needs and desires whenever they want" (Kourouthanassis and Roussos, 2003).All of these new technologies in the retail sector not only expanded the efficiency of retail business from the perspective of better stock management, but also improved customer experience due to better predictions of consumer behavior as well as customized and automated. This technology has reduced the advantages of acceleration to provide shopping services and loyalty programs. The special information adopted these days is that the software and equipment, understanding, creation and reading their activities, expand the human activities and form the basis of retail 4.0.

The position of retail businesses is changing as customers become more and more involved in the process, using real-time online applications to gather interesting, useful and engaging information. As a result, traditional methods of informing and preparing customers for buying opportunities are of little value. Clients retrieve information when they want it. On the other hand, the volume of data related to customer behavior gives marketers the ability to study and understand customer needs and desires at all levels. We use this data to help generate complete customer insights, predict customer buying behavior, and identify online refresh models that inspire and support customers. This means creating processes that continuously monitors customer service, analyze responses, generate incentives, and connect to business strategy and vendor models in real time.

The digital phenomenon of the Retail 4.0 era shows a very personal relationship with point of sale (POS), where the seller wants to know more about it, for personalized services. Highlighting the consumer's emotional side, brands will begin to integrate technology with digital catalogs, new payment methods that will facilitate the purchase and launch of mobile devices (Cotec Portugal,2015). Retail 4.0 aims to improve offline integration and the online world, which should exist together, as the online world has no 100% profit and product which has only a marketplace, and which is not compatible with technological changes, will also have difficulty in keeping the business. Trademarks should especially take place everywhere approach and additional personal contact with the customer and proper use strategies and devices. In this case, a good consumer experience on all channels (physical, social networks and e-commerce) should be ensured, where all products are available, as the customer can search the product online and complete offline purchases or vice versa. Brands should also value the digital interactions of their consumers and understand their feedback and recognition of brand value (Solutions, T. G., 2017). Nowadays digital marketing and social media are proving to be more influential. The customer relationship management system manages customer day to day data and provides personal information to them. Also, in-store self-examination and the usage of digital wallets are contributing to Retail 4.0. New ideas like dynamic prices which changes the price of a product depending on the required demand and supply of products in the store outlet are also contributors to this new retail revolution.

The internet of things shapes almost every business sector and reselling is one of them that makes marketing smarter than we think. The Internet of Things combines the ingenuity of machine learning with the exploration of useful data for advertisers. The best example of the Internet of Things is a domestic refrigerator that tells you how much milk you need and controls your air conditioner while sitting in your office. The Internet of Things is also at the peak of its retail transformation. A combination of machine-to-machine communication via Artificial intelligence converts data into useful resources for buyers and business. American clothing uses RFID tags to improve innovation management (Zhang, He & Xiao, 2013). Analysis of gray areas as stock level tracking and interpretation of consumer data will be improved via IoT (Drinkwater, 2016). Exhibition Room provide very useful information about the customer preferences, purchase pattern etc., besides, technology as sensors, video recording in the demo area will help track visitors and their shopping behaviour potential buyers. Sales statistics will provide more status image (Clark, 2016). Ocado tested its automated storage facilities and successful scanning 47000 Items with IoT and Robot. The retail industry is expected to grow to $ 4.4 trillion due to a combined need to assemble bricks and click stores with online shopping information. In this technology-driven era retailers can offer entertainment spirit to customers by connecting his online and in-store experience. (Drinkwater, 2016).The companies like American Apparel, Kroger, Tesco, and Walmart are using robots, RFID tags, fog computing, and cloud computing to improve and enhance customer experiences.

The emerging wave of the Internet of Things (IoT) requires support for the movement and distribution of geographic information in space and low latency. We believe that new stadiums are needed to meet their needs. Fog is a platform we call Fog Computing or Fog because it is a cloud near the ground. We also say so instead of using cloud computing (Bonomi, 2011). Fog computing enables the creation of new types of applications and services, and we see a beneficial relationship between the cloud and fog, especially when it comes to data management and analytics. The main objectives of introducing the fog computing paradigm are to achieve low energy consumption and latency, reduced cost, and enhanced

Quality of Services (QoS) of the service providers and Quality of Experience (QoE) of the end-users (Hazra et. al.,2023). The Internet of Things (IoT) is generating unprecedented amounts and diversity of data. However, you may no longer have the opportunity to take action while the data is being sent to the cloud for analysis. Therefore, fog computing, also known as edge computing, provides enhanced services to users at the end of the network. Extending cloud computing as Fog computing is appropriate and not replace it. As the number of devices connected to the Internet increases, next time the world is full of sensors, you will need a lot of hard-to-search data and cloud storage. So you can use fog. Fog computing is an efficient cloud component for the Internet of Things. Reduce delays and overcome security problems sending data towards the cloud.

4. FOG COMPUTING APPLICATIONS IN RETAIL INDUSTRY

The advent of online shopping has devastated the business industry. In fact, research shows that 67% of Millennials and 56% of Generation X are preferring to shop online. New access to online shopping is driving many consumers into the mainstream of online shopping. This is why retailers need to update their business structures to keep up with the times. As the retail industry faces these challenges, it must shift to a more flexible and secure IT infrastructure. The retail industry now sees opportunities associated with the growing evolution of the Internet of Things (IoT). IoT is the online connection of various device systems. Because of this, a lot of data can be used by the connection. This data can help the retailers to improve the delivery and improve their customer experience. This can entice customers to purchase in-store. This is where fog computing will come into play.

IoT growth in Retail 4.0 requires cloud and fog computing: Fog computing is essential at the retail edge of network. The rapid growth of the Internet of Things (IoT) is defining the way retailers help shoppers and manage their operations. It's an exciting time, but it also presents unique challenges. The amount of data IoT devices will generate in the market will grow much faster than the processing power of the network (Pan J, 2018). In this visible-to-virtual transition, how can businesses make a smooth transition? To keep pace with the growing IoT and future evidence of networks in Retail 4.0, marketers are gaining momentums in fog computing.

The concept of Fog computing: Fog computing is the standard that defines how edge computing works. Fog computing uses edge devices to do a significant amount of computing, storage, and communication locally. It facilitates compute, storage and network service operations between end devices and cloud computing. Fog computing serves as the jump off point for edge computing, as shown in Figure 1.

To expand your cloud computing network, fog computing is a process to add memory resources to edge devices. Besides, it requires pre-processing data collection in edge devices and send the combined outcomes to the cloud.

Several companies can help with something in this last step. They deliver unified data to the cloud using on-premises hybrid and cloud platforms. RESTful APIs provide integration with third-party platforms and then extend the way third-party code is deployed, authenticated, and monitored on edge devices. The combination of all company and third-party relationships allows users to securely connect to a wide variety of IoT devices.

Device Migration Requires Better Data Management: A long time ago, the store was able to pass the generic data warehouse. Nonetheless, the explosion of technology that generates a new need to provide a smart path that allows you to transfer priority data and provide a smart path that can send

Figure 1. Fog computing as a jump off point for edge computing

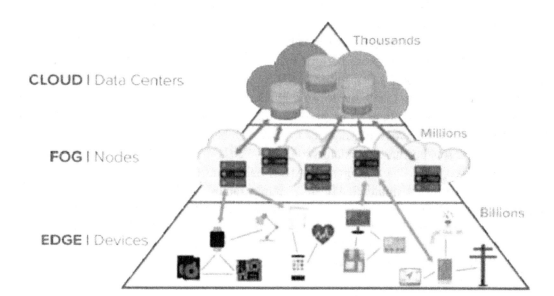

priority data and handle priority data more quickly in end or boundary devices. Quick-efficient Edge data processing uses all of these rich data to enhance the customer better and improve the sub-line. In real time, the application is an important fog calculation driver. For example, Bluetooth beacon has become a popular tool that retailers communicate and adapt to providing and providing customers from a store next to a store or a store next to a store. This beacon is just one example of many IoT devices that change the market environment. Digital logos, video stores, digital shopping carts, and public purchasing tools are becoming more and more popular. Fog computing at the edge allows retailers to process data from these devices as quickly and efficiently as possible (Vaquero LM, RoderoMerino L, 2014).

Fog computing is part of the network of the future: Because marketing officers are planned in advance for future network demands, they recognize emerging roles of fog computing that are creating networks. In the past, local technologies are generally limited to common computers and printers, and mobile devices were available in the store, with standard partnerships, central servers, firewalls, VPN connectors and SNMP control servers. However, now with mobile phones, cell phones and tablet, the vendor removes most applications and management features on the physical device of the cloud device. In future, the growth of edge devices will be dramatically increased. ATM, kiosk, camcorder, HVAC control, temperature sensor, digital signs, and new technologies in the store are connected. The cloud hosts network management, VPN providers, firewalls, applications, and more. To capture this kind of visual traffic, Edge devices are expected to handle more computers than ever before. Fog computing gives marketers the network flexibility and reliability they need to grow and evolve to the levels demanded by a highly competitive industry (Peralta G et al. 2017).

Data Management across All Platforms: IoT is rapidly changing the way stores operate. Here in fog computing it has been especially helpful in managing ever-growing visual data. The previous site was heavily censored by on-site technology but now with more useful devices such as mobile phones and tablets, vendors see the cloud as the best option for managing their data. Most of these peripheral devices will need good communication between them. And the flexibility of fog computing takes care of that.

Rapid Analysis of Useful Data: A lot of customer data is collected from IoT devices like wearables, blood sugar and blood pressure monitors. The problem lies in the integrity of this big data. All of this data is then stored in the cloud, which can take some time to recover from emergencies, especially. Now with the help of fog computing, all critical analysis can be done directly on the device itself. Thus, removing one central layer will improve performance speed (Basir R et al. 2019). By using a computer on the edge, all the complexities of customer needs data can be taken care of. That could be, getting smart data in a timely manner, the ability to work in a large area, and the privacy of customer data. In the retail industry, fog computing helps by introducing new ways to deal with real-time questions and problems. Stores may provide portable devices to staff members to check product information, check product lists, or have self-purchase calculators to improve customer information.

Members of Cisco, Dell, Intel, Microsoft, ARM, and Princeton University started the OpenFog Consortium in 2015. It aims to improve an open reference framework that expands and promotes the use of computer fog in all industries. The OpenFog Consortium (2018 OpenFog Consortium) introduced the concept of fog computing as a *"horizontal system-level architecture that brings compute, storage, control, and network functions closer to users on a cloud computing continuum"*.

The Need of Fog and Edge Computing in Retail Industry: The need of fog and edge computing in retail industry are listed below.

Increases Efficiency: To manage a retail business it can be tedious with so many moving parts. General trading companies use specialized applications as solutions for trading tasks such as assets handling, pricings, and scanning. It is a coherent system that can adapt to the changing nature of retail. Fog computing can do a wonderful job for marketing. With the help of computers on the edge, providers can increase the usage of IoT devices and big data that can pass in real time. In addition, fog &edge computing can maximize the effectiveness of the operating system using artificial intelligent technology (AI) and machine learning technology (HU B, 2018). Thanks to IoT device structures, Edge computing can interact with client devices. Customers will be able to create their own shopping list from anywhere. When they visit the shop, they can see how to get a product in the buy list in the right way and in the shortest time. Retailers can also effectively manage space based on client traffic to ensure traffic by placing sensors near shops. This is what Amazon Go has done in retail with cutting-edge technology. Shoppers download the app and use it to enter the store, buy what they need, and exit. This means no long queues, no more waiting and no cash. Their staff purchase IDs at the liquor store and answer customer questions. It is an example of how fog/edge computing can be used to improve store performance.

For unique customer experience: Along with operations, retailers can use peripheral computers to provide their customers with a unique experience when visiting a physical store. Imagine you are in a traditional clothing store where you are to get up, get dressed, and go out to buy and pay as you leave. Then imagine you are looking for the dress you want on your mobile phone, choose the one you want, choose your size, pay at the checkout and now wait for it to arrive. E-commerce looks very simple and easy, right? But what if you were able to make your store easier? Besides, what if you really enjoy shopping? Data captured by IoT devices can help marketers generate unique customer insights. Let's say you are using your mobile phone to find clothes on the Internet. Now you decide to go to the store to find out the price. With fog computing, nearby computers can communicate with the phone to find what they are looking for, and sellers can automatically give offer of the clothes at a promotional price. Clothing stores also sell augmented reality (AR) sunglasses so you can "try on" a dress without having to wear it. You can change colours, try different sizes, or check the stock. Also, you can check out some of the available items that you like. Connectivity and data enable retailers to make shopping easier for their customers. This can help retailers provide first-class customer service. Real-time data sharing is important to be able to provide features that can benefit customers (B. Cheng, G. et al. 2018). Remember that when customers shop, emotions go along. Retailers provide a fun and easy shopping experience, so customers are encouraged to visit the store and provide them excellent online reviews.

It helps in defining client styles: Along with unique customer experiences, fog computing can help identify consumer trends. Similarly, IoT data can help personalize customer interactions. IoT systems are designed to detect eye moments when shopping online (Yamamoto, 2016). It can also help to map purchasing patterns that can benefit internal processes such as warehouse management. Fog computing technology can now be used not just as a problem-solving tool, but to create strategies for how businesses can help driving innovation. Web and in-store usage data can provide insight into factors driving purchasing decisions or future trends. Retailers can also consider seasonal styles for shopping as well as marketing. Retailers can plan data ahead of time to track shopping trends. Data can be used to formulate marketing strategies. They can use personal email marketing to stimulate customer interest and increase conversions. However, consumers already know about email marketing strategies, so marketers shouldn't send out generic emails to get their attention. Good email marketing habits should include a balance between normal behaviour and personality.

It promotes safety and compliance: They use IoT and computing power at the edge to help retailers deliver the best products and services. However, their interaction comes with some security risks. If shoppers want the best shopping experience at their local grocery store, they need to connect their devices to the network. Alternatively, your store may have its own gadgets that you can provide when your customers visit your store. However, both of these situations pose a security risk. This means customers will be able to access data from their IT infrastructure. This is the reason; data security is so important when using fog computing. The good thing is that fog and edge computing can be integrated with near-source infrastructure, making it easy to set up, maintain, and control security measures to minimize communication risks (M Noor, W Haslina, 2019). Any device connected to the network can be damaged. To better control this very security threat, we need to strengthen the security of all connected devices. Additionally, security measures must be put in place on the edge computer infrastructure to protect the data of buyers and sellers. Meanwhile, some retailers are installing smart security cameras connected to nearby computers for quick, real-time surveillance. There are numerous any ways to use fog and edge computing to help marketers manage business security.

4.1 Case Study on Retail Shelf Management by ATOS Company

Approximately 90% of global retail sales comes from brick-and-mortar stores, and the number of sales and customer satisfaction depends on the departments being stopped. Shelf management is a major competitive driver to face e-commerce competition whether it is a question of internal process management issues, resource constraints or data breaches. The retail sector faces many problems that are managed manually on a daily basis. Real-time data analysis is essential for enabling optimal shelf management. Atos revolutionizes with all computer vision and artificial intelligence solutions powered by Bull Sequana edge (Atos,2020). The camera scans the shelves in the retail outlet and the information is then collected, sorted, stored and analyzed in the BullSequana edge server in real-time and continuously products are then detected and identified on the shelf using deep learning algorithms that can check availability selections space prices or promotions and automatically trigger internal notifications store teams can quickly fill up the shelves whenever needed. It is a solution that is fully self-contained, functional in all kinds of environments, controlled locally and remotely active in real-time for 24 hours each day for seven days in week. With BullSequana edge and edge computing vision solution to generate real-time alert system which supports rapid restocking of the shelves will increase the sales by three to five percent in all product categories. It securely analyses data near to IOT sources and not only ensures customer satisfaction but also prevents theft and avoids the old ways of physical store data storage and analysis systems. Figure 2 depicts the retail shelf management by ATOS company.

- **One complete solution** - To ensure complete shelf management, Atos innovates with edge computing vision, the BullSequana Edge. Smart camera scans store shelves. The ATOS BullSequana Edge Server collects, filters, stores and analyzes real-time data streams and identifies products on the shelf. Then you can check availability, selection, location, price, promotions and more. Then the internal app automatically activates the notification. Store groups can quickly replenish shelves as needed.
- **100% independent on the site installation-** BullSequana Edge operates outside of the data center environment. By installing it as close as possible to your IoT data, you can increase security and reduce data transmission delays. It works in all types of places, Location and remote control. The Edge Data Container solution can be a small on-site data center. Edge servers are rack mounted for more storage space.
- **The Technology Revolution in Edge Computing Vision solutions-** BullSequana Edge's edge computer vision solution meets vendor requirements for shelf management. It creates a real-time alert system and confirms immediately if a shelf is full or not which takes 30 mins as compared to 24 hours previously. This allows you to securely analyze ambient data from IoT sources and increase customer satisfaction to increase sales by 3-5% at specific product milestones.
- **Prevents theft by installation of cameras in self-payment-** In-depth reading algorithms are highly analytical which process huge quantities of complex video data in the real time. The motive is to find fraud while checking out and trying to steal and report it instantly.
- **Combats the Obsoleteness of in-store data-**It avoids expiry of storage and data analytics in stores, streamlines the number of servers used, and reduces energy consumption and costs. The goal is to bring value at the local level and highly effective analytics.

5. CONCLUSION

The retailers of today shall focus on building a robust business processes and delightful customer service. They should understand their customer completely -the customer's preferences, need and create a unique personalised shopping experience for them. The challenge before the brick and mortar store is technology adoption to take on the online shopping. Customers don't want to spend too much time in shops, they want smart, fast and efficient services be it online or in store. Retailers can increase computer use at the edge by providing a better experience for the customers. With fog computing all the retailers can have the flexibility of network and scalability which is necessary for its growth. Therefore, fog and edge

Figure 2. Atos device

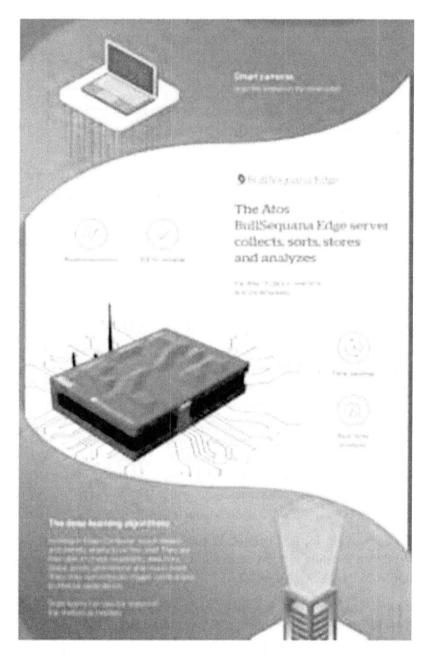

computing with IoT is one of the best ways to grow your business and bring customers back from the mall. Fog computing reduces the amount of data which is sent to the cloud thereby reducing the bandwidth consumption and the costs incurred. The response time is reduced due to better performance. Shoppers feel comfortable and efficient shopping, safe space and pleasant information in the retail store, so they will shop again soon. Using an end-to-end computer to connect your online shopping app to in-store devices can help upgrade your retail purchases. With the advent of various computer solutions, we can observe more technological advances and their use. The desire to use technology to provide consumers with a better sense of self-awareness sets the bar for other businesses.

REFERENCES

Aliyu, F., Abdeen, M. A., Sheltami, T., Alfraidi, T., & Ahmed, M. H. (2023). Fog computing-assisted path planning for smart shopping. *Multimedia Tools and Applications*, 1-26. doi:10.1007/s11042-023-14926-9ATOS

Basir, R., Qaisar, S., Ali, M., Aldwairi, M., Ashraf, M. I., Mahmood, A., & Gidlund, M. (2019). Fog computing enabling industrial internet of things: State-of-the-art and research challenges. *Sensors (Basel)*, *19*(21), 4807. doi:10.339019214807 PMID:31694254

Bonomi, F. (2011, October). Connected vehicles, the internet of things, and fog **computing**. *VANET*. https://www.sigmobile.org/mobicom/2011/vanet2011/program.html

Cheng, B., Solmaz, G., Cirillo, F., Kovacs, E., Terasawa, K., & Kitazawa, A. (2018). Fog Flow: Easy programming of IoT services over cloud and edges for smart cities. *IEEE Internet of Things Journal*, *5*(2), 696–707. doi:10.1109/JIOT.2017.2747214

Clark, J. (2016, March 22). What is Industry 4.0? *IBM Internet of Things blog*. https://www.ibm.com/blogs/internet-ofthings/industry-4-0/

Cotec Portugal. (2015). *The future of commerce: the new trends online and offline*. Cotec Portugal.

Drinkwater, D. (2016). *"The future of retail through the Internet of Things"*, *Internet of Business*. Beecham Research.

Ernst & Young. (2020, June 17). Digitalization key to helping Asian retailers emerge from Covid-19. *Retail News Asia*. https://www.retailnews.asia/digitalization-key-to-helping-asian-retailers-emerge-from-covid-19/

Fichman, R. G., Dos Santos, B. L., & Zheng, Z. E. (2014). Digital innovation as a fundamental and powerful concept in the information systems curriculum. *Management Information Systems Quarterly*, *38*(2), 329–353. doi:10.25300/MISQ/2014/38.2.01

Gautam, V., & Lanjewar, U. (2023). Fog computing: Analyzing challenges, unveiling opportunities, and maximizing benefits. *TIJER*, *10*(5), 1–15. doi:10.21276/tijer.2023.10.5.1

Har, L. L., Rashid, U. K., Te Chuan, L., Sen, S. C., & Xia, L. Y. (2022). Revolution of retail industry: From perspective of retail 1.0 to 4.0. *Procedia Computer Science*, *200*, 1615–1625. doi:10.1016/j.procs.2022.01.362

Hazra, A., Rana, P., Adhikari, M., & Amgoth, T. (2023). Fog computing for next-generation internet of things: Fundamental, state-of-the-art and research challenges. *Computer Science Review*, *48*, 100549. doi:10.1016/j.cosrev.2023.100549

Hu, B. (2018). A robust retail POS system based on blockchain and edge computing. In *International Publishing* (pp. 99–110). Springer. doi:10.1007/978-3-319-94340-4_8

Kourouthanassis, P., & Roussos, G. (2003). Developing consumer-friendly pervasive retail systems. *IEEE Pervasive Computing, 2*(2), 32–39. doi:10.1109/MPRV.2003.1203751

Li, H. L., Rashid, U. K., Chuan, L. T., Sen, S. C., & Xia, L. Y. (2022). Revolution of retail industry: From perspective of retail 1.0 to 4.0. *Procedia Computer Science, 200,* 1615–1625. doi:10.1016/j.procs.2022.01.362

Lumen Learning. (2020). *Introduction to retailing. The evolution of retail. Module of Retail Management.* Lumen Learning.

Mardiana, B. M., & Hassan, W. (2019). Current research on Internet of Things (IoT) security: A survey. *Computer Networks, 148,* 283-294.

NASSCOM. (2021). *Retail 4.0: India Story-Unlocking Value through Online+Offline Collaborations.* NASSCOM. https://www.nasscom.in/retail-4-0-india-story-unlocking-value-through-online-offline-collaborations

OECD. (2020). *Connecting businesses and consumers during COVID-19: trade in parcels.* OECD Policy Responses to Coronavirus (COVID-19). OECD. https://www.oecd.org/coronavirus/policy-responses/connecting-businesses-and-consumers-during-covid-19-trade-in-parcels-d18de131/

OpenFog Consortium. (2018). *IEEE Standard for Adoption of OpenFog Reference Architecture for Fog Computing.* IEEE.

Pan, J., & McElhannon, J. (2018). Future edge cloud and edge computing for internet of things applications. *IEEE Internet of Things Journal, 5*(1), 1–5. doi:10.1109/JIOT.2017.2767608

Peralta, G., Iglesias-Urkia, M., Barceló, M., Gómez, R., Morán, A., & Bilbao, J. (2017). Fog computing based efficient IoT scheme for the Industry 4.0. IEEE international workshop of electronics, control, measurement, signals and their application to mechatronics (ECMSM), (pp. 1-6). IEEE. doi:10.1109/ECMSM.2017.8085600

Reagan, J. R., & Singh, M. (2020). *Management 4.0: Cases and Methods for the 4th Industrial Revolution.* Springer. doi:10.1007/978-981-15-6751-3

Solutions, T. G. (2017). Retail 4.0. *The Retail Intelligence.* http://www.theretailintelligence.com/retail-4-0/

Susan Meyer. (2020). *The history and evolution of retail stores: from mom and pop to online shops.* Ecommerce News.

Vaquero, L. M., & Rodero-Merino, L. (2014). Finding your way in the fog: Towards a comprehensive definition of fog computing. *Computer Communication Review, 44*(4), 27–32. doi:10.1145/2677046.2677052

Yamamoto, Y., Kawabe, T., Tsuruta, S., Damiani, E., Yoshitaka, A., Mizuno, Y., & Knauf, R. (2016, July). IoT-aware online shopping system enhanced with gaze analysis. *2016 World Automation Congress (WAC),* (pp. 1-6). IEEE. 10.1109/WAC.2016.7583028

Zhang, F. Z., He, H. X., & Xiao, W. J. (2013). Application Analysis of Internet of Things on the Management of Supply Chain and Intelligent Logistics. [Trans Tech Publications.]. *Applied Mechanics and Materials*, *411*, 2655–2661. doi:10.4028/www.scientific.net/AMM.411-414.2655

Chapter 10
Remote Health Prediction System:
A Machine Learning–Based Approach

Pardhu Thottempudi
ⓘ https://orcid.org/0000-0002-9653-1951
BVRIT Hyderabad College of Engineering for Women, India

Nagesh Deevi
ⓘ https://orcid.org/0000-0001-6449-0609
BVRIT Hyderabad College of Engineering for Women, India

Amy Prasanna T.
BVRIT Hyderabad College of Engineering for Women, India

Srinivasarao N.
BVRIT Hyderabad College of Engineering for Women, India

Mahesh Babu Katta
BVRIT Hyderabad College of Engineering for Women, India

ABSTRACT

One of the many applications of machine learning in healthcare is the analysis of large amounts of data to reveal new therapeutic insights. Once doctors have this data, they can better serve their patients. Therefore, satisfaction can be raised by using deep learning to enhance the quality of care provided. This work aims to integrate machine learning and AI in healthcare into a single system. Predictive algorithms based on machine learning could revolutionize healthcare by allowing doctors to avoid unnecessary treatments. Various libraries, including those for machine learning algorithms, were used to develop this work. Because of its extensive library and user-friendliness, Python has emerged as the preferred language. syntax. The authors used various classification techniques to train machine learning models and then select the one that provided the best balance between accuracy and precision while avoiding prediction error and autocorrelation problems, the two main causes of bias and variance.

DOI: 10.4018/978-1-6684-4466-5.ch010

1. INTRODUCTION

In this era of information, where data is becoming the backbone of decision-making processes, it is crucial to comprehend and utilize the wealth of information at our disposal. This particularly applies to the healthcare industry, which generates colossal amounts of data daily. Properly analyzing and applying this data can significantly improve patient care and outcomes. With the advent of powerful computational tools and techniques such as Machine Learning (ML), one can now gain valuable insights from this data, leading to advances in disease diagnosis, treatment, and prediction. This chapter explores the intersection of machine learning and healthcare, primarily focusing on disease prediction.

Machine learning, a subfield of artificial intelligence, offers a unique way to process and learn from vast amounts of data without explicit programming. It involves training a model on data (Training phase) and then applying the model to new data to make predictions (Testing phase). ML algorithms, such as the Naive Bayes classifier, can be utilized in healthcare to predict diseases based on a patient's symptoms.

One of the major problems the healthcare industry grapples with is the effective and timely diagnosis of diseases. Traditionally, the identification of diseases has been heavily reliant on the expertise of medical professionals, often a time-consuming process with scope for human error. With the exponential growth in medical data - from patient records, medical imaging, genetic profiles, and more - it is increasingly challenging for clinicians to assimilate and interpret this information meaningfully. Furthermore, the nature of certain diseases demands swift identification and intervention, leaving little room for delays. This is where machine learning can play a transformative role.

This chapter presents the concept of disease prediction using machine learning. The project described herein leverages ML algorithms to predict diseases based on patient's symptoms and general information. The goal is to accurately identify the most probable diseases a patient might be afflicted with based on the given symptoms. This aids in early detection and intervention, often critical in successfully treating many medical conditions. By exploiting the predictive capabilities of machine learning algorithms like Naive Bayes, linear regression, and decision trees, one can forecast diseases like diabetes, malaria, jaundice, dengue, and tuberculosis. The system processes the patient's symptoms and delivers an output indicating the probability of the disease. It is a critical step forward in disease management, potentially providing life-saving information.

Through the course of this chapter, development of applications, benefits, and challenges of implementing machine learning in disease prediction is presented. Navigating the complexities of healthcare data and machine learning algorithms, underscore the potential of this convergence to revolutionize the healthcare industry. The fusion of machine learning with healthcare has the potential to herald a new age of medical diagnosis and treatment, significantly enhancing the capabilities of healthcare professionals to deliver top-tier care to their patients.

2. EXISTING SYSTEM

The traditional course of treatment often follows a standard protocol, which could sometimes be an overly complex and scattergun approach for certain conditions. The conventional methodology in medical practice commences with analyzing a patient's symptoms before any treatment is determined (Gavhane, et al, 2018). Doctors often mandate several tests to understand the patient's condition better. This process, which is time-consuming and resource-intensive, calls for significant resources. While traditional methods have proven effective in the past, they often fall short in addressing the needs of modern drug development (Hasija, et. al, 2017).

The methodology in the research by Bates, et.al, (2014) and Beam, et.al, (2018) leveraging burgeoning electronic health records and advanced clinical analytics to uncover valuable insights from big data. By focusing on six use cases, the authors illustrate how this data can be used to reduce healthcare costs. The approach necessitates appropriate data, analytical tools, and infrastructure to analyze the data and implement cost-saving strategies effectively.

However, this landscape is transforming with the advent of artificial intelligence (AI) technologies. Network pharmacology, bioinformatics, systems biology, computational biology, chemical informatics, machine learning, deep learning, image loading, and computer science have opened up a world of possibilities. (Patil, et al, 2019; Katarya, et al, 2020; Kohli, et al, 2018, Patil, et al, 2018; Yuan, 2016; Davenport, T, et.al, 2019).

Mujumdar and Vaidehi (2019) explore the application of various machine learning algorithms and identify the most effective ones. It use the K-means algorithm to categorize records into two clusters - "Age" and "Glucose" - assigning each record a value of 0 or 1, eliminating the possibility of correlation. Integrating big data in the medical field has dual benefits: it drives the growth of both domains. In healthcare, it enhances analysis accuracy, enables early disease prediction, provides patient-oriented data, ensures secure storage and versatile usage of medical data, and minimizes incomplete regional data. This concept aims to select a region, collect the hospital or medical data from that particular region, and analyze it using machine learning algorithms. This process, rooted in data mining techniques, aims at highly accurate disease prediction. The technique identifies and reduces the missing data based on latent factors.

A technique known as the Convolutional Neural Networks-Medicaid Drug Rebate Program (CNN-MDRP) algorithm is used to handle both structured and unstructured hospital data. This algorithm-based prediction has proven to yield highly accurate results, surpassing the accuracy of previous systems. One of this concept's main advantages is its improved feature description and high accuracy. However, a potential disadvantage is that it only applies to structured data, which might limit its effectiveness in disease description. Table 1 details the previous research on remote disease prediction (Ismaeel, et al, 2015; Dahiwade, et al, 2019; Jadhav, et al, 2019 ; Deo, 2015). It provides to explore this intersection of big data, machine learning, and healthcare, and to stand on the threshold of a transformative era in disease diagnosis and treatment.

The intersection of machine learning and healthcare harbours the promise to herald a novel epoch characterized by precise disease prediction and streamlined treatment procedures. Numerous esteemed authors have undertaken a plethora of investigative studies in this domain, with each one targeting distinct facets of disease prediction via the implementation of machine learning algorithms. Rashid, et al (2019) conducted a study using the random forest algorithm to predict diseases based on drugs. The main advantage of the research is resolving a significant problem among the youth using a machine learning model. However, a potential disadvantage of the study was the possibility of inaccurate drug prediction.

Shah, Patel, & Bharti (2020) used linear regression and K-nearest neighbors algorithms for heart disease prediction. The primary benefit of this approach was the ability to predict a wide range of heart diseases. A possible pitfall was that a small break in the model could render the entire project useless. Soni and Sunita (2020) revolved around predicting diabetes among Pima Indians aged 21 years and above using decision tree, random forest, Naïve Bayes, and support vector machine (SVM) algorithms. The foremost advantage of their research was giving patients the knowledge of whether they have diabetes at an early stage. The main drawback was similar to Gulati's study; any small break could waste the entire project.

Muhammad and Ibrahim (2019) developed a malaria disease prediction model using image processing on a specific set of photos. The main advantage was that people could medicate themselves and maintain proper hygiene based on predictions, but the image processing might sometimes interpret the wrong information, which was a limitation. Various other studies by distinguished authors, have also made significant contributions to this field.

While some have focused on heart disease prediction using hybrid machine learning, others have investigated muscular paralysis disease prediction based on hybrid features, brain tumour disease prediction, and the prediction of various symptoms using machine learning. Some studies have also tackled smart health predictions to avoid future diseases and applied machine learning to kidney disease prediction. The diversity of these studies showcases the vast potential and applicability of machine learning in the healthcare domain, from disease prediction to treatment optimization.

3. PROPOSED SYSTEM

Deep learning, a subset of artificial intelligence, involves the exploration of computational algorithms that can self-learn and progressively improve with time. The proposed system operates on the same principles as the existing model creation methodologies. Once all models are trained, the one yielding the highest accuracy is selected for deployment. This project primarily aims to predict critical health conditions such as diabetes, heart attacks, and strokes. If the predicted outcome is positive, users are provided vital information about symptoms, diet, and preventive measures. The system's functionality is visually represented in Figure 1 via a flowchart, while Figure 2 provides the Unified Modeling Language (UML) flowchart.

Our ML pipeline commences with the collection of data. Sourcing of datasets is done from Kaggle. Following the import, rigorously checking of each dataset for null values, improper values, and outliers is done. Standard scaling, normalization of features, and removal of correlated attributes is carried out. To circumvent data leakage, implementation of k-fold cross-validation is done, which forms a 'k' number of training and testing clusters.

The model construction phase involves the selection of appropriate algorithms. Optimization of the model parameters by applying hyper parameter tuning using grid search and randomized search is done. Following this, the algorithm exhibiting the highest accuracy is tested with the testing dataset. The results are evaluated using performance metrics, Area under Curve (AUC), and Receiver Operating Characteristic (ROC) curve. Finally, deployment of the project on the Heroku platform, as illustrated in Figure 3, which represents the use case diagram.

The use case diagram offers a visual interpretation of the whole process. Starting with data collection from the hospital dataset, we select suitable algorithms for the model. Upon introduction, the data undergoes processing, fed into the training and testing datasets model. The accuracy of these models is computed based on their performance. The entire procedure described so far constitutes the developer's tasks in building an efficient model. The last two steps involve user interaction, giving the symptoms as input and retrieving the predicted disease as output. This interaction tests the efficacy and reliability of the model in a real-world scenario.

Table 1. Previous research done on predicting the diseases remotely

Problem statement	Problem solution	Advantages and Limitations
Prediction of diseases by drugs using the random forest algorithm (Rashid, et.al, 2019).	Disease prediction, & drug that is commonly prescribed by doctor is suggested	Advantage: This is major problem of the youth, which is resolved using ML model. Limitation: Accurate drug may not be predicted.
Application of linear regression and k-nearest neighbors algorithm for prediction of heart disease (Gulati, 2022)	Prediction using input symptoms is addressed.	Advantage: Any kind of heart disease can be easily predicted, such as high heart rate, heart attack. Limitation: If there is small break in the model this total project goes waste
Diabetes prediction using, various ML techniques (Soni, M., et.al, 2020)	Using Pina Indians diabetes – whose age is more than 21 yrs.	Advantage: Early detection of diabetes is an advantage for the patients. Limitation: If there is small error, prediction is difficult.
Malaria disease prediction (Iradukunda, et.al, 2019)	Heterogeneous data set That works for only particular images	Advantage: People can medicate themselves and be in proper hygiene. Limitation: Sometimes image processing may understand the wrong information.
Heart disease prediction using hybrid ML (Mohan, et.al, 2019)	Exactness in cardiovascular problems.	Advantage: Used to detect heart-attack, high heart rate etc. Limitation: Classifiers may take more time to predict the output.
Prediction of muscular paralysis disease based on hybrid feature (Subramani, 2023)	Focused on muscular paralysis using Electromyography –EMG signals	Advantage: Hybrid features like muscle and bone testing is highly beneficial for the patients. Limitation: Sometimes this model may not be accurate.
Prediction of various diseases using advanced ML (Gomathy, et.al, 2021).	Age and gender was specified as part of dataset.	Advantage: Highly beneficial, & advantage the patient cannot go to the doctor always. Limitation: Not for all age groups, age and gender is specified.
Brain tumour disease prediction (Al-Ayyoub, et.al, 2012)	Multimodal disease risk prediction model with higher accuracy	Advantage: Use of neural network which has the perfect output. Limitation: Only regarding brain is predicted.
Prediction of various symptoms using ML (Hamsagayathri, & Vigneshwaran, 2021)	Age and gender was specified as part of dataset.	Advantage: Highly beneficial, & advantage the patient cannot go to the doctor always. Limitation: Not for all age groups, and gender is specified.
Smart health prediction for avoiding future diseases (Ponde, et.al, 2020)	Rapid use of analytics techniques.	Advantage: Use of analytics techniques. Limitation: Only a single classifier is used and it may not be accurate in all cases.
Machine learning applied to kidney disease prediction (Rabby, et.al 2019)	Research subject and instrumentation	Advantage: Early disease diagnosis. Limitation: Only a single disease is predicted.
Prediction of migration extraction with ML (Robinson, et.al. 2022)	Traditional migration and gravity radiation model.	Advantage: Migration can be identified early. Limitation: This may not be that accurate.

Figure 1. Working flow chart

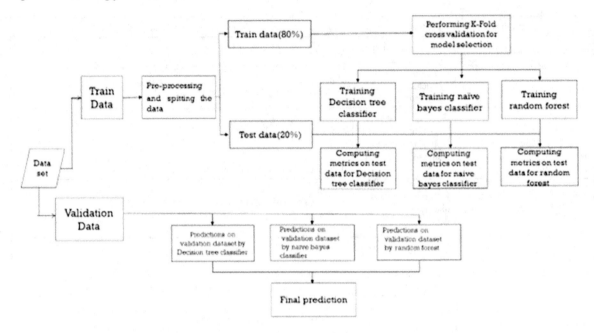

Figure 2. UML flow chart

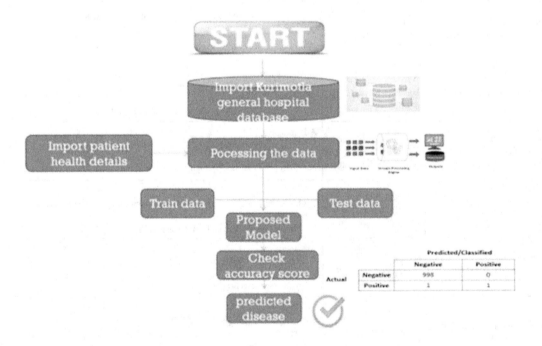

3.1 Class Diagram

A class diagram is a graphical representation that delineates the architecture model of a system. It displays the system's overall structure by illustrating the system's classes, properties, methods, activities,

Figure 3. Use case diagram

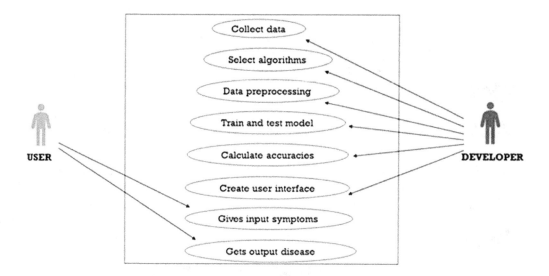

and relationships within the framework of the UML. One of the common uses of class diagrams is in constructing decision tree models, which typically involve two stages.

The first stage involves the integration of 'N' classification trees to produce a random forest. The second stage revolves around making predictions for each tree constructed in the initial stage. To better comprehend this process, let's break it down into simpler, step-by-step instructions:

1. Randomly select 'X' data points from the test dataset using probabilistic sampling.
2. With the selected data points, construct regression trees. Regression trees are decision trees that are used for predicting continuous variables.
3. Determine 'N', the number of decision trees you aim to create for the model.
4. Repeat steps 1 and 2 for 'N' several times, creating a 'random forest' of decision trees.
5. For additional data points, determine the predictions using each logistic regression tree. Finally, assign the data points to the classification with the most predictions.

This methodology provides a comprehensive yet flexible way to leverage the power of machine learning algorithms in prediction and classification tasks. Using class diagrams as decision tree models helps to demystify complex systems, enabling a clearer understanding and interpretation of the system's intricacies.

4. RESULTS AND DISCUSSIONS

The process begins once the symptoms are entered into the system. The backend takes this input and feeds it into the prediction function. The function, in turn, generates an outcome, essentially the prediction of the disease through three distinct classifiers. The interplay of this process is illustrated in Figure 4.

Figure 4. Web interface of disease prediction

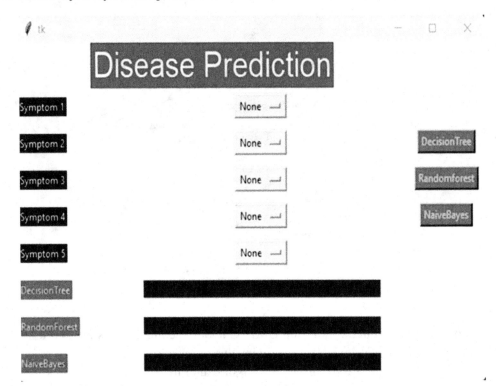

Figure 4 represents the interface designed for disease prediction. This interactive platform features five slots for symptom selection. This user-friendly arrangement facilitates ease of information input for the patients, allowing them to report their symptoms in a structured manner accurately. The prediction model springs into action once the symptoms have been selected and entered. The model is powered by three distinct algorithms that were previously installed. These algorithms decipher the underlying disease corresponding to the reported symptoms. The determined result, which identifies the disease the patient is likely suffering from, is displayed to the user.

The prediction process is further elucidated in Figure 5. The patient's symptoms are input into the system in this step-by-step depiction. Using the installed algorithms, the model assesses these symptoms to determine the potential disease afflicting the patient. The identified diseases are then displayed to the user, as shown in the figure.

This entire process illustrates a powerful intersection of healthcare and machine learning, harnessing the predictive capabilities of algorithms to assist in early disease detection and facilitating a proactive approach to health management.

5. CONCLUSION

Remote healthcare is a burgeoning field of research with the potential to transform traditional healthcare practices profoundly. This chapter illustrates the challenges and methodologies of developing a remote healthcare system. The remote health prediction system is designed to address the shortcomings of ex-

Figure 5. Disease prediction output

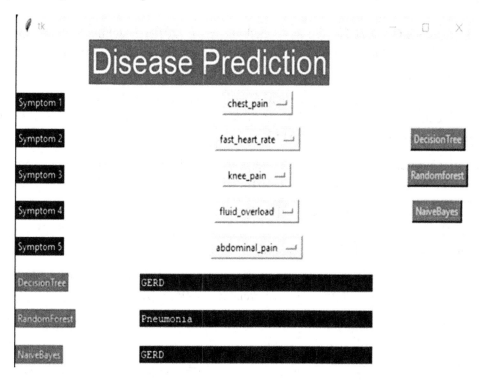

isting healthcare models. It is created using advanced ML techniques, enabling it to perform well under various input conditions. However, the system will require updates and enhancements in the future. It is focused solely on predicting diseases, but the goal is to incorporate additional functionalities like a seamless doctor appointment booking feature.

The focus of this chapter lies on two classic machine learning techniques that are widely used: decision tree and the Naive Bayes algorithm. In the proposed process, historical clinical symptom-related information is leveraged using the Naive Bayes approach to prepare datasets. The final model is generated once these statistics have been scrutinized and evaluated against the originating queries. This approach, grounded in empirical historical data, produces accurate predictions that provide patients with a clearer understanding of their health condition, enabling timely disease prediction. Moreover, patients can remotely consult with doctors suggested by the system. The recommended method could be invaluable when patients cannot physically access a specialist, when medical personnel are not immediately available, during late-night emergencies, or as a pre-examination tool for patients.

An inherent benefit of this automated system is its transparency, which allows users to comprehend their medical issues better. One possible future enhancement would be adapting this web application to an Android one. This would make the platform readily available on users' mobile devices, increasing its usage and making it more user-friendly. Furthermore, we plan to make this application accessible in rural areas with inadequate medical facilities. This shows ample research opportunities and scope for improvement in this application.

References

Al-Ayyoub, M., Husari, G., Darwish, O., & Alabed-alaziz, A. (2012). Machine learning approach for brain tumor detection. In: *Proceedings of the 3rd International Conference on Information and Communication Systems*, (pp. 1-4). ACM. 10.1145/2222444.2222467

Bates, D. W., Saria, S., Ohno-Machado, L., Shah, A., & Escobar, G. (2014). Big data in health care: Using analytics to identify and manage high-risk and high-cost patients. *Health Affairs*, *33*(7), 1123–1131. doi:10.1377/hlthaff.2014.0041 PMID:25006137

Beam, A. L., & Kohane, I. S. (2018). Big data and machine learning in health care. *Journal of the American Medical Association*, *319*(13), 1317–1318. doi:10.1001/jama.2017.18391 PMID:29532063

Dahiwade, D., Patle, G., & Meshram, E. (2019). Designing disease prediction model using machine learning approach. In: *Proceedings of the 3rd International Conference on Computing Methodologies and Communication*, (pp. 1211-1215). IEEE. 10.1109/ICCMC.2019.8819782

Davenport, T., & Kalakota, R. (2019). The potential for artificial intelligence in healthcare. *Future Healthcare Journal*, *6*(2), 94–98. doi:10.7861/futurehosp.6-2-94 PMID:31363513

Deo, R. C. (2015). Machine learning in medicine. *Circulation*, *132*(20), 1920–1930. doi:10.1161/CIRCULATIONAHA.115.001593 PMID:26572668

Gavhane, A., Kokkula, G., Pandya, I., & Devadkar, K. (2018). Prediction of heart disease using machine learning. In: *Proceedings of the Second IEEE International Conference on Electronics, Communication and Aerospace Technology*, (pp. 1275-1278). IEEE. 10.1109/ICECA.2018.8474922

Gomathy, C. K., & Naidu, A. R. (2021). The prediction of disease using machine learning. *International Journal of Scientific Research in Engineering and Management*, *5*(10), 1–7.

Hamsagayathri, P., & Vigneshwaran, S. (2021). Symptoms based disease prediction using machine learning techniques. In: *Proceedings of the Third IEEE International Conference on Intelligent Communication Technologies and Virtual Mobile Networks*, (pp. 747-752). IEEE. 10.1109/ICICV50876.2021.9388603

Hasija, Y., Garg, N., & Sourav, S. (2017). Automated detection of dermatological disorders through image-processing and machine learning. In: *Proceedings of the IEEE International Conference on Intelligent Sustainable Systems*, (pp. 1047-1051). IEEE. 10.1109/ISS1.2017.8389340

Iradukunda, O., Che, H., Uwineza, J., Bayingana, J. Y., Bin-Imam, M. S., & Niyonzima, I. (2019). Malaria Disease Prediction Based on Machine Learning. In: *Proceedings of the IEEE International Conference on Signal, Information and Data Processing*, (pp. 1-7). IEEE. 10.1109/ICSIDP47821.2019.9173011

Ismaeel, S., Miri, A., & Chourishi, D. (2015). Using the extreme learning machine (elm) technique for heart disease diagnosis. In: *Proceedings of the IEEE Canada International Humanitarian Technology Conference*, (pp. 1-3). IEEE. 10.1109/IHTC.2015.7238043

Jadhav, S., Kasar, R., Lade, N., Patil, M., & Kolte, S. (2019). Disease prediction by machine learning from healthcare communities. *International Journal of Scientific Research in Science and Technology*, *6*(3), 29–35. doi:10.32628/IJSRST19633

Katarya, R., & Srinivas, P. (2020). Predicting heart disease at early stages using machine learning: A survey. In: *Proceedings of the IEEE International Conference on Electronics and Sustainable Communication Systems*, (pp. 302-305). IEEE. 10.1109/ICESC48915.2020.9155586

Kohli, P. S., & Arora, S. (2018). Application of machine learning in disease prediction. In: *Proceedings of the 4th IEEE International Conference on Computing Communication and Automation*, (pp. 1-4). IEEE. 10.1109/CCAA.2018.8777449

Mohan, S., Thirumalai, C., & Srivastava, G. (2019). Effective heart disease prediction using hybrid machine learning techniques. *IEEE Access : Practical Innovations, Open Solutions*, 7, 81542–81554. doi:10.1109/ACCESS.2019.2923707

Mujumdar, A., & Vaidehi, V. (2019). Diabetes prediction using machine learning algorithms. *Procedia Computer Science*, 165, 292–299. doi:10.1016/j.procs.2020.01.047

Patil, M., Lobo, V. B., Puranik, P., Pawaskar, A., Pai, A., & Mishra, R. (2018). A proposed model for lifestyle disease prediction using support vector machine. In: *Proceedings of the 9th IEEE International Conference on Computing, Communication and Networking Technologies*, (pp. 1-6). IEEE. 10.1109/ICCCNT.2018.8493897

Ponde, S. S., & Padghan, S. V. (2020). Smart health prediction for avoiding future health risk by using machine learning. *International Journal of Scientific Development and Research*, 5(8), 355–362.

Rabby, A. K. M. S. A., Mamata, R., & Laboni, M. A., Ohidujjaman, & Abujar, S. (2019). Machine learning applied to kidney disease prediction: comparison study. In: *Proceedings of the 10th International Conference on Computing, Communication and Networking Technologies*, (pp. 1-7). IEEE. 10.1109/ICCCNT45670.2019.8944799

Rashid, M., Yousuf, M. M., Ram, B., & Goyal, V. (2019). Novel Big Data Approach for Drug Prediction in Health Care Systems. In: *Proceedings of the International Conference on Automation, Computational and Technology Management,* (pp. 325-329). IEEE. 10.1109/ICACTM.2019.8776823

Robinson, C., Chugg, B., Anderson, B., Ferres, J. M. L., & Ho, D. E. (2022). Mapping industrial poultry operations at scale with deep learning and aerial imagery. *IEEE Journal of Selected Topics in Applied Earth Observations and Remote Sensing*, 15, 7458–7471. doi:10.1109/JSTARS.2022.3191544

Shah, D., Patel, S., & Bharti, S. K. (2020). Heart disease prediction using machine learning techniques. *SN Computer Science*, 1(6), 345. doi:10.100742979-020-00365-y

Soni, M., & Varma, S. (2020, September). Diabetes prediction using machine learning techniques. *International Journal of Engineering Research & Technology (Ahmedabad)*, 9(9), 921–925.

Subramani, P., Srinivas, K., Kavitha Rani, B., Sujatha, R., & Parameshachari, B. D. (2023). Prediction of muscular paralysis disease based on hybrid feature extraction with machine learning technique for COVID-19 and post-COVID-19 patients. *Personal and Ubiquitous Computing*, 27(5), 831–844. doi:10.100700779-021-01531-6 PMID:33679282

Yuan, F. Q. (2016). Critical issues of applying machine learning to condition monitoring for failure diagnosis. In: *Proceedings of the IEEE International Conference on Industrial Engineering and Engineering Management*, (pp. 1903-1907). IEEE. 10.1109/IEEM.2016.7798209

Chapter 11
Comparison of Hybrid Artificial Neural Networks With GA, PSO, and RSA in Predicting COVID–19 Cases:
A Case Study of India

Balakrishnama Manohar
https://orcid.org/0000-0002-8929-8709
Vellore Institute of Technology, India

Raja Das
Vellore Institute of Technology, India

ABSTRACT

The objective of the current study is to choose the best model with the highest accuracy rate using three robust hybrid artificial intelligence-based models: the ANN-GA, ANN-PSO and ANN-RSA. To do so, a sample of COVID-19 confirmed cases in India between August 1, 2021, and July 26, 2022, is first compiled. A random allocation of 70% (30%) of the total observation has been chosen as training (testing) data. After that, the LM method is used to train an ANN model. Accordingly, the appropriate number of hidden neurons is determined to be 9 using the R^2 and RMSE criterion. To achieve the highest accuracy rate, ANN-GA, ANN-PSO, and ANN-RSA models are developed using the presented ANN model. The optimized model's R-values during the training and test phases, according to ANN-GA and ANN-PSO, are 0.99 and 0.95, respectively. The R-values for ANN-RSA varied from 0.99 to 0.96. hence, the ANN-RSA demonstrated superior performance in forecasting COVID-19 cases in India.

1. INTRODUCTION

A viral disease caused by a novel coronavirus (nCov) or 2019-nCov was first identified in Wuhan, China, at the end of December 2019. The person-to-person transfer of nCov is one of the epidemics

DOI: 10.4018/978-1-6684-4466-5.ch011

most difficult hurdles. Infected instances of the coronavirus (COVID-19) are increasing at an exponential rate all over the world. COVID-19 is a dangerous disease caused by the SARS-COV (Severe Acute Respiratory Syndrome Corona Virus) family, and it has become the world's worst health catastrophe of the twenty-first century. The World Health Organization (WHO) proclaimed it a global pandemic on March 11, 2020, just a few months after the first case was detected in Wuhan, China (Zou et al., 2020). Patients infected with COVID-19 suffered with common symptoms, including cough, fever, and respiratory problems. In the worst-case scenario, it could lead to major health problems such as kidney failure and pneumonia, which could lead to patient death. COVID-19 appears to be spread by coughs, sneezes, and human-to-human transmission (Zou et al., 2020). Between January 20, 2020 and August 28, 2022, approximately 600 million people were infected globally, resulting in more than 6.49 million deaths cases; in India, nearly 44.4 million people were infected positively, resulting in 0.528 million deaths cases; and in USA, China, UK, and France nearly 94 million, 0.948 million, 23.5 million, and 33.5 million people were infected positively, resulting in 0.401 million, 5226, 0.205 million, and 0.15 million deaths cases (*WHO Coronavirus (COVID-19) Dashboard | WHO Coronavirus (COVID-19) Dashboard With Vaccination Data*, n.d.).

The disease is spread by little droplets that become airborne when an infected person coughs or sneezes. These droplets drop on things and surfaces in the immediate vicinity of the afflicted person. COVID-19 can be contracted by touching certain objects or surfaces and then touching their eyes, nose, or mouth. If people inhale these airborne particles, they can get COVID-19. As a result, keeping a distance of about one meter (3 feet) from sick persons is crucial.

Mathematicians are primarily interested in investigating the mathematical and physical components of this disease in mathematics. Due to the general COVID-19 virus's complexity, there is less known information about it compared to the unknown data. It is also difficult to count all of the affected people for a number of reasons. The following are some of the main concepts: (i) Infected people are terrified of getting tested and then being admitted to the hospital. (ii) A small number of screenings, focused primarily on "suspicious" instances or those with significant symptoms, does not provide an accurate estimate of the number of people who could be infected without knowing it. This delay between the time of infection and the time of diagnosis can have serious ramifications for the epidemics spread, among other things. (Ojo et al., 2020).

Novel coronavirus (nCov) behavior can be explained by several scholars from several fields, including mathematics, chemistry, statistics, computer science, and health care, with the goal of discovering a cure (Fu et al., 2020). The dynamics of COVID-19 are studied using a variety of mathematical models. The Susceptible Infectious-Recovered (SIR) model is one of the most widely used models for disease dynamics. This model uses a system of time-dependent differential equations to predict epidemic growth. Researchers have extensively employed the SIR model and its different modified forms to study Ebola and AIDS infections (Khaleque et al., 2017; Zakary et al., 2016). Such models were recently employed to model the spread of the coronavirus outbreak. With testing and conditional quarantine, Berger et al. (Berger et al., 2020), utilized the SEIR infectious infection model. Using a stochastic epidemic SEIR model, Iwata et al. (Iwata et al., 2020) investigated the possible secondary transmission of Novel Coronavirus in an exported country. Godio et al.(Godio et al., 2020; Jena et al., 2021) studied the recent SARS-CoV-2 outbreak with a specific focus on Italy using an SEIR epidemiological model. The machine-learning based prognostication is presented by Zivkovic et al (Zivkovic et al., 2021). The COVID-19 new cases are predicted via a hybrid machine learning and beetle antennae search algorithms. They validate the proposed technique by using China and US data. With a R-squared of 0.9763, the authors concluded that the proposed model can be a robust forecaster of COVID-19 cases. Wieczorek et al. (Wieczorek et al., 2020) have predicted COVID-19 new cases using an autoregressive ANN model by considering coordinates. After pre-processing the input data, they developed two ANN architectures for the worldwide and countries. The proposed ANN was trained using Adam training algorithm. The findings disclosed that the proposed model can render a proper approximation of COVID-19 trend. A study conducted by Namasudra et al. (Namasudra et al., 2023) proposed nonlinear autoregressive neural network time series for predicting COVID-19 cases. They trained the model with various algorithms. The results indicated that Levenberg–Marquardt training algorithm is the most suitable technique for training the neural network. Manohar et al.(Manohar & Das, 2022a, 2022b) proposed the two explicit mathematical prediction models were used to forecasting the COVID-19 epidemic in India. A Boltzmann Function-based model and Beesham's prediction model are among these methods and also estimated using the advanced ANN-BP models. GAs is considered to be a subset of "computational models," which are models that are inspired by the concept of evolution(Ghamisi et al., 2015). Kennedy and Eberhart (Kennedy et al., 1995) introduced particle swarm optimization (PSO), a stochastic population-based method inspired by the intelligent collective behavior of some animals such as bird flocking or fish schooling. Laith Abuligah was introduced Reptile Search Algorithm (RSA), a unique nature-inspired meta-heuristic optimizer inspired by crocodile hunting. Encircling, which is accomplished by high walking or belly walking, and hunting, which is accomplished by hunting coordination or hunting cooperation, are the two primary phases of crocodile behaviors (Abualigah et al., 2022).

Several forecasting techniques exist. Many researchers have used linear regression models as their primary method of prediction or as a standard for comparison testing. It should be made clear that using linear regression methods to examine non-linear patterns among parameters is inappropriate. It is reasonable to assume that the linear approaches offer a reliable forecast when compared to the total set of COVID-19 variables. In other words, the total COVID-19 instances often have a linear form and increase over time. However, the daily COVID-19 new cases exhibit a clear non-linear pattern with several wave peaks in all nations, as illustrated in Figure 1. (For a better presentation, the countries are presents in same plots). The accurate forecasting of daily instances is crucial because it will enable policymakers to directly identify upcoming waves. As a result, for forecasting everyday instances, one may anticipate that linear models would have lower accuracy rates than models based on AI since AI approaches are designed to take into account non-linear interactions with a strong and flexible discerning eligibility. To put it another way, the output of an AI-based model (i.e., ANN) is re-trained using a new training method in order to boost the accuracy rate and optimize the weights acquired by ANN. In-dispersion-through AI-based models, the hybrid ones often enhance the accuracy rates. As a result, someone might assume that the hybrid models produce reliable forecasts of an output variable. Additionally, there is evidence that RSA is superior to algorithms derived from nature, such as PSO and GA, demonstrating its dependability and robustness in resolving all problems (Abualigah et al., 2022).

In that regard, the objective of this study aims to test the robustness of Artificial Neural Network-Genetic Algorithm (ANN-GA), the Artificial Neural Network-Particle Swarm Optimization (ANN-PSO), and the Artificial Neural Network-Reptile Search Algorithm (ANN-RSA) in predicting COVID-19 new cases across five nations. Based on the initial conjectures, it expresses the null hypothesizes as following:

H_0 There is no difference in prediction robustness of ANN with ANN-GA, ANN-PSO, and ANN-RSA.
H_1 There is no difference in prediction robustness of ANN-GA, ANN-PSO and ANN-RSA models.

Figure 1. The daily confirmed COVID-19 cases from 1, August, 2021 to 26, July, 2022

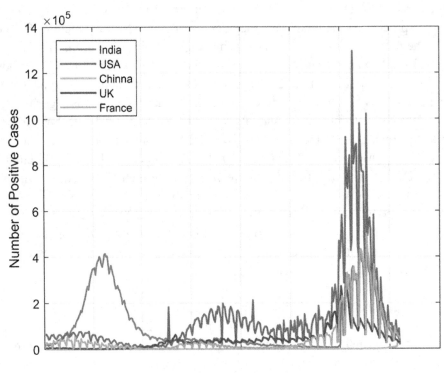

1 August 2021 to 26 July 2022

This study main contribution is to be divided into the following categories: (1) Offering three robust and effective models to simulate the illness trend. (2) Predicting COVID-19 new instances using a combination of three reliable metaheuristic methods and ANN to achieve the highest forecasting precision. (3) Rather than considering cumulative instances, this study concentrates on newly reported cases every day. Since attempts have been made to make the models both accurate and sparse, it can help health officials forecast wave peaks. (4) In the end, the proposed models will be tested using the daily data reported from all nations.

The following is how the rest of the article is structured. The basic structures of our ANN models are shown in Part 2, followed by a description of the GA, PSO, and RSA algorithms. The results are presented and analyzed in Part 3. Then come to certain conclusions in Part 4.

2. METHODOLOGY

2.1. Artificial Neural Network (ANN)

ANNs are built in the same way that human and animal brains are built. Basic scalar messages, simple processing components, a high degree of interconnection and adoptive interaction between units are the things which make them a type of multi-processor computer system (Rashidi et al., 2013). Actually, ANN provides a reasonably quick and flexible way of modeling, so it is appropriate for rainfall-runoff prediction (Asadi et al., 2013; Chiel et al., 2021). Layers of neurons make up an ANN as shown in Figure 2. One or more hidden layers of neurons connect the input layer of neurons to the output layer of neurons. The interconnecting link between the neuron layers is made up of connection weights. This method changes its weights throughout the training phase to reduce the errors between the projected result and the actual output using the Back Propagation algorithm (Aichouri et al., 2015; Jali et al., 2018) To get the best topology and weights, ANN is trained using experimental data and then evaluated with more experimental data whereas, bias refers to the weight that is provided directly to one neuron without being coupled to the prior neuron in specific circumstances. The most common type of ANN is the multilayer Perceptron (MLP). It also has one or more hidden layers feed forward neural network.

The network must be trained using an appropriate method before producing the required output (Maind et al., 2014). A feedforward network is often configured using the back-propagation training procedure. In the training step, the generated output is initially sent across the network since each node's output has the potential to become its succeeding node's input. The desired output is contrasted with the ANN output. At this stage, an error is disseminated. After that, the weights and bias can be changed by using the network feedback (also known as bias). This procedure helps the network in discovering the patterns between the input and output data (Schweighart & Sedwick, 2001). Multilayer Perceptron ANN with Levenberg-Marquardt training method has garnered a lot of uses in the interim. Each Perceptron, in general, is a binary processing unit that categorizes the acquired inputs. The next Perceptron will be given the signals (inputs) that have been processed. The weighted total of incoming signals (inputs) must be analyzed in order to establish the output. In order to do this, a stimulating function needs be applied to the hidden and output layers. The sigmoid transfer functions are primarily used in this context (Du & Stephanus, 2018). Each neuron's output is a function of the weighted sum of the inputs it got from the preceding levels plus an error value. Mathematically:

$$Output_k = \sum_{k=1}^{i=n} \left(W_{ik} X_i + B_i \right) \tag{1}$$

In Equation. 1, i is from neuron i of the prior layer, k refers to neuron k of the processing layer, W stands weight and B denotes for bias. As a result, the activation function of neuron S is generated using the sigmoid function shown below in Equation. 2:

$$S_k = \frac{1}{1 + e^{-output_k}} \tag{2}$$

2.2. Genetic Algorithm (GA)

GAs is considered to be a subset of "computational models," which are models that are inspired by the concept of evolution (Ghamisi et al., 2015). In a "chromosome-like" data model, these algorithms use "Potential Solutions," "Applicant Solutions," or "Possible Hypotheses" for a particular problem. by applying "Recombination Operators" to chromosome-like data structures, GA preserves important infor-

Figure 2. Artificial neural network modeling procedure

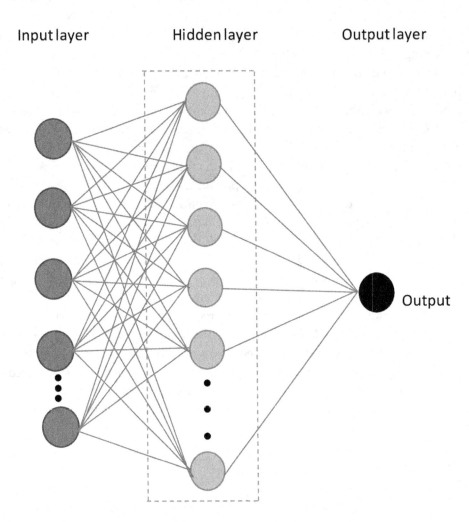

mation stored in these chromosome data models (Dineva et al., 2019; Mosavi et al., 2019; Mühlenbein et al., 1991). GAs is frequently used as "Function Optimizer" algorithms, which are algorithms that are used to optimize "Objective Functions." Furthermore, the GA can be used to solve problems in a wide range of situations (Horn et al., 1994; Mühlenbein et al., 1991).

A population of chromosomes is generally produced randomly and limited by the variables of the issue in order to begin the execution of a genetic algorithm (GA). It is at this stage that the chromosomes formed in the previous step are reviewed, and chromosomes that can better exhibit the ideal solution of the issue are more likely to be employed to create new ones. An answer's "goodness" is typically assessed by comparing it to the general population of candidates' responses (Ardabili et al., 2020; Houck et al., 1995; Jones et al., 1997; Whitley et al., 1990). Figure 3. illustrates the main algorithm of a GA process.

Figure 3. Flowchart of Genetic Algorithm

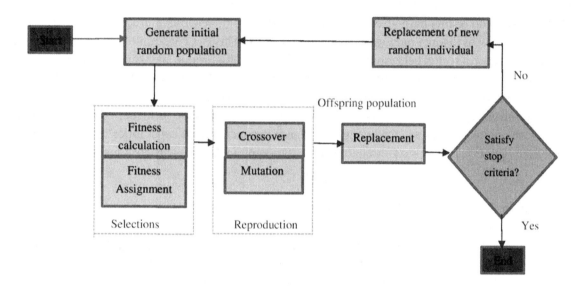

2.3. Particle Swarm Optimization (PSO)

Kennedy and Eberhart (Kennedy et al., 1995) initially proposed the Particle Swarm Optimization (PSO) technique in November 1995. They devised an algorithm named PSO based on the notion of swarming in nature, such as birds, fish, and other animals. Particles in the PSO are generated by natural swarms, and communications are based on evolutionary calculations. The PSO integrates individual experiences with social experiences. A proposed solution is displayed as a particle in this method. To attain to a global optimum, the algorithm uses a collection of flying particles (Modifying solutions) in a search space (current and prospective solutions) and moves towards a promising location. The particles displaying the solution candidates in the PSO begin their flight from random points in a search region. Particles change their location according to Equation 4. and move to a new position in each repetition. A fitness function that evaluates the quality of each solution has an impact on flying.

$$velocity_i^{t+1} = \chi\left(\omega.v_i^t + c_1.r_1\left(pbest_i - position_i^t\right) + c_2.r_2\left(gbest - position_i^t\right)\right) \tag{3}$$

$$position_i^{t+1} = position_i^t + velocity_i^{t+1} \tag{4}$$

In which $velocity_i^{t+1}$ = The Velocity of the ith Particle in t+1th Iteration, $position_i^{t+1}$ = The Position of the ith Particle in t+1th Iteration, $pbest_i$ = the best personal Position of the ith Particle, $gbest$ = Within the Swarm, the best Position.

$$\chi = 2k \Big/ \left| 2 - \phi - \sqrt{\phi^2 - 4\phi} \right|, \quad 0 < k < 1, \quad \phi = \phi_1 + \phi_2, \quad \phi > 4 \tag{5}$$

PSO includes a few dependent parameters: c_1 and c_2 are variables that balance the influence of self-best and social best while moving the particle towards the target, and they are commonly set to a value of 2, however, good results have also been obtained with $c_1 = c_2 = 4$(Balamurugan et al., 2016). Each repetition, r_1, and r_2 is distinct random values within 0 and 1. This is a constraint factor that reduces the velocity. ω Is a global search behavior that is first assigned to a high value and then dynamically lowered during the optimization process (which means a more personal search behavior).

The recommended range is 0.2<w<0.4. The Dynamic ω adjustment offers two benefits: first, it speeds up convergence to an ideal solution, and second, it modulates the influence of prior component velocities on ongoing velocities, managing the balance between swarm capabilities in local and global exploration. Figure 4. provides a flowchart representation of updating a particle's location in two iterations.

2.4. Reptile Search Algorithm (RSA)

The classic Reptile Search Algorithm (RSA) and its technique are presented in this section. The fundamental Reptile Search Algorithm (RSA) is explained in terms of its investigation (global search) and assault (local search) phases, which were influenced by real-life (Abualigah et al., 2022) crocodile encircle mechanics, stalking processes, and behavior patterns.

Figure 4. A Flowchart of Particle Swarm Optimization

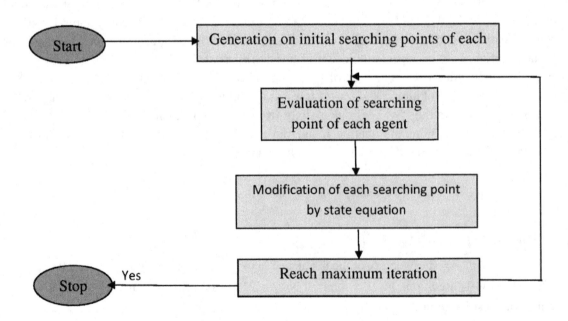

2.5. Phase of Encirclement (Exploration)

This section introduces the RSA's exploratory activity (encircling). Crocodiles encircle under one of two ways: high walking or belly walking, based on their encircling habit (Shinawi et al., 2021).

The RSA shifts between local and global search stages consisting of four scenarios: The number of iterations is divided into 4 parts; the entire number of repetitions is divided into 4 parts.; Based on two fundamental search approaches, the RSA investigation mechanisms analyze the search areas and approach to obtain a better solution.

Throughout this phase of the search, one criterion must be satisfied. The high walking search technique is carried out in accordance to $t \leq \dfrac{T}{4}$ and the tummy walking search is carried out in accordance to $t \leq 2\dfrac{T}{4}$ and $t > \dfrac{T}{4}$. Equation.6. depicts the position-updating procedure.

$$P_{(i,j)}(t+1) = \begin{cases} B_j(t) \times -\mu_{(i,j)}(t) \times \lambda - R_{(i,j)}(t) \times rand, & t \leq \dfrac{T}{4} \\ B_j(t) \times P_{(r_1,j)} \times E(t) \times rand, & t \leq 2\dfrac{T}{4} \ and \ t > \dfrac{T}{4} \end{cases} \tag{6}$$

Where $B_j(t)$ is the best-achieved solution, t is the ongoing repetition, r_1, r_2, r_3 and rand is the random values, and T is a maximum repetition. $\mu_{(i,j)}$ is a hunting operator calculated by Equation.7. $R_{(i,j)}$ is the decrease function and it is calculated by Equation 8. λ is an operator fixed to 0.1. $P_{(r_1,j)}$ is the random position. N is the candidate solutions. Equation 9. determines the probability parameter evolutionary sense (E(t)).

$$\mu_{(i,j)} = B_j(t) \times dp_{(i,j)}, \tag{7}$$

$$R_{(i,j)} = \frac{B_j(t) - P_{(r_2,j)}}{B_j(t) + \varepsilon}, \tag{8}$$

$$E(t) = 2 \times r_3 \times \left(1 - \frac{1}{T}\right), \tag{9}$$

Where ε is a small value, $dp_{(i,j)}$ difference operator calculated by Equation.10.

$$dp_{(i,j)} = \alpha + \frac{P_{(i,j)} - mbest(P_i)}{B_j(t) \times \left(Ub_{(j)} - Lb_{(j)}\right) + \varepsilon'} \tag{10}$$

Where $mbest(P_i)$ denotes the mean positions calculated using Equation 11. The upper and lower boundaries are denoted by $Ub_{(j)}$ and $Lb_{(j)}$. α is a parameter with a value of 0.1.

$$mbest\left(P_i\right)=\frac{1}{n}\sum_{j=1}^{n}P_{(i,j)},\tag{11}$$

2.6. Hunting Phase (Exploitation)

In this part, we'll look examine RSA's exploitative behaviors as shown in Figure 5. Crocodiles adopt two hunting strategies, as per their hunting behavior: hunting coordination and hunting teamwork (Shinawi et al., 2021).

The hunting in this phase (searching coordination) is implemented and calculated to $t\leq 3\frac{T}{4}$ and $t>2\frac{T}{4}$; otherwise, searching cooperation is implemented to $t\leq T$ and $t>3\frac{T}{4}$. The position-updating processes depicts Equation 12.

$$P_{(i,j)}\left(t+1\right)=\begin{cases} B_j(t)\times P_{(i,j)}\left(t\right)\times rand, & t\leq 3\frac{T}{4}\,and\,t>2\frac{T}{4} \\ B_j\left(t\right)\times\,-\mu_{(i,j)}\left(t\right)\times\varepsilon-R_{(i,j)}\left(t\right)\times rand, & t\leq T\,and\,t>3\frac{T}{4} \end{cases}\tag{12}$$

Where B_j (t) is the best-achieved solution, and $\mu_{(i,j)}$ is a hunting operator calculated by Equation8. $R_{(i,j)}$ is the decrease function and it is calculated by Equation 9. dp $_{(i,j)}$ difference operator calculated by Equation 10.

2.7. Evaluation Criteria

To determine the accuracy of model, Root Mean Square Error (*RMSE*), coefficient of estimation (R^2) and Mean Absolute Percentage Error (*MAPE*) are used in this work, statistically equations. (13-15):

$$RMSE=\sqrt{\frac{\sum_{i=1}^{n}\left(O_i-P_i\right)^2}{N}}\tag{13}$$

$$R^2=1-\frac{\sum_{i=1}^{n}\left(O_i-P_i\right)^2}{\sum_{i=1}^{n}\left(O_i-P_i\right)^2+\sum_{i=1}^{n}\left(P_i-\hat{O}\right)^2}\tag{14}$$

$$MAPE=\frac{100}{n}\sum_{i=1}^{n}\left|\frac{O_i-P_i}{O_i}\right|\tag{15}$$

Here, O_i denotes observed values, P_i denotes predicted values and $\hat{O}_i$ denotes observed average values and n is the total number of observations. Obviously, a higher value of R^2 will demonstrate more pre-dictability power. Conversely, a lower value of *RMSE* will guarantee the robustness of the developed models.

Figure 5. The flowchart representation for Reptile Search Algorithm

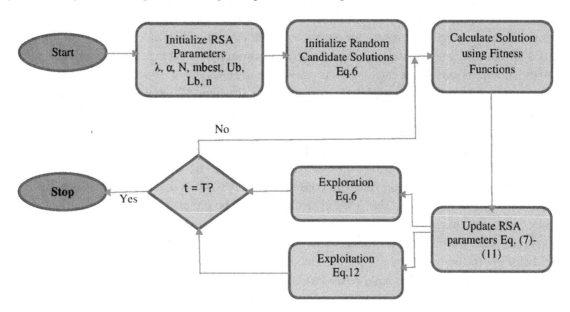

2.8. Developing Hybrid Models

In the framework of this article, three hybrid models i.e., ANN-GA, ANN-PSO and ANN-RSA are developed. In the beginning, MATLAB software is used to developed an ANN. The model is retrained with the new methods after initial training for the purpose of hybridizing. Figure 6. illustrates the hybrid modelling process. The output data are the daily COVID-19 new cases. In addition, the number of days (time) is taken into account as an input instance because the input data are unknown or may not have existed (Tran et al., 2019). A sample of 360 daily observations between the dates of 01 August 2021 and 26 July 2022 are gathered. The network is trained using 252 daily observations (70% of the total dataset) and with 108 observations (30% of the entire dataset) the model's robustness will be tested and validated.

3. RESULTS

3.1. Results For Modeling of ANN

Before beginning the hybrid modelling process, a Perceptron ANN with one hidden layer is created. For a sophisticated nonlinear issue, one hidden layer will be sufficient (Karsoliya., 2012). In addition, the Levenberg-Marquardt (LM) algorithm is used for network training. The LM method has been shown to be one of the best and most flexible training algorithms, and as it avoids computing the Hessian Matrix, it could be viewed as the fastest backpropagation technique (Gülcü, 2022; Saba & Elsheikh, 2020). The standard approach described in the literature (Koopialipoor et al., 2019; Yarsky, 2021; Zorlu et al., 2007) is used to find out the appropriate number of hidden neurons. In this regard, 24 ANN models (nodes) are created in the hidden layer. Each model is categorized according to R^2 and RMSE as a result of choosing the best option. A higher number is preferred for R^2. As a result, under this ranking method, the model with the highest R^2 obtains the highest score (i.e., the maximum score is 24). On the other hand, a smaller *RMSE* number will be suitable. Therefore, the model with the lowest RMSE value receives the highest rating. As a result, for each model, the overall rank is calculated by adding the two statistics for the train and test stages, independently. Accordingly, in Table 1. the overall ranks attributable to the simulated models are calculated. As can be regarded, Model No. 9 with 9 neurons has acquired the maximum total rank. In this model, the training stage is where R^2 (RMSE) is said to approach its maximum (minimum) value. As the number of neurons grows after this, R^2 will start to decline. Following that, this model is chosen as the best simulation based on the total rank. Figure 7 and Figure 8. contrasts real COVID-19 new cases from the training and testing phases with those that were anticipated during those periods (the values are normalized). As shown, during the testing phase, the suggested model had a good accuracy rate. But considering COVID-19's severe repercussions, increasing accuracy rate will be necessary. The ANN algorithms might be unable to identify the perfect solution in other cases. Reaching an extreme locally cannot ensure optimization. The relative minimum trap demonstrates that, for instance, *RMSE* is at its finest. However, in certain situations, using a hybrid model helps get the optimum value (i.e., the global extremum) (Yarsky, 2021). As a result, the chosen model is enlarged into the ANN-GA, AAN-PSO, and ANN-RSA models in the steps that follow. The countries data will be used to validate the suggested models, and in each instance, the effectiveness of hybrid models will be evaluated.

Figure 6. Flowchart of work procedure for hybrid modeling

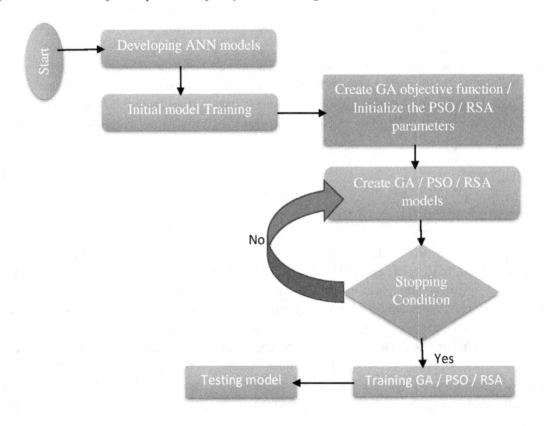

Table 1. Selecting the optimal ANN model with respect to neurons

Items	Neurons	Train		Test		Train-Rank		Test-Rank		Overall-Rank
		R^2	RMSE	R^2	RMSE	R^2	RMSE	R^2	RMSE	
1	1	0.908854	0.070426	0.812937	0.230797	3	3	3	3	12
2	2	0.955618	0.049781	0.882519	0.173615	4	4	17	20	45
3	3	0.956548	0.049287	0.904875	0.159849	5	6	21	21	53
4	4	0.966976	0.042537	0.887869	0.179621	10	9	19	19	57
5	5	0.790638	0.099674	0.754026	0.23552	2	1	2	2	7
6	6	0.972492	0.039450	0.843965	0.221047	11	11	5	5	32
7	7	0.962024	0.044202	0.859172	0.196751	8	8	8	10	34
8	8	0.973360	0.038628	0.911051	0.154897	12	12	22	22	68
9	**9**	**0.989768**	**0.023890**	**0.92497**	**0.151407**	**21**	**21**	**24**	**23**	**89**
10	10	0.988716	0.025178	0.877314	0.182992	20	20	15	17	72
11	11	0.976523	0.036207	0.862155	0.202924	13	13	11	9	46
12	12	0.981637	0.031933	0.858431	0.211556	16	16	7	7	46
13	13	0.992813	0.019904	0.876744	0.193740	22	22	14	11	69
14	14	0.786582	0.090723	0.657995	0.265135	1	2	1	1	5
15	15	0.980629	0.032971	0.85937	0.208507	15	15	9	8	47
16	16	0.977296	0.036200	0.860544	0.211731	14	14	10	6	44
17	17	0.961851	0.046338	0.876046	0.184853	7	7	13	16	43
18	18	0.956732	0.049670	0.867364	0.190463	6	5	12	14	37
19	19	0.996826	0.013330	0.88025	0.190687	24	24	16	13	77
20	20	0.983518	0.030426	0.923781	0.148725	18	18	23	24	83
21	21	0.964556	0.042143	0.858085	0.190219	9	10	6	15	40
22	22	0.996658	0.013668	0.904124	0.181772	23	23	20	18	84
23	23	0.983608	0.030217	0.885679	0.192118	19	19	18	12	68
24	24	0.982200	0.031554	0.835093	0.225458	17	17	16	4	42

3.2. Developing Hybrid Genetic Algorithm

As mentioned above, it is decided to build the ANN-GA model using the ANN optimum prediction with 9 neurons. The optimal number of populations needs to be determined in order to achieve this. It is a critical step because as the number of populations rises, so does their desire to find the best solution. The accuracy rate can decrease with a lower population, as would be expected logically.

However, a large number of populations will increase the computational time, which may not be related to a smaller RMSE. In order to compute the model, different populations and iterations are considered in order to determine the desired number of populations. Figure 9. displays the outcomes. With a population of between 20 and 90, there have been 200 iterations, according to this estimate. Most series will have converged after 60 iterations. In practical terms, as depicted in Figure 9. the solution will not be improved for populations greater than 30. The best ANN-GA model in this regard is decided to be

Figure 7. Regression analysis of the ANN optimal model training in predicting COVID-19 cases with India data

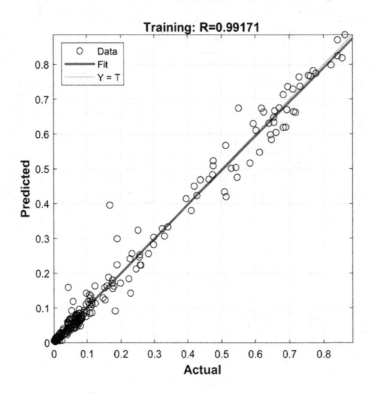

Figure 8. Regression analysis of the ANN optimal model test in predicting COVID-19 cases with India data

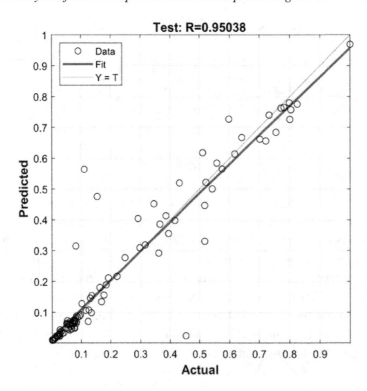

Figure 9. The ANN-GA models regarding number of populations and iteration

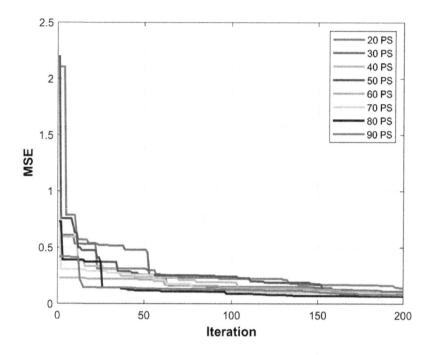

Figure 10. Regression analysis of the ANN- GA training in predicting COVID-19 cases with India data

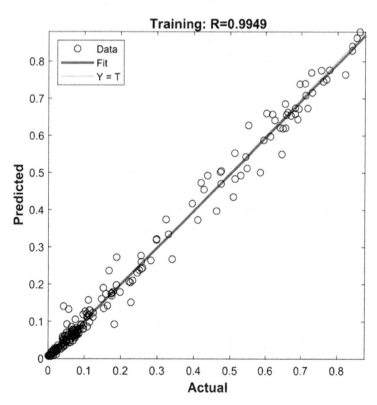

the model with 30 populations. the outcomes of the proposed model's prediction of COVID-19 new cases are shown in Figure 9. As a result, as compared to ANN, the ANN-GA displays good forecasting robustness in India throughout either the train and test stages. we simulated COVID-19 new instances using ANN-GA (Figure 10 and Figure 11). For the USA (Figure 12 and Figure 13), China (Figure 14 and Figure 15), the UK (Figure 16 and Figure 17), and France (Figure 18 and Figure 19). During the training phase, the R-value was in between 98% (the USA, China, UK, and France) and 0.99% (India) are shown in (Figures 10, 12, 14, 16, 18). In addition, the R-value of test stages varies from 92% (in the USA and China), 93% (in the UK), 94% (in France), and more than 95% (in India) are shown in (Figures 11, 13, 15, 17, 19).

3.3. Developing Hybrid Particle Swarm Optimization Algorithm

As previously, PSO incorporates the 9-neuron ANN model that has been suggested. Normally, the number of particles should be chosen to optimize the search area. Similar to the ANN-GA scenario, a huge insect number will increase the search space to discover the best result. As a result, the computation time might raise.

Thus, an investigation is carried out to choose the best model by taking into consideration 200 iterations as well as the number of particles varying from 20 to 90. The models have converged after around 50 iterations, as seen in Figure 20. The ANN-PSO with 20 particles is the most effective in this situation (i.e., with more particles, the computational time will increase but the solution is essentially the same).

Figure 11. Regression analysis of the ANN- GA test in predicting COVID-19 cases with India data

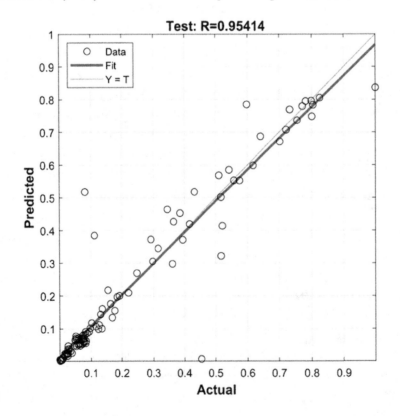

Figure 12. Regression analysis of the ANN- GA training in predicting COVID-19 cases with USA data

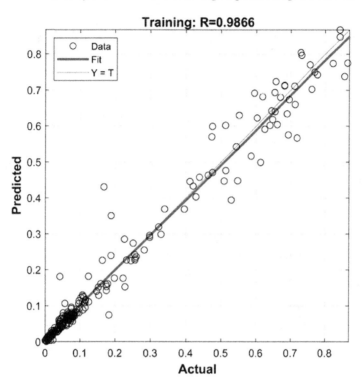

Figure 13. Regression analysis of the ANN- GA test in predicting COVID-19 cases with USA data

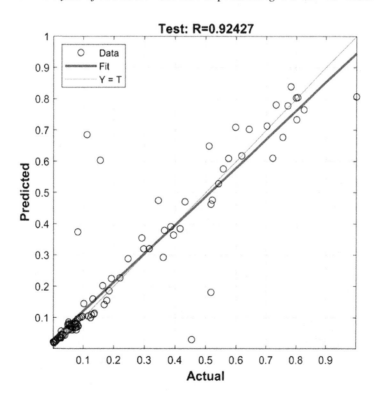

Figure 14. Regression analysis of the ANN- GA training in predicting COVID-19 cases with China data

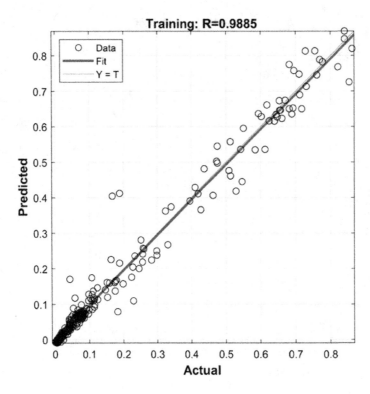

Figure 15. Regression analysis of the ANN- GA test in predicting COVID-19 cases with China data

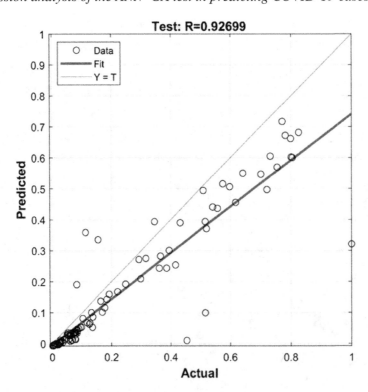

Figure 16. Regression analysis of the ANN- GA training in predicting COVID-19 cases with UK data

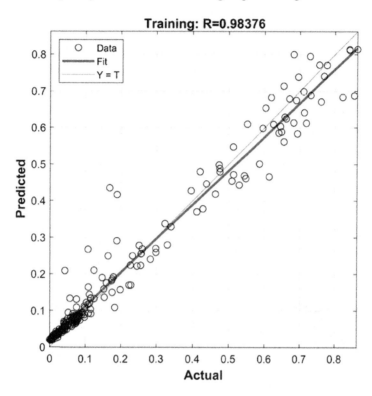

Figure 17. Regression analysis of the ANN- GA test in predicting COVID-19 cases with UK data

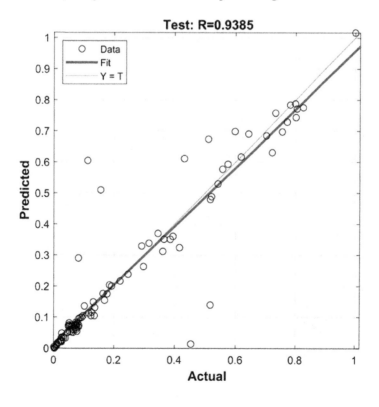

Figure 18. Regression analysis of the ANN- GA training in predicting COVID-19 cases with France data

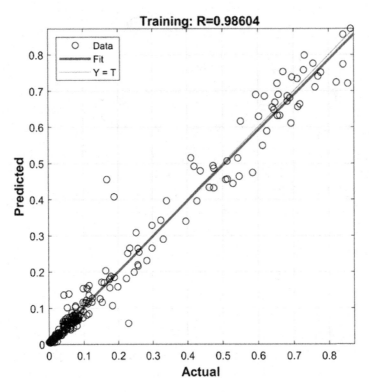

Figure 19. Regression analysis of the ANN- GA test in predicting COVID-19 cases with France data

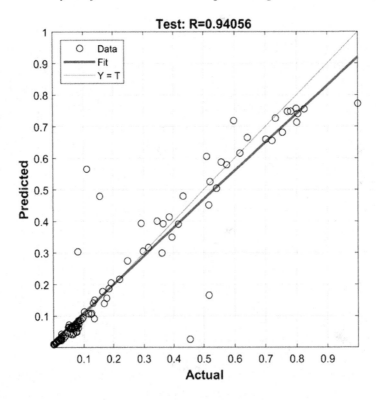

Figure 20. The ANN-PSO models regarding number of particles and iteration

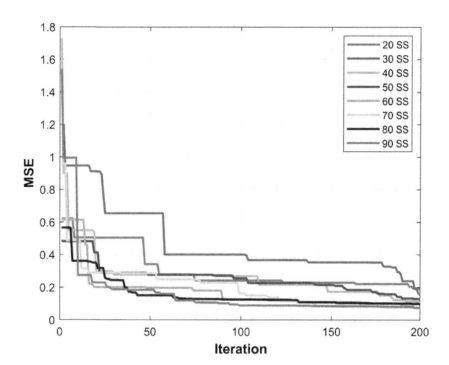

Figure 20. shows the outcomes using the suggested ANN-PSO model with 20 particles. Accordingly, the ANN-PSO has gained significant robustness in approximating the COVID-19 confirmed new instances in India (Figure 21 and Figure 22), with an R-value of more than 99% at both the train and test stages. Additionally, we used our ANN-PSO model to simulate additional case data from the USA (Figure 23 and Figure 24), China (Figure 25 and Figure 26), UK (Figure 27 and Figure 28), and France (Figure 29 and Figure 30). The R-value varies from 97% to 99% at the train stage (Figure 21, 23, 25, 27, 29), and the R-value varies from 92% to 95% at the test stage (Figure 22, 24, 26, 28, 30), demonstrating the ANN-PSO for simulating COVID-19 new cases data.

3.4. Developing Hybrid Reptile Search Algorithm

In order to compute the model, different populations and iterations are considered in order to determine the desired number of candidates. Figure 31. displays the outcomes. With a candidate of between 20 and 90, there have been 200 iterations, according to this estimate. Most series will have converged after 70 iterations.

In practical terms, as depicted in Figure 31. the solution will not be improved for candidates greater than 10. The best ANN-RSA model in this regard is decided to be the model with 10 candidates. The outcomes of the proposed model's prediction of COVID-19 new cases are shown in Figure 31. As a result, as compared to ANN, the ANN-RSA displays good forecasting robustness in India throughout either the train or test stages. We simulated COVID-19 new instances using ANN-RSA (Figure 32 and Figure 33). For the USA (Figure 34 and Figure 35), China (Figure 36 and Figure 37), the UK (Figure 38 and Figure 39), and France (Figure 40 and Figure 41). During the training phase, the R-value was in

Figure 21. Regression analysis of the ANN-PSO training in predicting COVID-19 cases with India data

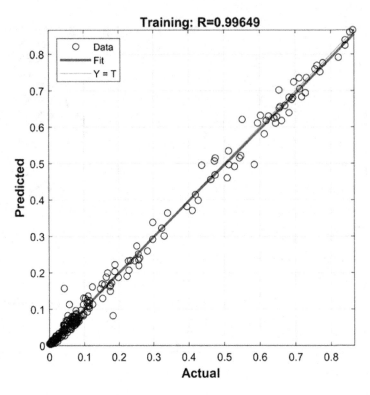

Figure 22. Regression analysis of the ANN- PSO test in predicting COVID-19 cases with India data

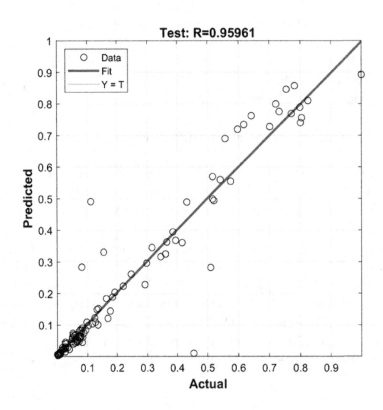

Figure 23. Regression analysis of the ANN-PSO training in predicting COVID-19 cases with USA data

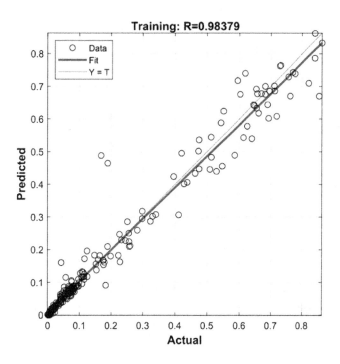

Figure 24. Regression analysis of the ANN- PSO test in predicting COVID-19 cases with USA data

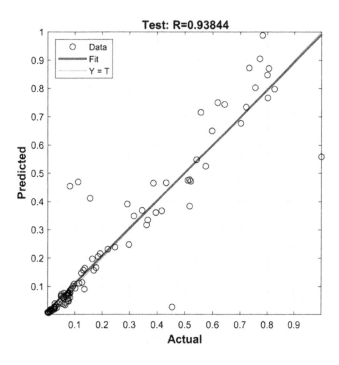

Figure 25. Regression analysis of the ANN- PSO training in predicting COVID-19 cases with China data

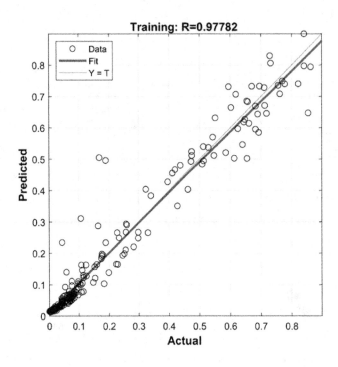

Figure 26. Regression analysis of the ANN-PSO test in predicting COVID-19 cases with China data

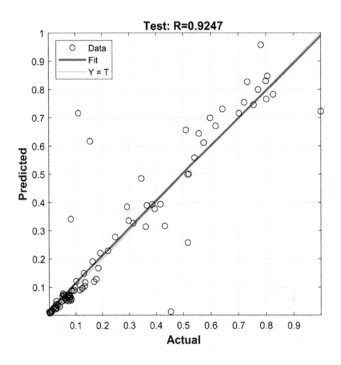

Figure 27. Regression analysis of the ANN-PSO training in predicting COVID-19 cases with UK data

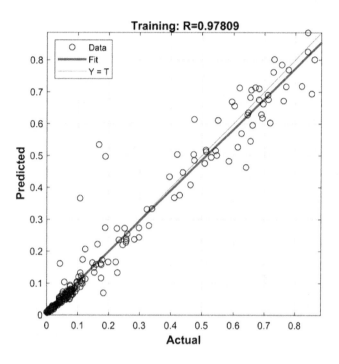

Figure 28. Regression analysis of the ANN- PSO test in predicting COVID-19 cases with UK data

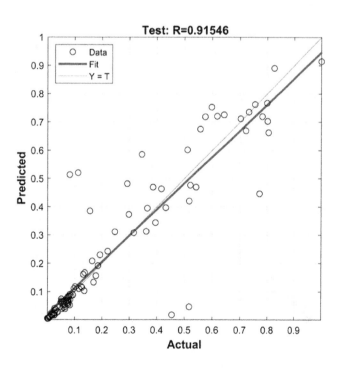

Figure 29. Regression analysis of the ANN- PSO training in predicting COVID-19 cases with France data

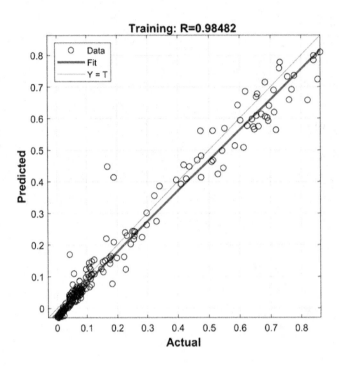

Figure 30. Regression analysis of the ANN-PSO test in predicting COVID-19 cases with France data

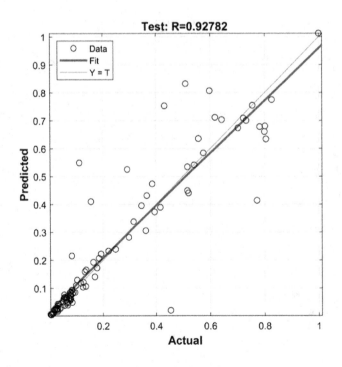

Figure 31. The ANN-RSA models regarding number of candidates and iteration

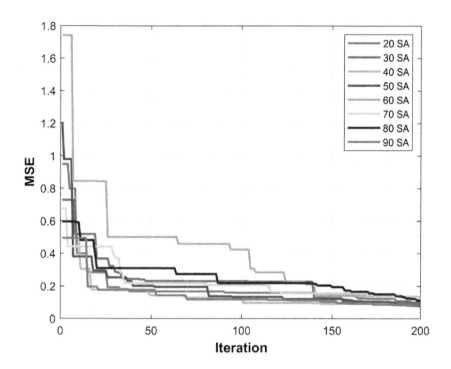

Figure 32. Regression analysis of the ANN-RSA training in predicting COVID-19 cases with India data

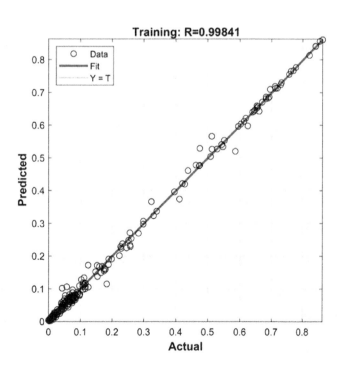

Figure 33. Regression analysis of the ANN- RSA test in predicting COVID-19 cases with India data

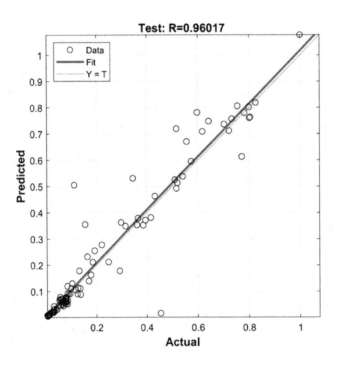

Figure 34. Regression analysis of the ANN-RSA training in predicting COVID-19 cases with USA data

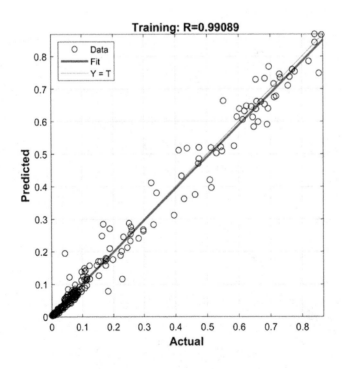

Figure 35. Regression analysis of the ANN- RSA test in predicting COVID-19 cases with USA data

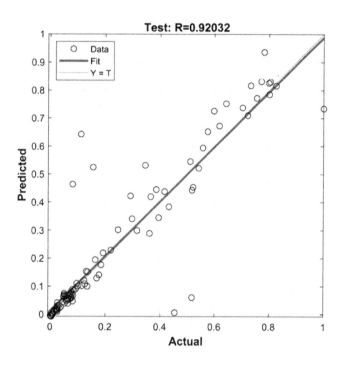

Figure 36. Regression analysis of the ANN- RSA training in predicting COVID-19 cases with China data

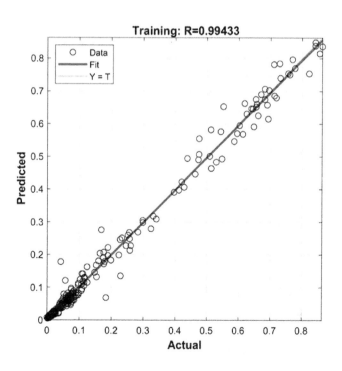

Figure 37. Regression analysis of the ANN-RSA test in predicting COVID-19 cases with China data

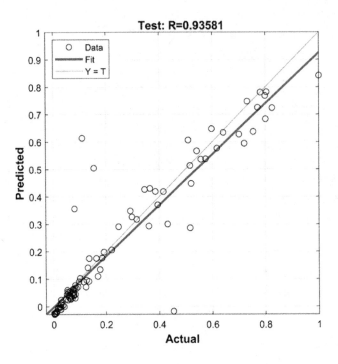

Figure 38. Regression analysis of the ANN-RSA training in predicting COVID-19 cases with UK data

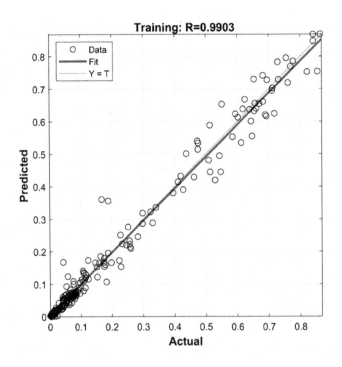

Figure 39. Regression analysis of the ANN- RSA test in predicting COVID-19 cases with UK data

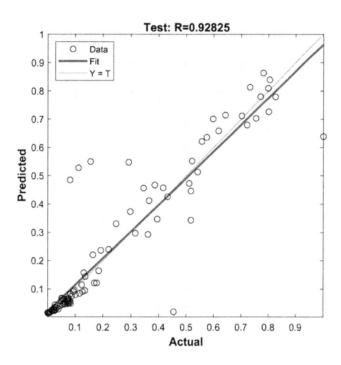

Figure 40. Regression analysis of the ANN- RSA training in predicting COVID-19 cases with France data

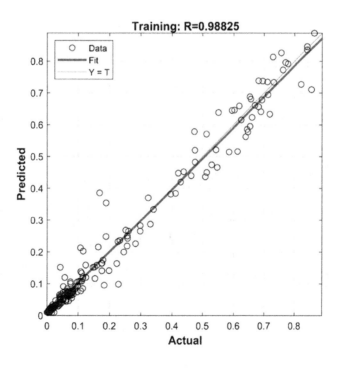

Figure 41. Regression analysis of the ANN-RSA test in predicting COVID-19 cases with France data

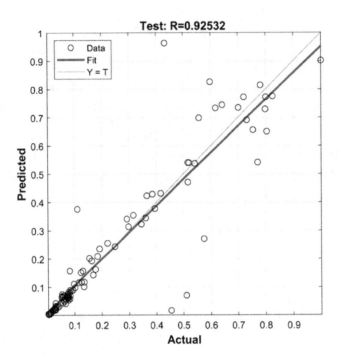

Table 2. Comparison of performance for ANN models in test stage on five selected countries

Models/Country		India	USA	China	UK	France
ANN-LM	RMSE	54984	56485	51889	36698	53890
	MAPE	0.0538	0.1269	0.0624	0.3581	0.2609
	R^2	0.97961	0.96532	0.96282	0.96581	0.96032
ANN-GA	RMSE	57827	58800	56147	42262	68647
	MAPE	0.4389	0.5355	0.5187	0.6901	0.39432
	R^2	0.98267	0.96790	0.97004	0.97018	0.96937
ANN-PSO	RMSE	60116	72939	57261	45760	68668
	MAPE	0.4977	0.5947	0.6025	1.5196	0.4287
	R^2	0.98385	0.96971	0.96188	0.95930	0.96772
ANN-RSA	RMSE	**30979**	**51814**	**43326**	**36278**	**48150**
	MAPE	**0.0409**	**0.1114**	**0.0428**	**0.0551**	**0.2491**
	R^2	**0.98693**	**0.97018**	**0.97677**	**0.97268**	**0.97239**

Figure 42. The overall R for the ANN-GA, ANN-PSO and ANN-RSA in five different countries

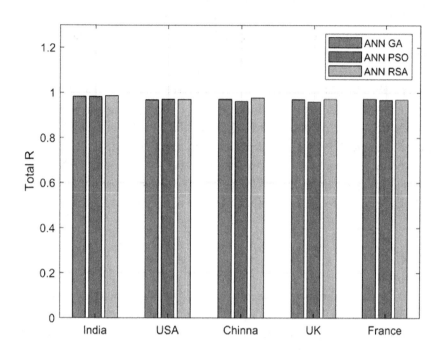

between 99% that shown in the India (Figure 32), USA (Figure 34), China (Figure 36), and UK (Figure 38) and 0.98% in France (Figure 40). In addition, the R-value of test stages varies from 92% are shown in the USA (Figure 35) and China (Figure 37) and France (Figure 41), 93% in the UK (Figure 39), and more than 96% in India (Figure 33).

4. DISCUSSION

The focus of this study was to develop three ANN-based models, the ANN-GA, ANN-PSO, and ANN-RSA, in order to achieve the highest prediction accuracy achievable in India. To achieve this, the train (70%) and test (30%) data from a sample of 360 COVID-19 daily confirmed cases were split at random. The ANN model was subsequently developed. A model with 9 hidden neurons was chosen for continued development in this stage (with an R-value for the train and test steps of 0.99 and 0.95, respectively). The global extremum might not be reached because of the relative extremum trap in ANN. The ANN-GA, ANN-PSO and ANN-RSA can improve the accuracy of ANN in this aspect. To improve the accuracy rate and the outcomes produced by ANN, we developed ANN-GA, ANN-PSO and ANN-RSA. First, the appropriate number of populations and iterations for ANN-GA modelling was determined to be 30 and 60, respectively. For India, the R-value for the train and test stages was almost 0.988. This ANN-GA model was also used to approximate COVID-19 data from other nations, such as the USA, China, UK, and France. The models often displayed an accurate approximation. The hybrid ANN-PSO model was also created in addition to that. A model with 20 particles and over 50 iterations was used in this instance. India's train and test stages had R-values of 0.995 and 0.955, respectively. Once more, we tested the robustness of our ANN-PSO model using a wide range of data. In several areas, the R-value varied from 95% to more than 99%. (Figure 42) displays the outcomes. The hybrid models consistently outperformed ANN. However, the difference between India and China is not significant. These findings show that for India, the USA, France and UK, the ANN-PSO performs better than the ANN-GA. There is no notable difference between the two models for COVID-19 prediction in France and China. Both models in France and China have shown a total R-value of more than 99%. The ANN-RSA has an overall R-value of more than 99% with respect to India. The two models perform satisfactorily for the US and UK, with the ANN-RSA outperforming ANN-GA and ANN-PSO. The results of the proposed ANN models are illustrated in Table 2. As the results indicate, in terms of RMSE, R^2, MAPE (Table 2), the ANN-RSA achieves better performance compared to the other ANN models (ANN, ANN-GA, ANN-PSO) in five countries such as the India, USA, China, UK, and France. Last but not least, the ANN-RSA performance significantly outperformed to ANN-PSO or is at least equivalent to it.

5. CONCLUSION

Currently, India and other nations are being affected by the COVID-19 epidemic, which has major repercussions and is transitioning quickly. The COVID-19 trends have been predicted by several researchers using a different model, including prophet models, machine-learning techniques, autoregressive integrated moving averages, and other methods. Most models have advantages and disadvantages. The aim of the research, and context, selecting the optimal model may not be achievable perse due to data limitations. The hybrid ANN models with GA, PSO, and RSA are now being used in many sectors and have proven to be very robust. Thus, we suggested three hybrid ANN-based models as part of this work to achieve the best predicting robustness of COVID-19 new cases in India. To formally express the results, we reject the null hypothesis. The three hybrid models outperformed the ANN; Thus, H_0 must be rejected. In the same way, the ANN-RSA outperformed the ANN-GA and ANN-PSO; Therefore, H_1 can be rejected. The use of these models for short-term forecasting should be noted. In other words, the level of public cooperation in disease control efforts and the decisions made by policymakers can change the pattern of an epidemic over a longer period of time. However, one of the strengths of our proposed models was their parsimony. They may also be used to create scenarios, such as vaccination or quarantine, by using these factors as input data or initialising the influence on the COVID-19 data for new instances. Hence, the three algorithms, ANN-GA, ANN-PSO, and ANN-RSA, are all reasonably effective in predicting pandemics, but ANN-RSA has the most promise to deliver for forecasting COVID-19 new cases in India, according to the data.

REFERENCES

Abualigah, L., Abd Elaziz, M., Sumari, P., Geem, Z. W., & Gandomi, A. H. (2022). Reptile Search Algorithm (RSA): A nature-inspired meta-heuristic optimizer. *Expert Systems with Applications*, *191*, 116158. doi:10.1016/j.eswa.2021.116158

Aichouri, I., Hani, A., Bougherira, N., Djabri, L., Chaffai, H., & Lallahem, S. (2015). River flow model using artificial neural networks. *Energy Procedia, 74,* 1007–1014. doi:10.1016/j.egypro.2015.07.832

Ardabili, S., Mosavi, A., & Várkonyi-Kóczy, A. R. (2020). Building Energy Information: Demand and Consumption Prediction with Machine Learning Models for Sustainable and Smart Cities. *Lecture Notes in Networks and Systems, 101,* 191–201. doi:10.1007/978-3-030-36841-8_19

Asadi, S., Shahrabi, J., Abbaszadeh, P., & Tabanmehr, S. (2013). A new hybrid artificial neural networks for rainfall-runoff process modeling. *Neurocomputing, 121,* 470–480. doi:10.1016/j.neucom.2013.05.023

Balamurugan, M., Narendiran, S., Sahoo, S. K., Das, R., & Sahoo, A. K. (2016). Application of particle swarm optimization for maximum power point tracking in PV system. *2016 3rd International Conference on Electrical Energy Systems, ICEES 2016,* (pp. 35–38). IEEE. 10.1109/ICEES.2016.7510591

Berger, D. W., Herkenhoff, K. F., Mongey, S., Griffin, K. C., & Post, W. (2020). *An seir infectious disease model with testing and conditional quarantine.* NBER. https://www.nber.org/papers/w26901

Chiel, H. J., Thomas, P. J., Zhang, L., Wang -, S., Zhu, S., Wang -, K., Shaw, R., Mishra, M., & Ranjan Jena, A. (2021). Knowledge mining in spreading pattern of COVID-19 and its impact on India economy. *Iopscience.Iop. Org, 12013.* doi:10.1088/1742-6596/1797/1/012013

Dineva, A., Mosavi, A., Faizollahzadeh Ardabili, S., Vajda, I., Shamshirband, S., Rabczuk, T., & Chau, K. W. (2019). Review of soft computing models in design and control of rotating electrical machines. *Energies, 12*(6), 1049. doi:10.3390/en12061049

Du, Y. C., & Stephanus, A. (2018). Levenberg-marquardt neural network algorithm for degree of arteriovenous fistula stenosis classification using a dual optical photoplethysmography sensor. *Sensors (Basel), 18*(7), 2322. doi:10.339018072322 PMID:30018275

El Shinawi, A., Ibrahim, R. A., Abualigah, L., Zelenakova, M., & Abd Elaziz, M. (2021). Enhanced adaptive neuro-fuzzy inference system using reptile search algorithm for relating swelling potentiality using index geotechnical properties: A case study at El Sherouk City, Egypt. *Mathematics, 9*(24), 3295. doi:10.3390/math9243295

Fu, L., Wang, B., Yuan, T., Chen, X., Ao, Y., Fitzpatrick, T., Li, P., Zhou, Y., Lin, Y., Duan, Q., Luo, G., Fan, S., Lu, Y., Feng, A., Zhan, Y., Liang, B., Cai, W., Zhang, L., Du, X., & Zou, H. (2020). Clinical characteristics of coronavirus disease 2019 (COVID-19) in China: A systematic review and meta-analysis. *The Journal of Infection, 80*(6), 656–665. doi:10.1016/j.jinf.2020.03.041 PMID:32283155

Ghamisi, P., Benediktsson, J. A., Ghamisi, P., & Benediktsson, J. A. (2015). Feature selection based on hybridization of genetic algorithm and particle swarm optimization. *Ieeexplore.Ieee. IEEE Geoscience and Remote Sensing Letters, 12*(2), 309–313. doi:10.1109/LGRS.2014.2337320

Godio, A., Pace, F., & Vergnano, A. (2020). SEIR modeling of the Italian epidemic of SARS-CoV-2 using computational swarm intelligence. *International Journal of Environmental Research and Public Health, 17*(10), 3535. doi:10.3390/ijerph17103535 PMID:32443640

Gülcü, Ş. (2022). Training of the feed forward artificial neural networks using dragonfly algorithm. *Applied Soft Computing, 124,* 109023. doi:10.1016/j.asoc.2022.109023

Horn, J., Nafpliotis, N., & Goldberg, D. E. (1994, June). A niched Pareto genetic algorithm for multi-objective optimization. In *Proceedings of the first IEEE conference on evolutionary computation. IEEE world congress on computational intelligence* (pp. 82-87). IEEE. 10.1109/ICEC.1994.350037

Houck, C. R., Joines, J., & Kay, M. G. (1995). A genetic algorithm for function optimization: a Matlab implementation. *Ncsu-ie tr, 95*(09), 1-10.

Iwata, K., & Miyakoshi, C. (2020). A simulation on potential secondary spread of novel coronavirus in an exported country using a stochastic epidemic SEIR model. *Journal of Clinical Medicine, 9*(4), 944. doi:10.3390/jcm9040944 PMID:32235480

Jali, B. R., Behura, R., Barik, S. R., Parveen, S., Mohanty, S. P., & Das, R. (2018). A brief review: Biological implications of naphthoquinone derivatives. *Research Journal of Pharmacy and Technology, 11*(8), 3698–3702. doi:10.5958/0974-360X.2018.00679.0

Jena, A. R., Pati, S., Chakraborty, S., Sarkar, S., Guin, S., Mallick, S., & Sen, S. K. (2021). *A Framework for Predicting Placement of a Graduate Using Machine Learning Techniques*, 197–206. Springer. doi:10.1007/978-981-16-4301-9_15

Jones, G., Willett, P., Glen, R. C., Leach, A. R., & Taylor, R. (1997). Development and validation of a genetic algorithm for flexible docking. *Journal of Molecular Biology, 267*(3), 727–748. doi:10.1006/jmbi.1996.0897 PMID:9126849

Karsoliya, S. (2012). Approximating number of hidden layer neurons in multiple hidden layer BPNN architecture. *International Journal of Engineering Trends and Technology, 3*(6), 714–717.

Kennedy, J., & Eberhart, R. (1995, November). Particle swarm optimization. In *Proceedings of ICNN'95-international conference on neural networks* (*Vol. 4*, pp. 1942-1948). IEEE. 10.1109/ICNN.1995.488968

Khaleque, A., & Sen, P. (2017). An empirical analysis of the Ebola outbreak in West Africa. *Scientific Reports, 7*(1), 42594. doi:10.1038rep42594 PMID:28205617

Koopialipoor, M., Noorbakhsh, A., Noroozi Ghaleini, E., Jahed Armaghani, D., & Yagiz, S. (2019). A new approach for estimation of rock brittleness based on non-destructive tests. *Nondestructive Testing and Evaluation, 34*(4), 354–375. doi:10.1080/10589759.2019.1623214

Maind, S. B., & Wankar, P. (2014). Research paper on basic of artificial neural network. *International Journal on Recent and Innovation Trends in Computing and Communication, 2*(1), 96–100.

Manohar, B., & Das, R. (2022a). Artificial neural networks for prediction of COVID -19 in India by using backpropagation. *Expert Systems: International Journal of Knowledge Engineering and Neural Networks, 40*(5), e13105. doi:10.1111/exsy.13105 PMID:36245831

Manohar, B., & Das, R. (2022b). Artificial Neural Networks for the Prediction of Monkeypox Outbreak. *Tropical Medicine and Infectious Disease, 7*(12), 424. doi:10.3390/tropicalmed7120424

Mosavi, A., Salimi, M., Faizollahzadeh Ardabili, S., Rabczuk, T., Shamshirband, S., & Varkonyi-Koczy, A. R. (2019). State of the art of machine learning models in energy systems, a systematic review. *Energies, 12*(7), 1301. doi:10.3390/en12071301

Mühlenbein, H., Schomisch, M., & Born, J. (1991). The parallel genetic algorithm as function optimizer. *Parallel Computing*, *17*(6-7), 619–632. doi:10.1016/S0167-8191(05)80052-3

Namasudra, S., Dhamodharavadhani, S., & Rathipriya, R. (2023). Nonlinear Neural Network Based Forecasting Model for Predicting COVID-19 Cases. *Neural Processing Letters*, *55*(1), 171–191. doi:10.100711063-021-10495-w PMID:33821142

Ojo, O. A., Ojo, A. B., Taiwo, O. A., & Oluba, O. M. (2020). Novel Coronavirus (SARS-CoV-2) main protease: Molecular docking of Puerarin as a Potential inhibitor. doi:10.21203/rs.3.rs-37794/v1

Rashidi, M. M., Ali, M., Freidoonimehr, N., & Nazari, F. (2013). Parametric analysis and optimization of entropy generation in unsteady MHD flow over a stretching rotating disk using artificial neural network and particle swarm optimization algorithm. *Energy*, *55*, 497–510. doi:10.1016/j.energy.2013.01.036

Saba, A. I., & Elsheikh, A. H. (2020). Forecasting the prevalence of COVID-19 outbreak in Egypt using nonlinear autoregressive artificial neural networks. *Process Safety and Environmental Protection*, *141*, 1–8. doi:10.1016/j.psep.2020.05.029 PMID:32501368

Sedwick, R., & Schweighart, S. (2001). Development and analysis of a high fidelity linearized J (2) model for satellite formation flying. In AIAA space 2001 Conference and exposition (p. 4744). AIAA.

Tran, T. T., Pham, L. T., & Ngo, Q. X. (2020). Forecasting epidemic spread of SARS-CoV-2 using ARIMA model (Case study: Iran). *Global Journal of Environmental Science and Management*, *6*(Special Issue (Covid-19)), 1–10.

Whitley, D., & Starkweather, T. computing, C. B.-P., & 1990, undefined. (1990). *Genetic algorithms and neural networks: Optimizing connections and connectivity.* Elsevier. https://www.sciencedirect.com/science/article/pii/016781919090086O

WHO Coronavirus (COVID-19) Dashboard. (n.d.). WHO. https://covid19.who.int/

Wieczorek, M., Siłka, J., & Woźniak, M. (2020). Neural network powered COVID-19 spread forecasting model. *Chaos, Solitons, and Fractals*, *140*, 110203. doi:10.1016/j.chaos.2020.110203 PMID:32834663

Yarsky, P. (2021). Using a genetic algorithm to fit parameters of a COVID-19 SEIR model for US states. *Mathematics and Computers in Simulation*, *185*, 687–695. doi:10.1016/j.matcom.2021.01.022 PMID:33612959

Zakary, O., Larrache, A., Rachik, M., & Elmouki, I. (2016). Effect of awareness programs and travel-blocking operations in the control of HIV/AIDS outbreaks: A multi-domains SIR model. *Advances in Difference Equations*, *2016*(1), 1–17. doi:10.118613662-016-0900-9

Zivkovic, M., Bacanin, N., Venkatachalam, K., Nayyar, A., Djordjevic, A., Strumberger, I., & Al-Turjman, F. (2021). COVID-19 cases prediction by using hybrid machine learning and beetle antennae search approach. *Sustainable Cities and Society*, *66*, 102669. doi:10.1016/j.scs.2020.102669 PMID:33520607

Zorlu, K., Gokceoglu, C., Ocakoğlu, F., Nefeslioglu, H. A., Zorlu, K., Gokceoglu, C., Ocakoglu, F., & Acikalin, S. (2007). Prediction of uniaxial compressive strength of sandstones using petrography-based models. *Elsevier*, *96*(3–4), 141–158. doi:10.1016/j.enggeo.2007.10.009

Zou, L., Ruan, F., Huang, M., Liang, L., Huang, H., Hong, Z., Yu, J., Kang, M., Song, Y., Xia, J., Guo, Q., Song, T., He, J., Yen, H.-L., Peiris, M., & Wu, J. (2020). SARS-CoV-2 viral load in upper respiratory specimens of infected patients. *The New England Journal of Medicine, 382*(12), 1177–1179. doi:10.1056/NEJMc2001737 PMID:32074444

Compilation of References

Aazam, M., Zeadally, S., & Harras, K. A. (2018). Offloading in fog computing for IoT: Review, enabling technologies, and research opportunities. *Future Generation Computer Systems*, *87*, 278–289. doi:10.1016/j.future.2018.04.057

Abba, S., Wadumi Namkusong, J., Lee, J. A., & Liz Crespo, M. (2019). Design and Performance Evaluation of a Low-Cost Autonomous Sensor Interface for a Smart IoT-Based Irrigation Monitoring and Control System. *Sensors (Basel)*, *19*(17), 3643. doi:10.339019173643 PMID:31438597

Abdelmoneem, R. M., Benslimane, A., & Shaaban, E. (2020). Mobility-Aware Task Scheduling in Cloud-Fog IoT-Based Healthcare Architectures. *Computer Networks*: .

Abdulkareem, K. H., Mohammed, M. A., Gunasekaran, S. S., Al-Mhiqani, M. N., Mutlag, A. H., Mostafa, S. A., Ali, N. S., & Ibrahim, D. A. (2019). A Review of Fog Computing and Machine Learning: Concepts, Applications, Challenges, and Open Issues. *IEEE Access : Practical Innovations, Open Solutions*, *7*, 153123–153140. doi:10.1109/AC-CESS.2019.2947542

Abdulqadir, H. R., Zeebaree, S. R. M., Shukur, H. M., Sadeeq, M. M., Salim, B. W., Salih, A. A., & Kak, S. F. (2021). A Study of Moving from Cloud Computing to Fog Computing. *Qubahan Academic Journal*, *1*(2), 60–70. doi:10.48161/qaj.v1n2a49

Abualigah, L., Abd Elaziz, M., Sumari, P., Geem, Z. W., & Gandomi, A. H. (2022). Reptile Search Algorithm (RSA): A nature-inspired meta-heuristic optimizer. *Expert Systems with Applications*, *191*, 116158. doi:10.1016/j.eswa.2021.116158

Ahad, A., Tahir, M., & Yau, K. L. A. (2019). 5G-based smart healthcare network: Architecture, taxonomy, challenges and future research directions. *IEEE Access : Practical Innovations, Open Solutions*, *7*, 100747–100762. doi:10.1109/ACCESS.2019.2930628

Ahmad, M., Khayal, M. S. H., & Tahir, A. (2022). Analysis of Factors Affecting Adoption of Volunteered Geographic Information in the Context of National Spatial Data Infrastructure. ISPRS International Journal of Geo-Information, 11(2). https://doi.org/10.3390/ijgi11020120

Ahmed, K. D., & Zeebaree, S. R. M. (2021). Resource allocation in fog computing: A review. *International Journal of Science and Business*, *5*(2), 54–63.

Aichouri, I., Hani, A., Bougherira, N., Djabri, L., Chaffai, H., & Lallahem, S. (2015). River flow model using artificial neural networks. *Energy Procedia*, *74*, 1007–1014. doi:10.1016/j.egypro.2015.07.832

Ajmi, M., Hamza, M. H., Labiadh, M., Yermani, M., Khatra, N. Ben, Al-Thubaiti, A. S., Moharrem, I. A., & Arrim, A. El (2014). Setting up a Spatial Data Infrastructure (SDI) for the ROSELT/OSS Network. *Journal of Geographic Information System*, *06*(02), 150–161. doi:10.4236/jgis.2014.62016

Aladwani, T. (2019). Scheduling IoT Healthcare Tasks in Fog Computing Based on their Importance. *Procedia Computer Science*, *163*, 560–569. doi:10.1016/j.procs.2019.12.138

Al-Ayyoub, M., Husari, G., Darwish, O., & Alabed-alaziz, A. (2012). Machine learning approach for brain tumor detection. In: *Proceedings of the 3rd International Conference on Information and Communication Systems*, (pp. 1-4). ACM. 10.1145/2222444.2222467

Aldağ, M., Kırsal, Y., & Ülker, S. (2022). An analytical modeling and QoS evaluation of fault-tolerant load balancer and web servers in fog computing. *The Journal of Supercomputing*, *78*(10), 12136–12158. doi:10.100711227-022-04345-2

Al-Doghman, F., Chaczko, Z., Ajayan, A. R., & Klempous, R. (2016). A review on Fog Computing technology. *2016 IEEE International Conference on Systems, Man, and Cybernetics (SMC)*. IEEE. 10.1109/SMC.2016.7844455

Ali, A., Imran, M., Jabeen, M., Ali, Z., & Mahmood, S. A. (2021). Factors influencing integrated information management: Spatial data infrastructure in Pakistan. Information Development. https://doi.org/10.1177/02666669211048483

Aliyu, F., Abdeen, M. A., Sheltami, T., Alfraidi, T., & Ahmed, M. H. (2023). Fog computing-assisted path planning for smart shopping. *Multimedia Tools and Applications*, 1-26. doi:10.1007/s11042-023-14926-9ATOS

Alli, A. A., & Muhammad, M. A. (2020). The fog cloud of things: A survey on concepts, architecture, standards, tools, and applications. *Internet of Things*, *9*, 100177. doi:10.1016/j.iot.2020.100177

Alraddady, S., Li, A. S., Soh, B., & AlZain, M. A. (2019). Deployment of Fog Computing During Hajj Season: A Proposed Framework. *Procedia Computer Science*, *161*, 1072–1079. doi:10.1016/j.procs.2019.11.218

Alzoubi, Y. I., Al-Ahmad, A., & Kahtan, H. (2022). Blockchain technology as a Fog computing security and privacy solution: An overview. *Computer Communications*, *182*, 129–152. doi:10.1016/j.comcom.2021.11.005

Ardabili, S., Mosavi, A., & Várkonyi-Kóczy, A. R. (2020). Building Energy Information: Demand and Consumption Prediction with Machine Learning Models for Sustainable and Smart Cities. *Lecture Notes in Networks and Systems*, *101*, 191–201. doi:10.1007/978-3-030-36841-8_19

Arifin, S., Silalahi, F. E. S., Prayitno, M., Majid, N. K., Amhar, F., & Gularso, H. (2023). Geospatial Big Data Management Testing Using Open Source Technology. *Mechanisms and Machine Science*, *121*, 29–42. doi:10.1007/978-3-031-09909-0_3

Asadi, S., Shahrabi, J., Abbaszadeh, P., & Tabanmehr, S. (2013). A new hybrid artificial neural networks for rainfall-runoff process modeling. *Neurocomputing*, *121*, 470–480. doi:10.1016/j.neucom.2013.05.023

Ashok Sasane, S., Jadhav, A. S., Barik, R. K., Krishnakumar, G., & Raghavswamy, V. (2019). Application of spatial technology in Malaria information infrastructure mapping with climate change perspective in Maharashtra, India. *Mausam (New Delhi)*, *70*(4), 787–806. doi:10.54302/mausam.v70i4.264

Aswad, S. A., & Sonuç, E. (2020). Classification of VPN network traffic flow using time related features on Apache Spark. In *2020 4th International Symposium on Multidisciplinary Studies and Innovative Technologies (ISMSIT)* (pp. 1-8), IEEE.

Atlam, H., Walters, R., & Wills, G. (2018). Fog Computing and the Internet of Things: A Review, Big Data. *Cognitive Computation*, *2*(2), 10–18.

Atlam, H., Walters, R., & Wills, G. (2018). Fog computing and the Internet of Things: A review. *Big Data and Cognitive Computing*, *2*(2), 10. doi:10.3390/bdcc2020010

Avedis, D. (2005). Evaluating the quality of medical care. Milbank *Memorial Fund Q. 1966; 44*(3), 166-206. *Reprinted in Milbank Q.*, *83*(4), 691–729.

Azar, A. T., Hassanien, A. E., & Kim, T. H. (2021). Expert system based on neural-fuzzy rules for thyroid diseases diagnosis. In *Computer Applications for Bio-technology, Multimedia, and Ubiquitous City* (pp. 94–105). Springer.

Baccarelli, E., Naranjo, P. G. V., Scarpiniti, M., Shojafar, M., & Abawajy, J. H. (2017). Fog of Everything: Energy-Efficient Networked Computing Architectures, Research Challenges, and a Case Study. *IEEE Access : Practical Innovations, Open Solutions*, 5, 9882–9910. doi:10.1109/ACCESS.2017.2702013

Badidi, E., Mahrez, Z., & Sabir, E. (2020). Fog computing for smart cities' big data management and analytics: A review. In Future Internet, 12(11). doi:10.3390/fi12110190

Bai, J., Chang, X., Ning, G., Zhang, Z., & Trivedi, K. S. (2020). Service availability analysis in a virtualized system: A Markov regenerative model approach. *IEEE Transactions on Cloud Computing*, 10(3), 2118–2130. doi:10.1109/TCC.2020.3028648

Bailey, E., Fuhrmann, C., Runkle, J., Stevens, S., Brown, M., & Sugg, M. (2020). Wearable sensors for personal temperature exposure assessments: A comparative study. *Environmental Research*, 180, 108858. doi:10.1016/j.envres.2019.108858 PMID:31708175

Bai, T., Pan, C., Deng, Y., Elkashlan, M., Nallanathan, A., & Hanzo, L. (2020). Latency Minimization for Intelligent Reflecting Surface Aided Mobile Edge Computing. *IEEE Journal on Selected Areas in Communications*, 38(11), 2666–2682. doi:10.1109/JSAC.2020.3007035

Balamurugan, M., Narendiran, S., Sahoo, S. K., Das, R., & Sahoo, A. K. (2016). Application of particle swarm optimization for maximum power point tracking in PV system. *2016 3rd International Conference on Electrical Energy Systems, ICEES 2016*, (pp. 35–38). IEEE. 10.1109/ICEES.2016.7510591

Banu, G. R. (2016). A Role of decision Tree classification data Mining Technique in Diagnosing Thyroid disease. *International Journal on Computer Science and Engineering*, 4(11), 64–70.

Barik, R. K., Dubey, H., Misra, C., Borthakur, D., Constant, N., Sasane, S. A., Lenka, R. K., Mishra, B. S. P., Das, H., & Mankodiya, K. (2018). Fog Assisted Cloud Computing in Era of Big Data and Internet-of-Things: Systems, Architectures, and Applications. In Studies in Big Data, 39. doi:10.1007/978-3-319-73676-1_14

Barik, R. K., Lenka, R. K., Simha, N. V. R., Dubey, H., & Mankodiya, K. (2017). *Fog computing based SDI framework for mineral resources information infrastructure management in India*. In arXiv.

Barik, R. K., Dubey, H., Mankodiya, K., Sasane, S. A., & Misra, C. (2019). GeoFog4Health: A fog-based SDI framework for geospatial health big data analysis. *Journal of Ambient Intelligence and Humanized Computing*, 10(2), 551–567. doi:10.100712652-018-0702-x

Barik, R. K., Dubey, H., Samaddar, A. B., Gupta, R. D., & Ray, P. K. (2017). FogGIS: Fog Computing for geospatial big data analytics. *2016 IEEE Uttar Pradesh Section International Conference on Electrical, Computer and Electronics Engineering, UPCON 2016*. IEEE. 10.1109/UPCON.2016.7894725

Barik, R. K., Muruga Perumal, K., Ajay-D-Vimal Raj, P., & Rajasekar, S. (2018). Development and implementation of renewable energy potential geospatial database mapping in India for cloud SDI using open source GIS. *Lecture Notes in Electrical Engineering*, 435, 419–428. doi:10.1007/978-981-10-4286-7_41

Barik, R. K., Priyadarshini, R., Lenka, R. K., Dubey, H., & Mankodiya, K. (2020). Fog computing architecture for scalable processing of geospatial big data. *International Journal of Applied Geospatial Research*, 11(1), 1–20. doi:10.4018/IJAGR.2020010101

Bartels, R. H., & Golub, G. H. (1969). The simplex method of linear programming using LU decomposition. *Communications of the ACM, 12*(5), 266–268. doi:10.1145/362946.362974

Basir, R., Qaisar, S., Ali, M., Aldwairi, M., Ashraf, M. I., Mahmood, A., & Gidlund, M. (2019). Fog computing enabling industrial internet of things: State-of-the-art and research challenges. *Sensors (Basel), 19*(21), 4807. doi:10.339019214807 PMID:31694254

Bates, D. W., Saria, S., Ohno-Machado, L., Shah, A., & Escobar, G. (2014). Big data in health care: Using analytics to identify and manage high-risk and high-cost patients. *Health Affairs, 33*(7), 1123–1131. doi:10.1377/hlthaff.2014.0041 PMID:25006137

Battula, S. K., O'Reilly, M. M., Garg, S., & Montgomery, J. (2020). A generic stochastic model for resource availability in fog computing environments. *IEEE Transactions on Parallel and Distributed Systems, 32*(4), 960–974. doi:10.1109/TPDS.2020.3037247

Beam, A. L., & Kohane, I. S. (2018). Big data and machine learning in health care. *Journal of the American Medical Association, 319*(13), 1317–1318. doi:10.1001/jama.2017.18391 PMID:29532063

Begum, A., & Parkavi, A. (March,2019). Prediction of thyroid disease using data mining techniques. In *2019 5th International Conference on Advanced Computing & Communication Systems (ICACCS)* (pp. 342-345), IEEE.

Berger, D. W., Herkenhoff, K. F., Mongey, S., Griffin, K. C., & Post, W. (2020). *An seir infectious disease model with testing and conditional quarantine.* NBER. https://www.nber.org/papers/w26901

Bermbach, D., Pallas, F., Pérez, D. G., Plebani, P., Anderson, M., Kat, R., & Tai, S. (2018). A research perspective on fog computing. In *Service-Oriented Computing – ICSOC 2017 Workshops* (pp. 198–210). Springer International Publishing. doi:10.1007/978-3-319-91764-1_16

Bernard, L., & Ostländer, N. (2008). Assessing climate change vulnerability in the arctic using geographic information services in spatial data infrastructures. *Climatic Change, 87*(1–2), 263–281. Advance online publication. doi:10.100710584-007-9346-0

Berwick, D. M. (2004). Lessons from developing nations on improving health care. *BMJ, 328* (7448), 1124–1129. doi:10.1136/bmj.328.7448.1R

Bhambri, P., Rani, S., Gupta, G., & Khang, A. (Eds.). (2022). *Cloud and fog computing platforms for internet of things.* CRC Press. doi:10.1201/9781003213888

Bhardwaj, A., & Krishna, C. R. (2021). Virtualization in cloud computing: Moving from hypervisor to containerization—a survey. *Arabian Journal for Science and Engineering, 46*(9), 8585–8601. doi:10.100713369-021-05553-3

Bhattacharya, D., & Painho, M. (2017). Smart cities intelligence system (SMACISYS) integrating sensor web with spatial data infrastructures (sensdi). isprs. *Annals of the Photogrammetry, Remote Sensing and Spatial Information Sciences, 4*(4W3). doi:10.5194/isprs-annals-IV-4-W3-21-2017

Bhusan Dash, B., Shekhar Patra, S., Nanda, S., Rani Jena, J., Rout, S., & Kumar Barik, R. (2023). *SFA4SDI: A Secure Fog Architecture for Spatial Data Infrastructure.* IEEE. doi:10.1109/iSSSC56467.2022.10051572

Bishop, I. D., Escobar, F. J., Karuppannan, S., Williamson, I. P., Yates, P. M., Suwarnarat, K., & Yaqub, H. W. (2000). Spatial data infrastructures for cities in developing countries. Lessons from the Bangkok experience. *Cities (London, England), 17*(2), 85–96. doi:10.1016/S0264-2751(00)00004-4

Bittencourt, L., Diaz-Montes, J., Buyya, R., Rana, O., & Parashar, M. (2018). Mobility aware application scheduling in fog computing. *IEEE Cloud Computing, 4*(2), 26-35.

Boerboom, I. (2010). *Integrating spatial planning and decision support system infrastructure and spatial data infrastructure.* GSDI 12 World Conference, Singapore. http://www.gsdi.org/gsdiconf/gsdi12/papers/82.pdf

Bonomi, F. (2011, October). Connected vehicles, the internet of things, and fog **computing**. *VANET.* https://www.sigmobile.org/mobicom/2011/vanet2011/program.html

Bonomi, F., Milito, R., Natarajan, P., & Zhu, J. (2014). Fog computing: A platform for internet of things and analytics. *Studies in Computational Intelligence, 546,* 169–186. Advance online publication. doi:10.1007/978-3-319-05029-4_7

Bonomi, F., Milito, R., Zhu, J., & Addepalli, S. (2012). Fog computing and its role in the internet of things. *Proceedings of the First Edition of the MCC Workshop on Mobile Cloud Computing.* ACM. 10.1145/2342509.2342513

Bordogna, G., Kliment, T., Frigerio, L., Brivio, P. A., Crema, A., Stroppiana, D., Boschetti, M., & Sterlacchini, S. (2016). A spatial data infrastructure integrating multisource heterogeneous geospatial data and time series: A study case in agriculture. *ISPRS International Journal of Geo-Information, 5*(5), 73. doi:10.3390/ijgi5050073

Bordoloi, D. (2022). *Deep Learning in Healthcare System for Quality of Service, Journal of care Engineering.* Hindawi. doi:10.1155/2022/8169203

Borzacchiello, M. T., & Craglia, M. (2013). Estimating benefits of spatial data infrastructures: A case study on e-Cadastres. *Computers, Environment and Urban Systems, 41,* 276–288. doi:10.1016/j.compenvurbsys.2012.05.004

Bouachir, O., Aloqaily, M., Tseng, L., & Boukerche, A. (2020). Blockchain and fog computing for cyberphysical systems: The case of smart industry. *Computer, 53*(9), 36–45. doi:10.1109/MC.2020.2996212

Brogi, A., & Forti, S. (2017). QoS aware deployment of IoT applications through the fog. *IEEE Internet of Things Journal, 4*(5), 1185–1192. doi:10.1109/JIOT.2017.2701408

Cabanillas, M. E., McFadden, D. G., & Durante, C. (2016). Thyroid cancer. *Lancet, 388*(10061), 2783–2795. doi:10.1016/S0140-6736(16)30172-6 PMID:27240885

Cai, J., Qin, B., Zheng, F., Li, S., Luo, Y., & Zhang, J. (2018, December). Design and application of innovative teaching platform based on fog computing. In *2018 2nd International Conference on Education Innovation and Social Science (ICEISS 2018)* (pp. 227-231). Atlantis Press. 10.2991/iceiss-18.2018.56

Cardellini, V., Mencagli, G., Talia, D., & Torquati, M. (2019). New landscapes of the data stream processing in the era of fog computing. *Future Generation Computer Systems, 99,* 646–650. doi:10.1016/j.future.2019.03.027

Cervantes, J., Garcia-Lamont, F., Rodríguez-Mazahua, L., & Lopez, A. (2020). A comprehensive survey on support vector machine classification: Applications, challenges, and trends. *Neurocomputing, 408,* 189–215. doi:10.1016/j.neucom.2019.10.118

Chakka, R. (1998). Spectral expansion solution for some finite capacity queues. *Annals of Operations Research, 79*(0), 27–44. doi:10.1023/A:1018974722301

Chandel, K., Kunwar, V., Sabitha, S., Choudhury, T., & Mukherjee, S. (2016). A comparative study on thyroid disease detection using K-nearest neighbor and Naive Bayes classification techniques. *CSI Transactions on ICT, 4*(2), 313–319. doi:10.100740012-016-0100-5

Chandio, J. A., Sahito, A., Soomrani, M. A. R., & Abbasi, S. A. (April,2016). TDV: Intelligent system for thyroid disease visualization. In 2016 International Conference on Computing, *Electronic and Electrical Engineering (ICE Cube)* (pp. 106-112). IEEE.

Chan, M., Estève, D., Fourniols, J. Y., Escriba, C., & Campo, E. (2012). Smart wearable systems: Current status and future challenges. *Artificial Intelligence in Medicine*, *56*(3), 137–156. doi:10.1016/j.artmed.2012.09.003 PMID:23122689

Chaturvedi, K., Matheus, A., Nguyen, S. H., & Kolbe, T. H. (2019). Securing Spatial Data Infrastructures for Distributed Smart City applications and services. *Future Generation Computer Systems*, *101*, 723–736. doi:10.1016/j.future.2019.07.002

Chaudhary, A., Kolhe, S., & Kamal, R. (2016). An improved random forest classifier for multi-class classification. *Information Processing in Agriculture*, *3*(4), 215–222. doi:10.1016/j.inpa.2016.08.002

Chemodanov, D., Calyam, P., & Palaniappan, K. (2020). Fog computing to enable geospatial video analytics for disaster-incident situational awareness. In *Fog Computing*. Theory and Practice. doi:10.1002/9781119551713.ch19

Cheng, B., Solmaz, G., Cirillo, F., Kovacs, E., Terasawa, K., & Kitazawa, A. (2018). Fog Flow: Easy programming of IoT services over cloud and edges for smart cities. *IEEE Internet of Things Journal*, *5*(2), 696–707. doi:10.1109/JIOT.2017.2747214

Chen, N., Chen, Y., Ye, X., Ling, H., Song, S., & Huang, C. T. (2017; Vol. 22). Smart City Surveillance in Fog Computing. In Studies in Big Data. doi:10.1007/978-3-319-45145-9_9

Chiel, H. J., Thomas, P. J., Zhang, L., Wang -, S., Zhu, S., Wang -, K., Shaw, R., Mishra, M., & Ranjan Jena, A. (2021). Knowledge mining in spreading pattern of COVID-19 and its impact on India economy. *Iopscience.Iop. Org*, *12013*. doi:10.1088/1742-6596/1797/1/012013

Choi, N., Kim, D., Lee, S.-J., & Yi, Y. (2017). A fog operating system for user-oriented IoT services: Challenges and research directions. *IEEE Communications Magazine*, *55*(8), 44–51. doi:10.1109/MCOM.2017.1600908

Choi, Y. J., Baek, J. H., Park, H. S., Shim, W. H., Kim, T. Y., Shong, Y. K., & Lee, J. H. (2017). A computer-aided diagnosis system using artificial intelligence for the diagnosis and characterization of thyroid nodules on ultrasound: Initial clinical assessment. *Thyroid*, *27*(4), 546–552. doi:10.1089/thy.2016.0372 PMID:28071987

Clark, J. (2016, March 22). What is Industry 4.0? *IBM Internet of Things blog*. https://www.ibm.com/blogs/internet-ofthings/industry-4-0/

Corti, P., Bartoli, F., Fabiani, A., Giovando, C., Kralidis, A. T., & Tzotsos, A. (2019). GeoNode: An open source framework to build spatial data infrastructures. *PeerJ*, *7*.

Cotec Portugal. (2015). *The future of commerce: the new trends online and offline*. Cotec Portugal.

Crompvoets, J., Bregt, A., Rajabifard, A., & Williamson, I. (2004). Assessing the worldwide developments of national spatial data clearinghouses. *International Journal of Geographical Information Science*, *18*(7), 665–689. doi:10.1080/13658810410001702030

Crompvoets, J., Vancauwenberghe, G., Bouckaert, G., & Vandenbroucke, D. (2011). Practices to develop spatial data infrastructures: Exploring the contribution to e-government. In *Practical Studies in E-Government*. Best Practices from Around the World. doi:10.1007/978-1-4419-7533-1_13

Croz, J. J. D., & Higham, N. J. (1992). Stability of methods for matrix inversion. *IMA Journal of Numerical Analysis*, *12*(1), 1–19. doi:10.1093/imanum/12.1.1

D'Oro, E. C., Colombo, S., Gribaudo, M., Iacono, M., Manca, D., & Piazzolla, P. (2019). Modeling and evaluating a complex edge computing based systems: An emergency management support system case study. *Internet of Things*, *6*, 100054. doi:10.1016/j.iot.2019.100054

Da Silva, T. P., Batista, T., Lopes, F., Neto, A. R., Delicato, F. C., Pires, P. F., & Da Rocha, A. R. (2022). Fog Computing Platforms for Smart City Applications: A Survey. *ACM Transactions on Internet Technology*, 22(4), 1–32. doi:10.1145/3488585

Dahiwade, D., Patle, G., & Meshram, E. (2019). Designing disease prediction model using machine learning approach. In*: Proceedings of the 3rd International Conference on Computing Methodologies and Communication*, (pp. 1211-1215). IEEE. 10.1109/ICCMC.2019.8819782

Dang, L. M., Piran, M. J., Han, D., Min, K., & Moon, H. (2019). A survey on internet of things and cloud computing for healthcare. *Electronics (Basel)*, 8(7), 768. doi:10.3390/electronics8070768

Dar, F., Liyanage, M., Radeta, M., Yin, Z., Zuniga, A., Kosta, S., Tarkoma, S., Nurmi, P., & Flores, H. (2023). Upscaling Fog Computing in Oceans for Underwater Pervasive Data Science using Low-Cost Micro-Clouds. *ACM Transactions on Internet of Things*, 4(2), 1–29. doi:10.1145/3575801

Das, J., Ghosh, S. K., & Buyya, R. (2021). Geospatial Edge-Fog Computing: A Systematic Review, Taxonomy, and Future Directions. In Mobile Edge Computing. doi:10.1007/978-3-030-69893-5_3

Dastjerdi, A. V., Gupta, H., Calheiros, R. N., Ghosh, S. K., & Buyya, R. (2016). Fog Computing: principles, architectures, and applications. In Internet of Things (pp. 61–75). Elsevier. doi:10.1016/B978-0-12-805395-9.00004-6

Davenport, T., & Kalakota, R. (2019). The potential for artificial intelligence in healthcare. *Future Healthcare Journal*, 6(2), 94–98. doi:10.7861/futurehosp.6-2-94 PMID:31363513

de Mendonça, F. F. Junior, Lopes Dias, K., d'Orey, P. M., & Kokkinogenis, Z. (2021). FogWise: On the limits of the coexistence of heterogeneous applications on Fog computing and Internet of Vehicles. *Transactions on Emerging Telecommunications Technologies*, 32(1). doi:10.1002/ett.4145

de Moura Costa, H. J., da Costa, C. A., da Rosa Righi, R., & Antunes, R. S. (2020). Fog computing in health: A systematic literature review. In Health and Technology, 10(5). doi:10.100712553-020-00431-8

De Sensi, D., De Matteis, T., Taranov, K., Di Girolamo, S., Rahn, T., & Hoefler, T. (2022). Noise in the Clouds: Influence of Network Performance Variability on Application Scalability. *Proceedings of the ACM on Measurement and Analysis of Computing Systems, 6*(3), 1-27.

Deo, R. C. (2015). Machine learning in medicine. *Circulation, 132*(20), 1920–1930. doi:10.1161/CIRCULATIONAHA.115.001593 PMID:26572668

Dev, A. & Malik, S. (2021). IoT and Fog Computing Based Prediction and Monitoring System for Stroke Disease. *Turkish Journal of Computer and Mathematics Education*, 12(12), 3211–3223.

Dineva, A., Mosavi, A., Faizollahzadeh Ardabili, S., Vajda, I., Shamshirband, S., Rabczuk, T., & Chau, K. W. (2019). Review of soft computing models in design and control of rotating electrical machines. *Energies, 12*(6), 1049. doi:10.3390/en12061049

Dittman, D., Khoshgoftaar, T. M., Wald, R., & Napolitano, A. (2011). Random forest: A reliable tool for patient response prediction. In *2011 IEEE International Conference on Bioinformatics and Biomedicine Workshops (BIBMW)* (pp. 289-296). IEEE. 10.1109/BIBMW.2011.6112389

Dizdarević, J., Carpio, F., Jukan, A., & Masip-Bruin, X. (2019). A survey of communication protocols for Internet of Things and related challenges of fog and cloud computing integration. *ACM Computing Surveys, 51*(6), 1–29. doi:10.1145/3292674

Doddapaneni, K. (2014). *Energy-aware performance evaluation of WSNs* [Doctoral dissertation, Middlesex University].

Donabedian, A. (2003). *An Introduction to Quality Assurance in Health Care*. Oxford University Press.

Drinkwater, D. (2016). *"The future of retail through the Internet of Things", Internet of Business*. Beecham Research.

Du, H., Leng, S., Wu, F., Chen, X., & Mao, S. (2020). A New Vehicular Fog Computing Architecture for Cooperative Sensing of Autonomous Driving. *IEEE Access : Practical Innovations, Open Solutions*, 8, 10997–11006. doi:10.1109/ACCESS.2020.2964029

Du, J., Zhao, L., Feng, J., & Chu, X. (2018). Computation offloading and resource allocation in mixed fog/cloud computing systems with min-max fairness guarantee. *IEEE Transactions on Communications*, 4(4), 1594–1608. doi:10.1109/TCOMM.2017.2787700

Du, Y. C., & Stephanus, A. (2018). Levenberg-marquardt neural network algorithm for degree of arteriovenous fistula stenosis classification using a dual optical photoplethysmography sensor. *Sensors (Basel)*, 18(7), 2322. doi:10.339018072322 PMID:30018275

Dwivedi, K., Sharan, H. O., & Vishwakarma, V. (2019). Analysis of Decision Tree for Diabetes Prediction [IJETR]. *International Journal of Engineering and Technical Research*, 9(6). doi:10.31873/IJETR.9.6.2019.64

El Shinawi, A., Ibrahim, R. A., Abualigah, L., Zelenakova, M., & Abd Elaziz, M. (2021). Enhanced adaptive neuro-fuzzy inference system using reptile search algorithm for relating swelling potentiality using index geotechnical properties: A case study at El Sherouk City, Egypt. *Mathematics*, 9(24), 3295. doi:10.3390/math9243295

Elhadad, A., Alanazi, F., Taloba, A. I., & Abozeid, A. (2022, March 15). Fog Computing Service in the Healthcare Monitoring System for Managing the Real-Time Notification. *Journal of Healthcare Engineering*, 5337733, 1–11. Advance online publication. doi:10.1155/2022/5337733 PMID:35340260

Elijah, O., Rahman, T. A., Orikumhi, I., Leow, C. Y., & Hindia, M. N. (2018, October). An Overview of Internet of Things (IoT) and Data Analytics in Agriculture: Benefits and Challenges. *IEEE Internet of Things Journal*, 5(5), 3758–3773. doi:10.1109/JIOT.2018.2844296

El-Sayed, H., Sankar, S., Prasad, M., Puthal, D., Gupta, A., Mohanty, M., & Lin, C. T. (2017). Edge of things: The big picture on the integration of edge, IoT and the cloud in a distributed computing environment. *IEEE Access : Practical Innovations, Open Solutions*, 6, 1706–1717. doi:10.1109/ACCESS.2017.2780087

Endeshaw, B. (2021). Health care service quality measurement models: A review. *Journal of Health Research, Emerald Publishing Limited*, 35(2), 106–117.

Ernst & Young. (2020, June 17). Digitalization key to helping Asian retailers emerge from Covid-19. *Retail News Asia*. https://www.retailnews.asia/digitalization-key-to-helping-asian-retailers-emerge-from-covid-19/

Evans, D. J. (1984). Parallel SOR iterative methods. *Parallel Computing*, 1(1), 3–18. doi:10.1016/S0167-8191(84)90380-6

Ever, E. (2007). *Performability modeling of homogenous and heterogeneous multiserver systems with breakdowns and repairs* [Doctoral dissertation, Middlesex University].

Fantacci, R., & Picano, B. (2020). Performance analysis of a delay constrained data offloading scheme in an integrated cloud-fog-edge computing system. *IEEE Transactions on Vehicular Technology*, 69(10), 12004–12014. doi:10.1109/TVT.2020.3008926

Fichman, R. G., Dos Santos, B. L., & Zheng, Z. E. (2014). Digital innovation as a fundamental and powerful concept in the information systems curriculum. *Management Information Systems Quarterly*, 38(2), 329–353. doi:10.25300/MISQ/2014/38.2.01

Font, X., English, R., Gkritzali, A., & Tian, W. (2021). Value co-creation in sustainable tourism: A service-dominant logic approach. *Tourism Management, 82*, 104200. doi:10.1016/j.tourman.2020.104200

Friha, O., Ferrag, M. A., Shu, L., Maglaras, L., & Wang, X. (2021). Internet of things for the future of smart agriculture: A comprehensive survey of emerging technologies. *IEEE/CAA Journal of Automatica Sinica, 8*(4), 718-752.

Fu, C., Lv, Q., & Badrnejad, R. G. (2020). Fog computing in health management processing systems. In Kybernetes, 49(12). doi:10.1108/K-09-2019-0621

Fu, L., Wang, B., Yuan, T., Chen, X., Ao, Y., Fitzpatrick, T., Li, P., Zhou, Y., Lin, Y., Duan, Q., Luo, G., Fan, S., Lu, Y., Feng, A., Zhan, Y., Liang, B., Cai, W., Zhang, L., Du, X., & Zou, H. (2020). Clinical characteristics of coronavirus disease 2019 (COVID-19) in China: A systematic review and meta-analysis. *The Journal of Infection, 80*(6), 656–665. doi:10.1016/j.jinf.2020.03.041 PMID:32283155

García, L., Parra, L., Jimenez, J. M., Lloret, J., & Lorenz, P. (2020). IoT-based smart irrigation systems: An overview on the recent trends on sensors and IoT systems for irrigation in precision agriculture. *Sensors (Basel), 20*(4), 1042. doi:10.339020041042 PMID:32075172

Gautam, V., & Lanjewar, U. (2023). Fog computing: Analyzing challenges, unveiling opportunities, and maximizing benefits. *TIJER, 10*(5), 1–15. doi:10.21276/tijer.2023.10.5.1

Gavhane, A., Kokkula, G., Pandya, I., & Devadkar, K. (2018). Prediction of heart disease using machine learning. In: *Proceedings of the Second IEEE International Conference on Electronics, Communication and Aerospace Technology*, (pp. 1275-1278). IEEE. 10.1109/ICECA.2018.8474922

Gerard, D. R. (2022). Quality Improvement Using the Donabedian Model. *EMS World*.

Ghamisi, P., Benediktsson, J. A., Ghamisi, P., & Benediktsson, J. A. (2015). Feature selection based on hybridization of genetic algorithm and particle swarm optimization. *Ieeexplore.Ieee. IEEE Geoscience and Remote Sensing Letters, 12*(2), 309–313. doi:10.1109/LGRS.2014.2337320

Ghosh, S., & Mukherjee, A. (2022). STROVE: Spatial data infrastructure enabled cloud–fog–edge computing framework for combating COVID-19 pandemic. *Innovations in Systems and Software Engineering*. doi:10.100711334-022-00458-2 PMID:35677629

Ghosh, S., Mukherjee, A., Ghosh, S. K., & Buyya, R. (2022). STOPPAGE: Spatio-temporal data driven cloud-fog-edge computing framework for pandemic monitoring and management. *Software, Practice & Experience, 52*(12), 2700–2726. doi:10.1002pe.3144

Gia, T. N. (2017). Low-cost fog-assisted health-care IoT system with energy efficient sensor nodes. *13th international wireless communications and mobile computing conference*. IEEE.

Gia, T. N., Jiang, M., Rahmani, A. M., Westerlund, T., Liljeberg, P., & Tenhunen, H. "Fog Computing in Healthcare Internet of Things: A Case Study on ECG Feature Extraction," 2015 IEEE International Conference on Computer and Information Technology; Ubiquitous Computing and Communications; Dependable, Autonomic and Secure Computing; Pervasive Intelligence and Computing, Liverpool, UK, 2015, pp. 356-363 10.1109/CIT/IUCC/DASC/PICOM.2015.51

Gia, T. N. (2018). Fog computing approach for mobility support in internet-ofthings systems. *IEEE Access : Practical Innovations, Open Solutions, 6*, 36064–36082. doi:10.1109/ACCESS.2018.2848119

Giuliani, G., Lacroix, P., Guigoz, Y., Roncella, R., Bigagli, L., Santoro, M., Mazzetti, P., Nativi, S., Ray, N., & Lehmann, A. (2017). Bringing GEOSS Services into Practice: A Capacity Building Resource on Spatial Data Infrastructures (SDI). *Transactions in GIS, 21*(4), 811–824. doi:10.1111/tgis.12209

Godio, A., Pace, F., & Vergnano, A. (2020). SEIR modeling of the Italian epidemic of SARS-CoV-2 using computational swarm intelligence. *International Journal of Environmental Research and Public Health*, *17*(10), 3535. doi:10.3390/ijerph17103535 PMID:32443640

Goh, K., Lavanya, J., Kim, Y., Tan, E., & Soh, C. (2005). A pda-based ecg beat detector for home cardiac care. *27th Annual International Conference of the Engineering in Medicine and Biology Society*, IEEE. 10.1109/IEMBS.2005.1616423

Goldstein, B. A., Navar, A., Pencina, M. J., & Ioannidis, J. (2017). Opportunities and challenges in developing risk prediction models with electronic health records data: a systematic review. *JAMIA, 24*(1):198-208. . doi:10.1093/jamia/ocw042

Gomathy, C. K., & Naidu, A. R. (2021). The prediction of disease using machine learning. *International Journal of Scientific Research in Engineering and Management*, *5*(10), 1–7.

Gomes, E., Costa, F., De Rolt, C., Plentz, P., & Dantas, M. (2021). A Survey from Real-Time to Near Real-Time Applications in Fog Computing Environments. In Telecom, 2(4). doi:10.3390/telecom2040028

Goswami, V., Sharma, B., Patra, S. S., Chowdhury, S., Barik, R. K., & Dhaou, I. B. (2023, January). IoT-Fog Computing Sustainable System for Smart Cities: A Queueing-based Approach. In *2023 1st International Conference on Advanced Innovations in Smart Cities (ICAISC)* (pp. 1-6). IEEE. 10.1109/ICAISC56366.2023.10085238

Greco, L., Percannella, G., Ritrovato, P., Tortorella, F., & Vento, M. (2020). Trends in IoT based solutions for health care: Moving AI to the Edge. *Pattern Recognition Letters*, *135*, 346–353. doi:10.1016/j.patrec.2020.05.016 PMID:32406416

Groene, O., Botje, D., Suñol, R., Lopez, M. A., & Wagner, C. (2013). A systematic review of instruments that assess the implementation of hospital quality management systems. *International Journal for Quality in Health Care*, *25*(5), 525–541. doi:10.1093/intqhc/mzt058 PMID:23970437

Groot, R., & McLaughlin, J. (2000). Geospatial data infrastructure : concepts, cases and good practice. In R. Groot & J. McLaughlin (Eds.), *GeoSpatial Data Infrastructure: Concepts, Cases and Good Practice*. Oxford University Press. https://research.utwente.nl/en/publications/geospatial-data-infrastructure-concepts-cases-and-good-practice

GSDI. (2004). Developing Spatial Data Infrastructures: The SDI Cookbook. In GSDI/Nebert.

Guerrero, C., Lera, I., & Juiz, C. (2019). Lightweight decentralized service placement policy for performance optimization in fog computing. *Journal of Ambient Intelligence and Humanized Computing*, *10*(6), 2435–2452. doi:10.100712652-018-0914-0

Guevara, J. C., Torres, R. da S., & da Fonseca, N. L. S. (2020). On the classification of fog computing applications: A machine learning perspective. *Journal of Network and Computer Applications*, *159*(102596), 102596. doi:10.1016/j.jnca.2020.102596

Gülcü, Ş. (2022). Training of the feed forward artificial neural networks using dragonfly algorithm. *Applied Soft Computing*, *124*, 109023. doi:10.1016/j.asoc.2022.109023

Habibi, P., Farhoudi, M., Kazemian, S., Khorsandi, S., & Leon-Garcia, A. (2020). Fog Computing: A Comprehensive Architectural Survey. *IEEE Access : Practical Innovations, Open Solutions*, *8*, 69105–69133. doi:10.1109/ACCESS.2020.2983253

Haghi Kashani, M., Rahmani, A. M., & Jafari Navimipour, N. (2020). Quality of service-aware approaches in fog computing. *International Journal of Communication Systems*, *33*(8), e4340. doi:10.1002/dac.4340

Hajibaba, M., & Gorgin, S. (2014). A review on modern distributed computing paradigms: Cloud computing, jungle computing and fog computing. *CIT. Journal of Computing and Information Technology*, *22*(2), 69. doi:10.2498/cit.1002381

Hall, P., Marshall, D., & Martin, R. (2002). Adding and subtracting eigenspaces with eigenvalue decomposition and singular value decomposition. *Image and Vision Computing*, 20(13-14), 1009–1016. doi:10.1016/S0262-8856(02)00114-2

Hamsagayathri, P., & Vigneshwaran, S. (2021). Symptoms based disease prediction using machine learning techniques. In: *Proceedings of the Third IEEE International Conference on Intelligent Communication Technologies and Virtual Mobile Networks*, (pp. 747-752). IEEE. 10.1109/ICICV50876.2021.9388603

Har, L. L., Rashid, U. K., Te Chuan, L., Sen, S. C., & Xia, L. Y. (2022). Revolution of retail industry: From perspective of retail 1.0 to 4.0. *Procedia Computer Science*, 200, 1615–1625. doi:10.1016/j.procs.2022.01.362

Hashmi, A., Ahmad, M. A., & Nawaz, M. A. (2021). The Role of Coordination, Decision Making and Spatial Data Infrastructure on the Disaster Management in Pakistan: Moderating Role of Information System. *Review of Applied Management and Social Sciences*, 4(1), 79–91. doi:10.47067/ramss.v4i1.100

Hasija, Y., Garg, N., & Sourav, S. (2017). Automated detection of dermatological disorders through image-processing and machine learning. In: *Proceedings of the IEEE International Conference on Intelligent Sustainable Systems*, (pp. 1047-1051). IEEE. 10.1109/ISS1.2017.8389340

Haverkort, B. R., & Niemegeers, I. G. (1996). Performability modeling tools and techniques. *Performance Evaluation*, 25(1), 17–40. doi:10.1016/0166-5316(94)00038-7

Hayford, T. B. (2017). Issues and Challenges in Measuring and Improving the Quality of Health Care. *Working Paper Series*. Congressional Budget Office Washington, D.C. doi:10.1377/hlthaff.16.3.7

Hazra, A., Rana, P., Adhikari, M., & Amgoth, T. (2023). Fog computing for next-generation internet of things: Fundamental, state-of-the-art and research challenges. *Computer Science Review*, 48, 100549. doi:10.1016/j.cosrev.2023.100549

Hendriks, P. H. J., Dessers, E., & van Hootegem, G. (2012). Reconsidering the definition of a spatial data infrastructure. In International Journal of Geographical Information Science, 26(8), 1479–1494. doi:10.1080/13658816.2011.639301

Higgins, C. I., Williams, J., Leibovici, D. G., Simonis, I., Davis, M. J., Muldoon, C., van Genuchten, P., O'Hare, G., & Wiemann, S. (2016). Citizen OBservatory WEB (COBWEB): A Generic Infrastructure Platform to Facilitate the Collection of Citizen Science data for Environmental Monitoring. *International Journal of Spatial Data Infrastructures Research*, 11. doi:10.2902/1725-0463.2016.11.art3

Higham, N. J. (2011). Gaussian elimination. *Wiley Interdisciplinary Reviews: Computational Statistics*, 3(3), 230–238. doi:10.1002/wics.164

Horn, J., Nafpliotis, N., & Goldberg, D. E. (1994, June). A niched Pareto genetic algorithm for multiobjective optimization. In *Proceedings of the first IEEE conference on evolutionary computation. IEEE world congress on computational intelligence* (pp. 82-87). IEEE. 10.1109/ICEC.1994.350037

Hosseini, E., Nickray, M., & Ghanbari, S. (2023). Energy-efficient scheduling based on task prioritization in mobile fog computing. *Computing*, 105(1), 187–215. doi:10.100700607-022-01108-y

Houck, C. R., Joines, J., & Kay, M. G. (1995). A genetic algorithm for function optimization: a Matlab implementation. *Ncsu-ie tr*, 95(09), 1-10.

Hu, B. (2018). A robust retail POS system based on blockchain and edge computing. In *International Publishing* (pp. 99–110). Springer. doi:10.1007/978-3-319-94340-4_8

Hu, P., Dhelim, S., Ning, H., & Qiu, T. (2017). Survey on fog computing: Architecture, key technologies, applications and open issues. *Journal of Network and Computer Applications*, 98, 27–42. doi:10.1016/j.jnca.2017.09.002

Hussein, W. N., Hussain, H. N., Hussain, H. N., & Mallah, A. Q. (2023). A deployment model for IoT devices based on fog computing for data management and analysis. *Wireless Personal Communications*, 1–13. doi:10.100711277-023-10168-y

Iftikhar, S., Gill, S. S., Song, C., Xu, M., Aslanpour, M. S., Toosi, A. N., Du, J., Wu, H., Ghosh, S., Chowdhury, D., Golec, M., Kumar, M., Abdelmoniem, A. M., Cuadrado, F., Varghese, B., Rana, O., Dustdar, S., & Uhlig, S. (2022). AI-based fog and edge computing: A systematic review, taxonomy and future directions. *Internet of Things*, *21*, 100674. doi:10.1016/j.iot.2022.100674

Indrajit, A., van Loenen, B., Suprajaka, Jaya, V. E., Ploeger, H., Lemmen, C., & van Oosterom, P. (2021). Implementation of the spatial plan information package for improving ease of doing business in Indonesian cities. *Land Use Policy*, *105*, 105338. doi:10.1016/j.landusepol.2021.105338

Iradukunda, O., Che, H., Uwineza, J., Bayingana, J. Y., Bin-Imam, M. S., & Niyonzima, I. (2019). Malaria Disease Prediction Based on Machine Learning. In: *Proceedings of the IEEE International Conference on Signal, Information and Data Processing*, (pp. 1-7). IEEE. 10.1109/ICSIDP47821.2019.9173011

Ismaeel, S., Miri, A., & Chourishi, D. (2015). Using the extreme learning machine (elm) technique for heart disease diagnosis. In: *Proceedings of the IEEE Canada International Humanitarian Technology Conference,* (pp. 1-3). IEEE. 10.1109/IHTC.2015.7238043

Iwata, K., & Miyakoshi, C. (2020). A simulation on potential secondary spread of novel coronavirus in an exported country using a stochastic epidemic SEIR model. *Journal of Clinical Medicine*, *9*(4), 944. doi:10.3390/jcm9040944 PMID:32235480

Iyapparaja, M., Alshammari, N. K., Kumar, M. S., Krishnan, S., & Chowdhary, C. L. (2022). Efficient Resource Allocation in Fog Computing Using QTCS Model. *Computers, Materials & Continua*, *70*(2), 2225–2239. doi:10.32604/cmc.2022.015707

Jacoby, S., Smith, J., Ting, L., & Williamson, I. (2002). Developing a common spatial data infrastructure between state and local government - An Australian case study. *International Journal of Geographical Information Science*, *16*(4), 305–322. doi:10.1080/13658810110096001

Jadhav, S., Kasar, R., Lade, N., Patil, M., & Kolte, S. (2019). Disease prediction by machine learning from healthcare communities. *International Journal of Scientific Research in Science and Technology*, *6*(3), 29–35. doi:10.32628/IJSRST19633

Jain, R., Gupta, M., Nayyar, A., & Sharma, N. (2021). Adoption of fog computing in healthcare 4.0. In *Fog computing for healthcare 4.0 environments* (pp. 3–36). Springer. doi:10.1007/978-3-030-46197-3_1

Jain, S., Gupta, S., Sreelakshmi, K. K., & Rodrigues, J. J. P. C. (2022). Fog computing in enabling 5G-driven emerging technologies for development of sustainable smart city infrastructures. *Cluster Computing*, *25*(2), 1111–1154. doi:10.100710586-021-03496-w

Jali, B. R., Behura, R., Barik, S. R., Parveen, S., Mohanty, S. P., & Das, R. (2018). A brief review: Biological implications of naphthoquinone derivatives. *Research Journal of Pharmacy and Technology*, *11*(8), 3698–3702. doi:10.5958/0974-360X.2018.00679.0

Jamil, B., Ijaz, H., Shojafar, M., Munir, K., & Buyya, R. (2022). Resource allocation and task scheduling in fog computing and internet of everything environments: A taxonomy, review, and future directions. *ACM Computing Surveys*, *54*(11s), 1–38. doi:10.1145/3513002

Javadzadeh, G., & Rahmani, A. M. (2020). Fog Computing Applications in Smart Cities: A Systematic Survey. *Wireless Networks*, *26*(2), 1433–1457. doi:10.100711276-019-02208-y

Jazieh, A. (2020). Quality Measures: Types, Selection, and Application. *Journal of Health Care Quality Assurance 26*(3), 269-78, 201.

Jena, A. R., Pati, S., Chakraborty, S., Sarkar, S., Guin, S., Mallick, S., & Sen, S. K. (2021). *A Framework for Predicting Placement of a Graduate Using Machine Learning Techniques*, 197–206. Springer. doi:10.1007/978-981-16-4301-9_15

Jeyashree, G., & Padmavathi, S. (2023). A Fog Cluster-Based Framework for Personalized Healthcare Monitoring. In Research Advances in Network Technologies. doi:10.1201/9781003320333-7

Jones, G., Willett, P., Glen, R. C., Leach, A. R., & Taylor, R. (1997). Development and validation of a genetic algorithm for flexible docking. *Journal of Molecular Biology*, *267*(3), 727–748. doi:10.1006/jmbi.1996.0897 PMID:9126849

Kamruzzaman, M. M., Yan, B., Sarker, M. N. I., Alruwaili, O., Wu, M., & Alrashdi, I. (2022). Blockchain and Fog Computing in IoT-Driven Healthcare Services for Smart Cities. *Journal of Healthcare Engineering*, *2022*, 1–13. doi:10.1155/2022/9957888 PMID:35126961

Karsoliya, S. (2012). Approximating number of hidden layer neurons in multiple hidden layer BPNN architecture. *International Journal of Engineering Trends and Technology*, *3*(6), 714–717.

Karvekar, S. B. (2019). *Smartphone-based human fatigue detection in an industrial environment using gait analysis*. Scholar Works. https://scholarworks.rit.edu/theses/10275/.

Kashyap, V. (2022). A Systematic Survey on Fog and IoT Driven Healthcare: Open Challenges and Research Issues. *Electronics*, 1-25.

Katarya, R., & Srinivas, P. (2020). Predicting heart disease at early stages using machine learning: A survey. In: *Proceedings of the IEEE International Conference on Electronics and Sustainable Communication Systems*, (pp. 302-305). IEEE. 10.1109/ICESC48915.2020.9155586

Keleş, A., & Keleş, A. (2017). ESTDD: Expert system for thyroid diseases diagnosis. *Expert Systems with Applications*, *34*(1), 242-246,2008.

Keleş, A., & Keleş, A. (2008). ESTDD: Expert system for thyroid diseases diagnosis. *Expert Systems with Applications*, *34*(1), 242–246. doi:10.1016/j.eswa.2006.09.028

Kennedy, J., & Eberhart, R. (1995, November). Particle swarm optimization. In *Proceedings of ICNN'95-international conference on neural networks* (*Vol. 4*, pp. 1942-1948). IEEE. 10.1109/ICNN.1995.488968

Khaleque, A., & Sen, P. (2017). An empirical analysis of the Ebola outbreak in West Africa. *Scientific Reports*, *7*(1), 42594. doi:10.1038rep42594 PMID:28205617

Khan, M. A., & Salah, K. (2018). IoT security: Review, blockchain solutions, and open challenges. *Future Generation Computer Systems*, *82*, 395–411. doi:10.1016/j.future.2017.11.022

Khan, S., Parkinson, S., & Qin, Y. (2017). Fog computing security: A review of current applications and security solutions. *Journal of Cloud Computing (Heidelberg, Germany)*, *6*(1), 19. doi:10.118613677-017-0090-3

Kharchenko, V., Ponochovnyi, Y., Ivanchenko, O., Fesenko, H., & Illiashenko, O. (2022). Combining Markov and Semi-Markov Modeling for Assessing Availability and Cybersecurity of Cloud and IoT Systems. *Cryptography*, *6*(3), 44. doi:10.3390/cryptography6030044

Kilbourne, A. M., Keyser, D., & Pincus, H. A. (2010). Challenges and Opportunities in Measuring the Quality of Mental Health Care. *Canadian Journal of Psychiatry*, *55*(9), 549–557. doi:10.1177/070674371005500903 PMID:20840802

Kirsal, Y. (2013). *Modeling and performance evaluation of wireless and mobile communication systems in heterogeneous environments* [Doctoral dissertation, Middlesex university].

Kirsal, Y. (2018). Analytical modeling and optimization analysis of large-scale communication systems and networks with repairmen policy. *Computing*, *100*(5), 503–527. doi:10.100700607-017-0580-7

Kirsal, Y., Ever, Y. K., Mapp, G., & Raza, M. (2021). 3D Analytical Modeling and Iterative Solution for High Performance Computing Clusters. *IEEE Transactions on Cloud Computing*, *10*(4), 2238–2251. doi:10.1109/TCC.2021.3055119

Ko, H., & Kyung, Y. (2022). Performance Analysis and Optimization of Delayed Offloading System with Opportunistic Fog Node. *IEEE Transactions on Vehicular Technology*, *71*(9), 10203–10208. doi:10.1109/TVT.2022.3179658

Kohli, P. S., & Arora, S. (2018). Application of machine learning in disease prediction. In: *Proceedings of the 4th IEEE International Conference on Computing Communication and Automation*, (pp. 1-4). IEEE. 10.1109/CCAA.2018.8777449

Kooistra, J. (2018). *Newzoo's 2018 Global Mobile Market Report: Insights into the World's 3 Billion Smartphone Users.* Newzoo. https://newzoo.com/insights/articles/newzoos-2018-globalmobile- market-report-insights-into-the-worlds-3-billion-smartphone-users/

Koopialipoor, M., Noorbakhsh, A., Noroozi Ghaleini, E., Jahed Armaghani, D., & Yagiz, S. (2019). A new approach for estimation of rock brittleness based on non-destructive tests. *Nondestructive Testing and Evaluation*, *34*(4), 354–375. doi:10.1080/10589759.2019.1623214

Kourou, K., Exarchos, T. P., Exarchos, K. P., Karamouzis, M. V., & Fotiadis, D. I. (2015). Machine learning applications in cancer prognosis and prediction. *Computational and Structural Biotechnology Journal*, *13*, 8–17. doi:10.1016/j.csbj.2014.11.005 PMID:25750696

Kourouthanassis, P., & Roussos, G. (2003). Developing consumer-friendly pervasive retail systems. *IEEE Pervasive Computing*, *2*(2), 32–39. doi:10.1109/MPRV.2003.1203751

Kranz, A., Dalton, S., Damberg, C., & Timbie, J. W. (2018). *Using Health IT to Coordinate Care and Improve Quality in Safety-Net Clinics, The Joint Commission.* Elsevier Inc.

Kugali, S. N. (2020). Vehicular ADHOC Network (VANET):-A Brief Knowledge. *International Journal of Engineering Research & Technology (Ahmedabad)*, *9*(6), 1026–1029. doi:10.17577/IJERTV9IS060784

Kumar, A., Upadhyay, A., Mishra, N., Nath, S., Yadav, K. R., & Sharma, G. (2022; Vol. 1030). Privacy and Security Concerns in Edge Computing-Based Smart Cities. In Studies in Computational Intelligence. doi:10.1007/978-3-030-96737-6_5

Kumar, A., Krishnamurthi, R., Nayyar, A., Sharma, K., Grover, V., & Hossain, E. (2020). A novel smart healthcare design, simulation, and implementation using healthcare 4.0 processes. *IEEE Access : Practical Innovations, Open Solutions*, *8*, 118433–118471. doi:10.1109/ACCESS.2020.3004790

Kumar, S., Nilsen, W., Pavel, M., & Srivastava, M. (2012). Mobile health: Revolutionizing healthcare through transdisciplinary research. *Computer*, *46*(1), 28–35. doi:10.1109/MC.2012.392

Laghari, A. A., Jumani, A. K., & Laghari, R. A. (2021). Review and state of art of fog computing. *Archives of Computational Methods in Engineering*. Archives of Computational Methods in Engineering, *28*(5), 3631–3643. doi:10.100711831-020-09517-y

Lai, K. L., Chen, J. I. Z., & Zong, J. I. (2021). Development of smart cities with fog computing and internet of things. [UCCT]. *Journal of Ubiquitous Computing and Communication Technologies*, *3*(01), 52–60. doi:10.36548/jucct.2021.1.006

Larson, E. C., Goel, M., Boriello, G., Heltshe, S., Rosenfeld, M., & Patel, S. N. (2012, September). SpiroSmart: using a microphone to measure lung function on a mobile phone. In *Proceedings of the 2012 ACM Conference on ubiquitous computing* (pp. 280-289). ACM. 10.1145/2370216.2370261

Larson, E. C., Lee, T., Liu, S., Rosenfeld, M., & Patel, S. N. (2011, September). Accurate and privacy preserving cough sensing using a low-cost microphone. In *Proceedings of the 13th international conference on Ubiquitous computing* (pp. 375-384). ACM. 10.1145/2030112.2030163

Lawal, M. A., Shaikh, R. A., & Hassan, S. R. (2020). An anomaly mitigation framework for IoT using fog computing. *Electronics (Basel)*, *9*(10), 1565. doi:10.3390/electronics9101565

Lawanont, W., Inoue, M., Mongkolnam, P., & Nukoolkit, C. (2018). Neck posture monitoring system based on image detection and smartphone sensors using the prolonged usage classification concept. *IEEJ Transactions on Electrical and Electronic Engineering*, *13*(10), 1501–1510. doi:10.1002/tee.22778

Lee, K., Kim, D., Ha, D., Rajput, U., & Oh, H. (2015). On security and privacy issues of fog computing supported Internet of Things environment. *2015 6th International Conference on the Network of the Future (NOF)*. ACM.

Lee, K., Kim, D., Ha, D., Rajput, U., & Oh, H. (2015). On security and privacy issues of fog computing supported Internet of Things environment. *2015 6th International Conference on the Network of the Future (NOF)*. IEEE.

Lillrank, P. (2015). Small and big quality in health care. *International Journal of Health Care Quality Assurance*, *28*(4), 356–366. doi:10.1108/IJHCQA-05-2014-0068 PMID:25982636

Lin, C.-C., & Yang, J.-W. (2018). Cost-efficient deployment of fog computing systems at logistics centers in industry 4.0. *IEEE Transactions on Industrial Informatics*, *14*(10), 4603–4611. doi:10.1109/TII.2018.2827920

Liu, B., Chang, X., Liu, B., & Chen, Z. (2017). Performance analysis model for fog services under multiple resource types. In *2017 International Conference on Dependable Systems and Their Applications (DSA)* (pp. 110-117). IEEE. 10.1109/DSA.2017.26

Liu, L., Xue, Y., Chen, H., Wang, Z., Fang, C., Sun, Y., & Sun, Y. (2021). Optimal Connected Cruise Control Design with Time-Varying Leader Velocity and Delays. *Journal of Sensors*, *2021*, 1–14. doi:10.1155/2021/5618538

Liu, X., Li, S., & Tong, W. (2015). A queuing model considering resources sharing for cloud service performance. *The Journal of Supercomputing*, *71*(11), 4042–4055. doi:10.100711227-015-1503-z

Lohr, K. (1990). Health, Health Care, and Quality of Care. In: *Medicare: A Strategy for Quality Assurance. Institute of Medicine. NAP.* https://books.nap.edu/openbook.php?record_id=1547&page=21

Lumen Learning. (2020). *Introduction to retailing. The evolution of retail. Module of Retail Management.* Lumen Learning.

Lutz, M., Sprado, J., Klien, E., Schubert, C., & Christ, I. (2009). Overcoming semantic heterogeneity in spatial data infrastructures. *Computers & Geosciences*, *35*(4), 739–752. doi:10.1016/j.cageo.2007.09.017

Machida, F., Zhang, Q., & Andrade, E. (2023). Performability analysis of adaptive drone computation offloading with fog computing. *Future Generation Computer Systems*, *145*, 121–135. doi:10.1016/j.future.2023.03.027

Maddah, E., & Beigzadeh, B. (2020). Use of a smartphone thermometer to monitor thermal conductivity changes in diabetic foot ulcers: A pilot study. *Journal of Wound Care*, *29*(1), 61–66. doi:10.12968/jowc.2020.29.1.61 PMID:31930943

Maheswaran, M., Yang, T., & Memon, S. (2019). A Fog Computing Framework for Autonomous Driving Assist: Architecture, Experiments, and Challenges. *CASCON '19: Proceedings of the 29th Annual International Conference on Computer Science and Software Engineering*, (pp. 24–33). IEEE.

Mahmud, R., Kotagiri, R., & Buyya, R. (2018). Fog computing: A taxonomy, survey and future directions. In *Internet of everything* (pp. 103–130). Springer. doi:10.1007/978-981-10-5861-5_5

Mahmud, R., Pallewatta, S., Goudarzi, M., & Buyya, R. (2022). iFogSim2: An extended iFogSim simulator for mobility, clustering, and microservice management in edge and fog computing environments. *Journal of Systems and Software*, *190*, 111351. doi:10.1016/j.jss.2022.111351

Mahmud, R., Ramamohanarao, K., & Buyya, R. (2021). Application Management in Fog Computing Environments. *ACM Computing Surveys*, *53*(4), 1–43. doi:10.1145/3403955

Mahmud, R., Srirama, S. N., Ramamohanarao, K., & Buyya, R. (2020). Profit aware application placement for integrated fog- cloud computing environments. *Journal of Parallel and Distributed Computing*, *135*, 177–190. doi:10.1016/j.jpdc.2019.10.001

Maind, S. B., & Wankar, P. (2014). Research paper on basic of artificial neural network. *International Journal on Recent and Innovation Trends in Computing and Communication*, *2*(1), 96–100.

Ma, K., Bagula, A., Nyirenda, C., & Ajayi, O. (2019). An IoT-based fog computing model. *Sensors (Basel)*, *19*(12), 2783. doi:10.339019122783 PMID:31234280

Manfré, L., Hirata, E., Silva, J. B., Shinohara, E. J., Giannotti, M., Larocca, A. P. C., & Quintanilha, J. (2012). An Analysis of Geospatial Technologies for Risk and Natural Disaster Management. *ISPRS International Journal of Geo-Information*, *1*(2), 166–185. doi:10.3390/ijgi1020166

Manju, A. B., & Sumathy, S. (2019). Efficient load balancing algorithm for task preprocessing in fog computing environment. In *Smart Intelligent Computing and Applications* (pp. 291–298). Springer Singapore. doi:10.1007/978-981-13-1927-3_31

Manohar, B., & Das, R. (2022b). Artificial Neural Networks for the Prediction of Monkeypox Outbreak. *Tropical Medicine and Infectious Disease*, *7*(12), 424. doi:10.3390/tropicalmed7120424

Manohar, B., & Das, R. (2022a). Artificial neural networks for prediction of COVID -19 in India by using backpropagation. *Expert Systems: International Journal of Knowledge Engineering and Neural Networks*, *40*(5), e13105. doi:10.1111/exsy.13105 PMID:36245831

Mansour, K. (2023). A two dimensional Markov chain model for aggregation-enabled 802.11 networks. *International Journal of Ad Hoc and Ubiquitous Computing*, *42*(4), 269–280. doi:10.1504/IJAHUC.2023.130467

Mardiana, B. M., & Hassan, W. (2019). Current research on Internet of Things (IoT) security: A survey. *Computer Networks*, *148*, 283-294.

Margariti, S. V., Dimakopoulos, V. V., & Tsoumanis, G. (2020). Modeling and simulation tools for fog computing—A comprehensive survey from a cost perspective. *Future Internet*, *12*(5), 89. doi:10.3390/fi12050089

Mas, L., Vilaplana, J., Mateo, J., & Solsona, F. (2022). A queuing theory model for fog computing. *The Journal of Supercomputing*, *78*(8), 11138–11155. doi:10.100711227-022-04328-3

Masser, I. (2005). GIS worlds: creating spatial data infrastructures, 338). ESRI press Redlands, CA.

Masser, I. (2009). Changing notions of a spatial data infrastructure. *SDI Convergence*, 219–228. http://drupal.gsdi.org/gsdiconf/gsdi11/SDICnvrgncBook.pdf#page=228

Masser, I. (1999). All shapes and sizes: The first generation of national spatial data infrastructures. *International Journal of Geographical Information Science*, *13*(1), 67–84. doi:10.1080/136588199241463

Ma, X., Li, Y., & Gao, Y. (2023). Decision model of intrusion response based on markov game in fog computing environment. *Wireless Networks*, 1–10. doi:10.100711276-023-03382-w

McLaughlin, J. D. (1991). Towards national spatial data infrastructure. *Proceedings of the Canadian Conference on GIS*, (pp. 1–5). IEEE.

Mekala, M. S., & Viswanathan, P. (2007). A Survey: Smart agriculture IoT with cloud computing. 2017 International conference on Microelectronic Devices, Circuits and Systems (ICMDCS). IEEE. 10.1109/ICMDCS.2017.8211551

Meng, Y., Naeem, M. A., Almagrabi, A. O., Ali, R., & Kim, H. S. (2020). Advancing the state of the fog computing to enable 5G network technologies. *Sensors (Basel)*, *20*(6), 1754. doi:10.339020061754 PMID:32245261

Miah, M. A., Kabir, M. H., Tanveer, M. S. R., & Akhand, M. A. H. (2015, December). Continuous heart rate and body temperature monitoring system using Arduino UNO and Android device. In *2015 2nd International Conference on Electrical Information and Communication Technologies (EICT)* (pp. 183-188). IEEE.

Mishra, S., Tadesse, Y., Dash, A., Jena, L., & Ranjan, P. (2021). Thyroid disorder analysis using random forest classifier. In *Intelligent and Cloud Computing* (pp. 385–390). Springer. doi:10.1007/978-981-15-5971-6

Mohammadi, H. (2008). The Integration of multi-source spatial datasets in the context of SDI initiatives. [PhD thesis. Department of Geomatics. The University of Melbourne].

Mohan, S., Thirumalai, C., & Srivastava, G. (2019). Effective heart disease prediction using hybrid machine learning techniques. *IEEE Access : Practical Innovations, Open Solutions*, *7*, 81542–81554. doi:10.1109/ACCESS.2019.2923707

Mokhtarian, A., Kampmann, A., Lueer, M., Kowalewski, S., & Alrifaee, B. (2021). A Cloud Architecture for Networked and Autonomous Vehicles. *IFAC-PapersOnLine*, *54*(2), 233–239. doi:10.1016/j.ifacol.2021.06.028

Molina, M., & Bayarri, S. (2011). A multinational SDI-based system to facilitate disaster risk management in the Andean Community. *Computers & Geosciences*, *37*(9), 1501–1510. Advance online publication. doi:10.1016/j.cageo.2011.01.015

Mosavi, A., Salimi, M., Faizollahzadeh Ardabili, S., Rabczuk, T., Shamshirband, S., & Varkonyi-Koczy, A. R. (2019). State of the art of machine learning models in energy systems, a systematic review. *Energies*, *12*(7), 1301. doi:10.3390/en12071301

Mouradian, C., Naboulsi, D., Yangui, S., Glitho, R. H., Morrow, M. J., & Polakos, P. A. (2018). A comprehensive survey on fog computing: State-of-the-art and research challenges. *IEEE Communications Surveys and Tutorials*, *20*(1), 416–464. doi:10.1109/COMST.2017.2771153

Moysiadis, V., Sarigiannidis, P., & Moscholios, I. (2018). Towards distributed data management in fog computing. *Wireless Communications and Mobile Computing*, *2018*, 1–14. doi:10.1155/2018/7597686

Mühlenbein, H., Schomisch, M., & Born, J. (1991). The parallel genetic algorithm as function optimizer. *Parallel Computing*, *17*(6-7), 619–632. doi:10.1016/S0167-8191(05)80052-3

Mujumdar, A., & Vaidehi, V. (2019). Diabetes prediction using machine learning algorithms. *Procedia Computer Science*, *165*, 292–299. doi:10.1016/j.procs.2020.01.047

Mukherjee, M., Matam, R., Shu, L., Maglaras, L., Ferrag, M. A., Choudhury, N., & Kumar, V. (2017). Security and Privacy in Fog Computing: Challenges. *IEEE Access : Practical Innovations, Open Solutions*, *5*, 19293–19304. doi:10.1109/ACCESS.2017.2749422

Mukherjee, M., Shu, L., & Wang, D. (2018). Survey of Fog Computing: Fundamental, Network Applications, and Research Challenges. *IEEE Communications Surveys and Tutorials*, *20*(3), 1826–1857. doi:10.1109/COMST.2018.2814571

Murdoch, T. B., & Detsky, A. S. (2013). The inevitable application of big data to health care. *Journal of the American Medical Association, 309*(13), 1351–1352. doi:10.1001/jama.2013.393 PMID:23549579

Mutlag, A. A., Abd Ghani, M. K., Arunkumar, N. A., Mohammed, M. A., & Mohd, O. (2019). Enabling technologies for fog computing in healthcare IoT systems. *Future Generation Computer Systems, 90*, 62–78. doi:10.1016/j.future.2018.07.049

Naha, R. K., Garg, S., Georgakopoulos, D., Jayaraman, P. P., Gao, L., Xiang, Y., & Ranjan, R. (2018). Fog computing: Survey of trends, architectures, requirements, and research directions. *IEEE Access : Practical Innovations, Open Solutions, 6*, 47980–48009. doi:10.1109/ACCESS.2018.2866491

Namasudra, S., Dhamodharavadhani, S., & Rathipriya, R. (2023). Nonlinear Neural Network Based Forecasting Model for Predicting COVID-19 Cases. *Neural Processing Letters, 55*(1), 171–191. doi:10.100711063-021-10495-w PMID:33821142

Naranjo, P. G. V., Pooranian, Z., Shojafar, M., Conti, M., & Buyya, R. (2019). FOCAN: A Fog-supported smart city network architecture for management of applications in the Internet of Everything environments. *Journal of Parallel and Distributed Computing, 132*, 274–283. doi:10.1016/j.jpdc.2018.07.003

NASSCOM. (2021). *Retail 4.0: India Story-Unlocking Value through Online+Offline Collaborations.* NASSCOM. https://www.nasscom.in/retail-4-0-india-story-unlocking-value-through-online-offline-collaborations

Nazir, S., Kumam, P., Nadeem, S., & García-Magariño, I. (2019). Internet of Things for Healthcare Using Effects of Mobile Computing: A Systematic Literature Review. *Wireless Communications and Mobile Computing, 2019*, 1–20. doi:10.1155/2019/5931315

Nemati, E., Rahman, M. M., Nathan, V., Vatanparvar, K., & Kuang, J. (2019, September). A comprehensive approach for cough type detection. In *2019 IEEE/ACM International Conference on Connected Health: Applications, Systems and Engineering Technologies (CHASE)* (pp. 15-16). IEEE.

Nguyen, H. L., Woon, Y. K., & Ng, W. K. (2015). A survey on data stream clustering and classification. *Knowledge and Information Systems, 45*(3), 535–569. doi:10.100710115-014-0808-1

Nguyen, N. D., Phan, L. A., Park, D. H., Kim, S., & Kim, T. (2020). ElasticFog: Elastic resource provisioning in container-based fog computing. *IEEE Access : Practical Innovations, Open Solutions, 8*, 183879–183890. doi:10.1109/ACCESS.2020.3029583

Nhamo, N., & Chikoye, D. (2017). Smart Agriculture: Scope, Relevance, and Important Milestones to Date. In *Smart Technologies for Sustainable Smallholder Agriculture* (pp. 1–20). Elsevier. doi:10.1016/B978-0-12-810521-4.00001-3

Ni, J., Zhang, K., Lin, X., & Shen, X. S. (2018). Securing fog computing for Internet of Things applications: Challenges and solutions. IEEE Commun. Surveys Tuts., 20(1), 601–628.

Ni, L., Zhang, J., Jiang, C., Yan, C., & Yu, K. (2017). Resource allocation strategy in fog computing based on priced timed Petri Nets. *IEEE Internet of Things Journal, 4*(5), 1216–1228. doi:10.1109/JIOT.2017.2709814

Nilashi, M., Ahmadi, H., Manaf, A. A., Rashid, T. A., Samad, S., Shahmoradi, L., & Akbari, E. (2020). Coronary heart disease diagnosis through self-organizing map and fuzzy support vector machine with incremental updates. *International Journal of Fuzzy Systems, 22*(4), 1376–1388. doi:10.100740815-020-00828-7

Ning, Z., Dong, P., Wang, X., Hu, X., Guo, L., Hu, B., Wilkinson, A. J., Qiu, T., & Kwok, R. Y. K. (2021). Mobile Edge Computing Enabled 5G Health Monitoring for Internet of Medical Things: A Decentralized Game Theoretic Approach. *IEEE Journal on Selected Areas in Communications, 39*(2), 463–478. doi:10.1109/JSAC.2020.3020645

OECD. (2020). *Connecting businesses and consumers during COVID-19: trade in parcels.* OECD Policy Responses to Coronavirus (COVID-19). OECD. https://www.oecd.org/coronavirus/policy-responses/connecting-businesses-and-consumers-during-covid-19-trade-in-parcels-d18de131/

Ojo, O. A., Ojo, A. B., Taiwo, O. A., & Oluba, O. M. (2020). Novel Coronavirus (SARS-CoV-2) main protease: Molecular docking of Puerarin as a Potential inhibitor. doi:10.21203/rs.3.rs-37794/v1

Ometov, A., Molua, O. L., Komarov, M., & Nurmi, J. (2022). A Survey of Security in Cloud, Edge, and Fog Computing. In Sensors, 22(3). doi:10.339022030927

OpenFog Consortium. (2018). *IEEE Standard for Adoption of OpenFog Reference Architecture for Fog Computing.* IEEE.

Ovretveit, J. (2004). Formulating a health quality improvement strategy for a developing country. *International Journal of Health Care Quality Assurance, 17*(7), 368–376. doi:10.1108/09526860410563177 PMID:15552392

Pan, J., & McElhannon, J. (2018). Future edge cloud and edge computing for internet of things applications. *IEEE Internet of Things Journal, 5*(1), 1–5. doi:10.1109/JIOT.2017.2767608

Parihar, V. R., Tonge, A. Y., & Ganorkar, P. D. (2017). Heartbeat and temperature monitoring system for remote patients using Arduino. *International Journal of Advanced Engineering Research and Science, 4*(5), 55–58. doi:10.22161/ijaers.4.5.10

Patil, M., Lobo, V. B., Puranik, P., Pawaskar, A., Pai, A., & Mishra, R. (2018). A proposed model for lifestyle disease prediction using support vector machine. In: *Proceedings of the 9th IEEE International Conference on Computing, Communication and Networking Technologies*, (pp. 1-6). IEEE. 10.1109/ICCCNT.2018.8493897

Peralta, G., Iglesias-Urkia, M., Barceló, M., Gómez, R., Morán, A., & Bilbao, J. (2017). Fog computing based efficient IoT scheme for the Industry 4.0. IEEE international workshop of electronics, control, measurement, signals and their application to mechatronics (ECMSM), (pp. 1-6). IEEE. doi:10.1109/ECMSM.2017.8085600

Pereira, P., Araujo, J., Melo, C., Santos, V., & Maciel, P. (2021). Analytical models for availability evaluation of edge and fog computing nodes. *The Journal of Supercomputing, 77*(9), 9905–9933. doi:10.100711227-021-03672-0

Pereira, P., Araujo, J., Torquato, M., Dantas, J., Melo, C., & Maciel, P. (2020). Stochastic performance model for web server capacity planning in fog computing. *The Journal of Supercomputing, 76*(12), 9533–9557. doi:10.100711227-020-03218-w

Pereira, P., Melo, C., Araujo, J., Dantas, J., Santos, V., & Maciel, P. (2022). Availability model for edge-fog-cloud continuum: An evaluation of an end-to-end infrastructure of intelligent traffic management service. *The Journal of Supercomputing, 78*(3), 1–28. doi:10.100711227-021-04033-7

Perera, C., Qin, Y., Estrella, J. C., Reiff-Marganiec, S., & Vasilakos, A. V. (2017). Fog computing for sustainable smart cities: A survey. *ACM Computing Surveys, 50*(3), 1–43. doi:10.1145/3057266

Peterson, S. J., Cappola, A. R., Castro, M. R., Dayan, C. M., Farwell, A. P., Hennessey, J. V., Kopp, P. A., Ross, D. S., Samuels, M. H., Sawka, A. M., Taylor, P. N., Jonklaas, J., & Bianco, A. C. (2018). An online survey of hypothyroid patients demonstrates prominent dissatisfaction. *Thyroid, 28*(6), 707–721. doi:10.1089/thy.2017.0681 PMID:29620972

Pierre, G., & Ahmed, A. (2020). Docker-pi: Docker container deployment in fog computing infrastructures. *International Journal of Cloud Computing, 9*(1), 6. doi:10.1504/IJCC.2020.105885

Ponde, S. S., & Padghan, S. V. (2020). Smart health prediction for avoiding future health risk by using machine learning. *International Journal of Scientific Development and Research, 5*(8), 355–362.

Pooranian, Z., Shojafar, M., Paola, G. V. N., Chiaraviglio, L., & Conti, M. (2016). A novel distributed fog-based networked architecture to preserve energy in fog data centres. In: *Proceedings of 14th IEEE International Conference on Mobile Ad Hoc and Sensor Systems*. IEEE.

Popović, I., Radovanovic, I., Vajs, I., Drajic, D., & Gligorić, N. (2022). Building Low-Cost Sensing Infrastructure for Air Quality Monitoring in Urban Areas Based on Fog Computing. *Sensors (Basel)*, 22(3), 1026. doi:10.339022031026 PMID:35161775

Poppe, K., & Glinoer, D. (2003). Thyroid autoimmunity and hypothyroidism before and during pregnancy. *Human Reproduction Update*, 9(2), 149–161. doi:10.1093/humupd/dmg012 PMID:12751777

Prerana, P. S., & Taneja, K. (2015). Predictive data mining for diagnosis of thyroid disease using neural network. *International Journal of Research in Management, Science & Technology*, 3(2), 75–80.

Purswani, J. M., Dicker, A. P., Champ, C. E., Cantor, M., & Ohri, N. (2019, October). Big data from small devices: The future of smartphones in oncology. []. WB Saunders.]. *Seminars in Radiation Oncology*, 29(4), 338–347. doi:10.1016/j.semradonc.2019.05.008 PMID:31472736

Qadri, Y. A., Nauman, A., Zikria, Y. B., Vasilakos, A. V., & Kim, S. W. (2020). The future of healthcare internet of things: A survey of emerging technologies. *IEEE Communications Surveys and Tutorials*, 22(2), 1121–1167. doi:10.1109/COMST.2020.2973314

Qi, Q., & Tao, F. (2019). A Smart Manufacturing Service System Based on Edge Computing, Fog Computing, and Cloud Computing. *IEEE Access : Practical Innovations, Open Solutions*, 7, 86769–86777. doi:10.1109/ACCESS.2019.2923610

Qiu, T., Chen, N., Li, K., Atiquzzaman, M., & Zhao, W. (2018). How can heterogeneous Internet of Things build our future: A survey. IEEE Commun. Surveys Tuts., 20(3). doi:10.1109/COMST.2018.2803740

Qureshi, H. N., Manalastas, M., Zaidi, S. M. A., Imran, A., & Al Kalaa, M. O. (2021). Service level agreements for 5G and beyond: Overview, challenges and enablers of 5G-healthcare systems. *IEEE Access : Practical Innovations, Open Solutions*, 9, 1044–1061. doi:10.1109/ACCESS.2020.3046927 PMID:35211361

Qu, Y., Gao, L., Luan, T. H., Xiang, Y., Yu, S., Li, B., & Zheng, G. (2020). Decentralized privacy using blockchain-enabled federated learning in fog computing. *IEEE Internet of Things Journal*, 7(6), 5171–5183. doi:10.1109/JIOT.2020.2977383

Quy, V. K., Van Hau, N., Van Anh, D., & Ngoc, L. A. (2022). Smart healthcare IoT applications based on fog computing: Architecture, applications and challenges. *Complex & Intelligent Systems*, 8(5), 3805–3815. doi:10.100740747-021-00582-9 PMID:34804767

Rabby, A. K. M. S. A., Mamata, R., & Laboni, M. A., Ohidujjaman, & Abujar, S. (2019). Machine learning applied to kidney disease prediction: comparison study. In: *Proceedings of the 10th International Conference on Computing, Communication and Networking Technologies*, (pp. 1-7). IEEE. 10.1109/ICCCNT45670.2019.8944799

Rabindra, B. (2017). CloudGanga: Cloud computing based SDI model for ganga river basin management in India. *International Journal of Agricultural and Environmental Information Systems*, 8(4), 54–71. doi:10.4018/IJAEIS.2017100104

Rahaman, S. H., & Biswas, S. (2020). Advantages of Internet of Things (IoT) and It's Applications in Smart Agriculture System. *Int. Res. J. Adv. Sci. Hub*, 2(10), 4–10. doi:10.47392/irjash.2020.181

Rahimi, M., Songhorabadi, M., & Kashani, M. H. (2020). Fog-based smart homes: A systematic review. *Journal of Network and Computer Applications*, 153, 102531. doi:10.1016/j.jnca.2020.102531

Rahmani, A. M., Gia, T. N., Negash, B., Anzanpour, A., Azimi, I., Jiang, M., & Liljeberg, P. (2018). Exploiting smart e-Health gateways at the edge of healthcare Internet-of-Things: A fog computing approach. *Future Generation Computer Systems*, *78*, 641–658. doi:10.1016/j.future.2017.02.014

Rajabifard, A., Binns, A., Masser, I., & Williamson, I. (2006). The role of sub-national government and the private sector in future spatial data infrastructures. *International Journal of Geographical Information Science*, *20*(7), 727–741. doi:10.1080/13658810500432224

Rajabifard, A., Feeney, M. E. F., & Williamson, I. P. (2002). Future directions for SDI development. *International Journal of Applied Earth Observation and Geoinformation*, *4*(1), 11–22. doi:10.1016/S0303-2434(02)00002-8

Rajabifard, A., Mansourian, A., Javad, M., Zoej, V., & Williamson, I. (2002). Developing Spatial Data Infrastructure to Facilitate Disaster Management. *Management.*

Rajaram, K., & Sundareswaran, R. (2020). IoT Based Crop-Field Monitoring and Precise Irrigation System Using Crop Water Requirement. *In International Conference on Computational Intelligence in Data Science,* Springer: Cham, Switzerland. 10.1007/978-3-030-63467-4_23

Rajendra, P., & Latifi, S. (2021). Prediction of diabetes using logistic regression and ensemble techniques. *Computer Methods and Programs in Biomedicine Update*, *1*, 100032. doi:10.1016/j.cmpbup.2021.100032

Rani, R., Kumar, N., Khurana, M., Kumar, A., & Barnawi, A. (2021). Storage as a service in Fog computing: A systematic review. *Journal of Systems Architecture*, *116*, 102033. doi:10.1016/j.sysarc.2021.102033

Rao, A. S. S., & Vazquez, J. A. (2020). Identification of COVID-19 can be quicker through artificial intelligence framework using a mobile phone-based survey in the populations when cities/towns are under quarantine. *Infection Control and Hospital Epidemiology*, *41*(7), 1–18. doi:10.1017/ice.2020.61

Rashidi, M. M., Ali, M., Freidoonimehr, N., & Nazari, F. (2013). Parametric analysis and optimization of entropy generation in unsteady MHD flow over a stretching rotating disk using artificial neural network and particle swarm optimization algorithm. *Energy*, *55*, 497–510. doi:10.1016/j.energy.2013.01.036

Rashid, M., Yousuf, M. M., Ram, B., & Goyal, V. (2019). Novel Big Data Approach for Drug Prediction in Health Care Systems. In: *Proceedings of the International Conference on Automation, Computational and Technology Management,* (pp. 325-329). IEEE. 10.1109/ICACTM.2019.8776823

Rawat, R., Chakrawarti, R. K., Vyas, P., Gonzáles, J. L. A., Sikarwar, R., & Bhardwaj, R. (2023). Intelligent Fog Computing Surveillance System for Crime and Vulnerability Identification and Tracing. *International Journal of Information Security and Privacy*, *17*(1), 1–25. doi:10.4018/IJISP.317371

Reagan, J. R., & Singh, M. (2020). *Management 4.0: Cases and Methods for the 4th Industrial Revolution.* Springer. doi:10.1007/978-981-15-6751-3

Rehman, A., Saba, T., Kashif, M., Fati, S. M., Bahaj, S. A., & Chaudhry, H. (2022). A revisit of internet of things technologies for monitoring and control strategies in smart agriculture. *Agronomy (Basel)*, *12*(1), 127. doi:10.3390/agronomy12010127

Robinson, C., Chugg, B., Anderson, B., Ferres, J. M. L., & Ho, D. E. (2022). Mapping industrial poultry operations at scale with deep learning and aerial imagery. *IEEE Journal of Selected Topics in Applied Earth Observations and Remote Sensing*, *15*, 7458–7471. doi:10.1109/JSTARS.2022.3191544

Rodrigo AC da Silva & Nelson LS da Fonseca. (2018). Resource allocation mechanism for a fog-cloud infrastructure. In: *Proceedings of the IEEE International Conference on Communications*, (pp. 1-6). IEEE.

Rodrigues, L., Rodrigues, J. J., Serra, A. D. B., & Silva, F. A. (2022). A queueing-based model performance evaluation for internet of people supported by fog computing. *Future Internet*, *14*(1), 23. doi:10.3390/fi14010023

Roldan Jimenez, C., Bennett, P., Ortiz Garcia, A., & Cuesta Vargas, A. I. (2019). Fatigue detection during sit-to-stand test based on surface electromyography and acceleration: A case study. *Sensors (Basel)*, *19*(19), 4202. doi:10.339019194202 PMID:31569776

Rosario Michel, G., Gonzalez-Campos, M. E., Manzano Aybar, F., Jiménez Durán, T., & Crompvoets, J. (2023). Identifying critical factors to enhance SDI performance for facilitating disaster risk management in small island developing states. *Survey Review*, *55*(389), 114–126. doi:10.1080/00396265.2021.2024969

Rouhani, M., & Mansouri, K. (2009). Comparison of several ANN architectures on the Thyroid diseases grades diagnosis. In *2009 International Association of Computer Science and Information Technology-Spring Conference* (pp. 526-528). IEEE.

Roy, C., Maheshwari, E., Pandey, M., Rautaray, S. S., & Barik, R. K. (2022). *GeoCloud4EduNet: Geospatial Cloud Computing Model for Visualization and Analysis of Educational Information Network*. doi:10.1007/978-981-19-0475-2_2

Saad, M. (2018). Fog computing and its role in the internet of things: Concept, security and privacy issues. *International Journal of Computer Applications*, *180*(32), 7–9. doi:10.5120/ijca2018916829

Saba, A. I., & Elsheikh, A. H. (2020). Forecasting the prevalence of COVID-19 outbreak in Egypt using nonlinear autoregressive artificial neural networks. *Process Safety and Environmental Protection*, *141*, 1–8. doi:10.1016/j.psep.2020.05.029 PMID:32501368

Saba, T., Rehman, A., & AlGhamdi, J. S. (2017). Weather forecasting based on hybrid neural model. *Applied Water Science*, *7*(7), 3869–3874. doi:10.100713201-017-0538-0

Saber, W., Eisa, R., & Attia, R. (2022). *Efficient Geospatial Data Analysis Framework in Fog Environment*. IEEE. doi:10.1109/ACCESS.2022.3231787

Sadri, A. A., Rahmani, A. M., Saberikamarposhti, M., & Hosseinzadeh, M. (2022). Data reduction in fog computing and internet of things: A systematic literature survey. *Internet of Things (Netherlands)*, *20*, 100629. Advance online publication. doi:10.1016/j.iot.2022.100629

Salimi, A., Ziaii, M., Amiri, A., Zadeh, M. H., Karimpouli, S., & Moradkhani, M. (2018). Using a feature subset selection method and support vector machine to address curse of dimensionality and redundancy in hyperion hyperspectral data classification. *The Egyptian Journal of Remote Sensing and Space Sciences*, *21*(1), 27–36. doi:10.1016/j.ejrs.2017.02.003

Samann, F. E., Abdulazeez, A. M., & Askar, S. (2021). Fog Computing Based on Machine Learning: A Review. *International Journal of Interactive Mobile Technologies*, *15*(12), 21. doi:10.3991/ijim.v15i12.21313

Santos, L., Cunha, B., Fé, I., Vieira, M., & Silva, F. A. (2021). Data processing on edge and cloud: A performability evaluation and sensitivity analysis. *Journal of Network and Systems Management*, *29*(3), 27. doi:10.100710922-021-09592-x

Sarker, I. H. (2021). Machine learning: Algorithms, real-world applications and research directions. *SN Computer Science*, *2*(3), 1–21. doi:10.100742979-021-00592-x PMID:33778771

Scholte, W. J., Zegelaar, P. W. A., & Nijmeijer, H. (2022). A control strategy for merging a single vehicle into a platoon at highway on-ramps. *Transportation Research Part C, Emerging Technologies*, *136*, 103511. doi:10.1016/j.trc.2021.103511

Sedwick, R., & Schweighart, S. (2001). Development and analysis of a high fidelity linearized J (2) model for satellite formation flying. In AIAA space 2001 Conference and exposition (p. 4744). AIAA.

Shafik, W., Matinkhah, S. M., & Ghasemazade, M. (2019). Fog-mobile edge performance evaluation and analysis on internet of things. *Journal of Advance Research in Mobile Computing, 1*(3), 1–17.

Shah, D., Patel, S., & Bharti, S. K. (2020). Heart disease prediction using machine learning techniques. *SN Computer Science, 1*(6), 345. doi:10.100742979-020-00365-y

Shaik, S., & Baskiyar, S. (2018). Hierarchical and autonomous fog architecture. *Proceedings of the 47th International Conference on Parallel Processing Companion.* ACM. 10.1145/3229710.3229740

Shaik, S., Hall, J., Johnson, C., Wang, Q., Sharp, R., & Baskiyar, S. (2022). PFogSim: A simulator for evaluation of mobile and hierarchical fog computing. *Sustainable Computing: Informatics and Systems, 35*, 100736. doi:10.1016/j.suscom.2022.100736

Sharma, A., Kosasih, E., Zhang, J., Brintrup, A., & Calinescu, A. (2022). Digital Twins: State of the art theory and practice, challenges, and open research questions. *Journal of Industrial Information Integration, 30*, 100383. Advance online publication. doi:10.1016/j.jii.2022.100383

Sharma, S., & Sajid, M. (2021). Integrated fog and cloud computing issues and challenges. [IJCAC]. *International Journal of Cloud Applications and Computing, 11*(4), 174–193. doi:10.4018/IJCAC.2021100110

Shukla, A., Tiwari, R., Kaur, P., & Janghel, R. R. (2009). Diagnosis of thyroid disorders using artificial neural networks. In *2009 IEEE International Advance Computing Conference* (pp. 1016-1020). IEEE. 10.1109/IADCC.2009.4809154

Sicotte, C. (1998). A Conceptual Framework for the Analysis of Health Care Organizations' Performance. *Sage Journals.* doi:10.1177/095148489801100106

Siddiqui, S. A., Zhang, Y., Feng, Z., & Kos, A. (2016). A pulse rate estimation algorithm using PPG and smartphone camera. *Journal of Medical Systems, 40*(5), 1–6. doi:10.100710916-016-0485-6 PMID:27067432

Silva, D. S., & Holanda, M. (2022). Applications of geospatial big data in the Internet of Things. In Transactions in GIS, 26(1). doi:10.1111/tgis.12846

Singh, J., Singh, P., & Gill, S. S. (2021). Fog computing: A taxonomy, systematic review, current trends and research challenges. *Journal of Parallel and Distributed Computing, 157*, 56–85. doi:10.1016/j.jpdc.2021.06.005

Singh, S., & Saini, B. S. (2021). Autonomous cars: Recent developments, challenges, and possible solutions. *IOP Conference Series. Materials Science and Engineering, 1022*(1), 012028. doi:10.1088/1757-899X/1022/1/012028

Sligo, J., Gauld, R., Roberts, V., & Villa, L. (2017). A literature review for large-scale health information system project planning, implementation and evaluation. *International Journal of Medical Informatics, 97*, 86–97. doi:10.1016/j.ijmedinf.2016.09.007 PMID:27919399

Solutions, T. G. (2017). Retail 4.0. *The Retail Intelligence.* http://www.theretailintelligence.com/retail-4-0/

Songhorabadi, M., Rahimi, M., MoghadamFarid, A. M., & Haghi Kashani, M. (2023). Fog computing approaches in IoT-enabled smart cities. *Journal of Network and Computer Applications, 211*, 103557. doi:10.1016/j.jnca.2022.103557

Song, X., Liu, Z., Li, L., Gao, Z., Fan, X., Zhai, G., & Zhou, H. (2021). Artificial intelligence CT screening model for thyroid-associated ophthalmopathy and tests under clinical conditions. *International Journal of Computer Assisted Radiology and Surgery, 16*(2), 323–330. doi:10.100711548-020-02281-1 PMID:33146848

Soni, M., & Varma, S. (2020, September). Diabetes prediction using machine learning techniques. *International Journal of Engineering Research & Technology (Ahmedabad), 9*(9), 921–925.

Sonuç, E. (2021). Thyroid Disease Classification Using Machine Learning Algorithms. Journal of Physics: Conference Series, 1963(1), 012140.

Sood, S. K., & Singh, K. D. (2018). An Optical-Fog assisted EEG-based virtual reality framework for enhancing E-learning through educational games. *Computer Applications in Engineering Education, 26*(5), 1565–1576. doi:10.1002/cae.21965

Souza, V. B., Masip-Bruin, X., Marín-Tordera, E., Sànchez-López, S., Garcia, J., Ren, G. J., Jukan, A., & Juan Ferrer, A. (2018). Towards a proper service placement in combined fog-to-cloud architectures. *Future Generation Computer Systems, 87*, 1–15. doi:10.1016/j.future.2018.04.042

Spatharakis, D., Dimolitsas, I., Dechouniotis, D., Papathanail, G., Fotoglou, I., Papadimitriou, P., & Papavassiliou, S. (2020). A scalable Edge Computing architecture enabling smart offloading for Location Based Services. *Pervasive and Mobile Computing, 67*, 101217. doi:10.1016/j.pmcj.2020.101217

Srirama, S. N., Dick, F. M. S., & Adhikari, M. (2021). Akka framework based on the Actor model for executing distributed Fog Computing applications. *Future Generation Computer Systems, 117*, 439–452. doi:10.1016/j.future.2020.12.011

Starfield, B. (2009). Primary care and equity in health: The importance to effectiveness and equity of responsiveness to peoples' needs. *Humanity & Society, 33*(1–2), 56–76. doi:10.1177/016059760903300105

Story, A., Aldridge, R. W., Smith, C. M., Garber, E., Hall, J., Ferenando, G., & Abubakar, I. (2019). Smartphone-enabled video-observed versus directly observed treatment for tuberculosis: A multicentre, analyst-blinded, randomised, controlled superiority trial. *Lancet, 393*(10177), 1216–1224. doi:10.1016/S0140-6736(18)32993-3 PMID:30799062

Subramani, P., Srinivas, K., Kavitha Rani, B., Sujatha, R., & Parameshachari, B. D. (2023). Prediction of muscular paralysis disease based on hybrid feature extraction with machine learning technique for COVID-19 and post-COVID-19 patients. *Personal and Ubiquitous Computing, 27*(5), 831–844. doi:10.100700779-021-01531-6 PMID:33679282

Sultana, T., & Wahid, K. A. (2019). Choice of application layer protocols for next generation video surveillance using Internet of video things. *IEEE Access : Practical Innovations, Open Solutions, 7*, 41607–41624. doi:10.1109/ACCESS.2019.2907525

Susan Meyer. (2020). *The history and evolution of retail stores: from mom and pop to online shops.* Ecommerce News.

Tang, B., Chen, Z., Hefferman, G., Pei, S., Wei, T., He, H., & Yang, Q. (2017). Incorporating Intelligence in Fog Computing for Big Data Analysis in Smart Cities. *IEEE Transactions on Industrial Informatics, 13*(5), 2140–2150. doi:10.1109/TII.2017.2679740

Thakur, A., & Malekian, R. (2019). Fog Computing for Detecting Vehicular Congestion, an Internet of Vehicles Based Approach: A Review. *IEEE Intelligent Transportation Systems Magazine, 11*(2), 8–16. doi:10.1109/MITS.2019.2903551

Tran, T. T., Pham, L. T., & Ngo, Q. X. (2020). Forecasting epidemic spread of SARS-CoV-2 using ARIMA model (Case study: Iran). *Global Journal of Environmental Science and Management, 6*(Special Issue (Covid-19)), 1–10.

Tripathi, A. K., Agrawal, S., & Gupta, R. D. (2020). Cloud enabled SDI architecture: a review. In Earth Science Informatics, 13(2). doi:10.100712145-020-00446-9

Tripathy, S. (2023). An Intelligent Health Care System in Fog Platform with Optimized Performance. *Sustainability, MDPI, 15,* 1862, 1-17.

Trivedi, K., & Bobbio, A. (2021). Reliability and Availability Analysis in Practice. Handbook of Advanced Performability Engineering, 501-522.

Trivedi, K. S., Dharmaraja, S., & Ma, X. (2002). Analytic modeling of handoffs in wireless cellular networks. *Information Sciences*, *148*(1-4), 155–166. doi:10.1016/S0020-0255(02)00292-X

Trivedi, K. S., Ma, X., & Dharmaraja, S. (2003). Performability modeling of wireless communication systems. *International Journal of Communication Systems*, *16*(6), 561–577. doi:10.1002/dac.605

Tuli, S., Mahmud, R., Tuli, S., & Buyya, R. (2019). FogBus: A blockchain-based lightweight framework for edge and fog computing. *Journal of Systems and Software*, *154*, 22–36. doi:10.1016/j.jss.2019.04.050

Umar Sidiq, D., Aaqib, S. M., & Khan, R. A. (2019). Diagnosis of various thyroid ailments using data mining classification techniques. *Int J Sci Res Coput Sci Inf Technol*, *5*, 131–136.

Umoh, V., Ekpe, U., Davidson, I., & Akpan, J. (2023). Mobile Broadband Adoption, Performance Measurements and Methodology: A Review. *Electronics (Basel)*, *12*(7), 1630. doi:10.3390/electronics12071630

Vancauwenberghe, G., & van Loenen, B. (2018). *Exploring the Emergence of Open Spatial Data Infrastructures: Analysis of Recent Developments and Trends in Europe*. Springer. doi:10.1007/978-3-319-59442-2_2

Vanderpump, M. P. (2011). The epidemiology of thyroid disease. *British Medical Bulletin*, *99*(1), 39–51. doi:10.1093/bmb/ldr030 PMID:21893493

Vaquero, L. M., & Rodero-Merino, L. (2014, October). Finding your way in the fog: Towards a comprehensive definition of fog computing. *Computer Communication Review*, *44*(5), 27–32. doi:10.1145/2677046.2677052

Varshney, P., & Simmhan, Y. (2017). Demystifying fog computing: Characterizing architectures, applications and abstractions. *2017 IEEE 1st International Conference on Fog and Edge Computing (ICFEC)*. IEEE.

Veillard, J., Garcia-Armesto, S., Kadandale, S., Klazinga, N., & Leatherman, S. (2010). International health system comparisons: From measurement challenge to management tool. Cambridge University Press, 641 672. doi:10.1017/CBO9780511711800.023

Veillard, J., Champagne, F., Klazinga, N., Kazandjian, V., Arah, O. A., & Guisset, A. L. (2005). A performance assessment framework for hospitals", The WHO regional office for Europe PATH project. *International Journal for Quality in Health Care*, *17*(6), 487–496. doi:10.1093/intqhc/mzi072 PMID:16155049

Vhaduri, S., Van Kessel, T., Ko, B., Wood, D., Wang, S., & Brunschwiler, T. (2019, June). Nocturnal cough and snore detection in noisy environments using smartphone-microphones. In *2019 IEEE International Conference on Healthcare Informatics (ICHI)* (pp. 1-7). IEEE. 10.1109/ICHI.2019.8904563

Vidal-Filho, J. N., Times, V. C., Lisboa-Filho, J., & Renso, C. (2021). Towards the Semantic Enrichment of Trajectories Using Spatial Data Infrastructures. *ISPRS International Journal of Geo-Information*, *10*(12), 825. doi:10.3390/ijgi10120825

Vilaplana, J., Solsona, F., Teixidó, I., Mateo, J., Abella, F., & Rius, J. (2014). A queuing theory model for cloud computing. *The Journal of Supercomputing*, *69*(1), 492–507. doi:10.100711227-014-1177-y

Wang, H., Liu, T., Kim, B., Lin, C.-W., Shiraishi, S., Xie, J., & Han, Z. (2020a). Architectural Design Alternatives based on Cloud/Edge/Fog Computing for Connected Vehicles. *IEEE Communications Surveys and Tutorials*, *22*(4), 2349–2377. doi:10.1109/COMST.2020.3020854

Wang, H., Wang, L., Zhou, Z., Tao, X., Pau, G., & Arena, F. (2019). Blockchain-based resource allocation model in fog computing. *Applied Sciences (Basel, Switzerland)*, *9*(24), 5538. doi:10.3390/app9245538 PMID:32944385

Wang, S., Guo, Y., Zhang, N., Yang, P., Zhou, A., & Shen, X. (2021). Delay-Aware Microservice Coordination in Mobile Edge Computing: A Reinforcement Learning Approach. *IEEE Transactions on Mobile Computing*, *20*(3), 939–951. doi:10.1109/TMC.2019.2957804

Wang, Y., Tao, X., Zhang, X., Zhang, P., & Hou, Y. T. (2019). Cooperative Task Offloading in Three-Tier Mobile Computing Networks: An ADMM Framework. *IEEE Transactions on Vehicular Technology*, *68*(3), 2763–2776. doi:10.1109/TVT.2019.2892176

Wang, Z., Guo, Y., Gao, Y., Fang, C., Li, M., & Sun, Y. (2020b). Fog-Based Distributed Networked Control for Connected Autonomous Vehicles. *Wireless Communications and Mobile Computing*, *2020*, 1–11. doi:10.1155/2020/8855655

Wani, U. I., Batth, R. S., & Rashid, M. (2019). Fog computing challenges and future directions: A mirror review. *2019 International Conference on Computational Intelligence and Knowledge Economy (ICCIKE)*. IEEE. 10.1109/ICCIKE47802.2019.9004428

Wen, Z., Yang, R., Garraghan, P., Lin, T., Xu, J., & Rovatsos, M. (2017). Fog orchestration for Internet of Things services. *IEEE Internet Computing*, *21*(2), 16–24. doi:10.1109/MIC.2017.36

Whitley, D., & Starkweather, T. computing, C. B.-P., & 1990, undefined. (1990). *Genetic algorithms and neural networks: Optimizing connections and connectivity*. Elsevier. https://www.sciencedirect.com/science/article/pii/016781919090086O

WHO Coronavirus (COVID-19) Dashboard. (n.d.). WHO. https://covid19.who.int/

Wieczorek, M., Siłka, J., & Woźniak, M. (2020). Neural network powered COVID-19 spread forecasting model. *Chaos, Solitons, and Fractals*, *140*, 110203. doi:10.1016/j.chaos.2020.110203 PMID:32834663

Wigren, T. (2023). Recursive identification of a nonlinear state space model. *International Journal of Adaptive Control and Signal Processing*, *37*(2), 447–473. doi:10.1002/acs.3531

Wilkinson, M. D., Dumontier, M., Aalbersberg, I. J., Appleton, G., Axton, M., Baak, A., Blomberg, N., Boiten, J. W., da Silva Santos, L. B., Bourne, P. E., Bouwman, J., Brookes, A. J., Clark, T., Crosas, M., Dillo, I., Dumon, O., Edmunds, S., Evelo, C. T., Finkers, R., & Mons, B. (2016). The FAIR Guiding Principles for scientific data management and stewardship. *Scientific Data*, *3*(1), 160018. doi:10.1038data.2016.18 PMID:26978244

Winnie, Y., Umamaheswari, E. & Ajay. D. M. (2018). Enhancing Data Security in IoT Healthcare Services Using Fog Computing, International *Conference on Recent Trends in Advance Computing*. IEEE.

Wobker, C., Seitz, A., Mueller, H., & Bruegge, B. (2018). Fogernetes: Deployment and management of fog computing applications. *NOMS 2018 - 2018 IEEE/IFIP Network Operations and Management Symposium*.

Yadav, D. C., & Pal, S. (2019). To generate an ensemble model for women thyroid prediction using data mining techniques. *Asian Pacific Journal of Cancer Prevention*, *20*(4), 1275. PMID:31031212

Yadav, D. C., & Pal, S. (2020). Prediction of thyroid disease using decision tree ensemble method. *Human-Intelligent Systems Integration*, *2*(1), 89–95. doi:10.100742454-020-00006-y

Yamamoto, Y., Kawabe, T., Tsuruta, S., Damiani, E., Yoshitaka, A., Mizuno, Y., & Knauf, R. (2016, July). IoT-aware online shopping system enhanced with gaze analysis. *2016 World Automation Congress (WAC)*, (pp. 1-6). IEEE. 10.1109/WAC.2016.7583028

Yarsky, P. (2021). Using a genetic algorithm to fit parameters of a COVID-19 SEIR model for US states. *Mathematics and Computers in Simulation*, *185*, 687–695. doi:10.1016/j.matcom.2021.01.022 PMID:33612959

Yigitoglu, E., Mohamed, M., Liu, L., & Ludwig, H. (2017). Foggy: A framework for continuous automated IoT application deployment in fog computing. In: *Proceedings of IEEE International Conference on AI Mobile Services*, (pp. 38-45). IEEE. 10.1109/AIMS.2017.14

Yin, L., Luo, J., & Luo, H. (2018). Tasks scheduling and resource allocation in fog computing based on containers for smart manufacturing. *IEEE Transactions on Industrial Informatics*, *14*(10), 4712–4721. doi:10.1109/TII.2018.2851241

Yi, S., Hao, Z., Qin, Z., & Li, Q. (2015). Fog computing: Platform and applications. *2015 Third IEEE Workshop on Hot Topics in Web Systems and Technologies (HotWeb)*. IEEE. 10.1109/HotWeb.2015.22

Yuan, F. & Chung, K. C. (2016). Defining Quality in Health Care and Measuring Quality in Surgery, American Society of Plastic Surgeons. *PRSJ Journal*, 1635-1644. doi:10.1097/PRS.0000000000002028

Yuan, F. Q. (2016). Critical issues of applying machine learning to condition monitoring for failure diagnosis. In: *Proceedings of the IEEE International Conference on Industrial Engineering and Engineering Management*, (pp. 1903-1907). IEEE. 10.1109/IEEM.2016.7798209

Zaadoud, B., & Chbab, Y. (2021). The Performance Measurement Frameworks in Health Care: Appropriateness Criteria for Measuring and Evaluating the Quality-of-Care Performance through a Systematic Review. *Management Issues in Healthcare System*, *7*(7), 11–34. doi:10.33844/mihs.2021.60603

Zakary, O., Larrache, A., Rachik, M., & Elmouki, I. (2016). Effect of awareness programs and travel-blocking operations in the control of HIV/AIDS outbreaks: A multi-domains SIR model. *Advances in Difference Equations*, *2016*(1), 1–17. doi:10.118613662-016-0900-9

Zhang, M., & Berghäll, S. (2021). E-commerce in agri-food sector: A systematic literature review based on service-dominant logic. In Journal of Theoretical and Applied Electronic Commerce Research, 16(7). doi:10.3390/jtaer16070182

Zhang, F. Z., He, H. X., & Xiao, W. J. (2013). Application Analysis of Internet of Things on the Management of Supply Chain and Intelligent Logistics. [Trans Tech Publications.]. *Applied Mechanics and Materials*, *411*, 2655–2661. doi:10.4028/www.scientific.net/AMM.411-414.2655

Zhang, H., Xiao, Y., Bu, S., Niyato, D., Yu, F. R., & Han, Z. (2017). Computing resource allocation in three-tier IoT fog networks: A joint optimization approach combining stackelberg game and matching. *IEEE Internet of Things Journal*, *4*(5), 1204–1215. doi:10.1109/JIOT.2017.2688925

Zhang, Y., Qu, Y., Gao, L., Luan, T. H., Zheng, X., Chen, S., & Xiang, Y. (2019). APDP: Attack-Proof Personalized Differential Privacy Model for a Smart Home. *IEEE Access : Practical Innovations, Open Solutions*, 1–13. doi:10.1109/ACCESS.2019.2943243

Zhou, Z., Liao, H., Wang, X., Mumtaz, S., & Rodriguez, J. (2020). When Vehicular Fog Computing Meets Autonomous Driving: Computational Resource Management and Task Offloading. *IEEE Network*, *34*(6), 70–76. doi:10.1109/MNET.001.1900527

Zivkovic, M., Bacanin, N., Venkatachalam, K., Nayyar, A., Djordjevic, A., Strumberger, I., & Al-Turjman, F. (2021). COVID-19 cases prediction by using hybrid machine learning and beetle antennae search approach. *Sustainable Cities and Society*, *66*, 102669. doi:10.1016/j.scs.2020.102669 PMID:33520607

Zorlu, K., Gokceoglu, C., Ocakoğlu, F., Nefeslioglu, H. A., Zorlu, K., Gokceoglu, C., Ocakoglu, F., & Acikalin, S. (2007). Prediction of uniaxial compressive strength of sandstones using petrography-based models. *Elsevier*, *96*(3–4), 141–158. doi:10.1016/j.enggeo.2007.10.009

Zou, L., Ruan, F., Huang, M., Liang, L., Huang, H., Hong, Z., Yu, J., Kang, M., Song, Y., Xia, J., Guo, Q., Song, T., He, J., Yen, H.-L., Peiris, M., & Wu, J. (2020). SARS-CoV-2 viral load in upper respiratory specimens of infected patients. *The New England Journal of Medicine*, *382*(12), 1177–1179. doi:10.1056/NEJMc2001737 PMID:32074444

About the Contributors

Debi Prasanna Acharjya received his Ph.D. in computer science from Berhampur University, India. He has been awarded with Gold Medal in M. Sc. from NIT, Rourkela. Currently, he is working as a Professor in the School of Computing Science and Engineering, at VIT University, Vellore, India. He has authored many national and international journal papers, book chapters, and five books to his credit. Additionally, he has edited seven books to his credit. He is a reviewer of many international journals such as Fuzzy Sets and Systems, Knowledge-Based Systems, and Applied Soft Computing. He has been awarded Gold Medal from NIT, Rourkela; the Eminent Academician Award from Khallikote Sanskrutika Parisad, Berhampur, Odisha; the Bharat Vikas Award from the Institute of Self Reliance, Bhubaneswar; Outstanding Educator and Scholar Award from National Foundation for Entrepreneurship Development, Coimbatore, and Lifetime Achievement Award from NFED, Coimbatore. Dr. Acharjya is actively associated with many professional bodies like CSI, ISTE, IMS, AMTI, ISIAM, OITS, IACSIT, CSTA, IEEE, and IAENG. He was the founder secretary of the OITS Rourkela chapter. His current research interests include rough sets, formal concept analysis, knowledge representation, data mining, granular computing, bio-inspired computing, and business intelligence.

Kauser Ahmed P. is an Assistant Professor in the School of Computing Sciences and Engineering, VIT, Vellore, India. His research interests include bio-inspired computing, big data analytics, and computational intelligence. He has published a number of research papers in peer-reviewed international journals and conferences. He is associated with many professional bodies like CSI, ISTE, IEEE, IRSS, and IAENG. He has been involved in a number of conferences and workshops in various capacities.

Nirase Fathima Abubacker is an Associate Professor at the Asia Pacific University in Malaysia. She received a Bachelor Degree in Mathematics (BSc) and a Master Degree in Computer Applications (MCA) in 1997. After serving in the teaching industry for a few years in Malaysia & Saudi Arabia, she obtained her Master of Philosophy in Computer Science (M.Phil) in 2008. She enrolled for a PhD in computing in January 2011, specialising in the field of Intelligent Systems at the University Putra Malaysia and received her PhD in 2016. Since 1997, she has been a lecturer and then a senior lecturer in the field of computing and IT for both the undergraduate and postgraduate courses in Malaysia and Saudi Arabia. From 2017, She worked as an Associate Professor in Dublin City University, Ireland as well as a visiting professor at United Arab Emirates University, Abu Dhabi. She has published more than 20 research papers in both ISI and Scopus journals focusing on the field of medicine. Her current research interests include data science, image processing, and computer vision using machine learning and artificial intelligence. She also serves as a reviewer for various indexed journals and has actively participating in dealing with industrial projects.

Aditi Acharjya is currently perusing B. Tech. (Computer Science and Engineering) at SRM Institute of Science & Technology, Chennai, India. She has actively involved in research and development in computer science and engineering. Besides, she has published few papers in conferences.

Munir Ahmad is a Ph.D. in Computer Science. over 23 years of extensive experience in spatial data development, management, processing, visualization, and quality control. He is dedicated expertise in open data, crowdsourced data, volunteered geographic information and spatial data infrastructure. A seasoned professional with extensive knowledge in the field, having served as a trainer for the latest spatial technologies. With a passion for research and over 25 publications in the same field. In 2022, he got PhD degree in Computer Science from Preston University Rawalpindi, Pakistan. He is dedicated to advancing the industry and spreading knowledge through my expertise and experience. #SpatialData #GIS #GeoTech

Asmat Ali is PhD in Remote Sensing & GIS. He is Director at Survey of Pakistan. In, 1998 he earned Professional Master Degree in Geoinformatics from Faculty of Geo-Information Science and Earth Observation (ITC), University of Twente, Enschede The Netherlands. Later on, he got MSc Degree in Geo-information Science and Earth Observation, with Specialization in Geo-Information Management from the same university. In 2022, he got PhD degree in Remote Sensing and GIS from PMAS-Arid Agriculture University Rawalpindi, Pakistan. He has 34 years of experience in geospatial information production and management discipline as practitioner, trainer and educator. He has served on a number of operational, administrative and instructional appointments. He was in-charge of the team which started GIS mapping and digital cartography at Survey of Pakistan in 1999. His more than 25 research papers including two book chapters and articles on Spatial Data Infrastructure (SDI), GIS, Remote Sensing, E-governance, as well as Land Administration have been published in various international conferences and renowned journals. In 2008, SDI Asia-Pacific identified him as focal point for SDI development in Pakistan. GSDI in 2016, acknowledged and awarded him as SDI implementer from Pakistan. He is on the visiting faculty of Bahria University Islamabad and PMAS- Arid Agriculture University Rawalpindi, Pakistan.

Priyanka Bharti, received B.E., M. Tech and PhD Degree in Computer Science & Engg. She is currently working as an Assistant Professor in School of Computer Science & Engineering, REVA University, Bengaluru, INDIA. She is reviewer of several international/national Journals published by Elsevier, IEEE, ACM, Springer, etc. She has been technical program committee member of more than 5 National/International Conferences.

Himadri Biswas is Professor & HOD at the Department of Information Technology (CSE), Budge Budge Institute of Technology, Kolkata, W.B. INDIA. He also has 21 years of teaching experience and has served in several institutions. He's done his M. Tech in Computer Science & Engineering and Ph.D. degree from the University of Kalyani, Nadia, West Bengal, India. He has published several Patents, Journal Papers, Conference Papers and Book Chapters. His research interests include cloud computing, mobile computing, Data Science and Machine Learning.

Raja Das is working as an Assistant Professor (Department of Mathematics) at Vellore Institute of Technology Vellore, Tamilnadu –632014, India. He had published more than 68 papers in various International journals and Conferences. His research interest includes Medical Imaging, Electrical Discharge Machining, Artificial Intelligence, Machine Learning, and Deep Learning.

Swati Das is presently working as an Assistant Professor in the Department of Computer Applications at Rourkela Institute of Management Studies. Prior to this assignment She worked as Lecturer at SKDAV Polytechnic College, Rourkela for three years. She completed her M.Tech programme in Computer Science and Engineering in the year 2016 from State Technical University- Biju Patnaik University of Technology, Odisha, India . She has published few research papers national journals of repute. Her research areas of interest are Data Mining, IoT, Cloud Computing & Fog Computing. She has qualified the UGC-NET examination.

Bikash Ranjan Debata is an academic and consultant in the area of medical tourism, controversial advertisement, knowledge management, marketing analytics, green sustainability, customer experience and service quality standards. He is a Post Doc fellow to University of Macau, China. In his corporate tenure he had worked with big data as a moderator to ensure the necessary data is captured and later translated into actionable recommendations. In addition, he had designed and delivered more than 3000 hours of behavioural skill training program in India and abroad to blue chips such as Steel Authority of India Limited, Cognizant Technology Solutions, Satyam Computers (Now Tech-Mahindra), Idea Cellular, Avenion India, RPG and Royal Sundaram. Bikash has twenty-five research papers published in reputed international journals, such as Journal of Cleaner Production, Benchmarking - An international Journal, International Journal of Process Management and Benchmarking, International Journal of Services and Operations Management, International Journal of Indian Culture and Business Management. He has published two books on Medical Tourism Service Quality and emerging trends in marketing respectively with international publishers. Bikash has an MBA from Southern New Hampshire University, USA and a Ph.D. from National Institute of Technology, India. He is also in the editorial board of reputed journals of repute. He is affiliated to Kirloskar Institute of Management as Professor of Marketing.

Rema Gopalan is presently working as an Associate Professor in the Department of Management Studies, CMR Institute of Technology (CMRIT), Bengaluru, and has more than thirteen years of academic, research, and administrative experience. She has also worked with reputed institutes such as Jagdish Sheth School of Management (IFIM B School) and Rourkela Institute of Management Studies. She qualified for the National Eligibility Test conducted by University Grant Commission, India. She received a Doctorate of Philosophy in Management (Marketing) from Sambalpur University, Odisha. Her research interests include Multi-Criteria Decision Making, Service Quality Evaluation, Machine Learning, Business Analytics, and related areas of marketing. She has published around thirteen research papers in various international and national journals and conferences.

Amrut Ranjan Jena has completed his M.Tech., in IT from Jadavpur University, India. He has completed his Ph.D. in computer science from VIT Vellore, India. At present, Dr. Jena is working as an Associate Professor in the CSE department at Guru Nanak Institute of Technology, JIS Group, Kolkata, India. He has eighteen years of academic experience to date including seven years of research experience. He has published many research papers in journals, book chapters, and conference proceedings. His area of research includes machine learning, neural computing, and fog computing. He is the convener of ISACS 2021 and ISACS 2022 international conference.

Yonal Kirsal received a graduate degree from the Electrical and Electronic Engineering Department, Eastern Mediterranean University (EMU), Fagamusta, Cyprus, in 2006, and the MSc and PhD degrees from Middlesex University, London, U.K., in 2008 and 2013, respectively. He joined the Electrical and Electronic Engineering Department, the European University of Lefke, as an assistant professor, in 2014. He has been elected head of the Electronics & Communication Engineering Department, since October 2017. He was appointed as associate professor, in 2019. His main research is in the field of modelling heterogeneous wireless networks, performance evaluation, queueing theory, network design and evaluation, and Intelligent Transportation Systems (ITS).

Sreekumar is presently working as a Professor in Decision Science at Rourkela Institute of Management Studies, Rourkela. His areas of interest include application of Data Envelopment Analysis, Multi-criteria Decision-Making, Decision Making in Fuzzy Environment, Service Quality Evaluation etc. He has 29 years of teaching experience in the areas of Management Science. He has published more than 60 research papers in various International and National conferences and journals of repute. He has also authored two text books. He is the reviewer of a few International journals of repute including publications like Inderscience, Emerald, Elsevier and IGI. In addition, he is a visiting faculty to many business schools in India. He has conducted many workshops and has been invited as resource person for AICTE sponsored training programs. He was exposed to International Business at De La Salle University, Manila. He is also guiding research scholars for their Ph.D programme in Management under various State University.

Nancy Kumari received her Ph.D. in Computer Science and Engineering from VIT Vellore, Tamil Nādu, India; M.Tech. degree in Computer Science and Engineering from Galgotia's University, U.P., India; and B.Tech. in Information Technology from the Women's Institute of Technology, India. She has an academic experience of 3 years and has also worked for the National Assessment and Accreditation Council (NAAC); she has authored many impact-factor journal papers with reputed publishers like Elsevier, Springer, and Wiley. In addition to that, she has published many conference papers and book chapters to her credit. During her Ph.D., she received the Raman Research Award from VIT, Vellore, for publishing research papers in reputed journals. She is acting as a reviewer for some international journals. Dr. Nancy has been a keynote speaker in various faculty development programs and has organized several workshops. She is associated with many professional bodies, including CSI, ISTE, IMS, AMTI, CSTA, IEEE, and IAENG. Her current research interests include computational intelligence, soft computing, bioinspired algorithms, data analytics, ambient intelligence, reinforcement learning, and healthcare informatics.

Balakrishnama Manohar is a full-time Ph.D., Research Scholar (Institute Fellowship Category) in the Department of Mathematics at Vellore Institute of Technology Vellore, Tamilnadu–632014, India. He has completed his master's in Mathematics from Sree Vidyanikethan PG College, Tirupati, A.P. (Affiliated to S. V. University), India. He is an M.Sc. Gold Medalist. His research interest includes Machine Learning and Deep Learning.

Punyaban Patel, PhD(CSE), Professor in the department of Computer Science & Engineering, CMR Technical Campus (An Autonomous Engineering College), Hyderabad, India. He has published more than 80 research papers in national, international conferences, journals and 7 patents and a book in image processing. He has 24 years of research and teaching experience in UG and PG courses in Computer Science and Engineering. He has completed his PGDBM (2 years course) in Business Management from NMIMS, Mumbai. He is a member of many professional societies and Fellow member of The Institution of Engineers(India). He has research interest in Image Processing, Pattern Recognition ML and Health care.

Riyam Patel, male, a B.Tech(AI & ML) student of Department of Computer Science and Engineering, SRM Institute of Science and Technology, Chennai, India. He has published 05 research paper in international conferences and Journals in the field of Computer science and Engineering along with 02 patents. His specializations are AI, ML. He has research interest in AI, ML, data Mining and Health care. He is an IEEE student member.

Mafas Raheem is a Senior Lecturer at the Asia Pacific University of Technology & Innovation of Malaysia. He received his bachelor's degree in Applied Sciences majoring in Computer Science (BSc) in 2007 and a master's degree in Business Administration (MBA) in 2016. Further, he obtained his master's degree in Data Science & Business Analytics (MSc) in 2018. Currently, he is enrolled for a PhD in computing, specialising in the field of Natural Language Processing/Machine Learning at the Asia Pacific University of Technology & Innovation of Malaysia. Since 2009, he has been a lecturer and then a senior lecturer in the field of computing and Business IT for both undergraduate and postgraduate courses in Sri Lanka and Malaysia. From 2022, he is working as a senior lecturer at the Asia Pacific University of Technology & Innovation of Malaysia. He conducted several corporate training programs for a significant number of companies which includes OCBC and Crystal, Malaysia. He actively take part and won many international & national level awards in data mining competitions by mentoring his students including America and Germany. He has published more than 15 research papers in ISI, WOS and Scopus-indexed journals and more than 30 other indexed journal articles focusing on the field of data mining and business analytics, especially in the domain of retail business. His current research interests include natural language processing, using machine/deep learning and artificial intelligence for eCommerce.

Muhammad Ehsan Rana is an accomplished academic professional with over 20 years of experience in academic management, lecturing, and quality assurance. He holds a PhD in Software Engineering from Universiti Putra Malaysia, as well as additional qualifications including a PGD in Quality Management, an MSc in Mathematics, and a Master's degree in Computer Science. He has been associated with the Asia Pacific University of Technology & Innovation (APU) Malaysia since December 2008, currently serving as an Associate Professor. His responsibilities encompass teaching, research and engagement with industry and professional bodies. Prior to his academic career, Dr Ehsan worked as a Software Quality Manager for an international software development company specializing in ERP solutions. In this role, he successfully managed and implemented organization-wide quality policies, quality assurance plans, and risk management strategies. As an active researcher, Dr Ehsan focuses on areas such as Software Architecture, Cloud Computing, IoT, and Blockchain. He has made significant contributions to the field, having authored and co-authored more than 100 journal papers, conference publications, and book chapters. He also serves as a reviewer for various indexed journals and has actively participated in organizing IEEE and other international conferences.

Bibhudatta Sahoo is a Professor in the Department of Computer Science & Engineering at the National Institute of Technology Rourkela, India, where he has been a faculty member since 2000. He is a Communication and Computing Research Group member and a Professor in charge of the Cloud Computing Research Laboratory. His research interests lie in Parallel and Distributed Systems, Cloud Computing, Sensor Networks, Algorithms for VLSI Design, the Internet of Things, Software-defined networks, Multicore Architecture, 5g Networks, Web Engineering and Algorithmic Engineering. Dr Sahoo is a Fellow of the Institution of Electronics and Telecommunication Engineers (IETE), the Computer Society of India (CSI), the Indian Society for Technical Education (ISTE), the Indian Science Congress Association (ISCA), and the Orissa Science Academy. Dr Sahoo is also a member of IEEE, and professional member of ACM, and the author or co-author of over 250 publications, book chapters, research monographs and reference books.

Gopal Krishna Shyam, received B.E., M. Tech and PhD Degree in Computer Science & Engg. from Visveswaraya Technological University, Belagavi. He is currently working as a Professor and HoD in School of Computer Engineering, Presidency University, Bengaluru, INDIA. He has experience of around 17 years in teaching and research. He is involved in research in areas of Cloud/Grid computing, E-commerce, Protocol engineering, and Artificial intelligence applications.

Malik Sikandar Hayat Khiyal born at Khushab, Pakistan, is currently Professor of Faculty of Computer Science, Preston University, Islamabad. He remained Chairman Department of Computer Sciences and Software Engineering in Fatima Jinnah Women University Pakistan from 2007 to 2012 and in International Islamic University, Islamabad from 2002 to 2007. He Served Pakistan Atomic Energy Commission for 25 years (1978-2002) and continuously was involved in different research and development projects of the PAEC. He developed software for underground flow and advanced fluid dynamic techniques. He was also associated with teaching at Computer Training Centre (PAEC) and International Islamic University. His areas of interest are Numerical Analysis, Analysis of Algorithms, Theory of Automata and Theory of Computation. He has more than hundred and fifty research publications to his credit in National and International Journals and Conference proceedings. He has supervised four PhD and more than one hundred and fifty research projects at graduate and postgraduate levels. He is a member of SIAM, ACM, Informing Science Institute, IACSIT. He is associate editor of IJCTE, IJMO, JACN, LNSE and Coeditor of the journals JATIT and International Journal of Reviews in Computing. He is reviewer of Journals, IJCSIT, JIISIT, IJCEE and CEE of Elsevier.

Borra Sivaiah, Associate professor of the Department CSE in CMR College of Engineering & Technology and. He has completed B. Tech (CSE), M. Tech (CSE) from JNTU, Hyderabad and pursuing his Ph.D. (CSE) in Data Mining and Big Data from JNTUK, Kakinada, AndraPradesh State, India. He has published more than 10 papers in International, National Journals and conferences with few patents. He is an eminent academician and has more than 19 years of experience in teaching and administration. He certified in Data Science and Big Data analytics by DELL EMC.

Madhusmita Mishra completed her M. Tech. in IT from Jadavpur University, West Bengal, India, and B. Tech. in CSE from BPUT, Odisha, India. Currently pursuing Ph.D. in CSE from VIT Vellore. She is currently working as an Assistant Professor in CSE at DSCSITSC, JIS Group, Kolkata, India. She has published several research papers in various journals. Her research interest includes machine learning, data mining, information retrieval, and bioinspired computing.

T. Amy Prasanna received MTech degree in Embedded systems and VLSI from Malla Reddy Engineering college for women, Hyderabad, India in 2016. She is currently working as an Assistant Professor in BVRITHYDERABAD College of engineering for women, Hyderabad, India. Her Research works include VLSI design, Embedded systems & IOT.

Pardhu Thottempudi was born in Luxettipet village in Adilabad district in Telangana state, India. He completed Batchelor's degree B.Tech in the stream of Electronics and Communication Engineering in 2011 from MLR Institute of Technology, Hyderabad, India. He has done his master's degree M.Tech in Embedded systems from Vignan's University, Vadlamudi in 2013. He is pursuing Ph.D in the stream of RADAR signal processing from VIT University His Research Includes Human Motion Analysis Behind walls using Optimized Deep Learning Algorithms. His major fields of interests include Digital Signal Processing, RADAR communications, Embedded systems, and implementation of signal processing on applications in FPGA. He is working as assistant professor of department of Electronics and Communication Engineering in BVRIT HYDERABAD College of Engineering for Women, Hyderabad, India since 2023. he was associated with SR University, Warangal, MLR Institute of Technology, St.Peters Engineering College, Marri Laxman Reddy Institute of Technology & Management as Assistant professor. He also worked as project intern in Research Centre Imarat, Hyderabad. He published 35+ research papers on VLSI, image processing, Antennas, signal processing, RADAR communications in reputed international journals and various IEEE conferences. Pardhu Thottempudi is the life member of ISTE, associate member of IETE from 2015, Member of IAENG, ISOC. He is the reviewer of many international reputed journals like WSEAS transactions, AIRCCSE.

Index

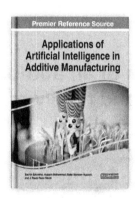
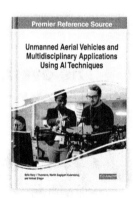

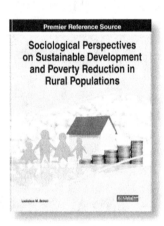

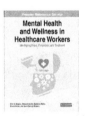

Printed in the United States
by Baker & Taylor Publisher Services